Ship Passenger Lists

The South

1538-1825

Carl Boyer, 3rd

HERITAGE BOOKS
2007

HERITAGE BOOKS
AN IMPRINT OF HERITAGE BOOKS, INC.

Books, CDs, and more—Worldwide

For our listing of thousands of titles see our website
at
www.HeritageBooks.com

Published 2007 by
HERITAGE BOOKS, INC.
Publishing Division
65 East Main Street
Westminster, Maryland 21157-5026

Other books by the author:

Ship Passenger Lists: National and New England (1600-1825)
Ship Passenger Lists: New York and New Jersey (1600-1825)
Ship Passenger Lists: Pennsylvania and Delaware (1641-1825)

International Standard Book Number: 978-0-940-90726-3

CONTENTS

PREFACE

Ship passenger lists have been described by Michael Tepper as "the delight of the genealogist," containing the first records of an immigrant in America as well as the evidence of his emigration. To bridge the Atlantic is important, for an insight into origins as well as information concerning age, occupation, physical description, religion, and, perhaps, reasons for emigration. Yet, but for some of the well known tools, including Hotten's *Persons* and the work of Strassburger and Hinke, most of these lists have been used far too little.

It is a curious fact that since the publication of Harold Lancour's *A Bibliography of Ship Passenger Lists, 1538-1825* in 1937, the job of putting the lists themselves into print again has been accomplished at a snail's pace. While a number of books, and some lengthy journal articles, were reprinted over a period of years by the Genealogical Publishing Company, it was not until 1975 that the consolidation of articles from journals into reprint volumes was begun in earnest. Such consolidation is important because of the common indexing, which is in many respects as helpful as making the articles easily attainable once more.

The publication of this volume, which is the third to be completed in a series, meets a need perceived when the editor was working seriously upon the ancestral lines of his wife and himself, which have seen print in *Slade-Babcock Genealogy* (1971) and *Ancestral Lines* (1975). Limited to lists mentioned in the third edition of Lancour, it deals with twelve kinds of material which are commonly called, simply for convenience, ship passenger lists.

Of two hundred fifty lists found in Lancour, covering immigrants through 1825, seventy-five in number, or thirty per cent of the total, are emigrant lists, that is, records made in ports of embarcation. These are particularly noticeable in *Ship Passenger Lists: National and New England (1600-1825)* (1977), for the people listed sailed in a number of different ships to many ports in America. Sadly this volume, which has sold tremendously well since its publication (if "tremendously well" may be defined as two or three copies a day, consistently!), is not as valuable as the other volumes, which often include more precise details about their subjects in more useful respects.

Somewhat more than ten per cent of the lists mentioned by Lancour are immigrant lists made in the port of arrival. Records kept by occupation (somewhat less than five per cent) dealt with apprentices, liverymen and others and were sometimes found in guildhalls, while works on settlers of specific locations (little more than twenty per cent) were often derived from early church records. Forty-six of the two hundred fifty cited by Lancour and Wolfe in 1963 actually dealt with ship lists, while the remaining resources concerned convicts and paupers, naturalization records, customs lists and legal papers, petitions, oaths and early census records of varying types and degrees of accuracy, as this compiler has discussed in a previous preface.

Now, with new volumes from the Genealogical Publishing Company reintroducing appropriate articles from the larger and better known journals, and the present volume again putting into print the lists from the lesser known (and often extremely difficult to locate) sources, insofar as they pertain to the South (from Maryland to Louisiana), the work remains to be done only for Pennsylvania and Delaware, and that is in progress.

It might be pointed out that the sources treated in the present book were originally published in a wide variety of sizes and typefaces, including German Gothic, which few Americans these days can read at all, thus calling for a new type. Logically it would have been nice to entrust the work to a printer, who could have produced justified pages at reasonable cost, and quite quickly. However, the need for accuracy was too great, and this editor's experience has been that even extremely careful proofreading, done six times over by as many people, will not uncover all the errors inherent in copying by amateurs. For that matter, in places it was important that errors in the originals be preserved (and there are many). This compiler then sat down to the task of editing (only for the removal of material in lengthy works having little to do with ship passengers, not for errors), typing and indexing all the articles himself.

Once a book is ready for publication the choice of a title becomes important. No work can help anyone if all the copies sit in a garage, unsold. The compiler must have some reward for his time and some funds for publication of the next volume, and the researcher considering purchase must be given some information with which to make a decision. Thus the misnomer, "Ship Passenger Lists," came into use. This was taken from the title of Lancour's bibliography more than from the content of the books, not because of any intent to deceive the public (which has never complained), but because the lists, articles, excerpts and extracts of materials dealing with trans-Atlantic migration had come to be known, collectively, as ship lists or ship passenger lists, in part from the title of Lancour's slim but immensely useful volume.

Of course this work is not intended as an index to one's immigrant ancestors. Such an index is forthcoming, hopefully, from another source in the relatively near future. Such an index will not eliminate the need to consult the lists themselves, not only to determine what additional information may be available concerning an immigrant whose name is at hand, but whether some of his fellow passengers might be people about whom more is known, thus providing some valuable clues.

Even when the previously published lists are all actively in circulation by way of reprints, computerization of the passenger and customs lists kept until recently in the National Archives, and now at Temple University, Philadelphia, will remain to be done.

Errors, omissions and inconsistencies must be dealt with comprehensively (Meredith B. Colket, Jr., has completed a useful volume dealing with immigrants to 1657). Some of the editions of Hotten's *Persons* were sloppily done (with early reprints made from the poor 1880 edition). Different passengers with the same name must be identified, and it should not be forgotten that some people made the crossing twice, or a number of times.

While the need for this work is great, it is hampered, unfortunately, by unreasonably restrictive laws relating to vital records in an increasing number of states. This compiler suspects that a number of lower level archivists (to use the term very loosely) are frankly too darn lazy to earn their keep, and, bugged increasingly by some unthinking genealogists beyond the call of duty, have used the cozy relationship between public employees and their respective legislatures to close down the vital records on flimsy pretexts of privacy.

No, the records should not be opened to genealogists at the expense of the taxpayer or the working conditions of public service personnel, but reasonable safeguards supported by sensible search fees can be initiated without unreasoning overreaction.

In closing this researcher would like to thank the growing number of librarians who are actively building genealogical collections, particularly those who carefully await the reviews so that the unwary will not be reading the works of the unschooled and unskilled.

Carl Boyer, 3rd

P. O. Box 333 (24200 Cheryl Kelton Place)
Newhall, California 91322

December 21, 1978

Note concerning the second printing:

With the exception of the ISBN number being added to the copyright, three missing numbers being added to page 229, and the following page being brought up to date, there have not been any changes made in this printing but for the imprint on the title page.

The reception of this work has been quite gratifying.

Carl Boyer, 3rd

Newhall
August 5, 1980

Note concerning the third printing:

With the exception of a minor correction to the index on page 233, involving the correct spelling of "Nansemond" and its order in the alphabet, no changes have been made in this printing except for the omission of other books from this compiler having been listed previously on this page. Those interested in having a list of currently available books may drop a card requesting it to the undersigned.

On this day a note was received from P. William Filby, stating that in response to an article on immigrant lists published in the current *Genealogical Helper* he had received 230 letters within a short time asking for information on where the books he listed, including this series, could be obtained.

Thus it would be well to note, for the reader's information, that the books from this publisher are listed in *Books in Print* and other industry bibliographical sources, as well as *Genealogical & Local History Books in Print*, and can be ordered through any bookstore.

Carl Boyer, 3rd

P. O. Box 333 (24200 Cheryl Kelton Place)
Newhall, California 91322
9 September 1983

SHIP PASSENGER LISTS

J. Thomas Scharf. *History of Maryland from the Earliest Period to the Present Day*. Baltimore: John Piet, 1879 (I:66) [Lancour No. 198E].

The following excerpt from Scharf refers to the passengers on *The Ark* and *The Dove*, who went to Maryland in 1633 with Governor Leonard Calvert.

In them embarked nearly two hundred "gentlemen adventurers and their servants." Many of them were persons of wealth and consideration at home. Some of the names of the "gentlemen" which have been preserved, are: Leonard Calvert, the governor, and George Calvert [George Calvert went to Virginia and, it is stated, acted in the interest of Claiborne, and died before the year 1653], his brother. Two persons were joined with them in the commission, as counsellors, Jerome Hawley and Thomas Cornwallys. There also accompanied them Richard Gerard, son to Sir Thomas Gerard, knight and baronet; Edward Wintour and Frederick Wintour, sons of Lady Anne Wintour; Henry Wiseman, son of Sir Thomas Wiseman, knight; John Saunders, Edward Cranfield, Henry Greene, Nicholas Fairfax, John Baxter, Thomas Dorrell, Captain John Hill, John Medcalfe and William Saire. Among those who, it is supposed, came with the first colonists, were: Thomas Wills, Robert Simpson, Mary Jennings, John Hilliord, Robert Shorly, Rogers, John Hill, Christopher Carnock, John Bryant, William Ashmore, Richard Lusthead, Nicholas Hardy, Robert Edwards, Thomas Charinton, William Edwyn, Thomas Grigsta, Richard Duke, Henry Bishop, Thomas Heath, John Tomson, James Thornton, Lewis Fremond, Richard Nevill, John Hollis, Richard Cole, John Eckin, Thomas Hodges, Thomas Green, Anam Bonam, Thomas Cooper, John Hallowos, John Holder, Roger Walter, Roger Morgan, Josias Walter; and two Jesuit priests, Andrew White and John Altham. Richard Thompson at the same time brought into the colony Mathias Tousa, a "mulato," who he no doubt brought from the Island of Barbadoes, where the *Ark* and the *Dove* stopped on their voyage to Maryland.

After the objections raised by the Virginia Commissioners had been heard by the Privy Council..., and determined, the following order was issued by that body:

"Whereas the good ship called the *Ark* of Maryland of the burthen of about 350 tons, whereof one Lowe is Master, is set forth by our very good Lord, the Lord Baltimore for his Lordship's plantation at Maryland in America and manned with about 40 men. For as much as his Lordship hath desired, that the men belonging to his said ship, may be free from press or interruption, these are to will and require you, to forbear to take up, or press any, the officers, seamen, mariners or others belonging to his Lordship's said ship either in her voyage to Maryland, or in her return for England, and that you permit and suffer her quietly to pass and return without any let or hindrance, stay or interruption whatsoever [MSS. in London State Paper Office]."

On the 19th of October Lord Coke, the British Secretary of State informed Admiral Pennington "that the *Ark*, Richard Lowe, master, carrying men for Lord Baltimore to his new plantation in or about New England, had sailed from Gravesend contrary to orders, the company in charge of Capt. Winter not having taken the oath of allegiance," [In consequence of the bull issued by Pope Pius V., freeing all English subjects from allegiance to the King of England, after the Gun-Powder Plot, all persons sailing to the British colonies were required to take the oath of allegiance.—*Neill*] and instructed him [to have the *Ark* and the *Dove*, the latter a pinnace of twenty tons, brought back].

Gordon Ireland. "Servants to Foreign Plantations from Bristol, England, 1654-1686," *The New York Genealogical and Biographical Record*, 79 (1948), 65-75 [Lancour No. 199].

This material is readily available in the new Michael Tepper edition of ship passenger lists reprinted from *The Record*, and was extracted from materials in R. Hargreaves-Mawdsley's *Bristol and America*, which is generally available in a 1970 reprint, and is scheduled for another reprint (1978) by Genealogical Publishing Co., 111 Water Street, Baltimore, Maryland 21202.

J. Thomas Scharf. [Names of Aliens Naturalized by Special Acts of the Provincial Legislature, 1666-1750, in] *History of Maryland from the Earliest Period to the Present Day*. Baltimore: John B. Piet, 1879 (II:11) [Lancour No. 200].

Peter Achillis, John Alward, Abraham Ambrose, Moentz Anderson, Peter Anleton, Cornelius Arenson, Isaac de Barrette, Peter Bayard, Stephen Beeson, Michael Bellicane, Samuel Berry, Paul Berte, Garret Vansweringen, Barbara de Barette, Robert Roeland, Jean Jourdain, John Vanheeck, Charles de la Roche, Peter Johnson, Paul Barteaud, William Blankenstein, Lewis Blaney, Francis Rudolph Bodieu, Henry Bouquet, Cornelius Boys, Anthony Brispoe, James Broord, Hermanns Schee, Isaac Vanbibber, Mathias Vanbibber, Derrick Colieman, Sebastian Oley, Christopher Smithers, Arnold Livers, John Jowert, Derrick Browne, Lewis de Roch Brune, Herman van Buckele, Leonard Camperson, Matthew Cartwright, Laurence Christian, Andrew Clements, William Cody, Oliver Colke, Cornelius Comegys, Alexander Dhyniossa, Thomas Turner, Matthias Peterson, Jacob Clause de Young, Ham Jacob de Ring, Rutgerson Garretts, John Lederer, John Elexon, Nicholas Fountaine, Anthony Demouderer, Andrew Toulson, Hester Cordea, John Cosins, Matthias de Costa, Joseph Crismand, Michael Curtis, Benjamin Daffour, Xtopher Dangerman, Daniel Danison, Jasper Dauntrees, John Debrater, John Delamaire, John des Jardins, Peter Dowdee, Jacob Duhattoway, Claudius Dutitree, John Edgar, Henry Enloes, Peter Fernando, Alexander Forbes, Peter Fowcate, Stephen Francis, Henry Freeman, Christian Geist, Peter Golley, John Gotee, John Gontee, Arnoldus de la Grange, Henry Green, Albert Greening, Joshua Guibert, Samuel Guichard, Anna Hack, Hans Hanson, Thomas Harvey, Henry Henderson, John Hendrickson, Augustine Hermann, Gustavus Hesselius, John Francis Holland, Jeoffrey Jawbson, John Jarbo, Andrew Imbert, Albert Johnson, Bernard Johnson, Cornelius Johnson, John Johnson, Peter Johnson, Simon Johnson, Jean Jourdain, Herman Kinkee, Justus Englehead Kitchin, John Lamee, John Lavielle, Joseph Lazear, John Lecount, John Lederer, Arnold Livers, Jacob Lockerman, Jacob Looton, Peter Mannadoe, Rowland Mans, Andrew Matson, Henry Matthews, Matthias Matthiason, Daniel Maynadier, Peter Mills, Peter Moize de Moizne, Nicholas de la Montagne, Peter Montgomery, Christopher Mounts, Martin Mugenbourg, Andrew Poulson *alias* Mullock, John Samuel Mynkie, James Neale, Ambrose Nelson, William Nengfinger, John Nomers, John Oeth, John Oldson, Peter Oldson, Otho Othoson, Peter Owerard, Daniel Packet or Pacquet, David Paget, James Parandier, James Peane, Christian Peters, Cornelius Peterson, Stephen Rashoon, William Rayman, Onerio Razolini, Stephen Rich, James Richard, James Robert, Charles de la Roche, Peter Saunders, Peter Scamper, Jacob Seth, Peter Slayter, George Sleecombe, Hendrick Sluyter, Christopher Smithers, John Haus Steelman, Axel Stille, John Swineyard, Christian Swormstead, Marius Syserson, John Tavert, William Tick, Thomas Turner, John Baptist Tyler, Michael Ury, John de Vagha, Matthias Vanderheyden, Nicholas Verbrack, Frederick Victor, Gerardus Weeffels, John Woolf, John Peter Zenger.

Edward Duffield Neill. [Passengers on the *American Merchant*, 1714, in] *Terra Mariae; or Threads of Maryland Colonial History.* Philadelphia: J. B. Lippincott & Co., 1867 (202) [Lancour No. 201].

There were shipped on board the American Merchant, thirty-five women, thirty boys, and twenty-eight men. Subjoined are the names and occupations of some of the men and boys:

Names of Men.	*Occupation.*
William Colvin	Cooper
Arch'd Williamson	Smith
Peter Campbell	Coppersmith
John Kennedy	Wright
James Adamson	Sailor
Daniel Millar	Shoemaker
Henry Hunter	Tailor
James Chrystie	Farmer

Names of Boys.	*Occupation.*
Alex'r Campbell	Tailor
Charles Swinton	Weaver
Wm. Watson	Barber
Peter Graham	Glover
Henry McMillan	Butcher
John Toward	Painter
James Porteous	Baker
Wm. Brown	Shoemaker
Thos. Falconer	Farmer

J. Thomas Scharf. *History of Maryland from the Earliest Period to the Present Day.* Baltimore: John Piet, 1879 (I:386-387) [Lancour No. 202].

"A List of Rebbells Transported in the Shipp the *Friendship* of Belfast, Michael Mankin, Comander, the 20th of August, 1716:

Rebbells' Names.	*Purchasers' Names.*
John Pitter,	
James Nithery,	
Dugail Macqueen,	Wm. Holland, Esq.
Alex. Smith,	Samuel Chew, Jr.
Abraham Lowe,	Thomas Larkin
Henry Wilson,	
Alexander Gorden,	John Gresham.
John Hay,	William Homes.
William Simm,	
Alex'der Spalding,	Wm. Nicholson.
Leonard Robinson,	Thomas Doccora.
John Blondell,	Benjamin Wharfield.
John Sinclear,	Joseph Hill.
William Grant,	Thomas Davis.
Thomas Spark,	Philip Dowell.
James Webster,	Steph. Warman.
Wm. Cumins,	
Allin Maclien,	
John Robertson,	Thos. Macnemara.
Farq. Macgilvary,	Saml. Young, Esq.
David Mills,	Evan Jones.
Patrick Cooper,	Albertus Greening.
Jeremiah Dunbarr,	Hugh Kenneday.
John Degedy,	
William McBean,	
Thomas Lawry,	Phile. Lloyd, Esq.
John Glaney,	Hugh Spedden.

Wm. Macgilvary,	Robt. Ungle, Esq.
Alexandre Nave,	Thomas Broadhurst.
James Hindry,	John Oldham.
William Mobbery,	Henry Tripp.
James Small,	
James White,	Samuel Peele.
John Macbayn,	John Ford.
Rot. Henderson,	Edward Penn.
Thomas Potts,	
George Thompson,	
John Ramsey,	
Alexandre Reind,	
Thomas Forbus,	Wm. Bladen, Esq.
William Davidson,	Mordecai Moor.
James Mitchell,	
James Lowe,	Benjamin Tasker.
James Denholme,	John Clark.
James Allein,	Eliz. Brown.
James White,	Benjamin Dufour.
Thomas Donolson,	John Cheney.
James Hill,	Humphrey Godman.
David Steward,	
Henry Lumsdale,	Jacob Henderson.
Arch. Macdonall,	
alias Kenneday,	W. Fitz Redmond.
Charles Donalson,	
William Mare,	
Hector Macqueen,	Aaron Rawlings.
John Maclean,	Edward Parish.
John Mac Intire,	
William Onan,	
Alex. Macqueen,	
Alex. Macdugall,	Daniel Sherwood.
David Macqueen,	
John Macdonald,	Robert Grundy.
John Poss,	Edgar Webb.
Robert Stobbs,	John Valliant.
Finley Cameron,	Wm. Elbert.
John Mertison,	Peter Anderson.
Alex. Swinger,	Phil Sherwood.
Wm. Macgilvary,	Thomas Mackell.
Patrick Hunter,	James Calston.
Henry Farchaser,	Darley Dullany.
Alex. Mortimore,	Henry Ernallse.
Jas. Robertson,	Joseph Hopkins.
Thomas Butter,	
Andrew Davidson,	Francis Bullock.
Thos. Smith,	Joseph Bullock.
Thos. Mac Nabb,	Wm. Thomas.

James Shaw,	
Donald Robertson,	Thos. Robbins.
Andrew Daw,	Roger Woolforde.
John Coucham,	Philip Kersey.
Henry Murry,	Wm. Holland, Esq.

In all 80 Rebells.

J. Thomas Scharf. *History of Maryland from the Earliest Period to the Present Day*. Baltimore: John Piet, 1879 (I:388-389) [Lancour No. 203].

"A List of the Rebell prisoners transported into this province in the Ship the *Good Speed*, on the 18th Day of October, Anno Domini 1716, with the names of the persons who purchased them:

[The prisoners listed below, mostly Scots, were taken "in the late Rebellion at Preston, and Imported in the Ship the *Good Speed*, of Liverpoole, whereof Arthur Smith is Comander...."]

Prisoners' Names.	*Purchasers.*
Wm. Macferson,	
Tho. Shaw,	
Miles Beggs,	Michael Martin.
John Macgregier,	
Daniel Steward,	Rich'd Eglin.
Duncan Ferguson,	
John Mackewan,	John Fendall.
David Graham,	
Wm. Johnson,	
Jas. Mallone,	
Geo. Nuelson,	
John Chambers,	Charles Digges.
James Sinclare,	
Alexr. Orrach,	Henry Wharton.
James Crampson,	Francis Clavo.
John Stewart,	John Middleton.
Patt Smith,	Gustavus Brown.
Geo. Hodgson,	John Nelly.
Malcolm Maccolm,	John Wilder.
James Mac Intosh,	Henry H. Hawkins.
John Cameron,	Wm. Penn.
David Lander,	Francis Goodrich.
Francis Macbean,	Charles Born.
Wm. Simpson,	John Rogers.
John Kennery,	Marmaduke Simms.
James Bowe,	John Philpott.
Laughlin McIntosh,	Henry Miles.

Alexr. McIntosh,	Daniel Steward.
Wm. Ferguson,	
James Dixon,	John Bruce.
Richd. Withington,	
Tho. Berry,	
Jas. Maclearn,	Randall Garland.
Rowl'd Robertson,	
Ninian Brown,	Thomas Jameson.
Daniel Kennedy,	
Patrick Mackoy,	
Angus Macdormott,	John Courts.
James Mac Intosh,	
Hugh Macdugall,	Robt. Hanson.
John Maccollum,	
Wm. Shaw,	John Hawkins.
Hugh Mac Intire,	John Vincent.
Finloe Mac Intire,	John Penn.
Richd. Birch,	Benj. Tasker.
James Shaw,	Jno. Donalson.
Danl. Grant,	Wm. Macchonchia.
Hugh White,	Danl. Bryant.
James Rutherford,	Arthur Smith.
Tho. Hume,	Judith Bruce.
James Renton,	Unsold.
Alexr. Macgiffin,	Runaway.
Humphrey Sword,	---- ----
James Sumervill,	---- ----
John Shaftoe,	Dead.

Frank F. White, Jr. "A List of Convicts Transported to Maryland," *Maryland Historical Magazine*, 43 (1948), 55-60 [Lancour No. 204].

Footnotes are omitted from the excerpts which follow.

A list of one hundred fifteen convicts and felons transported by Andrew Reid [the contractor for the transportation of Newgate felons from April, 1739, to March, 1757] in 1740, a recent anonymous gift to the library of the Maryland Historical Society, is a document exceedingly rich in social and economic history....

Maryland received more convicts and felons than any other province in the eighteenth century.... Scharf estimates that the total number of criminals sent to Maryland was about 20,000, with over six hundred a year coming in between the years 1737 and 1767. In all probability, the majority of those so transported were not political offenders. Clearly, then, Maryland became a dumping ground for the objectionable subjects of the realm.

Most of these "seven-year" criminals were the ordinary criminals of the British Isles. Those transported included both men and women of all ages and descriptions. Their crimes ranged from merely stealing a loaf of bread to armed robbery. The more serious offenders were not transported but were executed shortly after their sentences were imposed. The Act of 1718 provided that persons who had been convicted of clergyable offenses such as burglary, robbery, perjury, or theft, be sent to America for seven years. James Went, for instance, one of those on the list, was guilty of robbing a house [*Gentleman's Magazine*, 9:325], while John Wells, William Snowd, and William Cardell, were charged with highway robbery [*Ibid.*, 10:34, 9:404]. Jarvis Hare, a mere lad of fourteen years, was sentenced for stealing a horse [*Ibid.*, 9:325], while Thomas Henning enlisted a man for the King of Prussia [*Ibid.*, 9:551]. Sarah Kingman picked a pocket [9:383]. Thus, the British Government perceived the great need for "servants" who might improve the colonial plantations and at the same time make themselves more useful to His Majesty.

These felons and convicts...often...languished in the jails...for as much as nine months....

Sheriffs were not allowed to deliver criminals to the transporters without license. The transporters themselves in turn had to give security that the felons would not return to England until their terms of banishment had expired....

Because of the great demand for indentured servants, many of the transporters made tremendous wealth. Captain Anthony Bacon was but one of those who chose to earn his living in this manner....

Marylanders tolerated the shipment of convicts simply because they had to. They protested the intrusion of convicts, but were unable to do much about it. They imposed a duty on the numbers of convicts brought in and not infrequently kidnapped them and spirited them away. The planter class appears to have been the only group which from the first favored the importation of convict labor. This group did, however, resent the King's making Maryland the dumping ground for his objectionable subjects, but were influential in forcing the passage of the 1728 Maryland law which, among other things, made compulsory written testimonials from each shipmaster as to the offense, the sentence, and the time each convict had to serve. Eventually, the agitation against convict labor became so great that the British Government were forced to look elsewhere for the site of a penal colony. This eventually became Botony Bay, Australia.

.... *The Historical Register* faithfully listed for many years the numbers of those to be transported, but none of those on the ship *York* could be traced through this journal. *The Gentleman's Magazine* also chronicled the names of those condemned, but usually these entries were in the briefest possible form. Those to be transported seldom appeared in the latter journal, but their offenses were usually listed with a remark such as "condemned and ordered to be transported four men and three women."

The list follows.

Blackwall March 22nd 1739/40.

A List of One Hundred and Fifteen Felons & Convicts Shipped from Newgate by Andrew Reid Esqr on board the York Capt Anthony Bacon Commander, bound for Maryland, vizt:

1 James Wood
2 Richard Merring
3 Myers Samuel
4 Elizabeth Ward
5 Mary Wood
6 Daniel Sullivan
7 James Evans
8 Ann (Johanna) Price
9 Thomas Watson
10 Richard Land
11 James Meredith
12 James Stuart
13 Elizabeth Jackson
14 Richard Markloud
15 Benjamin Dunkersly
16 John Plummer
17 Thomas Ward
18 Thomas Deane
19 Ephraim Hubbard
20 John Cooke
21 Sarah Stanley
22 William Turner
23 Richard Underwood
24 William Maxwell
25 John Anderson
26 Cesar Franklin
27 John Brown
28 James Eakins
29 John Warren
30 John Myers
31 Mary Johnson
32 Samuel Peartree
33 Lucy Hughes
34 John Irving
35 Jacob Edmunds
36 James Bartley
37 Michael Smith
38 William Jones
39 Thomas Henning
40 William Cardell
41 Jarvis Hare
42 James Went
43 Sarah Kingman
44 Sarah Sumners
45 Margaret Betts
46 William Burchmore
47 John Hastings
48 William Green
49 John Matthews
50 Sarah Withers
51 John Morgan
52 Mary Hardcastle
53 Francis Smith
54 John Deacon
55 Sarah Jones
56 Samuel Powell
57 William Stewart
58 Mary Castle
59 John Delane
60 John Duggen
61 Ann Groom
62 Elizabeth Price
63 Diana Cole
64 Elizabeth Fowles
65 James Brockwell
66 John Tizzard
67 Elizabeth Green
68 Alice Faulkner
69 John Patterson
70 Moses Beesely
71 Ann Stringer
72 William Shaw
73 Sarah Liddiard
74 Joshua Blackett
75 Henry Chapman
76 James Downes
77 Isaac Gaytes
78 Arnold Reynolds
79 Rebecca Peake
80 John Smith
81 John Mitchell
82 James Anderson
83 Hannah Thompson
84 William Graves
85 William Brown
86 Ann Wilson
87 Thomas Davis
88 James Stiles

89 John Patterson
90 William Berry
91 John Claxton
92 Charles Groom
93 Elianor Bolton
94 Elizabeth Smith
95 Martha Abbott
96 Margaret Ellis
97 Thomas Winter
98 John Wicks
99 Edward Groves
100 William Peake
101 John Blake
102 Marmaduke Bignoll
103 Richard Ford
104 Ann Williams
105 William Seale
106 Thomas Street
107 Francis Flack
108 Mary Heckman
109 Benjamin Bellgrove (Dead)
110 John Potter
111 William Kipps
112 Mary Elliott
113 George Vaughan
114 William Snowd
115 Joseph Wells

Blackwell March 22d 1739/40.
I Anthony Bacon Master of the Ship York, now lying in the River of Thames & bound for Maryland in America do hereby humbly certify that the above named Persons being in Number One Hundred & Fifteen were this day all received on board my said Ship (except Benjamin Bellgrove who died in Newgate) by the Order of Andrew Reid Esqr. to be immediately & effectually transported to Maryland, one of His Majesty's Plantations in America, pursuant to the Acts of Parliament for the purpose made & provided.

Antho: Bacon

Witness
Jno Nicholls
John Davis

[Followed by further affidavits concerning security for delivery.]

J. Thomas Scharf. [Scotch prisoners deported to Maryland on the ship *Johnson*, 1747, in] *History of Maryland from the Earliest Period to the Present Day*. Baltimore: John B. Piet, 1879 (I: 435) [Lancour No. 205].

After the suppression of [the] rebellion [of the partisans of Prince Charles Edward, "the Young Pretender,"] the participators in it were punished with vindictive severity. Great numbers were put to death, and multitudes transported. The Scottish prisoners were taken to England for trial, lest their own countrymen should be disposed to deal with them too leniently; and at one time there were no less than three hundred and eighty-five crowded in Carlisle jail. Of these the rank and file were permitted to cast lots, one man out of every twenty to be tried and hanged, and the rest to be transported. One ship-load of the latter were sent to Maryland. They came by the ship *Johnson*, of Liverpool, William Pemberton, master, and arrived at the port of Oxford, on July 20, 1747.

Their names, taken from a worm-eaten, certified list among the records at Annapolis, are as follows [given in paragraph form in original note]:

John Grant	Robert -------	Adam Norvil
John ---nald	James Erwyn	Peter Ruddoch
John Newton	Dunkin Farguson	David Russell
John Cameron	Dunham Farguson	Naile Robertson
----- Stutton	Allen Grant	Alexander Smith
Patrick Ferguson	Peter Gardiner	William Stewart
Thomas Ross	John Gray	James Simson
William Cowan	John Hector	Michael Steele
----- Naccoon	----- Hamilton	John Suter
Patrick Macintergall	James King	John Taylor
Mary Shaw	Dunham Macgregor	Andrew Fillery
Alice Pimmarrage	Alexander ------	Saunders Taylor
James Allen	Patrick Murray	Minnian Wise
William Beverley	Archi MacAnnis	John Warair
John Brandy	William Melvil	George Walson
John Bowe	William Murdock	John Watt
Alexander Buchanan	John Mean	Sanders Walker
John Burnett	John Magregor	William Yeats
Robert Boy	Roderick Macquerrist	Alexander -------
Robert Craigin	Roderick Macferrist	Adam Sutherland
Alexander ----agie	John Macdaniel	Augus Maccleod
William Connell	John Maquerrist	Archi Macintire
Duncan Cameron	John Macnabb	---- Macdaniel
John Cameron	Dan'l MacDaniel	Augus Grant
Donald -------	Hugh Macclean	Alexander Maccelod
James Chapman	Peter Maccloughton	Daniel Mageliis
Thomas Claperton	James Macluff	---- Macintosh
Sanders Campbell	Patrick Morgan	Donald Macintosh
William -------	Peter Maccoy	Gilbert Maccullum
Charles Davidson	James Mill	----- Gwyn
John Dunham	John Macgregor	John Cameron
John Duff	John Nesmith	John Arbuthnot

"Naturalization of Maryland Settlers in Pennsylvania," *Maryland Historical Magazine*, 5 (1910), 72 [Lancour No. 206].

The reports of the Pennsylvania authorities to the British Board of Trade, copies of which are contained in the Pennsylvania Historical Library, show that the following Marylanders went to Pennsylvania for naturalization in the latter days of the Province, most of them being naturalized at York: 1767—Jacob Werryfield, Jacob Bowman, Christian Whitmore, John Yeager, Henry Inkle, Samuel Wolgamode and Paul Werkslagen, all affirmed; 1768—Frederick Cramer, Stephen Wink, Michael Miller, Conrad Fox, Jacob Snyder, Simon Schicky, and Jacob Miller, all affirmed; 1769—George Pooderbach, affirmed; 1770—Lawrence Shook, took oath; 1771—George Yerkardt and Peter Naffager, both affirmed; 1772—Michael Huber, Christopher Miller, and Philip Fishbourne, all took oath; and John Erdman Doritz and Henry Worman, both affirmed.

Those who affirmed were probably Dunkers or Mennonites.

Kate Singer Curry. "Naturalizations—during the Court Sessions of January, 1798, Washington Co., Maryland," *National Genealogical Society Quarterly*, 23 (1935), 111-113 [Lancour No. 207].

Henry Adam of Hagerstown, a German and formerly a subject of Prince of Hesse.

Michael Beard, native of Germany.

Conrad Bleutlingers, of Hagerstown, native of Switzerland.

Henry Bowser, of Salisbury District, Washington Co. Md. Native of Switzerland.

Frederick Clinch, laborer, of Hagerstown. Native of Germany.

Daniel Cline of Funkstown, formerly a subject of the Emperor of Germany.

Henry Cline, butcher, of Hagerstown, formerly subject of the Emperor of Germany.

George Creager, of Hagerstown, of German & formerly a subject of Prince of Hanover.

Henry Delman, weaver of Hagerstown, native of Holland.

Christian Fightig, shoemaker of Funkstown, formerly subject of Emperor of Germany.

Francis Garmyer, shoemaker near Antietam, formerly subject of Emperor of Germany.

George Crisman, butcher of Hagerstown. Native of Germany.

John Goll, near Hagerstown, German, formerly subject of Prince of Landgrave.

Henry Hickroat, of Williamsport, German, formerly subject of Prince of Hesse.

Charles Holbrick, blacksmith, Antietam Hundred. Native of Germany.

John Johnson, farmer near Gilbert's Mills. Native of Ireland.

Gregorius Kempff, clock maker of Hagerstown. Native of Germany.

John Leight, of Hagerstown, tinner, formerly subject of Emperor of Germany.

John Longemon, residence Washington Co. Md. Native of Germany.

John Miller, baker, of Hagerstown, formerly a subject of Emperor of Germany.

John Neitzell, of Williamsport, cooper. Native of Germany.

Conrad Null, of Hagerstown, of German, formerly subject of the Prince of Hesse.

Ralph Ormston near Booth's Mills, farmer. Native of Great Britain.

Vendel Oyer, near Williamsport, laborer, Formerly subject of Emperor of Germany.

Samuel Ross, shoemaker, Williamsport. An Irishman.

William Seagler, of Marsh Hundred, Washington Co., Md. Native of Germany and formerly a subject of the Prince of Hesse.
Henry Schrader, of Marsh Hundred, formerly subject of King of Prussia.
Charles Seltzer, of Hagerstown, and formerly a subject of the Prince of Hesse.
Conrad Shafer, of Boonsberry, Washington Co., Md., formerly a subject of the Prince of Hesse.
Conrad Shane, of Hagerstown, whitesmith, formerly a subject of the Emperor of Germany.
William Shiker, rear [*sic*] Hagerstown, formerly subject of the King of Prussia.
Matthias Shold, tailor near Antietam. Native of Germany.
John Smith, of Hagerstown, bricklayer & stonemason. Native of Ireland.
Adam Smotz (?), farmer Lower Antietam. Native of Germany.
Henry Snyder, farmer near Hagerstown. Native of Germany.
Christian Stemple, of Hagerstown, of German & formerly subject of Prince of Wurtemburg.
Christian Stinebrenner, of Hagerstown. Native of Germany.
Henry Strouse, stone cutter. Native of Germany.
Christopher Swope, of Hagerstown, formerly subject of Emperor of Germany.
Edward Augustus Thomas, surveyor, near Booth's Mills. Native of England.
John Wagenor, native of France.
Jacob Weber, laborer of Hagerstown. Native of Germany.
Adam Weller, native of Germany, residing in Washington Co., Md.
John Jacob Werner, bookbinder of Hagerstown. Native of Germany.
James Wilson, of Boonsberry, carpenter. Native of Ireland.

Robert Armistead Stewart. "Ancient Planters" (in Nell Marion Nugent's *Cavaliers and Pioneers; Abstracts of Virginia Land Patents and Grants, 1623-1666* [Baltimore: Genealogical Publishing Company, 1974]) [Lancour No. 208].

Pages xxviii to xxxiv of Nugent's first volume contain the lists, which deal with those who came before 1616, with the date of arrival and the name of the ship where known. A second volume of Nugent's work, indexed by Claudia R. Grundman and covering the period 1666-1695, was published in Richmond in 1977, forty-three years after the original printing of the first volume.

"Lists of the Livinge & the Dead in Virginia February 16, 1623" (in *Colonial Records of Virginia* [Richmond: R. F. Walker, Superintendent of Public Printing, 1874]) [Lancour No. 208-1].

Apparently this title was reprinted in Baltimore in 1964 but is now out of print. The following lists, less the footnotes, are taken from pages 37-66.

A List of the Livinge.

At the Colledg Land.

[These lands were located on the northern side of the James River, from the falls down to Henrico, ten miles in length.]

Thomas Marlett,
Christopher Branch,
Francis Boot,
William Browning,
Walter Cooper,
William Welder,
Leonard More,
Daniell Shurley,
Peeter Jorden,
Nicholas Perse,
William Dalbie,
Isaias Rawton,
Theoder Moises,
Robert Champer,
Thomas Jones,
David Williams,
William Walker,
Edward Hobson,
Thomas Hobson,
John Day,
William Cooksey,
Robert Farnell,
Nicholas Chapman,
Mathew Edlow,
William Price,
Gabriell Holland,
John Wattson,
Ebedmeleck Gastrell,
Thomas Osborne.

Att the Neak of Land.

[Location not definitely known.]

Luke Boys,
Mrs. Boys,
Robert Halam,
Joseph Royall,
John Dods,
Mrs. Dods,
Elizabeth Perkinson,
William Vincent,
Mrs. Vincent,
Allexander Bradwaye,
his wife Bradwaye,
John Price,
his wife Price,
Robert Turner,
Nathaniell Reeve,
Serjeant William Sharp,
Mrs. Sharp,
Richard Rawse,
Thomas Sheppy,
William Clemens,
Ann Woodley,
Thomas Harris,
his wife Harris,
Margaret Berman,
Thomas Farmer,
Hugh Hilton,
Richard Taylor,
uxor Taylor,
Joshua Chard,
Christopher Browne,
Thomas Oage,
uxor Oage,
infant Oage,
Henry Coltman,
Hugh Price,
uxor Price,
infant Price,
Mrs. Coltman,
Robert Greene,
uxor Greene,
infant Greene.

Att West & Sherlow Hundred.

[Located about thirty seven miles above James City.]

John Harris,
Dorothe Harris,
Infants Harris, Harris,
Thomas Floyd,
Ellias Longe,
William Nichollas,
Roger Ratcliffe,
Robert Milver,
Robert Parttin,
Margaret Parttin,
infantes Parttin, Parttin,
Henry Benson,
Nicholas Blackman,
Nathanell Tattam,
Mathew Gloster,
Symon Surgis,
Nicholas Baley,
Ann Bayley,
Eliner Phillips,

Thomas Paulett,
Thomas Baugh,
Thomas Packer,
Jonas Bayley,
John Truffell,
Christopher Beane,
John Cartter,
Henry Bagwell,

Thomas Bagwell,
Edward Gardiner,
Richard Biggs,
Mrs. Biggs,
William Biggs,]
Thomas Biggs,] Sons.
Richard Biggs,]
William Askew,

Henry Carman,
Andrew Dudley,
James Gay,
Anthony Burrows,
Rebecca Rosse,
sons Rosse,
Rosse,
Petters, a maid.

Att Jordan's Jorney.

[Perhaps relates to Jordan's Point.]

Siselye Jordan,
Temperance Bayliffe,
Mary Jordan,
Margery Jordan,
William Farrar,
Thomas Williams,
Roger Preston,
Thomas Brookes,
John Peede,
John Freme,
Richard Johnson,
William Dawson,
John Hely,
Robert Mannell,

Ann Linkon,
William Besse,
Mrs. Besse,
Christopher Saford,
uxor Saford,
John Caminge,
Thomas Palmer,
Mrs. Palmer,
fil Palmer,
Richard English,
Nathaniel Causey,
Mrs. Causey,
Lawrence Evans,
Edward Clarke,

uxor Clarke,
infant Clarke,
John Gibbs,
John Davies,
William Emerson,
Henry Williams,
uxor Williams,
Henry Fisher,
uxor Fisher,
infant Fisher,
Thomas Chapman,
uxor Chapman,
infant Chapman,
Edith Hollis.

Att Flourdieu Hundred.

Richard Gregory,
Edward Alborn,
Thomas Dellimager,
Thomas Hack,
Anthony Jones,
Robert Guy,
William Strachey,
John Browne,
Annis Boult,
William Baker,
Theoder Beriston,
Walter Blake,
Thomas Watts,
Thomas Doughty,
George Deverell,
Richard Spurling,
John Woodson,
William Straimge,
Thomas Dune,
John Landman,
Leonard Yeats,

George Levet,
Thomas Harvay,
Thomas Filenst,
Robert Smith,
Thomas Garmder,
Thomas Gaskon,
John Olives,
Christopher Pugett,
Robert Peake,
Edward Tramorden,
Henry Linge,
Gibert Pepper,
Thomas Mimes,
John Linge,
John Gale,
Thomas Barnett,
Roger Thompson,
Ann Thompson,
Ann Doughty,
Sara Woodson,
Negors,

Negors,
6 Negors,
Negors,
Negors,
Negors,
Grivell, Pooley, Minister.
Samuel Sharp,
John Upton,
John Wilson,
Henry Rowinge,
Nathaniell Thomas,
William Barrett,
Robert Okley,
Richard Bradshaw,
Thomas Sawell,
John Bramford,
Anthony,
William, Negors men.
John,
Anthony,
A Negors Woman. 224

The rest at West and Sherlow Hundred Island.

Capt Fackt Maddeson,
Mary Maddeson,
Thomas Wattson,
James Wattson,
Francis West,
Roger Lewis,
Richard Domelow,
William Hatfeild,

Thomas Fossett,
Ann Fossett,
Jenkin Osborne,
William Sismore,
Martha Sismore,
Stephen Braby,
Elizabeth Braby,
Edward Temple,

Daniel Vergo,
William Tathill, boy,
Thomas Haile, boy,
Richard Mosewood [?],
Edward Sparshott,
Barnard Jackson,
William Brocke,
James Mayro.

At Chaplain's Choise.

[Perhaps located near Jordan's Point.]

Isacke Chaplaine,
Mrs. Chaplaine,
John Chaplaine,
Walter Priest,
William Weston,
John Duffy,
Ann Michaell,
Thomas Phillipps,

Henry Thorne,
Robert Hudson,
Isacke Baugton,
Nicholas Sutton,
William Whitt,
Edward Butler,
Henry Turner,
Thomas Leg,

John Browne,
John Trachern,
Henry Willson,
Thomas Baldwin,
Allexander Sanderson,
David Ellis,
Sara More,
Ann, a maid.

Att James citie and within the Corporation thereof.

Sir Francis Wyatt, Govr
Margarett, Lady Wyatt,
Hant Wyatt, minister,
Kathren Spencer,
Thomas Hooker,
John Gather,
John Matcheman,
Edward Cooke,
George Nelson,
George Hall,
Lane Burtt,
Elizabeth Powell,
Mary Woodward,
Sir George Yeardley, knight,
Temperance Lady Yeardley,
Argall Yeardley,
Frances Yeardley,
Elizabeth Yeardley,
Kilibett Hitchcocke,
Austen Combes,
John Foster,
Richard Arrundell,
Susan Hall,
Ann Grimes,

Elizabeth Lyon,
——— Younge,
negro, negro women,
Alice Davison, *vidua*,
Edward Sharples,
Jone Davies,
George Sands, Treas^r,
Capt. William Perce,
Joan Perce,
Robert Hedges,
Hugh Win,
Thomas Moulston,
Henry Farmer,
John Lightfoote,
Thomas Smith,
Roger Ruese,
Allexander Gill,
John Cartwright,
Robert Austine,
Edward Bricke,
William Ravenett,
Jocomb Andrews,
uxor Andrews,
Richard Alder,
Ester Evere,
Angelo, a negar,
Doctor John Pott,

Elizabeth Pott,
Richard Townsend,
Thomas Leister,
John Kullaway,
Randall Howlett,
Jane Dickinson,
Fortune Taylor,
Capt. Roger Smith,
Mrs. Smith,
Elizabeth Salter,
Sara Macocke,
Elizabeth Rolfe,
Christopher Lawson,
uxor Em. Lawson,
Francis Fouler,
Charles Waller,
Henry Booth,
Capt. Raph Hamor,
Mrs. Hamor,
Joreme Clement,
Elizabeth Clement,
Sara Langley,
Sisely Greene,
Ann Addams,
Elkinton Ratclife,
Francis Gibson,
James Yemanson,
John Pountes,

Christopher Best,
Thomas Clarke,
Mr. Reignolds,
Mr. Hickmore,
uxor Hickmore,
Sara Ruddell,
Edward Blaney,
Edward Hudson,
uxor Hudson,
William Hartley,
John Shelley,
Robert Bew,
William Ward,
Thomas Mentis,
Robert Whitmore,
Robert Channtree,
Robert Sheppard,
William Sawyer,
Lanslott Dansport,
Mathew Loyd,
Thomas Ottway,
Thomas Crouth,
Elizabeth Starkey,
Elinor,
Mrs. Perry,
infant Perry,
Frances Chapman,
George Graues,
uxor Graues,
Rebecca Snowe,
John Isgrane,
Mary Astombe, *vidua*,
Benamy Bucke,
Gercyon Bucke,
Peleg Bucke,
Mara Bucke,
Abram Porter,
Brigett Clarke,
Abigall Ascombe,
John Jackson,
uxor Jackson,
Ephraim Jackson,
Mr. John Burrows,
Mrs. Burrows,
Anthony Burrows,
John Cooke,
Nicholas Gouldsmith,
Elias Gaile,
Andrew Howell,
Ann Ashley,
John Southern,
Thomas Pasmore,
Andrew Ralye,
Nathaniel Jefferys,
uxor Jefferys,
Thomas Hebbs,
Clement Dilke,
Mrs. Dilke,
John Hinton,
Richard Stephens,
Wassell Rayner,
uxor Rayner,
John Jackson,
Edward Price,
Osten Smith,
Thomas Spilman,
Bryan Cawt,
George Minify,
Moyes Ston,
Capt. Holmes,
Mr. Calcker,
Mrs. Calcker,
infant Calcker,
Peceable Sherwood,
Anthony West,
Henry Barker,
Henry Scott,
Margery Dawse,
Mr. Cann (or Cam),
Capt. Hartt,
Edward Spalding,
uxor Spalding,
puer Spalding,
puella Spalding,
John Helin,
uxor Helin,
puer Helin,
infant Helin,
Thomas Graye,
uxor Graye,
Jone Graye,
William Graye,
Richard Younge,
uxor Younge,
Jone Younge,
Rendall Smallwood,
John Greene,
William Mudge,
Mrs. Sothey,
Ann Sothey,
Elin Painter,
Goodman Webb.

In the Maine.

Richard Atkins,
uxor Atkins,
William Baker,
Edward Oliver,
Samuell Morris,
Robert Davis,
Robert Lunthorne,
John Vernie,
Thomas Wood,
Thomas Rees,
Michael Batt,
uxor Batt,
vidua Tindall,
Mr. Stafferton,
uxor Stafferton,
John Fisher,
John Rose,
Thomas Thornegood,
John Badston,
Susan Blackwood,
Thomas Rinston (or f),
Robert Scottismore,
Roger Kid,
Nicholas Bullington,
Nicholas Marttin,
John Carter,
Christopher Hall,
David Ellis,
uxor Ellis,
John Frogmorton,
Robert Marshall,
Thomas Snow (orig. Swnow),
John Smith,
Lawrance Smalpage,
Thomas Crosse,
Thomas Prichard,
Richard Crouch,

Christopher Redhead,
Henry Booth,
Richard Carven,
uxor Carven,
John Howell,
William Burtt,
William Stocker,
Nicholas Roote,
Sara Kiddall,
infants Kiddall,
Kiddall,
Edward Fisher,
Richard Smith,
John Wolrich,
Mrs. Wolrich,
Jonathin Giles,
Christopher Ripen,
Thomas Banks,
Frances Butcher,
Henry Daivlen,
Arthur Chandler,
Richard Sanders,
Thomas Helcott,
Thomas Hichcocke,
Griffine Greene,
Thomas Osbourn,
Richard Downes,
William Laurell,
Thomas Jordan,
Edward Busbee,
Henry Turner,
Joshua Crew,
Robert Hutchinson,
Thomas Jones,
uxor Jones,
Reignold Morecocke,
uxor Morecocke,
Richard Bridgewater,
uxor Bridgewater,
Mr. Thomas Bun,
Mrs. Bun,
Thomas Smith,
Elizabeth Hodges,
William Kemp,
uxor Kemp,
Hugh Baldwine,
uxor Baldwine,
John Wilmose,
Thomas Doe,
uxor Doe,
George Fryer,
uxor Fryer,
Stephen Webb.

In James Island.

John Osbourn,
uxor Osbourn,
George Pope,
Robert Cunstable,
William Jones,
uxor Jones,
John Johnson,
uxor Johnson,
infants Johnson,
Johnson,
John Hall,
uxor Hall,
William Cooksey,
uxor Cooksey,
infant Cooksey,
Alice Kean,
Robert Fitts,
uxor Fitts,
John Reddish,
John Grevett,
uxor Grevett,
John West,
Thomas West,
Henry Glover,
Goodman Stocks,
uxor Stocks,
infant Stocks,
Mr. Adams,
Mr. Leet,
William Spence,
uxor Spence,
infant Spence,
James Tooke,
James Roberts,
Anthony Harlow,
Sara Spence,
George Shurke,
John Booth &
Robt Bennett.

The Neck of Land.

Mr. Kingsmeale,
uxor Kingsmeale,
infants Kingsmeale,
Kingsmeale,
Raph Griphin,
Frances Compton,
John Smith,
John Filmer,
Edward, a negro,
Thomas Sulley,
uxor Sulley,
Thomas Harwood,
George Fedam,
Peter Staber,
Thomas Popkin,
Thomas Sides,
Richard Perse,
uxor Perse,
Allen, his man,
Isabell Pratt,
Thomas Allnutt,
uxor Allnutt,
John Paine,
Roger Redes,
Elinor Sprad.

Over the River.

John Smith,
uxor Smith,
infant Smith,
John Pergo,
Richard Fenn,
William Richardson,
Robert Lindsey,
Richard Dolsemb,
John Bottam,
John Elliott,
Susan Barber,
Thomas Gates,

uxor Gates,
Percevall Wood,
Anthony Burrin,
William Bedford,
William Sands,
John Proctor,
Mrs. Proctor,
Phettiplace Close,
Henry Home,
Richard Home,
Thomas Flower,
William Bullocke,
Ellias Hinton,
John Foxen,
Edward Smith,
John Skimer,
Martine De Moone,
William Naile,
Thomas Fitts,
Elizabeth Abbitt,
Alice Fitts.

At the Plantation over against James Cittie.

[Perhaps located on the other side of the water.]

Capt. Samuel Mathews,
Benjamin Owin,
Rice Ax^{r} Williams,
John, a negro,
Walter Parnell,
William Parnell,
Margaret Roades,
John West,
Francis West, *vidua*,
Thomas Dayhurst,
Robert Mathews,
Arthur Gouldsmith,
Robert Williams,
Morice Loyd,
Aron Conway,
William Sutton,
Richard Greene,
Mathew Haman,
Samuell Davies,
John Thomas,
John Docker,
Abram Wood,
Michaell Lupworth,
John Davies,
Lewis Baly,
James Daries,
Alice Holmes,
Henry Barlow,
Thomas Button,
Edmond Whitt,
Zacharia Crispe,
John Burland,
Thomas Hawkins,
Thomas Phillips,
Paul Reinolds,
Nicholas Smith,
Elizabeth Williams,
Hugh Cruder,
Edward Hudson,
Robert Sheppard,
Thomas Ottawell,
Thomas Crouth,
Robert Bew,
John Russell,
Robert Chantry,
George Rodgers,
Lanslott Damport,
John Shule,
Nathaniell Loyd,
William Sawyer,
William Ward,
William Hartley,
Jereme Whitt,
Livetenant Purfrey,
Edward Grindall,
Mr. Swift,
William Hames,
George Gurr,
Henry Wood,
John Baldwine,
John Needome,
William Bricks,
Nicholas Thompson,
John Dency,
Erasmus Cartter,
John Edwards,
George Bayley,
George Sparke,
Nicholas Comin,
Nicholas Arras,
Marttin Turner,
John Stone, infant,
Davy Mansfield,
John Denmarke,
Elizabeth Rutten,
Goodwife Bincks,
A servant of Mr. Moorewood's.

The Glase Howse.

["A place in the woods neare a myle from Iames Toune."]

Vincentio,
Bernardo,
Ould Sheppard,
his sonn,
Richard Tarborer.
Mrs. Bernardo.

At Archer's Hoop.

[Archer's Hope Creek empties into the James River a short distance below Jamestown.]

Lieutenant Harris,
Rowland Lottis,
uxor Lottis,
John Elison,
uxor Elison,
George Sanders,
Thomas Corder,
Joseph Johnson,
George Pran,
John Bottom,
Thomas Farley,
uxor Farley,
a child,
Nicholas Shotton.

At Hogg Island.

[Located six or eight miles below Jamestown Island.]

David Sanders, minister,
John Utie,
Mrs. Utie,
John Utie, infant,
Willam Tyler,
Elizabeth Tyler,
Richard Whitby,
William Ramshaw,
Rice Watkins,
Thomas Foskew, lost,
Hener Elsword,
Thomas Causey,
George Union,
Henry Woodward,
Roger Webster,
John Donston,
Joseph Johnson,
Richard Crocker, child,
William Hitchcocke, lost,
George Prowse,
Robert Parramore,
John Jarvice, als. Glover,
John Browne,
William Burcher,
John Burcher,
John Fulwood,
Thomas Bransby,
Thomas Colly,
Thomas Simpson,
Thomas Powell,
Nicholas Longe.

At Martin's Hundred.

[Located between Hog Island and Mulberry Island, on a small stream named Skies Creek, on the north side of the James River.]

William Harwood,
Samuell March,
Hugh Hues,
John Jackson,
Thomas Ward,
John Stevans,
Humphrey Walden,
Thomas Doughtie,
John Hasley,
Samwell Weaver,
vidua Jackson,
filia Jackson,
Mrs. Taylor,
Ann Windor,
Elizabeth Bygrane,
Mr. Lake,
Mr. Burren,
John Stone,
Samwell Cultey,
John Helline,
uxor Helline,
A Frenchman *et uxor*,
Thomas Siberg.

At Warwick Squrake.

[Located on the south side of the James River, fourteen miles below Hogg Island.]

John Batt,
Henry Prinfse,
Wassell Weblin,
Anthony Read,
Frances Woodson,
Henry Phillips,
Petter Collins,
Christopher Reinolds,
Edward Mabin,
John Maldman,
Thomas Collins,
George Rushmore,
Thomas Spencer,
George Clarke,
Richard Bartlett,
Francis Banks,
John Jenkins,
Thomas Jones,
William Denham,
Peter,]
Anthony,]
Frances,] negroes,
Margrett,]
John Bennett,
Nicholas Skinner,
John Atkins,
John Pollentin,
Rachell Pollentin,
Margrett Pollentin,
Mary, a maid,
Henry Woodward,
Thomas Sawyer,
Thomas, a Boye.

At the Indian Thickett.

Henry Woodall,
Gregory Dory,
John Foster,
John Greene,
John Ward,
Christopher Wendmile,
Richard Rapier,
Cutbert Pierson,
Adam Rumell,
Richard Robinson,
James, a French man.

At Elizabeth Cittye.

[Location includes the peninsula formed by the Chesapeake and the James River.]

Capt. Isacke Whittakers,
Mary Whittakers,
Charles Atkinson,
Charles Calthrop,
John Lankfeild,
Bridges Freeman,
Nicholas Wesell,
Edward Loyd,
Thomas North,
Anthony Middleton,
Richard Popely,
Thomas Harding,
William Joye,
Raph Osborne,
Edward Barnes,
Thomas Thorugood,
Ann Atkinson,
——— Lankfeild,
——— Medclalfe,
George Nuce,
Elizabeth Whittakers,
George Roads,
Edward Josnson (sic.), (qy. Johnson,)
William Fouller,
Reinold Goodwyn,
James Larmount,
John Jackson,
vidua Johnson,
vidua Fowler,
Two Frenchmen,
George Medcalfe,
Walter Ely,
Thomas Lane,
Barthelmew Hopkins,
John Jefferson,
Robert Thresher,
John Rowes,
Mr. Yates,
Robert Goodman,
uxor Ely,
infant Ely,
Capt. Rawleigh Crashaw,
Robert Wright,
James Sleight,
John Welchman,
John More,
Henry Potter,
Mr. Roswell,
William Gawntlett,
Osborne Smith,
uxor More,
uxor Wright,
uxor Wright,
filia Wright,
Thomas Dowse,
Samwell Bennett,
William Browne,
William Allen,
Lewis Welchman,
Robert More,
Mrs. Dowse,
uxor Bennett,
pueri [Bennett,
[Bennett.

At Bricke Row.

Thomas Flint,
John Hampton,
Richard Peirsby,
William Rookins,
Rowland Williams,
Steven Dixon,
Thomas Risby,
Henry Wheeler,
James Brooks,
Samuel Bennett,
John Carning,
Thomas Neares,
Robert Salvadge,
William Barry,
Joseph Hatfield,
Edward Marshall,
Ambrose Griffith,
Petter Arrundell,
Anthony Bonall,]
——— La Geurd,] Frenchmen,
James Bonall, a Frenchm.,
John Arrundell,
John Haine,
Nicholas Row,
Richard Althrop,
John Loyd,
uxor Haine (or Hame),
uxor Hampton,
Elizabeth Arrundell,
Margret Arrundell.

At Bass's Choice.

Capt. Nathaniel Basse,
Samwell Basse,
Benjamin Simmes,
Thomas Sheward,
Benjamin Handcleare,
William Barnard,
John Shelley,
Nathaniell Moper,
Nath. Gammon,
Margrett Giles,
Richard Longe,
uxor Longe,
infant Longe,
Richard Evans,
William Newman,
John Army,
Peter Langden,
Henry,
Andrew Rawley,
Peter.

More at Elizabeth Cittie.

Lieutenant Sheppard,
John Powell,
John Wooley,
Cathren Powell,
John Bradston,
Francis Pitts,
Gilbert Whitfield,
Peter Hereford,
Thomas Faulkner,
Esaw de la Ware,
William Cornie,
Thomas Curtise,
Robert Brittaine,
Roger Walker,
Henry Kersly,
Edward Morgaine,
Anthony Ebsworth,
Agnes Ebsworth,
Elinor Harris,
Thomas Addison,
William Longe,
William Smith,
William Pinsen,
Capt. William Tucker,
Capt. Nick Martean,
Leftenant Ed. Barkly,
Daniell Tanner,
John Morris,
George Thomson,
Paule Thomson,
William Thomson,
Pasta Champin,
Stephen Shere,
Jeffery Hall,
Rich. Jones,
William Hutchinson,
Richard Apleton,
Thomas Evans,
Weston Browne,
Robert Mounday,
Steven Colloe,
Raph Adams,
Thomas Phillips,
Francis Barrett,
Mary Tucker,
Jane Brackley,
Elizabeth Higgins,
Mary Mounday,
Chouponke, an Indian,

Anthony,]
Isabella,] negroes.
Lieut. Lupo,
Phillip Lupo,
Bartholmew Wethersby,
Henry Draper,
Joseph Haman,
Elizabeth Lupo,
Albiano Wethersby,
John Laydon,
Ann Laydon,
Virginia Laydon,
Alice Laydon,
Katherine Laydon,
William Evans,
William Julian,
William Kemp,
Richard Wither,
John Jornall,
Walter Mason,
Sara Julian,
Sara Gouldocke,
John Salter,
William Soale,
Jeremy Dickenson,
Lawrance Peele,
John Evans,
Marke Evans,
George Evans,
John Downeman,
Elizabeth Downeman,
William Baldwin,
John Sibley,
William Clarke,
Rice Griffine,
Joseph Mosley,
Robert Smith,
John Cheesman,
Thomas Cheesman,
Edward Cheesman,
Peter Dickson,
John Baynam,
Robert Sweet,
John Parrett,
William Fouks,
John Clackson,
John Hill,
William Morten,
William Clarke,

Edward Stockdell,
Elizabeth Baynam,
George Davies,
Elizabeth Davies,
Ann Harrison,
John Curtise,
John Walton,
Edward Oston,
Toby Hurt,
Cornelius May,
Elizabeth May,
Henry May, child,
Thomas Willowbey,
Oliver Jenkinson,
John Chandeler,
Nicholas Davies,
Jone Jenkins,
Mary Jenkins,
Henry Gouldwell,
Henry Prichard,
Henry Barber,
Ann Barber,
John Hutton,
Elizabeth Hutton,
Thomas Baldwin,
John Billiard,
Reynold Booth,
Mary,
Elizabeth Booth, child,
Capt. Thomas Davies,
John Davies,
Thomas Huges,
William Kildrige,
Alex[r] Mountney,
Edward Bryan,
Percivall Ibotson,
John Penrice,
Robert Locke,
Elizabeth & Ann Ibotson,
Edward Hill,
Thomas Best,
Hanna Hill,
Elizabeth Hill,
Robert Salford,
John Salford,
Phillip Chapman,
Thomas Parter,

Mary Salford,
Francis Chamberlin,
William Hill,
William Harris,
William Worldige,
John Forth,
Thomas Spilman,
Rebecca Chamberlin,
Alice Harris,
Pharow Phlinton,
Arthur Smith,
Hugh Hall,
Robert Sabin,
John Cooker,
Hugh Dicken,
William Gayne,
Richard Mintren, Junr,
Joane Hinton,
Elizabeth Hinton,
Rebecca Coubber,
Richard Mintren, Senr,
John Frye,
William Brooks,
Sibile and William Brooks,
Thomas Crispe,
Richard Packe,
Miles Prichett,
Thomas Godby,
Margery Prichett,
Jone Goodby,
Jone Grindry,
John Iniman,
Mary Grindry,
John Grindry, child,
John Waine,
Ann Waine,
Mary Ackland,
George Ackland,
John Harlow,
William Cappe,
Edward Watters,
Paule Harwood,
Nick. Browne,
Adam Througood,
Richard East,
Stephen Read,
Grace Watters,
Willm Watters,
Willm Ganey,
Henry Ganey,
John Robinson,
Robert Browne,
Thomas Parrish,
Edmund Spalden,
Roger Farbracke,
Theodor Jones,
William Baldwin,
Luke Aden,
Anna Ganey,
Anna Ganey, *filia*,
Elizabeth Pope,
Rebecca Hatch,
Thomasin Loxmore,
Thomas Garnett,
Elizabeth Garnett,
Susan Garnett,
Frances Michell,
Jonas Stockton,
Timothee Stockton,
William Cooke,
Richard Boulten,
Frances Hill,
John Jackson,
Richard Davies,
Ann Cooke,
Dictras Chrismus,
Thomas Hill,
Arthur Davies,
William Newcome,
Elizabeth Chrismus,
Joan Davies,
Thomas Hethersall,
William Douglas,
Thomas Douthorn,
Elizabeth Douthorn,
Samuel Douthorn, a boy,
Thomas, an Indian,
John Hazard,
Jone Hazard,
Henry,
Frances Mason,
Michaell Wilcocks,
William Querke,
Mary Mason,
Mandlin Wilcocks,
Mr. Keth, minister,
John Bush,
John Cooper,
Jonadab Illett,
John Barnaby,
John Seaward,
Robest Newman,
William Parker,
Thomas Snapp,
Clement Evans,
Thomas Spilman,
Thomas Parrish.

At the Eastern Shore.

Capt. William Epps,
Mrs. Epps,
Peter Epps,
William,
Edmond Cloake,
William Bribby,
Thomas Cornish,
John Fisher,
William Dry,
Henry Wilson,
Peter Porter,
Christopher Cartter,
John Sunnfill (or Sumfill),
Nicholal Graunger,
James Vocat Piper,
Edward,
John,
Thomas,
George,
Charles Farmer,
James Knott,
John Ascomb,
Robert Fennell,
Phillip,
Daniell Cogley,
William Andrews,
Thomas Granes,
John Wilcocks,
Thomas Crampe,
William Coomes,
John Parsons,
John Coomes,

James Chambers,
Robert Ball,
Goodwife Ball,
Thomas Hall,
Ismale Hills,
John Tyers,
Walter Scott,
Goodwife Scott,
Robert Edmonds,
Thomas Hichcocke,
John Evans,
Henry Wattkins,
Peregree Wattkins,
Daniell Watkins,
John Blower,
Gody Blower,
John,
A boy of Mr. Cans,
John How,
John Butterfeild,
William Davies,
Peter Longman,
John Wilkins,
Goodwife Wilkins,
Thomas Powell,
Gody Powell,
Thomas Parke,
William Smith,
Edward Drew,
Nicholas Hoskins,
and his child,
William Williams,
Mrs. Williams,
John Throgmorton,
Bennanine Knight,
Chad Gunston,
Abram Analin,
Thomas Blacklocke,
John Barnett,
Thomas Savadge,
William Beane,
Salamon Greene,
John Wasborne,
William Quills. 1277

The End of the List of the Living.

A LIST OF THE NAMES OF THE DEAD IN VIRGINIA SINCE APRIL LAST. Feby 16th, 1623.

Colledge.

William Lambert,
John Wood, killed,
William More, killed,
Thomas Naylor, killed,
James Howell, killed.

At the Neck of Land.

Moses Conyers,
Greorge Grimes,
William Clements,
Thomas Fernley, killed,
Edward.

At Jordain's Jorney.

Roger Much,
Mary Reese,
Robert Winter,
Robert Woods,
Richard Shriese,
Thomas Bull,
John Kinton,
Daniell.

At West & Sherlow Hundred.

Samwell Foreman,
Zorobabell,
2 Indians,
One negar,
Thomas Roberts,
John Edmonds,
John Lasey,
Daniell Francke,
Capt. Nath. West,
Christopher Harding, killed.

At Flower de Hundred.

John Mayor,
William Waycome,
Thomas Prise,
Robert Walkin,
John Fetherston,
John Ax. Roberts,
Richard Jones,
Richard Griffin,
Richard Ranke,
William Edger,
John Fry,
Dixi Carpenter,
William Smith,
James Cindnare,
Edward Temple,
Sara Salford,
John Stanton,
Christo. Evans.

At James Cittie.

Mr. Sothey,
John Dumpont,
Thomas Browne,
Henry Sothey,
Thomas Sothey,
Mary Sothey,

Elizabeth Sothey,
Thomas Clarke,
Margarett Shrawley,
Richard Walker,
Vallentyne Gentler,
Peter Brishitt,
Humphrey Boyse,
John Watton,
Arthur Edwards,
Thomas Fisher,
William Spence,]
Mrs. Spence,]
lost,
George Sharks,
John Bush,
Mr. Collins,
uxor Collins,
Mr. Peyden,
Peter De Maine,
Goodman Ascomb,
Goodman Witts,
William Kerton,
Mr. Atkins,
Thomas Hakes,
Peter Gould,
Robert Ruffe,
Ambrose Fresey,
Henry Fry,
John Dinse,
Thomas Trundall,
Richard Knight,
John Jefferys,
John Hamun,
John Meridien,
John Countivane,
Thomas Guine,
Thomas Somersall,
William Rowsley,
Elizabeth Rowsley,
a maid of theirs,
Robert Bennett,
Thomas Roper,
Mr. Fitziefferys,
Mrs. Smith,
Peter Martin,
James Jakins,
Mr. Crapplace,
John Lullett,
Ann Dixon,
William Howlett,
Mr. Furlow's child,
Jacob Prophett,
John Reding (or Reeing)
Ritchard Atkins,
his child,
John Bayly,
William Jones,
his son and
John, Mr. Pearis' servant,
Josias Hartt,
Judith Sharp,
Ann Quarle,
——— Reignolds,
William Dier,
Mary Dier,
Thomas Sexton,
Mary Brawdrye,
Edward Normansell,
Henry Fell,
——— Enims,
Roger Turnor,
Thomas Guine,
John Countway,
John Meriday,
Benjamine Usher,
John Haman,
John Jefferyes,
Richard Knight,
John Walker,
Hosier,
William Jackson,
William Apleby,
John Manby,
Arthur Cooke,
Stephen.

At the Plantation over ag^{t} James Cittie.

Humphrey Clough,
Morris Chaloner,
Samuell Betton,
John Gruffin,
William Edwards,
William Salisbury,
Mathew Griffine,
Robert Adwards,
John Jones,
Thomas Prichard,
Thomas Morgaine,
Thomas Biggs,
Nicholas Bushell,
Robert Williams,
Robert Reynolds,
Edward Huies,
Thomas Foulke,
Mathew Jenings,
Richard Morris,
Frances Barke,
John Ewins,
Samwell Fisher,
John Ewins,
James Cartter,
Edward Fletcher,
Aderton Greene,
Morice Baker,
Robert, Mr. Ewins' man,
Robert Pidgion,
Thomas Triggs,
James Thursby,
Nicholas Thimbleby,
Frances Millett,
John Hooks,
Thomas Lawson,
William Miller,
Nicholas Fatrice,
John Champ,
John Maning,
Richard Edmonds,
David Collins,
Thomas Guine,
John Vicars,
John Meredie,
Beng. Usher,
John Cantwell,
Richard Knight,
Robert Hellue,
Thomas Barrow,
John Enines,
Edward Price,
Robert Taylor,
Richard Butterey,
Mary Lacon,
Robert Baines,
Joseph Arthur,

Thomas Mason,
John Beman,
Christo. Pittman,
Thomas Willer,
Samwell Fulshaw,
John Walmsley,
Abram Colman,
John Hodges,
Naamy Boyle.

At Hogg Island.

William Brakley,
Peter Dun,
John Long.

At Martin's Hundred.

Henry Bagford,
Nicholas Gleadston,
Nicholas Dornigton,
Raph Rogers,
Richard Frethram,
John Brogden,
John Beanam,
Francis Atkinson,
Robert Atkinson,
John Kerill,
Edward Davies,
Percivall Mann,
Mathew Staneling,
Thomas Nicholls,
2 children of the Frenchmen,
John Pattison,]
uxor Pattison,] killed,
Edward Windor,
Thomas Horner,
John Walker,
Thomas Pope,
Richard Ston,
John Catesby,
Richard Stephens,
William Harris,
Christo. Woodward,
Joseph Turner.

At Warwick Squrake.

Josias Collins,
Clement Wilson,
William Robinson,
Christo. Rawson,
Thomas Winslow,
uxor Winslow,
infant Winslow,
Alex[r] Sussames,
Thomas Prickett,
Thomas Maddox,
John Greene,
Nathaniel Stanbridg,
John Litton,
Christo. Ash,
uxor Ash,
infant Ash,
Nethaniel Lawe,]
Jane Fisher,] killed.
Phillip Jones,
Edward Banks,
John Symons,
Thomas Smith,
Thomas Griffin,
George Cane,
Robert Whitt,
Symon, an Italien.

At Elizabeth Cittie.

Charle Marshall,
William Hopkicke,
Dorothie Parkinson,
William Robertts,
John Ferrar,
Martin Cuffe,
Thomas Hall,
Thomas Smith,
Christo. Robertts,
Thomas Browne,
Henry Fearne,
Thomas Parkins,
Mr. Huffy,
James Collis,
Raph Rockley,
William Geales,
George Jones,
Andrew Allinson,
William Downes,
Richard Gillett,
Goodwife Nonn,
Hugo Smale,
Thomas Wintersall,
John Wright,
James Fenton,
Cisely, a maid,
John Gavett,
James,]
John,] Irishmen,
Jocky Armestronge,
Wolfston Pelsant,
Sampson Pelsant,
Cathrin Capps,
William Elbridg,
John Sanderson,
John Bewbricke,
John Baker, killed,
William Lupo,
Timothy Burley,
Margery Frisle,
Henry West,
Jasper Taylor,
Brigett Searle,
Anthony Andrew,
Edmond Cartter,
Thomas ———,
William Gauntlett,
Gilbert ———, killed,
Christopher Welchman,
John Hilliard,
Gregory Hilliard,
John Hilliard,
William Richards,
Elizabeth, a maid,
Capt. Hickcocke,
Thomas Keinnston,
Capt. Lincolne,

Chad. Gulstons,
uxor Gulstons,
infant Gulstons,
George Cooke,
Richard Goodchild,
Chrisenus, his child,
Elizabeth Mason,
Symon Wither,
Whitney Guy,
Thomas Brodbanke,
William Burnhouse,
John Sparkes,
Robert Morgaine,
John Locke,
William Thompson,
Thomas Fulham,
Cutberd Brooks,
Innocent Poore,
Edward Dupper,
Elizabeth Davies,
Thomas Buwen,
Ann Barber,
William Lucott,
Nicholas ———, killed,
Henry Bridges,
Henry Payton,
Richard Griffin,
Raph Harrison,
Samwell Harvie,
John Boxer,
Benjaimine Boxer,
Thomas Servant,
Frances Chamberline,
Bridgett Dameron,
Isarell Knowles,
Edward Bendige,
William Davies,
John Phillips,
Daniell Sandwell,
William Jones,
Robert Ball's wife,
Robert Leaner,
Hugh Nickcott,
John Knight.

Out of the Ship called The Furtherance.

John Walker,
——— Hosier,
William Jackson,
William Apleby,
John Manby,
Arthur Cooke,
Steven.

Out of the God's Gift.

Mr. Clare, master.
William Bennett.

Out of the Margrett & John.

Mr. Langley,
Mr. Wright.

The Guner of the *William & John.* 371

[The following list was originally published in Neil's *History of the Virginia Company*, and then reprinted in *Colonial Records*.]

"Here following is set downe a true list of the names of all those that were massacred by the treachery of the Savages in Virginia, the 22nd March last [1622].

"To the end that their lawfull heyres may take speedy order for the inheritinge of their lands and estates there. For which the honourable Company of Virginia are ready to do them all right and favour:"

At Captaine Berckley's Plantation, seated at Falling Creeke, some 66 miles from James Citie, in Virginia.

John Berkley, Esquire,
Thomas Brasington,
John Sawyer,
Roger David,
Francis Gowsh,
Bartholmew Peram,
Giles Peram,
John Dowler,
Laurence Dowler,
Lewis Williams,
Richard Bascough,
Thomas Holland,
John Hunt,
Robert Horner Mason,
Phillip Barnes,
William Swandal,
Robert Williams, his Wife and Childe,
Giles Bradshawe, his Wife and Childe,
John Howlet and his sonne,
Thomas Wood and Col-

lins his man, Joseph Fitch, apothecary to Doctor Pots.

At Master Thomas Sheffield Plantation, some three miles from the Falling Creeke.

Master Th: Sheffield [son of William Sheffield] and Rachel his wife,
John Reeve,
William Tyler, a boy,
Samuel Reeve,
John Ellen,
Robert Tyler, a boy,
Mathew ———,
Judeth Howard,
Thomas Poole,
Methusalem ———,
Thomas Taylor,
William Tyler.

At Henrico Iland, about two miles from Sheffield's Plantation.

——— Atkins,
——— Weston,
Philip Shatford,
William Perigo,
Owen Jones, one of Capt. Berkley's people.

Slaine of the Colledge People, about two miles from Henrico-Citie.

Samuel Stringer,
George Soldan,
William Basset,
John Perry,
Edward Ember,
Jarrat Moore,
Thomas Xerles,
Thomas Freeman,
John Allen,
Thomas Cooke,
John Clements,
James Faulkoner,
Christopher Henley,
William Jordan,
Robert Davis,
Thomas Hobson,
William Bailey.

At Apo-mattucke River, at Master Abraham Pierce his Plantation, some five miles off the Colledge People.

William Charte,
Jo: Waterhowse,
John Barker, a boy.
Robert Yeoman.

At Charles-Citie and about the precincts of Capt. Smith's Company.

Roger Royal,
Thomas Jones,
Robert Marvel,
Edward Heydon,
Henry Bushel.

At other Plantations next adioyning.

Richard Plat and his Brother,
Henry Milward, his wife, his Childe and his Sister,
Richard, a boy,
Goodwife Redhead.

At Mr. William Farrar's House.

Master John England and his man,
John Bel,
Henricke Peterson and Alice, his Wife, and William, her sonne,
Thomas, his man,
James Woodshaw,
Mary and Elizabeth, Maid servants.

At Berkley-Hundred, some five miles from Charles-Citie.

Capt. George Sharpe, Esq., one of his Maiesties Pentioners.
John Rowles,
Richard Rowles, his Wife and Childe,
Giles Wilkins,
Giles Bradway,
Richard Fereby,
Thomas Sharpe,
Robert Jordan,
Edward Painter.

At Westover, about a mile from Berkley-Hundred.

And First at Cap. Fr. West's Plantation:

James English, Richard Dash.

At Master John West's Plantation:

Christopher Turner, David Owen.

At Capt. Nathanael Wests:

Michael Aleworth, John Wright.

At Lieutenant Gibs his Dividend:

John Paly, Thomas Ratcliffe, Michael Booker, John Higglet, Nathanael Earle, John Gibbes, William Parker, Richard Wainham, Benomy Keyman, Thomas Gay, James Upsall, Daniel, M[r] Dombelowes man.

At Mr. Richard Owen's House:

Richard Owen, Stephen Dubo, Francis, an Irishman, Thomas Paine, One old Maid called blinde Margaret, William Reeve,

At Master Owen Macar's House:

Owen Macar, Garret Farrel, Richard Yeaw, One Boy.

At Master Macock's Dividen:

Capt. Samuel Macock, Esquire, Edward Lister, Thomas Browne, John Downes.

At Flowerdieu-Hundred, Sir George Yeardley's Plantation.

John Philips, Thomas Nuson, John Braford, Robert Taylor, Samuel Jarret, Elizabeth Bennet.

At the other side of the River, opposite to Flowerdieu-Hundred.

Master Hobson and his wife, Richard Storks, John Slaughter, Thomas Philips, Richard Campion, Anne Greene.

At Mr. Swinhowe his House.

Mistris Swinhow and Thomas and George Swinhow, her sonnes, Richard Mosse, John Larkin, William Blyth, Thomas Grindal.

At Mr. William Bikar's House.

William Bykar, Math. Hawthorn and his wife, Edward Pierce, Nicholas Howsdon.

At Weynoack of Sir George Yeardley his people.

Nathaniel Elie, John Flores, Henry Gape, ——— Buckingham, William Puffet, William Walker, John Gray, James Boate, John Suersby, Thomas Evans, Thomas ap-Richard, Henry Haynes, John Blewet, Henry Rice, ——— Hurt, Jonas Alpart, Thomas Stephens, Samuel Goodwine, John Snow and his Boy, Margery Blewet.

At Powle-Brooke.

Capt. Nath. Powle, Esq., and his wife, Daughter to Mr Tracey,
Mistris Bray,
Adam Rayner's wife,
Barbara Burges,
William Head,
Thomas Woolcher,
William Meakins,
Robert ———,
Peter Jordan,
Nathanael Leydon,
Peter Goodale.

At Southampton Hundred.

Robert Goffe and his wife,
William Larkum,
John Davis,
William Mountfort.

At Martin Brandons.

Lieutenant Sanders,
Ensigne Sherley,
John Taylor and his wife,
2 Boyes,
Mathew, a Polander.

At Captaine Spilman's House.

John Basingthwayte,
Walter Shawe.

At Ensigne Spence his House.

William Richmond,
John Fowler,
Alexander Bale,
William Fierfax,
The Tinker.

Persons slaine at Martins-Hundred, some seaven miles from James-Cities.

Lieutenant Rich: Kean,
Master Tho: Boise & Mistris Boise, his wife & a sucking Childe, 4 of his men, A Maide, 2 Children,
Nathanael Jefferies wife,
Margaret Davies,
3 servants,
Master John Boise,
his wife,
A Maide,
4 Men-servants,
Laurence Wats,
his Wife,
2 Men servants,
Timothy Moise,
his Man,
Henry Bromage,
his Wife,
his Daughter,
his Man,
Edward How,
his Wife,
his Childe,
A child of John Jackson,
4 Men servants,
Josua Dary,
his wife,
Richard Staples,
his wife,
and Childe,
2 Maides,
6 Men and Boyes,
Walter Davies & his brother,
Christopher Guillam,
Thomas Combar,
A Man,
Ralphe Digginson,
his Wife,
Richard Cholser,
George Jones,
Cisby Cooke,
his wife,
David Bons,
John Benner,
John Mason,
William Pawmet,
Thomas Bats,
Peter Lighborrow,
James Thorley,
Robert Walden,
Thomas Tolling,
John Butler,
Edward Rogers,
Maximilian Russel,
Henry, a Welchman.

At Mr. Thomas Pierce his House over against Mulberry Iland.

Master Tho: Pierce,
his Wife,
and Childe,
John Hopkins,
John Samon,
A French Boy.

At Mr. Edward Bennets Plantation.

Mastter Th: Brewood,
his wife,
his Childe,
Robert Gray,
John Griffin,
Ensigne Harrison,
John Costard,
David Barry,
Thomas Sheppard,
Henry Price,
Robert ———,
Edward Jolby,
Richard ———,
Alice Jones,
Thomas Cooke,
Philip Worth,
Mathew a maid,
Francis Winder,
Thomas Conly,
Richard Woodward,
Humfrey Cropen,
Thomas Bacon,
Evan Watkins,
Richard Lewis,
Edward Towse,
2 Servants,
Thomas Ferris,
George Cole,
Remember Michel,
——— Bullocke,
Richard Chandler,
Henry Moore,
Nicholas Hunt,
John Corderoy,
Richard Cockwell,
John Howard,
Mistris Harrison,
Mary Dawks,
Annie English,
Rebecca ———,
Master Prowse,
Hugh ———,
John ———,
Edward ———,
Mistris Chamberlin,
Parnel a maid,
Humfrey Sherbrooke,
John Wilkins,
John Burton.
John Scotchmore,]
Edward Turner,] Mr John Pountis his men.
Edward Brewster, Lieutenant Pierce his man.
Thomas Holland, Capt. Whittakers man.

At Master Walters his house.

Master Edward Walters,
his wife,
a Childe,
a Maid,
a Boy.

The whole number 347.

"Census of Inhabitants: Names of the First Settlers at Jamestown, 1607; Names of Those Who Came in the First Supply; Names of Those Who Came in the Second Supply; Names of Inhabitants of Jamestown in 1624" (in Lyon Gardiner Tyler's *The Cradle of the Republic: Jamestown and James River* [Richmond: The Hermitage Press, 1906], pages 101-104) [Lancour No. 209].

Names of those who came in the First Supply:

(From Smith, *Works*, [Arber's ed.] p. 411).

Mathew Scrivener appointed to be one of the Councell.

Gentlemen.

Michaell Phittiplace.
William Phittiplace.
Ralph Morton.
Richard Wyffing.
John Taverner.
William Cantrell.
Robert Barnes.
Richard Featherstone.
George Hill.
George Pretty.
Nathaniell Causy.
Peter Pory.
Robert Cutler.
Michaell Sicklemore.
William Bentley.
Thomas Coe.
Doctor Russell.
Jeffrey Abbot.
Edward Gurgana.
Richard Worley.
Timothy Leeds.
Richard Killingbeck.
William Spence.
Richard Prodger.
Richard Pots.
Richard Mullinax.
William Bayley.
Francis Perkins.
John Harper.
George Forest.
John Nichols.
William Grivell.

Laboroures.

Raymond Goodison.
William Simons.
John Spearman.
Richard Bristow.
William Perce.
James Watkins.
John Bouth.
Christopher Rods.
Richard Burket.
James Burre.
Nicholas Ven.
Francis Perkins.
Richard Gradon.
Rawland Nelstrop.
Richard Savage.
Thomas Savage.
Richard Milmer.
William May.
Vere.
Michaell.
Bishop Wiles.

Taylers.

Thomas Hope.
William Ward.
John Powell.
William Yonge.
William Beckwith.
La(w)rence Towtales.

Apothecaries.

Thomas Field.
John Harford.

Dani: Stallings, Jeweller.
Will. Dawson, a refiner.

Wil. Johnson, a Goldsmith.
Peter Keffer, a gunsmith.
Rob: Alberton, a perfumer.
Richard Belfield, a Goldsmith.
Post Ginnat, a Chirurg(ion).
John Lewes, a Cooper.
Robert Cotton, a Tobacco-pipemaker.
Richard Dole, a Blacksmith.

And divers others to the number of 120.

Names of those who came in the Second Supply:

(From Smith, *Works*, [Arber's ed.] p. 445).

Captaine Peter Winne] were appointed to be of the
Captaine Richard Waldo] Councell.
Master Francis West, brother to the Lord Le Warre.

Gent.

Thomas Graves.
Raleigh Croshaw.
Gabriel Beadle.
John Beadle.
John Russell.
William Russell.
John Cuderington.
William Sambage.
Henry Leigh.
Henry Philpot.
Harmon Harrison.
Daniel Tucker.
Henry Collings.
Hugh Wolleston.
John Hoult.
Thomas Norton.
George Yarington.
George Burton.
Thomas Abbay.
William Dowman.
Thomas Maxes
Michael Lowick.
Master Hunt.
Thomas Forrest.
John Dauxe.

Tradesmen (i. e., *Artizans*).

Thomas Phelps.
John Prat.
John Clarke.
Jeffrey Shortridge.
Dionis Oconor.
Hugh Winne.
David ap Hugh.
Thomas Bradley.
John Burras.
Thomas Lavander.
Henry Bell.
Master Powell.
David Ellis.
Thomas Gibson.

Labourers.

Thomas Dawse.
Thomas Mallard.
William Tayler.
Thomas Fox.
Nicholas Hancock.
Walker.
Williams.
Floud.
Morley.
Rose.
Scot.
Hardwyn.

Boyes.

Milman.
Hilliard.

Mistresse Forrest, and Anne Burras her maide; eight Dutch men and *Poles*, with some others, to the number of seaventie persons, &c.

Names of inhabitants of Jamestown in 1624:

(From Hotten, *Lists of Emigrants to America*, 173-178.)

Sir Francis Wyatt, Governor
Margaret, Lady Wyatt
Hawt Wyatt, Minister
Kathren Spencer
Thomas Hooker
John Gather
John Matheman
Edward Cooke
George Nelson
George Hall
Jane Burtt
Elizabeth Pomell
Mary Woodward

———

Sir George Yeardley, Knight
Temperance, Lady Yeardley
Argall Yardley
Frances Yeardley
Elizabeth Yeardley
Kilibett Hichcocke
Austen Combes
John Foster
Richard Arrundell
Susan Hall
Ann Grimes
Elizabeth Lyon
Younge
——— Negroe] Women
——— Negroe]

———

Alice Davison—vid
Edward Sharples
Jone Davies
George Sands, Treasurer
Captain William Perce
Jone Perce
Robert Hedges
Hugh Wms. (Williams)
Thomas Moulston
Henry Farmor
John Lightfoote
Thomas Smith
Roger Ruese
Alexander Gill
John Cartwright,
Robert Austine
Edward Bricke
William Ravenett
Jocomb Andrews
vx Andrews
Richard Alder
Ester Evere
Angello A Negar

———

Doct. John Pott
Elizabeth Pott
Richard Townsend
Thomas Leister
John Kullaway
Randall Howlett
Jane Dickenson
Fortune Taylor

Capt. Roger Smith
Mrs. Smith
Elizabeth Salter
Sarah Macocke
Elizabeth Rolfe
Chri Lawson
vxor eius Lawson
Francis Fouler
Charles Waller
Henry Booth

Capt. Ralph Hamor
Mrs. Hamor
Jereme Clement
Elizabeth Clement
Sarah Langley
Sisley Greene
Ann Addams
Elkinton Ratcliffe
Frances Gibson
James Yemanson

John Pontes
Christopher Best
Thomas Clarke
Mr. Reignolds
Mr. Hickmore
vx Hickmore
Sarah Riddall

Edward Blaney
Edward Hudson
vx Hudson
William Hartley
John Shelley
Robert Bew
William Ward
Thomas Mentis
Robert Whitmore
Robert Chauntree
Robert Sheppard
William Sawier
Lanslott Damport
Math. Loyd
Thomas Ottway
Thomas Crouch
Elizabeth Starkey
Elinor

Mrs. Perry
Infans Perry
Frances Chapman
George Graves
vx Graves
Rebecca Snowe
Sarah Snowe
John Isgraw (Isgrave)
Mary Ascombe vid
Banamy Bucke
Gercyon Bucke
Peleg Bucke
Mara Bucke
Abram Porter
Bridget Clarke
Abigall Ascombe
John Jackson
vx Jackson
Ephraim Jackson

Mr. John Burrows
Mrs. Burrows
Anthony Burrows
John Cooke
Nicholas Gouldsmith
Elias Gaill
Andrew Howell
An Ashley

John Southern
Thomas Pasmore
Andrew Ralye

Nath. Jefferys
vx. Jefferys
Thomas Hebbs

Clement Dilke
Mrs. Dilke
John Hinton

Richard Stephens
Wassell Rayner
vx. Rayner
John Jackson
Edward Price
Osten Smith
Thomas Spilman
Bryan Cawt

George Menify
Moyes Ston

Capt. Holmes
Mr. Calcker
Mrs. Calcker
infans Calcker
Peceable Sherwood
Anthony West
Henry Barker
Henry Scott
Margery Dawse

Mr. Cann
Capt. Hartt
Edward Spalding
vx. Spalding
Puer Spalding
Puella Spalding
John Helin
vx. Helin
puer Helin
infans Helin
Thomas Graye et vx.
Jone Graye
William Graye
Richard Younge
vx. Younge
Jone Younge
Randall Smalwood
John Greene
William Mudge

Mrs. Southey
Ann Southey
Elin Painter

Goodman Webb

In James Island.

John Osbourn
vx. Osbourn
George Pope
Robert Constable

William Jones
vx. Jones
John Johnson
vx. Johnson
infans
Johnson
Johnson
John Hall
vx. Hall
William Cooksey
vx. Cooksey
infans Cooksey
Alice Kean

Robert Fitts
vx. Fitts
John Reddish
John Grevett
vx. Grevett
John West
Rhomas West
Henry Glover

Goodman Stoiks
vs. Stoiks
infans Stoiks
Mr. Adams
Mr. Leet
William Spence
vx. Spence
infans Spence
James Tooke
James Roberts
Anthony Harlow

Sarah Spence
George Shurke
John Booth
Robert Bennett

"Musters of the Inhabitants in Virginia 1624/1625" (in Annie Lash Jester and Martha Woodroof Hiden's *Adventurers of Purse and Person; Virginia, 1607-1625* [Princeton: Princeton University Press, 1956], pages 5-69) [Lancour No. 210].

The following list is actually taken from the second edition of 1964, copyright by the Order of the First Families of Virginia, and reference must be made to this work to ascertain what additional information is readily available therein.

Name of passenger	Name of ship	Date given
Daniell Sherley	*Bona Nova*	1619
Peter Jorden	*London Marchannt*	1620
Richard Davis	*Jonathan*	1620
Robert Lapworth	*Abigaile*	
John Watson	*William & Thomas*	
Edward Hobson	*Bona Nova*	1619
Christopher Branch	*London Marchannt*	
Mary his wife	*London Marchannt*	
Thomas his sonne	*London Marchannt*	
William Browninge	*Bona Nova*	
Mathew Edlow	*Neptune*	1618
William Weldon	*Bona Nova*	1619
Francis Wilton	*Jonathan*	
Ezekiah Raughton	*Bona Nova*	
Margaret his wife	*Warwick*	
William Price	*Starr*	
Robert Campion	*Bona Nova*	
Leonard Moore	*Bona Nova*	
Thomas Baugh	*Supply*	
Thomas Parker	*Neptune*	

Theoder Moyses	*London Marchannt*	
Luke Boyse	*Edwine*	May 1619
Allice his wife	*Bona-Nova*	April 1622
Robert Hollam	*Bonaventure*	August 1620
Joseph Royall	*Charitie*	July 1622
Josuah Chard	*Seaventure*	May 1607
Ann his wife	*Bony besse*	August 1623
John Dods	*Susan Constant*	April 1607
William Vincene	*Mary & James*	
Thomas Harris	*Prosperous*	May
Adria his wife	*Marmaduke*	November 1621
Elizabeth [servant]	*Margaret & John*	1620
John Price	*Starr*	May
Ann his wife	*Francis Bonaventure*	August 1620
Hugh Hilton	*Edwine*	May 1619
Richard Taylor	*Mary Margrett*	September 1608
Dorothy his wife	*London Marchannt*	May 1620
Christopher Browne	*Dutie*	May 1620
Thomas Oage	*Starr*	May
Ann his wife	*Neptune*	August 1618
Robert Greenleafe	*Tryall*	August 1610
Susan his wife	*Jonathan*	May 1620
Henery Coltman	*Noah*	August 1610
Ann his wife	*London Marchannt*	May 1620
Hugh Price	*William & John*	January 1618
Judith his wife	*Marygold*	May 1619
Thomas Farmer	*Tryall*	1616
Thomas Sheppey	*Supply*	January 1620
Alexander Bradway	*Supply*	January 1620
Sisley his wife	*Jonathan*	May 1620
William Sharp	*Starr*	May
Elizabeth his wife	*Bonaventure*	August 1620
Richard Vause	*Jonathan*	May 1620
Richard Biggs	*Swann*	August 1610
Sarah his wife	*Marygold*	May 1618
Thomas Turner	*Marygold*	1616
Susan Old	*Marygold*	1616
James Guy	*Marygold*	1622
William Brock	*Margrett*	May 1622
Edward Temple	*Margrett*	May 1622
Mary Peeters	*London Marchant*	May 1620
William Baley	*Prosperous*	May 1610
Mary his wife	*George*	1617
Robert Partin	*Blessinge*	June 1609
Margrett his wife	*George*	1617
Thomas Hale	*George*	October 1623
Ellin Cooke	*London Marchannt*	June 16
Christopher Woodward	*Tryall*	June 162-
John Higgins	*George*	1616
Rice Howe	*Gifte*	1618

Mathew Gloster	*Warwick*	1621
William Totle	*George*	1623
John Canon	*Abigaile*	1622
Amias Bolte	*Neptune*	August 1618
John Collins	*Suply*	1620
Susan his wife	*Treasurer*	1613
Henery Benson	*Francis Bonaventure*	August 1620
Nicholas Blackman	*Francis Bonaventure*	August 1620
Thomas Pawlett	*Neptune*	August 161-
John Trussell	*Southampton*	1622
William Askew	*Prosperous*	May 1610
Rebecca Rose [Widow]	*Marygold*	May 1619
Marmaduke Hill, child	*Marygold*	May 1619
Jane Hill, child	*Marygold*	May 1619
Mary Madison [Widow]	*Treasurer*	1618
James Watson	*George*	1623
Roger Lewes	*Edwin*	May 1617
Henery Bagwell	*Deliverance*	1608
Symon Turgis	*William & Thomas*	1618
Randall Bawde	*Due Returne*	1623
Charles, servant	*Jacob*	1624
Robert Milner	*Francis Bonaventure*	Augu-
John Passeman	*Jonathan*	May 1620
Jenkin Osborn	*George*	1617
William Weston	*Jonathan*	May 162-
John Throgmorton	*William & Thomas*	1618
Chyna Boyse	*Georg*	May 1617
Edward Sparshott	*Seafloure*	1621
Francis Downing	*Returne*	March 1624
Ellis Ripping	*Returne*	1624
Roger Ratlife	*Georg*	May 1619
Ann his wife	*George*	May 1619
Nathaniell Tatam	*George*	May 1619
Katherine Benett	*Abigall*	1622
Randall Crew	*Charles*	1621
Andrew Dudley	*Truelove*	1622
Ralph Freeman	*Margrett and John*	1622
Mr William Benet	*Seafloure*	1621
James Crowder	*Returne*	1623
Daniell Viero	*George*	1623
Barnard Jackson	*Margrett & John*	1623
Thomas Weston	*George*	1623
William Ferrar	*Neptune*	August 1618
Sisley Jordan	*Swan*	August 1610
William Dawson	*Discovery*	March 1621
Robert Turner	*Tryall*	June 1619
John Hely	*Charles*	November 1621
Roger Preston	*Discoverie*	March 1621
Robert Manuell	*Charles*	November 1621
Thomas Williams	*Dutie*	May 1618

Richard Johnson	*Southampton*	1622
William Hatfeild	*Southampton*	1622
John Pead	*Southampton*	
John Freame	*Southampton*	
Thomas Palmer	*Tyger*	November 1621
Joane his wife	*Tyger*	
Richard English	*James*	1622
Robert Fisher	*Elsabeth*	May 1611
Katherine his wife	*Marmaduk*	October 1621
Idye Halliers	*Jonathan*	1619
John Claye	*Treasuror*	February 1613
Ann his wife	*Ann*	August 1623
William Nicholls	*Dutie*	May 1619
Christopher Safford	*Treasuror*	1613
John Gibbs	*Supply*	1619
Henery Lane	*Southampton*	1623
Henery Williams	*Treasuror*	1613
Susan his wife	*William & Thomas*	
William Branlin	*Margrett & John*	1620
Ann his wife	*Truelove*	1622
John Fludd	*Swan*	1610
Margrett his wife	*Supply*	1620
Frances Finch	*Suply*	1620
Thomas Chapman	*Tryall*	1610
Ann his wife	*George*	1619
Joseph Bull	*Abigaile*	1622
John Davis	*George*	1617
William Emerson	*Sampson*	1618
William Popleton	*James*	1622
Eustice Downes	*Abigall*	1622
Thomas Cawsey	*Francis Bonaventure*	1620
Thomas Iron Monger		
Richard Milton	*Suply*	1620
Nathaniell Cawsey	*Phoenix*	1607
Thomasine his wife	*Lyon*	1609
Edward Denison	*Truelove*	1623
James Bonner	*Truelove*	1623
James Dore	*Bona Nova*	1621
Laurance Evans	*James*	1622
Joane Winscomb	*George*	1618
Lidia Sherley	*George*	1623
Isack Chaplaine	*Starr*	1610
Mary his wife	*James*	1622
John Chaplaine	*James*	1622
Robert Hudson	*James*	1622
Henery Thorne	*James*	1622
John Duffill	*James*	1622
Ivie Banton	*James*	1622
Ann Mighill	*George*	1619
Walter Price	*Willm & Thomas*	1618

Henery Turner	*John & Francis*	1615
Edward Fallowes	*Hopewell*	1623
Thomas Keie	*Prosperous*	June 1619
Sarah his wife	*Truelove*	1622
John Browne	*Bona Nova*	Aprill 1621
John Trehearne	*Truelove*	1622
David Jones	*Truelove*	1622
John Box	*Truelove*	1622
Henery Wilson	*Truelove*	1622
Nicholas Sutton	*James*	1622
Nicholas Baldwin	*Truelove*	1622
William Barnett	*Truelove*	1623
Samuell Sharpe	*Seaventure*	1609
Elizabeth his wife	*Margrett and John*	1621
Henery Carman	*Duty*	1620
Grivell Pooley	*James*	1622
John Chambers	*Bona Nova*	1622
Charles Magner	*George*	1623
Humfrey Kent	*George*	1619
Joane his wife	*Tyger*	1621
Margrett Arrundell	*Abigaile*	1621
Christopher Beane	*Neptune*	1618
Thomas Doughtie	*Marigold*	1619
Ann his wife	*Marmaduke*	1621
Edward Auborn	*Jonathan*	1620
William Baker	*Jonathan*	1609
John Woodson	*George*	1619
Sarah his wife	*George*	1619
Edward Threnorden	*Diana*	1619
Elizabeth his wife	*George*	1619
Nicholas Baly	*Jonathan*	1620
Ann his wife	*Marmaduke*	1621
John Lipps	*London Marchannt*	1621
Anthony Pagitt	*Southampton*	1623
Saloman Jackman	*Southampton*	1623
John Davies	*Southampton*	1623
Clement Roper	*Southampton*	1623
John Bates	*Southampton*	1623
Thomas Abbe	*Southampton*	1623
Thomas Brooks	*Southampton*	1623
William Jones	*Southampton*	1623
Peeter Jones	*Southampton*	1623
Pierce Williams	*Southampton*	1623
Robert Graves	*Southampton*	1623
Edward Hubberstead	*Southampton*	1623
John Lathrop	*Southampton*	1623
Thomas Chambers	*Southampton*	1623
Walter Jackson	*Southampton*	1623
Henery Sanders	*Southampton*	1623
William Allen	*Southampton*	1623

Georg Dawson		1623
John Upton		1622
John Bamford		1622
William Garrett		1619
Thomas Sawell		1619
Henery Rowinge		1621
Nathaniell Thomas		1621
Richard Broadshaw		
Robert Okley		1618
Allice Thorowden		1623
Katherine Loman		1623
Adam Dixon	*Margarett & John*	
Joseph Ryale	*William & Thomas*	
George Frier	*William & Thomas*	
Ursula his wife	*London Marchant*	
Allen Keniston	*Margarett & John*	
Robert Paramour	*Swan*	
William Kemp	*George*	
Margrett his wife	*George*	
Richard Bridgwatter	*London Marchannt*	
Isbell his wife	*London Marchannt*	
Hugh Haward	*Starr*	
Susan his wife	*George*	
Henery Turner	*London Marchannt*	
Joseph Crew	*London Marchannt*	
Thomas Jones	*London Marchannt*	
Margrett his wife	*London Marchannt*	
Edward Bourbicth	*London Marchannt*	
Revoll Morcock	*Jonathan*	
Edward Fisher	*Jonathan*	
Sarah his wife	*Warwick*	
John Moone	*Returne*	1623
Julian Hallers	*Truelove*	1623
Giles Martin	*Truelove*	1623
Clinion Rush	*Truelove*	1623
Richard Smith	*London Marchannt*	
Thomas Jorden	*Diana*	
John Milnhouse	*London Marchannt*	
Richard Sanders	*Francis Bonaventure*	
Griffin Winne	*Francis Bonaventure*	
Arthure Chandler	*Jonathan*	
William Dorrell	*Truelove*	
Christopher Ripping	*Francis Bonaventure*	
Thomas Osborn	*Francis Bonaventure*	
George Nelson	*Francis Bonaventure*	
Francis Butler	*Francis Bonaventure*	
Thomas Blancks	*Francis Bonaventure*	
Henery Dowtie	*Francis Bonaventure*	
John Swarbeck		
Thomas Marloe	*Bona Nova*	

John Smith	*Abigaile*	
Thomas Smith	*Abigaile*	
Thomas Jones	*Bona Nova*	
James Robesonn	*Swann*	
Elizabeth Hodges	*Abigaile*	
Thomas Swinhow	*Diana*	
Lawrance Smalepage	*Abigaile*	
John Carter	*Prosperous*	
David Ellis	*Mary Margrett*	
Margrett his wife	*Margrett & John*	
James Tooke		
William Binks	*George*	
Ann his wife	*George*	
Michaell Batt	*Hercules*	
Ellin his wife	*Warwick*	
Robert Lince	*Treasuror*	
Hugh Baldwine	*Tryall*	
Susan his wife		
Robert Scotchmore	*George*	1623
Thomas Kniston	*George*	1623
Roger Kidd	*George*	1623
Robert Cholmle	*Charitie*	
James Standish	*Charitie*	
Roger Stanley	*Abigaile*	1620
Thomas Pritchard	*Abigaile*	1620
Henery Crocker	*Abigaile*	1620
Thomas Crosse	*Abigaile*	1620
John Trye	*Abigaile*	1620
Walter Beare	*Abigaile*	1620
Randall Holt	*George*	1620
Sr Francis Wyatt K^{t}	*George*	1621
Christopher Cooke	*George*	1621
Georg Hall	*Suply*	1620
Jonathan Giles	*Triall*	1619
John Matheman	*Jonathan*	1619
Jane Davis	*Abigaile*	1622
Sr George Yearlley K^{t}	*Deliverance*	1609
Temperance Lady Yearlley	*Faulcon*	1608
Richard Gregory	*Temperance*	1620
Anthony Jones	*Temperance*	1620
Thomas Dunn	*Temperance*	1620
Thomas Phildust	*Temperance*	1620
Thomas Hatch	*Duty*	1619
Robert Peake	*Margrett & John*	1623
William Strange	*George*	1619
Roger Thompson	*London Marchannt*	1620
Ann his wife		
Richard Arrundell	*Abigall*	1620
George Deverill	*Temperannce*	1620

Thomas Barnett	*Elsabeth*	1620
Theophilus Beriston	*Treasuror*	1614
Susan Hall	*William & Thomas*	1618
Ann Willis	*Temperance*	1620
Elizabeth Arrundell	*Abigall*	1620
Doctor John Pott	*George*	1620
mrs Elizabeth Pott	*George*	1620
Richard Townshend	*Abigaile*	1620
Thomas Wilson	*Abigaile*	1620
Osmond Smith	*Bona Nova*	1620
Susan Blackwood	*Abigaile*	1622
Capt Roger Smith	*Abigaile*	1620
mrs Joane Smith	*Blessinge*	
Elizabeth Salter	*Seafloure*	
Charles Waller	*Abigaile*	1620
Christopher Bankus	*Abigaile*	1622
Henery Booth	*Dutie*	
Henery Lacton	*Hopewell*	1623
John Lightfoote	*Seaventure*	
Francis Gibbs	*Seaflower*	
Capt William Pierce	*Sea-venture*	
mrs Jone Pierce	*Blessinge*	
Thomas Smith	*Abigaile*	
Henery Bradford	*Abigaile*	
Ester Ederife	*Jonathan*	
Angelo a Negro Woman	*Treasuror*	
mr Abraham Peirsey	*Susan*	1616
Elizabeth his daughter	*Southampton*	1623
Mary his daughter	*Southampton*	1623
Christopher Lee	*Southampton*	1623
Richard Serieant	*Southampton*	1623
Alice Chambers	*Southampton*	1623
Annis Shaw	*Southampton*	1623
mr Edward Blaney	*Francis Bonaventure*	
Robert Bew	*Dutie*	
John Russell	*Bona Nova*	
Robert Poole		
James Hicmott	*Bonaventure*	
John Southern	*George*	1620
Thomas Crust	*George*	1620
Randall Smalewood		
George Grave	*Seaventure*	
Elnor his wife	*Susan*	
Edward Cadge	*Marmaduke*	
Nathaniell Jeffreys	*Gift*	
John Jackson		
Thomas Alnutt	*Gifte*	
His wife	*Marygold*	

Roger Roeds	*Bony bess*	
Peeter Langman	*William & Thomas*	
Mary his wife		
Abraham Porter		
Thomas Sawier		
mr John Burrowes		
Bridgett his wife		
Elizabeth Soothey	*Southampton*	
John Jefferson	*Bona Nova*	
Walgrave Marks	*Margrett & John*	
William Mutch	*Jonathan*	
Margery his wife	*George*	1623
Richard Steephens	*George*	1623
Wassell Rayner		
Thomas Spillman	*George*	1623
Edward Prise	*George*	1623
Joane Rayner wife of Wassell Rayner		
George Minifie	*Samuell*	July 1623
John Griffin	*William & John*	1624
Edward Williams	*William & John*	
John Barnett	*Jonathan*	1620
John Stoaks	*Warwick*	
Ann his wife	*Warwick*	
Richard Tree	*George*	
Silvester Bullen		
Willm Lasey	*Southampton*	1624
Susan his wife	*Southampton*	1624
John West	*Bony bess*	
Thomas Crompe		
John Greevett		
Ellin his wife		
Thomas Passmore	*George*	
Jane his wife	*George*	
Thomas Kerfitt	*Hopewell*	
Robert Julian	*Jacob*	
John Buckmuster	*Hopewell*	
Christopher Hall		
Robert Fitt	*George*	
Ann his wife	*Abigaile*	
George Onion	*Francis bona venture*	
Elizabeth his wife	*Francis bona venture*	
John Hall	*John & Francis*	
Susan his wife	*London Marchant*	
Robert Marshall	*George*	
Ann his wife	*George*	
Thomas Grubb	*George*	
John Osborn		
Mary his wife		

William Spencer	*Sarah*	
Allice his wife		
Thomas Graye		
Margrett his wife		
Gabriell Holland	*John & Francis*	
Rebecca his wife	*John & Francis*	
Josias Tanner		
Andrew Railey		
Richard Kingsmell	*Delaware*	
Jane his wife	*Susan*	
Horten Wright	*Susan*	
John Jackson	*Abigall*	
Isbell Pratt	*Jonathan*	
John Smith	*Bonaventure*	
Thomas Bagwell		
Thomas Benett	*Bona Nova*	
Margery his wife	*Guift*[e]	
John Reddish		
Richard Pierce	*Neptune*	
Elizabeth his wife	*Neptune*	
Thomas Bransby	*Charitie*	
Chadwallader Jones	*Marmaduk*	1623
Robert Crew	*Marmaduk*	1623
John Ellison	*Prosperous*	
Ellin his wife	*Charitie*	
John Badeley	*Hopewell*	1623
Thomas Farley	*Ann*	1623
Jane his wife	*Ann*	
Nicholas Shotten	*Ann*	1623
Joseph Johnson	*William & Thomas*	
Margrett his wife	*Abigaile*	
George Prouse	*Diana*	
John Smith	*Elizabeth*	1611
Susanna his wife	*Bona Nova*	1619
John Ellatt	*Margrett & John*	1621
George Pelton	*Furtherance*	1622
Richard Richards	*London Marchant*	1620
Richard Dolphinbe	*Guift*	1618
John Proctor	*Seaventure*	1607
Allis his wife	*George*	1621
Richard Grove	*George*	1623
Edward Smith	*George*	1621
William Nayle	*Ann*	1623
Phettiplace Close	*Starr*	1608
Daniell Wattkins	*Charles*	1621
Martin Demon	*George*	1617
John Skinner	*Marmaduk*	1621
Thomas Gates	*Swan*	1609
Elizabeth his wife	*Warwick*	1620
William Bedford	*James*	1621

Francis Chapman	*Starr*	1608
Rice Watkins	*Francis bonaventure*	
Nathaniell Floid	*Bona Nova*	
George Rogers	*Bona Nova*	
John Shelley	*Bona Nova*	
Thomas Ottowell	*Bona Nova*	
Thomas Crouch	*Bona Nova*	
Robert Sheppeard	*Hopwell*	
William Sawier	*Hopwell*	
Robert Chauntrie	*George*	
William Hartley	*Charles*	
Lawley Damport	*Duty*	
William Ward	*Jonathan*	
Jeremy White	*Tyger*	
John Hacker	*Hopwell*	
Robert Whitmore	*Duty*	
Capt Samuell Mathews	*Southampton*	1622
mr David Sands	*Bonaventure*	1620
Minister	*Southampton*	1622
Roger Williams	*Southampton*	1622
Samuel Davies	*Southampton*	1622
Henery Jones	*Southampton*	1622
Aaron Conaway	*Southampton*	1622
John Thomas	*Southampton*	1622
Michaell Lapworth	*Southampton*	1622
William Feild	*Charles*	1621
Peeter Montecue	*Charles*	1621
Robert Fernall	*London Marchant*	1619
Walter Coop	*Jonathan*	1619
William Walters	*Bona Nova*	1618
Nicholas Chapman	*Jonathan*	1619
Gregory Spicer	*Triall*	1618
Nicholas Peirse	*Falcon*	1619
Robert Penn	*Abigaile*	1620
William Dalby	*Furtherance*	1622
Thomas Hopson	*Bona Nova*	1618
Abraham Wood	*Margrett & John*	1620
William Kingsley	*Marmaduk*	1623
Thomas Bridges	*Marmaduk*	1623
Arthure Goldsmith	*Diana*	1618
mr Hugh Crowder	*Bona Nova*	1619
Richard Ball	*George*	1617
Thomas Hawkins	*James*	1622
Paule Renalles	*Tryall*	1619
Nicholas Smith	*Bona Nova*	1621
John Verin	*George*	1623
mr Georg Sandis	*George*	1621
Martin Turner	*George*	1621
George Bailife	*George*	1621
John Sparks	*George*	1621

John Dancy	*George*	1621
John Edwards	*George*	1621
Nicholas Tompson	*George*	1621
Rosamus Carter	*George*	1621
John Stone a boy	*George*	1621
Nicholas Comon	*Guifte*	1622
Nicholas Eyres a boy	*Guifte*	1622
David Mansfeild	*Bona Nova*	1619
John Claxon	*Bona Nova*	1619
Thomas Swifte	*Tyger*	1622
John Baldwine	*Tyger*	1622
Robert Sheaperd	*George*	1621
James Chambers	*Dutie*	1620
John Parsons	*Marygold*	1619
William Benge	*Marygold*	1619
John Evens	*Marygold*	1619
Robert Edmunds	*Marygold*	1619
John Comes	*Marygold*	1619
John Tyos	*Bona Nova*	1620
William Pilkinton	*Bona Nova*	1620
Elias Longe	*Bona Nova*	1620
Thomas Hall	*Bona Nova*	1620
Zachary Cripps	*Margrett & John*	1621
Edward White	*Bona Nova*	1620
Mathew Hamon	*Southampton*	1622
Phillip Kithly	*Furtherance*	1622
Anthony West	*James*	1622
Jefferey Hull	*George*	
Mordecay Knight	*William & John*	
Thomas Doleman	*Returne*	
Elkinton Ratliffe	*Seafloure*	
Thomas Powell	*Seafloure*	
Thomas Cooper	*Returne*	
John Davies	*Guifte*	
Liuetennt Edward Barkley	*Unitie*	
m^rs^ Jane Barkley	*Seafloure*	
Thomas Phillips	*Bona Nova*	
Francis Barrett	*Bona Nova*	
Robert Martin	*George*	
Katherin Davies	*Southampton*	
John Uty	*Francis Bonaventure*	
Ann his wife	*Seafloure*	
John his Sonn	*Seafloure*	
William Burt	*Bony besse*	
William Stocker	*Bony besse*	
Richard Bickley	*Returne*	
John Chew	*Charitie*	
Sarah his wife	*Seafloure*	
Roger Delk	*Southampton*	

Samuell Parson	*Hopewell*	
Walter Haslewood	*Due Returne*	
Henery Elwood	*Francis Bonaventure*	
William Ramshaw	*Francis Bonaventure*	
John Stone	*Swann*	
Sisly his wife	*Seafloure*	
Henery Crocker	*Marygold*	
Jone his wife	*Swan*	
Henery Woodward	*Diana*	
Thomas Hitckock	*Marygold*	
Maximilian Stone	*Temperance*	1620
Elizabeth his wife	*Temperance*	
Robert Guy	*Swan*	1619
Edward Yates	*Duty*	1619
Cesar Puggett	*Diana*	1619
Allexander Sanders	*Truelove*	1623
William Strachey	*Temperance*	1620
George Whitehand	*Temperance*	1620
Henery King	*Jonathan*	1620
John Day	*London Marchannt*	1620
The wife of John Day	*London Marchannt*	
John Root	*Guift*	
Walter Blake	*Swan*	
Thomas Watts	*Treasuror*	
m[r] William Harwood	*Francis Bonaventure*	
Hugh Hughs	*Guifte*	
Ann his wife	*Abigall*	
Thomas Doughtie	*Abigall*	
John Hasley	*Abigall*	
Samuell Weaver	*Bony bess*	
Elizabeth Bygrave	*Warwick*	
Ellis Emerson	*George*	1623
Ann his wife	*George*	1623
Thomas his sonn	*George*	1623
Thomas Goulding	*George*	1623
Martin Slatier	*Swan*	1624
Robert Addams	*Bona Nova*	
Augustine Leak	*Bona Nova*	
Winifred Leak his wife	*George*	1623
Richard Smith	*George*	1623
Stephen Barker	*James*	
Humphrey Walden	*Warwick*	
John Jackson	*Warwick*	
Ann his wife	*Warwick*	
Thomas Ward	*Warwick*	
John Steephens	*Warwick*	
Samuel March	*William & Thomas*	
Collice his wife	*Ann*	1623

Samuell Culley	*London Marchamt*	
Robert Scotchmore		
Richard Attkins	*London Marchannt*	
Abigall his wife	*Abigall*	
William Baker	*Abigall*	
Robert Aston	*Treasuror*	
Hugh Wing	*George*	1620
Robert Lathom	*George*	1620
Richard Aldon	*George*	1620
Thomas Wood	*George*	1620
Robert Ruce	*Charles*	
Allexander Gill	*Bony bess*	
Samuel Morris	*Abigall*	
Thomas Rose	*Jonathan*	
Robert Hedges		
John Virgo	*Treasuror*	
Susan his wife	*Treasuror*	
John Gatter	*George*	1620
William Richardson	*Edwine*	
Richard Fine	*Neptune*	
John Nowell	*Margrett & John*	
Richard Downes	*Jonathan*	
John Cranich	*Marygold*	
Percevall Wood	*George*	
Ann his wife	*George*	
William Raymont	*Neptune*	
William Bullock	*Jonathan*	
Anthony Baram	*Abigall*	
Elizabeth his wife	*William & Thomas*	
Thomas Harwood	*Margrett & John*	1622
Grace his wife	*George*	
Henery Pinke	*London Marchannt*	1619
John Bate	*Addam*	1621
Peeter Collins	*Addam*	1621
Wassell Webling	*James*	1621
Antonio a Negro	*James*	1621
Christopher Reynolds	*John & Francis*	1622
Luke Chappman	*John & Francis*	1622
Edward Maybank	*John & Francis*	1622
John Attkins	*Guifte*	1623
William Denum	*Guifte*	1623
Francis Banks	*Guifte*	1623
Mary a Negro Woman	*Margrett & John*	1622
Nathaniell Basse	*Furtherance*	1622
William Barnard	*Furtherance*	1622
Edward Wigge	*Abigall*	1621
Thomas Phillipes	*William and Thomas*	1618
Elizabeth Phillipes	*Sea Flower*	1621
Thomas Bennett	*Neptune*	1618
Mary Bennett	*Southampton*	1622

Roger Heford	*Returne*	1623
Beniamine Simes		
Richard Longe		
Alice Longe	*London Merchant*	1620
Richard Evands	*Neptune*	1618
William Newman	*Furtherance*	1622
John Army	*Furtherance*	1622
Henrie Woodward		
John Browninge	*Abigall*	1621
Ambrose	*Marmiducke*	1621
Peeter	*Margett and John*	1620
William Wadsworth	*Flyinge Harte*	1621
William Foockes	*Flyinge Harte*	1621
Thomas Curtis	*Flyinge Harte*	1621
Peeter Sherwood	*Flyinge Harte*	1621
Gilbert Whitfild	*Flyinge Harte*	1621
Rise Griffin	*Flyinge Harte*	1621
William Smith	*Flyinge Harte*	1621
Anthonie Ebsworth	*Flyinge Harte*	1621
Edmond Morgan	*Providence*	1623
William Clarke	*Providence*	1623
Joseph Mosley	*Providence*	1623
Capt William Tucker	*Mary and James*	[16]10
Mirs Mary Tucker	*George*	1623
George Tomson	*George*	1623
Paule Tomson	*George*	1623
William Thomson	*George*	1623
Pascoe Champion	*Ellonor*	1621
Strenght Sheere	*Ellonor*	1621
Thomas Evands	*George*	1623
Stephen Collowe	*George*	1623
Robart Munday	*George*	1623
Mathewe Robinsonn	*greate hopewell*	1623
Richard Appleton	*James*	1622
John Morris	*Bona Nova*	1619
Mary Morris	*George*	1623
William Hutchinson	*Diana*	1618
Peeter Porter	*Tyger*	1621
John Downeman	*John and Francis*	1611
Elizabeth Downeman	*Warwicke*	1621
Moyses Stones	*Bone Bes*	1623
John Laydon	*Susan*	1606 [*sic*]
Anne Laydon	*Mary Margrett*	1608
William Cole	*Neptune*	1618
Francis Cole	*Susan*	1616
Roger Farbrase	*Elzabeth*	1621
Miles Prickett	*Starr*	1610
Francis Mitchell	*Neptune*	1618
Maudlin Mitchell	*Bona Nova*	1620
Richard Yonge	*George*	1616

Joane Yonge	*Guifte*	1618
Susan	*Swan*	1624
Albiano Lupo	*Swan*	1610
Elizabeth Lupo	*George*	1616
Henrie Draper	*George*	1621
Joseph Ham	*Warwicke*	1621
John Powell	*Swallowe*	1609
Kathren Powell	*flyinge Hart*	1622
Thomas Prater	*Marie Providence*	1622
Larence Peale	*Margett and John*	1620
William Smith	*Jacob*	1624
Robart Brittin	*Edwin*	1618
Mihell Wilcockes	*Prosporouse*	1610
Elzabeth Willcockes	*Concord*	1621
John Slater	*George*	1617
Anne Slater	*Guyft*	1622
James Feild	*Swan*	1624
John Jornall	*Ann*	1623
Theodore Joones	*Margett and John*	1620
Joseph Cobb	*Treasoror*	1613
Elzabeth Cobb	*Bone Bes*	1623
John Snowood		
Cornelius May	*Providence*	1616
William Morgan	*Starr*	1610
William Julian	*Hercules*	1609
Sara Julian	*Neptune*	1618
William Kemp	*William and Thomas*	1618
Thomas Sully	*Sara*	1611
Maudlyn Sully	*London Marchant*	1620
Thomas Flower	*George*	1623
Wyatt Masonn	*Ann*	1623
Thomas Purfry	*George*	1621
Christopher Cole-thorpe	*Furtherance*	1622
Danniell Tanner	*Sampson*	1618
Henrie Feeldes	*Jacob*	1624
John Barnabie	*London Marchant*	1620
John Hazard	*William and Thomas*	1618
Abraham Pelteare	*Swan*	1624
Jerimiah Dickinson	*Margett and John*	1620
Elzabeth Dickinson	*Margett and John*	1623
Phillip Lupo	*George*	1621
Thomas Willoby	*Prosporouse*	1610
John Chaundler	*Hercules*	1609
Thomas	*greate hopewell*	1623
Robert Bennett	*Jacob*	1624
Niccolas Davis	*Mariegould*	1618
John Hatton	*Tresorer*	1613
Olive Hatton	*Abigall*	1620
Mr George Keth	*George*	1617

James Whitinge	*George*	1617
John Keth	*George*	1617
Susan Bush	*George*	1617
Clement Evands	*Edwin*	1616
William Parker	*Charles*	1616
John Seward	*Geife [Guift]*	1622
Gilbert Marburie	*Southampton*	1622
Thomas Killson	*Truelove*	1623
Niccolas Martue	*Francis Bonaventure*	
Peter Eccallowe	*Southampton*	
William Stafford	*furtherance*	
John Banum	*Susan*	1616
Elzabeth Banum	*Bona Nova*	1620
Robart Sweete	*Neptune*	1618
Niccolas Thredder	*Katherin*	1623
Richard Robisonn	*Bona nova*	1620
John Hill	*Bona Nova*	1620
William Morton	*Margett and John*	1620
James Pascoll	*Warwicke*	1621
Robart Draper	*Jacob*	1624
Sara Gouldinge	*Ann*	1623
Richard Mintrene	*Margett and John*	1620
William Beane	*Diana*	1618
Edward Mintrene	*Margett and John*	1620
John Inman	*Falcon*	1619
William Browne	*Southampton*	1622
Anthoney Burroes	*George*	1617
John Waine	*Neptune*	1618
Amyte Waine	*Swan*	1610
John Harlow	*Sampson*	1619
Robart Sabyn	*marget and John*	1622
Phillip Chapman	*flyinge hart*	1621
Mr Robart Salford	*John and Francis*	1611
John Salford	*George*	1616
Mary Salford	*Bona Nova*	1620
William Ellison	*Swan*	1624
Thomas Faulkner	*Mary Providense*	1622
Bartholemew Wethers-bie	*Providence*	1616
Dorythie Wethersbie	*London Marchant*	1620
Richard Boulton	*Mary and James*	1610
Richard	*Swan*	1624
John Gundrie	*Starr*	1610
Marie Gundrie	*George*	1618
Francis Mason	*John and Francis*	1613
Alice Mason	*Margett and John*	1622
William Querke	*Marmaducke*	1621
Thomas Worthall	*Marmaducke*	1621
William Stafford	*furtherance*	1622
Henrie Gany	*Dutie*	1619

John Robinson	*Margett and John*	1622
Farrar Flinton	*Elzabeth*	1612
Joane Flinton	*Elzabeth*	1612
William Bentlie	*Jacob*	1624
Arthur Smyth	*Marget and John*	1622
Hugh Hall	*Marget and John*	1622
Mathew Hardcastell	*Jacob*	1624
Henrie Nasfeild	*Swan*	1624
Francis Huff	*Swan*	1624
James Sleight	*Tryall*	1610
John Chisman	*flyinge hart*	1621
Edward Chisman	*Providence*	1623
Thomas Spilman	*George*	1616
Hanna Spilman	*Bona Nova*	1620
Robart Browne	*Marygould*	1618
Rebecca Browne	*Southampton*	1623
Thomas Parrish	*Charity*	1622
John Harris	*Jacob*	1624
Oliver Jinkines	*mary James*	1610
Joane Jinkines	*George*	1617
Robart Newman	*Neptune*	1618
William Gayne	*Bona Nova*	1620
John Taylor	*Swan*	1610
Rebecca Taylor	*Margett and John*	1623
Richard Packe	*Warwick*	1621
Abraham Avelin	*Elzabeth*	1620
Arthur Avelin	*Elzabeth*	1620
Thomas Godby	*Delivrance*	1608
Joane Godby	*Flyinge Hart*	1621
John Curtis	*Flyinge Hart*	1621
Christopher Smith	*Returne*	1624
Edward Waters	*Patience*	1608
Grace Waters	*Diana*	1618
William Hampton	*Bona Nova*	1620
Joane Hampton	*Abigall*	1621
Thomas Lane	*Treasorer*	1613
Alice Lane	*Bona Nova*	1620
Thomas Thornebury	*George*	1616
Adam Thorogood	*Charles*	1621
Niccolas Browne	*Charles*	1621
Paule Harwood	*Bona Nova*	1622
Stephen Reede	*George*	1618
Mathias Francisco	*Jacob*	1624
Robart Penrise	*Bona nova*	1620
Capt Thomas Davis	*John and Francis*	1623
Thomas Hewes	*John and Francis*	1623
Francis Chamberlin	*Marmaducke*	1621
Rebecca Chamberlin	*Bona Nova*	1622
John Forth	*Bona Nova*	1622
William Worlidge	*Bona Nova*	1622

sionell [Lionel?] Rowlston	*Gods Guifte*	1623
Richard Burton	*Swan*	1624
Percivall Ibottson	*Neptune*	1618
Elzabeth Ibottson	*Flyinge Hart*	1621
John Davis	*John and Francis*	1623
William Greene·	*Hopewell*	1623
Robart Locke	*Warwicke*	1621
Thomas Bouldinge	*Swan*	1610
William Coxe	*Godspeede*	1610
Richard Edwards	*Jacob*	1624
Niccolas Dale	*Jacob*	1624
Reynold Booth	*Hercules*	1609
Elizabeth Booth	*Ann*	1623
George Levett	*Bona Nova*	1619
Thomas Seywell	*Tyger*	1623
Thomas Garnett	*Swan*	1610
Elzabeth Garnett	*Neptune*	1618
Ambrose Gyffith	*Bona Nova*	1619
Joyse Gyffith	*Jacob*	1624
Thomas Dunthorne	*Margett and John*	1620
Elzabeth Dunthorne	*Tryall*	1610
William Tomson	*Swan*	1624
George Turnor	*Swan*	1624
George Banckes	*Swan*	1624
Elzabeth Joones	*Patience*	1609
Thomas Stepney	*Swan*	1610
Jonas Stockton	*Bona Nova*	1620
Richard Popeley	*Bona Nova*	1620
Richard Davis	*Bona Nova*	1620
Walter Barrett	*Bona Nova*	1620
Timothey Stockton	*Bona Nova*	1620
William Duglas	*Margett and John*	1621
John Watson	*Swan*	1624
Tobias Hurst	*Treasurer*	1618
William Gany	*George*	1616
Anna Gany	*Bona Nova*	1620
Thomasin Eester	*Falcon*	1617
Elizabeth Pope	*Abbigall*	1621
John Wright	*Ambrose*	1623
William Clarke	*Ambrose*	1623
Hather Tomson	*Ambrose*	1623
Thomas Savadge	*Ambrose*	1623
Alexand^r Mountney	*Mary James*	1610
Lenord Mountney	*Bona Nova*	1620
John Walton	*Elzabeth*	1621
Bryan Rogers	*Elzabeth*	1621
John Washborne	*Jonathan*	1619
Capt Francis West	*Mary Ann Margett*	1610

M[rs] Francis West Widdowe	*Supply*	1620
Joane Fairchild	*George*	1618
Beniamin Owin	*Swan*	1623
William Parnell	*Southampton*	1622
Walter Couper	*Neptune*	1618
Reinould Godwin	*Abigall*	1620
John Pedro a Neger	*Swan*	1623
Cap[t] John Martin	*Swan*	1624
Sackford Wetherell	*Swan*	1624
John Smith	*Swan*	1624
John Howard	*Swan*	1624
John Anthonie	*Swan*	1624
Sara Medcalfe	*Hopewell*	1624
Edward Johnson	*Abigall*	1621
	Bona Nova	1621
John Lauckfild	*Bona Nova*	1621
Alice Lauckfild	*Abbigall*	1621
Sammuell Kennell	*Abigall*	1621
William Fowler	*Abigall*	1621
Margrett Fowler	*Abigall*	1621
Elzabeth Ely	*Warwicke*	1622
William Tiler	*Francis Bonaventure*	1620
Elizabeth Tiler	*Francis Bonaventure*	1620
Robart More	*Providence*	1622
William Browne	*Providence*	1622
Robart Todd	*Hopewell*	1622
Anthonie Burt	*Hopewell*	1622
Samiell Bennett	*Providence*	1622
Joane Bennett	*providence*	1622
Thomas Flynt	*Diana*	1618
Thomas Merres	*Francis Bonaventure*	1620
Henrie Wheeler	*Tryall*	1620
John Brocke	*Bona Nova*	1619
James Brookes	*Jonathan*	1619
Robart Savadge	*Elzabeth*	1621
John Ward	*Elzabeth*	1621
Adam Rimwell	*Bona Nova*	1619
Christopher Wynwill	*Bona Nova*	1619
Ann Potter	*London Marchant*	
Robart Goodman	*Bona Nova*	1619
Gregorie Dorie	*Bona Nova*	1620
John More	*Bona Nova*	1620
Elizabeth More	*Abigall*	1622
William Barry	*Bona Nova*	1619
Richard Frisbie	*Jonathan*	1619
William Rookins	*Bona Nova*	1619
Joseph Hattfild	*Bona Nova*	1619
Cutbert Seirson	*Bona Nova*	1619
John Gibbes	*Abigall*	1621

Francis Hill	*Bona Nova*	1619
John Vaghan	*Bona Nova*	1619
Edward Marshall	*Abigall*	1621
William Joyce	*Abigall*	1621
William Evands	*Bona Nova*	1619
Ralph Osborne	*Bona Nova*	1619
Morris Stanley	*hopewell*	1624
Niccolas Weasell	*Abigall*	1621
Stephen Dickson	*Bona Nova*	1619
Thomas Calder	*Bona Nova*	1619
William Hampton	*Bona Nova*	1621
John Arndell	*Abigall*	1621
Anthonie Bonall	*Abigall*	1621
Elias Legardo	*Abigall*	1621
Robart Wright	*Swan*	1608
William Binsley	*Jacob*	1624
Robart Godwin	*Swan*	1624
Virbritt [French]	*Abigall*	1622
Oble Hero [French]	*Abigall*	1622
Robart Thrasher	*Bona Nova*	1620
Roland Williames	*Jonathan*	1623
John Sacker	*Marget and John*	1623
John Haney	*Margett and John*	1621
Elzabeth Haney	*Abigall*	1622
Nicholas Rowe	*Elzabeth*	1621
Mary Rowe	*London Marchant*	1620
Thomas Moreland	*Abigall*	1621
Ralph Hoode	*Abigall*	1621
Capt William Epes	*William and Thomas*	
Margrett Epes	*George*	1621
Niccholas Raynberd	*Swan*	1624
William Burditt	*Susan*	1615
Thomas Cornish	*Dutie*	1620
Peeter Porter	*Tiger*	1621
John Baker	*Ann*	1623
Edward Rogers	*Ann*	1623
Thomas Warden	*Ann*	1623
Beniamine Knight	*Bona Nova*	1620
Niccolas Granger	*George*	1618
William Munnes	*Sampson*	1619
Henrie Wilson	*Sampson*	1619
James Blackborne	*Sampson*	1619
Nicholas Sumerfild	*Sampson*	1619
Capt John Willcockes	*Bona Nova*	1620
Henrie Charlton	*George*	1623
Thomas Savage	*John and Francis*	1607
Ann Savage	*Sea Flower*	1621
John Washborne	*Jonathan*	1620
Capt Thomas Graves	*Mary and Margrett*	1607
Walter Scott	*Hercules*	1618

Apphia Scott	*Gift*	1618	
Thomas Powell	*Samson*	1618	
William Smith	*Samson*	1618	
Edward Drewe	*Samson*	1618	
Charles Harman	*Furtherance*	1622	
John Askume	*Charles*	1624	
Robert Fennell	*Charles*	1624	
James Knott	*George*	1617	
Nicholas Hodgskines	*Edwin*	1616	
Temporance Hodgskines	*Jonathan*	1620	
Solloman Greene	*Diana*	1618	
Thomas Gaskoyne	*Bona Nova*	1619	
William Andros	*Treasuror*	1617	
Danniell Cugley	*London Marchant*	1620	
John Blore	*Star*	1610	
Francis Blore	*London Marchant*	1620	
John Parramore	*Bona Venture*	1622	
Robart Ball	*London Marchant*	1619	
William Bibbie	*Swan*	1621	[or 1620]
Thomas Sparkes	*Susan*	1616	
John Home	*Margerett and John*	1621	
John Wilkines	*Mary gould*	1618	
Briggett Wilkines	*Warwicke*	1621	
Perregrim Watkines	*George*	1621	
William Davis	*William and Thomas*	1618	

The reader should note that the above list was compiled from entries as they stood in the printed text. Some names are listed without a ship, generally resulting from a listing including the notation "came over in" but omitting a ship name. In one case the name of a person was missing. Refer to Jester and Hiden for the very few additional details in their book, including many ages, and names of inhabitants born in Virginia living in the same communities, as well as others obviously born elsewhere but with no ship listed.

"Burgesses of the Assembly Convened at Jamestown, October 16, 1629" (in Edward Duffield Neill's *Virginia Carolorum: The Colony under the Rule of Charles the First and Second, A. D. 1625-A. D. 1685, Based upon Manuscripts and Documents of the Period* [Albany: Joel Munsell's Sons, 1886], pages 71-74) [Lancour No. 211].

College Plantation or Henrico.

Lt. Thomas Osborne. Arrived in 1619, in *Bona Nova*, and was now 35 years old. Justice in 1632.

Mathew Edlowe. Came in 1618 in *Neptune*, died in 1668, his wife Tabitha in 1670. His son John was under the guardianship of Col. Robert Wynne.

Neck of Land, Charles City Corporation.

Serg't Sharpe. Samuel Sharpe came in 1610, with Gates and Somers, and had been a member of the first legislature in 1619.

He married a girl who came in 1621.

Chene Boise. Arrived in 1617, in the *George*, and was now 35 years old.

Shirley Hundred Island.

Mr. Thomas Palmer. He, and his wife, and daughter seven years old, came in 1621, in the *Tiger*. Justice in 1632.

John Harris. Had been several years in Virginia.

Henry Throgmorton's Plantation.

William Allen. Came in 1623, in *Southampton*.

Jordan's Journey Charles City.

William Popleton. Came in 1622, in the *James* as a servant of John Davies.

Chaplain's Choice Charles City.

Walter Price. Came in 1618, in *William and Thomas*.

Westover, Charles City.

Christopher Woodward. Aged 35 came in 1620 in *Trial*.

Fleur Dieu Hundred.

Anthony Pagett. Aged 40, came in 1623, a servant in *Southampton*.

James City.

Mr. Menefie. Arrived in July 1623, in the *Samuel*. A merchant.

Mr. Kingsmell. Perhaps Kingswell came in the *Delaware*. His wife in the *Susan*.

Paces Pains, James City.

Lt. William Perry.

John Smyth. Came in 1611, in *Elizabeth*.

Over the River.

Capt. John West. Brother of the late Lord Delaware, and Gov. Francis West.

Capt. Rob't Fellgate.

Pasbehay, James City.

Thomas Bagwell. An old settler.

Neck of Land, James City.

Richard Brewster.

Archer's Hope, James City.

Theodore Moyses, Came in *London Merchant*.
Thomas Doe.

Between Archer's Hope, and Martin's Hundred.

Mr. John Utie. Came in the *Francis Bona Ventura*. A man of influence.

Richard Townsend. Now about 24 years old. Came in the *Abigail*, 1620, had been a servant of Dr. John Pott.

Hog Island.

John Chew. Came in the *Charity*. A merchant.

Richard Tree. Arrived in the *George*, with his son twelve years old.

Martin's Hundred.

Thomas Kingston. In the colony several years.

Thomas Fawcett. In the colony several years.

Mulberry Island.

Thomas Harwood. Came in 1623, in *Margaret and John*.

Phettiplace Close. An old settler, who came in the *Star*.

Warwick River.

Christopher Stokes. Had been five years in colony.

Thomas Ceeley. A county justice in 1632.

Thomas Flint. Came in 1618, in *Diana*, a county justice in 1632.

Zachary Cripps. Came in 1621 in *Marg't and John*, a county justice in 1632.

Warosquoyake.

Capt. Natt Basse. Was about 40 years old and came in 1622, in *Furtherance*.

Richard Bennett. Afterwards Councillor.

Robert Savin.

Thomas Jordan. Justice in 1632.

Nutmeg Quarter.

William Cole. Now about 31 years old, came in 1618 in *Neptune*. His wife came in 1616, in *Susan*.

William Bentley. About 41 years of age, came as a hired man in 1624, in the *Jacob*.

Elizabeth City.

Lt. Thompson.
Adam Thorowgood. Came in 1621, when 18 years old.
Mr. Rowlston. Came in 1623 in *God's Gift*.
John Browning. About 27 years old, came in 1621, in *Abigail*.
John Downeman. When a boy, came in 1611, married a maid sent out in 1621, in *Warwick*.

"Muster of the Inhabitants in Virginia. Taken in 1625. Total, 1,095. The Muster of the Inhabitants at Wariscoyack, Taken the 7th of February, 1625," *William and Mary College Quarterly Historical Magazine*, 7 (1899), 217-218 [Lancour No. 212].

The Muster of Mr. Edward Bennett's Servants.

Henry Pinke came in the London Marchannt 1619, John Bate in the Addam 1621, Peter Collins in the Addam 1621, Wassell Webbling, Antonio, a negro, in the James 1621, Christopher Reynold's, Luke Chappman, Edward Maybank, in the John & Francis 1622, John Attkins, William Denum, Francis Banks, in the Guifte 1623, Mary, a negro woman, in the Margrett & John 1622.

A Muster of the Inhabitants of Basses Choyse.

Capt. Nathaniell Basse his Muster.

Nathaniell Basse, aged 35, in the *Furtherance* 1622.
William Barnard, aged 21, in the *Furtherance* 1622.
Edward Wigge, aged 22, in the *Abigall* 1621.

The Muster of Thomas Phillipes.

Thomas Phillipes, aged 26, in the *William and Thomas* 1618.
Elizabeth Phillipes, aged 23, in the *Sea Flower* 1621.

The Muster of Thomas Bennett.

Thomas Bennett, aged 38, in the *Neptune* 1618.
Mary Bennett, aged 18, in the *Southampton* 1622.
Roger Heford, aged 22, in the *Returne* 1623.
Beniamine Simes [Syms], aged 33 in the ——.

Richard Longe His Muster.

Richard Longe, aged 33, in the ——.
Alice Longe, aged 23, in the *London Marchant* 1620.
Robert Longe, a child borne in Virginia.

Richard Evand's His Muster.

Richard Evand's, age 35, in the *Neptune* 1618.

William Newman His Muster.

William Newman, aged 35, in the *Furtherance* 1622.

John Army, aged 35, in the *Furtherance* 1622.

Henrie Woodward His Muster.

Henrie Woodward, aged 30, in the ——.
John Browninge, aged 22, in the *Abigall* 1621.

Servants.

Ambrose, aged 25, in the *Marmiducke* 1621.
Peeter, aged 19, in the *Margett and John* 1620.
Total muster living at Basse's and Warrascoyack, 31.

A List of the Dead in Wariscoyack 1624 (25).

John Selley, Nathaniell Haukworth [or Hankworth], Thomas Sherwoud, Beniamin Handcleare, Margrett Symes; Nathaniell, Thomas, servants; of Mr Bennett's men slayne by the Indianes, five.

Winifred Lovering Holman. "Marriages of Emigrants to Virginia," *The Virginia Magazine of History and Biography*, 40 (1932), 80 [Lancour No. 213].

The following marriages taken from Volume XIV of the Hampshire, England, marriages, p. 32, may be of interest:

Newport, Isle of Wight, Parish Registers begin 1541: p. 32, 11 Feb. 1620-21, Henry Bushell & Alice Crocker, Christopher Cradocke & Alice Cooke, Edward Marshall & Mary Michell, Walter Beare & Ann Greene, Robert Gullever & Joan Pie. "All which last fyve coupple were for virgenia".

"Mr. Danniell Gookines Muster" (in Frederick William Gookin's *Daniel Gookin, 1612-1687* [Chicago: F. W. Gookin, 1912], pages 47-48) [Lancour No. 214].

This list contains the names listed on page 57, above, William Wadsworth through Joseph Mosley, with their ages, all from 21 through 26, along with the names of names of nine others, aged 19 through 44, for whom no ship is given.

"Minutes of the Council and General Court, 1622-1624," *The Virginia Magazine of History and Biography*, 19 (1911?), 113-148 [Lancour No. 215].

Following is an excerpt from pages 131-134. Much of the material below is given as a footnote in the original.

[51]

Court held 8 ——— 1624?
(torn)
Lt Pott The oathes of Supremacy & aleg
To these whose names are underwritten
of the A[nn] Thomas Fairlay of Worcester in Worcestershire gent
which arrived at James Owen Dawson of St. Martins in the fields
Cittye the 5 of Septr jovner & fren [torn]
Ralph Buckridge of Sutten in Barkshire gent
John Crampton of Bolton in the moore in Lancashire
William Poole of Preston in Andernesse in Lankeshire
Thomas Crompton of Bolton in the moore in Lankashire
Simon Withe of London, bricklayer
Thomas Sisson of London, haberdasher
William Kempe of Howes in Leicestershire, ge[n']
10 Thomas Warden of Ely in Hampshire, husband[man]
Edward Rogeres of Porbery in Somershire, carye[r]
William Jones (about 17 aged) in London joyner
William Kelloway aged about 20 of Poorchmouth, husbandm[an]
15 John Gowton of Harfield in Surrey, gent
John Downes of London, Grocer
Thomas Roper of Milden in the County of bedfordshire, gen'

Of the Bonny Bess wch came to James Citty the 12 of Sep^{r}
John Bath of London a Leatherseller
Willm Fitzgeffrey of Staple Inne gen'
George Syberrye of London Tallow-chandler
Henry Fell of Christchurch in Oxford, student.
Theodore Pettus of Norwich gen'
Robert Collins of London, haberdasher
John Pegden of London gen'
Josyas Harr of London, haberdasher
John Eman of London, goldsmith
George Fitzgeffrey of Howton Conquest in bedfordshire gen'
Henry Cheyney of York, marchant
14 Robert Constable of North Allerton in Yorkshire gen'

[52]

George Pacy of London, grocer
John West of Witley in Surrey, husbandman
Austen Smith of London, Carpenter
Edward Hosyer of Raschiffe, vintner

Henry Syberrye of London, chandler
Thomas West of London, coop[er]
James Holt of London, Carpenter
Alexander Gill of Maldon in Bedfordshire
Ralph Martin of Bachain Somershire, husbandman
John Dyer of London, Carpenter
John Priest of Langport in Somersetshire, tayler
Richard Crouch of Howton, in Bedfordshire
Carpenter aged about 27 [Qy? faded]
Samuell Weauer of London aged about 18
Roger Rodes of Dowton in Wilshire, Mr. Fitzgeffrey his servant aged about 19 basle [torn]
Thomas Sexton of London, one of Christs Hospitall age about 17
16 Moyses Stone of Longworth in Barkshire aged about 18

[Footnote from page 131:] These emigrants came before February, 1622-23, for many of the names appear in the census taken in that month.

From the earliest period of the settlement it had been the law that all new-comers should register their names, birthplaces, occupation and take the oath of allegiance. This law was often re-encited after the Colony came under royal government. In February, 1631-32, the Assembly passed a law which required that the commander of the fort at Point Comfort should go aboard all ships as soon as they arrived "and there require the cammander, captayne or mayster, of the shipp or shipps, to deliver unto him a true list of all such persons, which were embarqued in theire shipp, at theire coming out of England, together with their ages, countryes and townes where they were borne, and to keep record of the same; and be the sayd commander of the ffort to administer unto them the oaths of supremacy and allegiance," (*Hening*, I, 166). The two lists here given appear to be the only ones which remain of the great number which must have once existed. Probably most of them were kept at Elizabeth City and were destroyed along with all the other early records there.

Thomas Farley, who came in the *Ann*, in 1623, was living at Archer's Hope, with his wife Jane and daughter Ann in 1623, (*Hotten*, 230). He was a Burgess for the plantations between Harrop and Archer's Hope and Martin's Hundred at the session of March, 1629-30, and for Archer's Hope, February, 1631-32.

Simon With died at Elizabeth City between March, 1622 and February, 1623.

There were apparently two persons named William Kemp living in Virginia in 1624-25. One, who arrived in the *George* with his wife Margaret, had a son Anthony, seven weeks old at the date of the census, and was living at Pashbebays or the Main near Jamestown. The other, aged 33 at the time of the census, came in the *William and Thomas*, in 1618, and was living at Elizabeth City. William Kempe was J. P. for Elizabeth City in 1628, and Burgess for the Upper Parish of that county, 1629-30.

At the census of 1624-25, Thomas Warden, aged 24, who came in the *Ann*, in 1623, was among the servants of Capt. William Epes on the Eastern Shore and Edward Rogers was in the same position.

Between July, 1622 and May, 1623, the Virginia Company issued a patent for land to "Mr. Roper, Mr. Fitz Jeffreys and others." Thomas Roper died at James City in the year predeeding [*sic*] the census of February, 1623.

One "Mr. Fitz Jeffreys" died at James City during the year preceding February, 1623.

Thomas Siberry was living at Martin's Hundred, February, 1623.

Henry Fell died at James City during the year preceding February, 1623. He appears in Foster's *Alumni Oxonienses* as Henry Fell, of London, gent., who matriculated at St. Albans Hall, June 5, 1618, aged 18, and was B. A. from Christ Church, June 20, 1620.

Theodore Pettus was doubtless of the family of Pettus, baronets (now extinct or dormant) who were closely connected with Norwich.

"Mr. Collins" and wife and "Mr. Pegden," died at James City during the year preceding February, 1623.

"Robert Cunstable" was living in James Island, February, 1623.

"Osten Smith" was living at James City, February, 1623.

——— Hosier died at James City during the year preceding February, 1623.

This John West, who came in the *Bonny Bess*, was living at James City, 1624-25; Thomas West died in 1624.

At the census of 1624-25, Alexander Gill, aged 20, was one of the servants of Capt. William Pierce at Mulberry Island.

Richard Crouch was living at James City, February, 1623.

Samuel Weaver, aged 30 (in 1624-25), was then living as one of William Harwood's servants at Martin's Hundred.

Thomas Sexton died at James City during the year preceding February, 1623.

Moyses Stone was living at Elizabeth City, 1624-25.

George Cabell Greer. *Early Virginia Immigrants*. Baltimore: Genealogical Publishing Co., 1973 [Lancour No. 216].

This 376 pages work contains 25,000 names taken from the records of the Virginia Land Office for the period 1623-1666.

H. G. Somerby. "Passengers for Virginia, 1635," *The New England Historical and Genealogical Register*, 2 (1848), 111ff. [Lancour No. 217].

This series is now readily available in *Passengers to America; a Consolidation of Ship Passenger Lists from The New England Historical and Genealogical Register*, edited by Michael Tepper and published in Baltimore, 1977, by the Genealogical Publishing Co., Inc. The list cited here appears on pages 80-107. The entire book includes mention of some 18,000 names, is well indexed (excepting for place names), and pertains primarily to New England.

William Glover Stanard. *Some Emigrants to Virginia: Memoranda in Regard to Several Hundred Emigrants to Virginia During the Colonial Period Whose Parentage is Shown or Former Residence Indicated by Authentic Records*, second edition, enlarged, reprint. Baltimore: Genealogical Publishing Co., 1976 [Lancour No. 218].

This is an alphabetical list of emigrants to Virginia, 1635-1800, 94 pages, in wrappers.

Martha W. Hiden, editor. "Accompts of the Tristram and Jane," *The Virginia Magazine of History and Biography*, 62 (1954), 424-447 [Lancour No. 219].

A Booke of Accompts for the Shippe called the Tristram and Jeane of London which came from Virginia Anno Domini 1637. Exhibit 26th Aprilis 1637.

An Abstract of the Cargazoune of goods laden aboard the good shippe called the Tristram and Jane of London, Daniell Hopkinson, Merchant, and Joseph Blowe, Master, bound for Virginia, and what Tobacco was received for the said goods by Joseph Clifton Executor of the Said Hopkinson the 22th of Aprill 1637.

Fol: Mr. Withers as per his Accompt....

Mr. Henry Greene as per his Accompt....

Capt Batten as per Mr. Andrew Battens Accompt....

Mr. Steed as per Contrary his Accompt....

Given by Joseph Clifton....

Mr. Minifries accompt sould by Dan: Hopkinson....

For a servant named Tho: Moorton....

Bought by Dan: Hopkinson of John Watts Vizt....

Sould more of Mr. Rolfes and Mr. Watts his stockings....

Mr. Abraham Hopkinson's 8th part of the Cargazoune was disposed amongst the passingers as per a book of one John Lee's wrighting a passinger may appeare being clothes, shirts etc.

Mr. James Pickering's 16th part....

For 3 fowling peeces of Mr. Wallers....

....

The Names of the Servants and to what Masters they were turn'd over unto in Virginia.

		Tob. *li*	*Masters.*
	James Miller,* Cooper for his and his wifes passage	0900	
	Servants.		
1	William Browne	0550	James Miller*
2	John Scoffin*		
3	Walter Willis*		
4	Samuell Fenne*		
5	Thomas Dodge*		
6	Cornelius Sanders*		
7	Judith Hobbes a maid		
8	Thomas Horiman	3500	John Davis*
9	Robert Lord		
10	Francis Berry a maid	1000	William Worlich*
11	Roger Shillito	00500	Thomas Maleigh
12	Edward Hartuppe*		
13	Anthony Lentall*		
14	Dorothy Moore a maid	01800	Timothy Stockdell Account
		08250	
15	John Grigges		
16	Dorothy Scott a maid	01200	Robert Partin*
17	Anne Hartford maid	00600	Anthony Panton,* Clarke
18	Francis Seymer* Mr. Wallers servant at London		
19	Thomas Cordell	01000	John Neale
20	Sarah Cole* a maid	00600	Thomas Sully*
21	Thomas Mooreton	00600	George Minifry*
22	Richard Buckland	00525	John Smith
23	Thomas Purser	00600	Brasheers*
24	Robert Lord		
25	Elinor Felton maid	01050	Gookines*
26	John Swancoat Mr. Wallers man. London		
27	Anne Turner a maid	01100	Gresham Coffeld*
28	Richard Baxter*		
29	William Abraham		
30	Anne Dennis a maid	01800	Cooke
31	John Compton		
32	Anne Underwood a maid	01200	Harris*
	Total	18525	Verte Fol: [Turn page]
33	John Trevone		
34	Andrew Minstrid		
35	John Jones		
36	Jeremy Damford		

*Discussed in notes which follow documents.

37	John Tailour	03000	John Howe*
38	Elizabeth Keltridge maid		
39	David Fluellin	00550	Cornelius Lloid*
40	Rachell Dill a maid	00550	Joseph More*
41	Howell David		
42	James Thornton		
43	Robert Nicholls		
44	John Tomson		
45	John Briscoe	02500	Cornwallis*
46	John Jollitt		
47	Richard Carter*	01100	Nathaniel Floyd*
48	Alice Mason a maid	00500	Ralph Wyatt*
49	Katherin Teage a maid	00450	William Armstead*
50	Michael Vincklee*	00580	Nicholas Smith
51	Arthur Raymond*	00500	William Croppe
52	Griffin Atkins	00550	Christopher Thomas
53	John Mocaye	00450	William Freeman
54		00500	Richard Preston*
55	Peter Rigglesworth*	00500	Robert Glascocke*
		11730	
56	Ellen Fetherstone* maid	00500	Thomas Trotter
57	Walter Blake*	00500	James Knatt*
58	Robert Ashbury	00550	Martin Baker*
59	Thomas Mason	00550	John Ward*
60	Edward Thornicraft* Mr. Wallers servant London	00720	Ellis Tailour*
61	Robert Spratling* Mr. Wallers servant London	00560	Thomas Rochester
62	Vincent Paton		
63	William Workuppe	00900	Thomas Hart
64	John Hall*	00465	William Walder
65	John Lee*	00450	Richard Tomson
		16925	
	On the former leafe Total	18525	
	Totall both	35450	Verte Fol: [Turn page]
	On the other leafe	35450	
66	Priscilla Norman maid		
67	William Beeby	01100	Arthur Haslerton*
68	Anne Merriott a maid	00500	Drewe
69			
70	2 servants	01100	Robert Lucas*
71			
72	2 servants	01100	Liuetenant Cheesman*
73	Richard Turner	00400	Samuell Fermont
74	Thomas Green	00500	Parson Caynhoo*
	Total	40050	
	To deduct out for 4 of Mr. Wallers servants	02280	
	Rest per 70 men	37770	

Memorandum there is recorded amongst the Tobacco for Mr. Wallers 4 servants 1190 li which may be paid out of the hhds marked with I K remembering their dietting aboard being sick and the maid also.

A Coppy of all the Debts owing by bills and without bills in Virginia for all the goods written in this booke Vizt.

		Tob li
	Partin per bills	04039
	Pore per Davis	00400
Masters	Causy* per Davis	00046
	Cage* per Davis	00642
	Ransham* & Merriman*	00310
	Thomas Hart	02305
	Wilson*	00600
	James Miller	01040
	Harris	00236
	Arthur Haslerton	00600
		10218
	Per foot of Account beneath Masters is	28628
	Read	00349
	Parry*	00291
	Cage	01000
	Marme	00100
	Mason*	00117
	Maleigh the bill left with Capt. Hooke	00550
	Hadarell the bill* left with Robt. Lucas	00585
	Drewe	00400
	Smith	00710
	Thomas	01112
Masters	Lewin*	00200
	Chum[i]nge*	00206
	Parson Panton*	00700
	Hegnam besides 4 tunne of hogsheads	00369

		li
	Hutchinson	00059
	Seawell*	00666
	Brasheere	01971
		16611
	Finch	00200
	Wyat	00230
Masters	Gookins	00270
	Worlich	00380
	Parson Caynhoo	03091
	Howe	05744
	Welton	00090
	Codd*	01263
	Ray*	00149
	Ward	00600
		28628
	Gilbert Symonds*	00075
	Francis Lassard	00045
	Trussell*	00170
	Dennis Russell*	00050
	Mr. Ouldis*	00090
	Hampton & Warren the bill left with James Stone*	00360
	Bland	00120
	Watkins	00052
	Fermont	00400
Masters	Minifry	01465
	Totall of debts per bills and without bills	34455

[The following tobacco accounts mention Nathaniel Withers, Henry Greene, Capt. Batten, Thomas Steed, Daniell Hopkinson, Abraham Hopkinson, James Pickering, all referred to as "Mr."]

[The last account is signed by Joseph Clifton.]

[There follows the will of Daniell Hopkinson which mentions "my beloved brother, Joseph Clifton to be my full and lawfull executor" and "my beloved wife Sarah" as well as "Father Clifton and Mother Clifton," "Mother Katherine Hopkinson," "brother Abraham," "brother Michael Markland," "brother and sister Sole," "Sister Barbery Clifton," "Mr. Reeves," "Mr. Hart." The will was dated 21 November 1636 and witnessed by Robert Reeves and Thomas Nant [Hart?].

"A Booke of Accounts for the Shippe called the Tristram and Jeane of London which came from Virginia Anno Domini 1637" (Public Record Office, London, HCA 30 635, 13 sheets) is one of the interesting bits of Virginiana unearthed by Mr. Francis L. Berkeley, Curator of Manuscripts at the Alderman Library, University of Virginia, while doing research in Great Britain. It is the earliest account of a trading voyage to Virginia that this writer has seen and contains numerous items of interest. Like voyages to the Near and Far East described in "John Offley's Book" (*Virginia Magazine of History and Biography*, L (1942), 1-12), it was a joint stock venture with each member putting up either a certain amount of money or of commodities, repayable at the end of the voyage with a proportionate share of the profits. In this case there were eight shares divided among seven persons as follows: Mr. Nathaniel Withers, one-eighth; Mr. Henry Greene, one-eighth; Captain Batten, one-sixteenth; Mr. Thomas Steed, one-eighth; Mr. Daniell Hopkinson, the so-called "Merchant" but acting more like a supercargo, three-eighths; his brother, Mr. Abraham Hopkinson, one-eighth; and Mr. James Pickering, one-sixteenth. Daniell Hopkinson died in Virginia testate leaving his brother-in-law, Joseph Clifton, his executor. Hopkinson's will was probated in London (P.C.C. (52) Goare 1636 in the Principal Probate Registry, Somerset House, London). The account book was among the papers filed in the settlement of the estate.

The *Tristram and Jane* probably left England in late summer or early fall of 1636, arriving in Virginia in time to take on the tobacco which was ready for market by December. On the homeward voyage the vessel probably reached London the latter part of March 1637 for Daniell Hopkinson's will was probated April 8, 1637. The ship took back to England 99 hogsheads of tobacco totalling 31,800 pounds or an average of slightly over 321 pounds to the hogshead. Besides this, the partners shipped on the *Unity* of the Isle of Wight two hogsheads weighing 550 pounds. Their total poundage was, therefore, 32,350, which at fourpence per pound equals £539-3-4. The profits of the voyage cannot be learned from this "book of accompts" for it does not give the cost of all the articles comprising the cargo....

We return now to passengers of the *Tristram and Jane*. A check of the land patents in Nell Marion Nugent's *Cavaliers and Pioneers* [from this point many footnotes are omitted] was made to learn if possible what became of them. It is possible that two persons having the same name may be confused in some of the identifications.

James Miller, the first passenger named was a cooper by trade, an important trade in a country where tobacco, the main crop, was generally handled in hogsheads. James Miller paid 900 pounds of tobacco for his and his wife's passage. On October 23, 1637, he took up 100 acres in Charles River (now York) County lying on the great Otterdams at the head of the new Poquoson, due him for "the personal adventure of himself and his wife Mary." He purchased a servant from the *Tristram*, William Browne, of whom we have no further mention.

John Davis on August 26, 1637, patented 250 acres in James City County lying on the Chickahominy River for his own transportation and that of four servants, three of whom Samuel Fenn, Walter Willis, and Thomas Lodge (Lodge being likely a misreading for Dodge as the name appears in the "Accompt") had come over on the *Tristram*. John Davis had purchased two other servants, John Scoffin and Cornelius Sanders. Scoffin he likely sold to Nicholas Hill whose patent for land in Elizabeth City County on November 25, 1637, claims as a headright "a servant called John Coffin (or Scoffin)." Davis also sold Sanders whose right was not used until some sixteen years later. Then on April 27, 1653, Captain Robert Abrahall patented 400 acres in Gloucester County for the transportation of eight persons whose rights had been "assigned by Captain Barnehouse," among them appears the name "Cor. Sanders."

William Worlich, who bought two servants, patented on May 7, 1637, 150 acres lying "in Warwick County commonly called the broadneck." There is no record of the servant Robert Lord whom Worlich had purchased from the *Tristram*.

Timothy Stockdell appears in the "Accompt" as purchasing Edward Hartuppe and Anthony Lentall. He soon sold them, for, on February 6, 1637/38, Humphry Higgenson, Gent., patented 700 acres called by the name of Tuttey's Neck adjacent to Harrop, "upon a branch of Archer's Hope Creek parting it from Kingsmell's Neck." "Said land graunted unto Elizabeth his now wife by order of Court October 4, 1637, whose right is transferred to said Higgenson, and alsoe due for the adventure of 14 persons, Eliza. Higgenson, Edward Hartop, Anth. Lenton," etc. Anthony Lentall (Lenton, Lynton, Linton) is doubtless progenitor of the family later in Lower Norfolk and still later in Stafford and Prince William counties.

We learn of Robert Partin and John Neale, who bought two servants each, through the following items. Captain Francis Hook, Esquire, on August 9, 1637, patented 100 acres in Elizabeth City County adjoining Thomas Oldis and John Neale, "the said land being in the tenure and occupation of Robert Partin and Gresham Covell." On November 24, 1637, Robert Partin leased 40 acres in Elizabeth City County between the great house and Widow Thompson's land, south on the fort field, west on Robert Brasheare, and north to the church for a term of 21 years. John Neale, merchant, on February 12, 1632, had taken a 21 year lease on 50 acres lying upon the Strawberry Banks within the precincts of Elizabeth City, east upon the land of Lieutenant Edward Waters, west along the great river. (The great river would be the part of Hampton Roads lying between Hampton Creek and Salter Creek. Strawberry Banks is the site of the present Kecoughtan Veterans' Facility.)

Anthony Panton, clarke, later called in the "Accompts" Parson Panton, was the minister of York and Chiskiack Parishes in York County. He was persecuted by Governor John Harvey for disparaging remarks about Richard Kemp, secretary of the colony, and banished from the colony on October 8, 1638. Governor Francis Wyatt, Harvey's successor, restored him to his parish. York Parish extended from Poquoson River to Morgan's Creek and Chiskiack from Morgan's Creek to Queen's Creek.

Thomas Sully, according to the "Accompts," purchased Sarah Cole, but sold her to Walter Chiles, merchant, for on May 2, 1638, she is one of the headrights listed in a patent issued to Walter Chiles for 250 acres on the Appomattox River, Charles City County. Thomas Sully on August 14, 1624, had patented six acres "within the Island of James City, east upon block house field, cleared in the time of the Government of Sir Thomas Gates, extending to the new block house lately built, part of his first divident for his personal adventure." He is described as "of the Neck of Land in the Corporation of James City, Yeoman and old planter." ("Old" or "Ancient Planter" was the term for those who had come prior to 1616, and were therefore entitled to 100 acres instead of the 50 acres due later arrivals.)

George Menifee (Minifry, Menefee), who is mentioned several times as a purchaser both of commodities and a servant, was a merchant who came in 1622 in the *Samuel*. On February 4, 1624/25, he patented land, "having been in this country almost 3 years." George Menifee resided some eight miles east of Williamsburg, a state historical marker on U. S. Route 60 now designates the location. His land adjoined that of Richard Kingsmill. In 1953 the Kingsmill tract, then comprising a much longer acreage than early patents called for, became the property of Colonial Williamsburg, Inc.

The Brasheare who paid 600 pounds of tobacco for Thomas Purser is presumably the person named in the following: Peter Johnson's patent for 600 acres in Warrisquicke County June 1, 1636, land abutting on Nansemond River, "Renewed in the name of Robert Brasseur and Peter Ray."

The Gookines who bought two servants may be either John or Daniel Gookins; the former patented on October 17, 1636, 500 acres on Nansemond River, the latter also owned land in this vicinity, for on November 24, 1637, William Fookes patented 450 acres "at Nansemond River joining to the land of Mr. Daniel Gookins." ("Mr." in the seventeenth century was used to denote social position and was not applied generally.)

Gresham Coffeld, who bought two servants, is identical with "Gresham (Gressom) Coffield" who on August 14, 1638, patented in partnership with Thomas Stamp 200 acres in Isle of Wight County. "Coffield" is the same as "Covell," and this is the same person previously mentioned as holding land in Elizabeth City County with Robert Partin.

A Cooke bought Richard Baxter and William Abraham, but evidently sold the former, who is listed in a patent to Thomas Clipwell dated November 15, 1638, for 600 acres lying in James City County on the Chickahominy River.

The Harris who bought two servants is possibly Thomas Harris an "Ancient Planter" and prominent citizen.

Captain John Howe who was in Accomack County prior to October 24, 1637, at which time he patented land "upon Cherrystone Creek" is probably identical with the John Howe who invested in six servants as noted in the "Accompts."

Cornelius Lloyd who purchased a servant had a patent on July 2, 1635, for 800 acres lying upon Elizabeth River. He had come to Virginia with his brother Colonel Edward Lloyd, before the Massacre. Cornelius died childless, but Edward removed to Maryland and became the founder of a distinguished family.

Joseph Moore is mentioned in the following items. John Robins the younger of the Back River in the Corporation of Elizabeth City, planter, son and heir of his father John Robins the elder deceased, patented 300 acres at said Back River on September 7, 1632. Among his headrights was Joseph Moore who came over in the *Margaret and John* in 1622. Joseph Moore patented on June 2, 1636, 200 acres in Elizabeth City County at the old Poquoson River. (In 1632 the division of the colony into four corporations was still in force and Elizabeth City was one; when the corporations were abandoned and the colony divided into eight shires or counties, Elizabeth City was one. In 1952 the county became the City of Hampton.)

A Cornwallis is shown in the "Accompts" as buying five servants, he is probably the person referred to in an order of the York County Court held in January 1645/6 in Beverley Fleet's *Virginia Colonial Abstracts*: "Thomas Bushrod to have an attachment against the estate of Captain Thomas Cornwallis to cover debt of 3030 pounds of tobacco."

On August 18, 1627, Lieutenant Gilbert Peppett patented 250 acres on the southerly side of Warwick River parting it from the land of Captain Samuel Matthews now in the tenure "of Thomas Attowell (or Howell) and Nathaniell Floyd." Nathaniel Floyd patented on November 20, 1637, 250 acres in Isle of Wight County, claiming as headrights, among others, Richard Carter, whom he had purchased from the *Tristram*.

No patent has been found for Ralph Wyatt, but he was a landholder prior to December 31, 1636, as on that date he executed a lease for 21 years to Richard Johnson, Roger Davis, and Abraham Wood, planters, for land lying on Sizemore's Creek near Appomattox River, reserving to said Wyatt ten acres.

William Armistead who bought for 450 pounds of tobacco a maid servant Katherin Teage is presumably the same person who on July 7, 1636, took out a patent for 450 acres in Elizabeth City County.

Richard Preston in an undated patent, but probably issued in November, 1637, received 100 acres upon the uppermost end of Thomas Jordan's great Indianfield Neck for the transportation of Michael

Vinkles and Walter Brute. The latter may be the unnamed servant he bought from the *Tristram*. The right of Michael Vincklee he had purchased later, since Nicholas Smith was the person buying him from the *Tristram*.

Arthur Raymond, though bought by William Croppe, appears as a headright for William Burdett who patented on March 18, 1639, 1050 acres in Accomack County.

Peter Rigglesworth, purchased by Robert Glascocke, was a land owner by 1652 when Robert Grimes patenting 300 acres lying at the head of the westernmost branch of Elizabeth River describes it as adjoining Peter Rigglesworth. ("The westernmost branch of Elizabeth River" is now usually called "Western Branch.") Robert Glascocke received a patent on October 7, 1635, for 200 acres lying in Elizabeth City County adjoining Lieutenant Cheeseman. (The Glascock, like many other Warwick and Elizabeth City County families, somewhat later moved to the Northern Neck of Virginia which lies between the Rappahannock and Potomac rivers.)

Ellen Fetherstone, a maid, sold to Thomas Trotter, appears later as a headright for William Warren, who on August 10, 1642, received 650 acres lying on the north side of Charles River.

James Knott who purchased Walter Blake used him as one of his headrights to purchase on August 18, 1637, 1550 acres in the Upper County of New Norfolk. (This area later became Nansemond County.)

Martin Baker purchased Robert Ashbury of whom we have no trace. Martin Baker on April 24, 1635, took out a patent for 600 acres lying upon Captain Martin's lands.

John Ward before 1633 had taken up land for in that year he secured a 21 year lease on 25 acres adjacent to his own holdings.

Ellis Tailour [Elias Taylor] who purchased Edward Thornicraft used him as one of his headrights to secure 100 acres in Accomack County at Nassawaddox Creek on July 10, 1640.

Robert Spratling, purchased by Thomas Rochester appears as a headright some years later for Nicholas Waddilowe, who patented on September 15, 1649, 400 acres in Northampton County lying on Occahannock Creek.

John Hall purchased by William Walders was a headright for James Warradine, when he patented 350 acres in Charles City lying on Bailey's Creek on November 3, 1637. (This land was on the south side of James River.)

Richard Tomson purchased John Lee but probably sold him to Robert Bennett, for Lee appears as a headright in a patent issued August 18, 1637, to Bennett for 700 acres in the Upper County of New Norfolk about a mile and a half up a creek near the mouth of the Nansemond River.

Arthur Haslerton (Haslington) took out a patent on December 23, 1636, for 200 acres in Warrisquicke (later Isle of Wight) County, due for his personal adventure and the transportation of three persons. It was renewed July 18, 1640, in the name of Gresham Cofeild.

Robert Lucas, who purchased two servants, secured 150 acres in Charles River County lying on the New Poquoson River on April 30, 1636.

John Cheesman, Gent. of Kicoughton, had a patent on September 2, 1624, for the transportation of four servants who came in the *Southampton* in 1622. As Lieutenant John Cheeseman on November 21, 1635, he patented 600 acres in Charles River County. (The Chisman family has long been prominent in lower York and Elizabeth City counties.)

Parson Caynhoo of the "Accompts" has not been identified, unless he is the William Canhooe who on September 10, 1639, patented 300 acres in Charles River County at the New Poquoson upon Cheesman's Creek, which tract apparently escheated later.

The Causy who owned a small bill in the "Accompts" is likely Thomas Causey who took out a patent on April 18, 1635, for 150 acres in Charles City County "in the Indian field comonly soe called," lying due north upon Jordan's Journey, west upon the main woods, south upon Chaplin's Choice, and due east upon the main river.

The Cage mentioned in the "Accompts" is probably the person named in the lease of Dictoris Christmas, planter, of Elizabeth City, assigned to Lyonell Rowlston, Gent. of the same place, on September 29, 1628, in the presence of William Claibourne and Edward Cage. The title of the lease he had received on August 20, 1627, from Sir George Yeardley for 50 acres on the Strawberry Banks where "I now dwell."

Of the Ransham and Marriman, also debtors, Ramsham may be either William or Thomas Ramshaw, both of whom took out patents in July 1635 in Elizabeth City County. The Merriman is likely James Merriman who patented 150 acres in Charles City County adjoining Weyanoke, on November 6, 1635, for the personal adventure of himself and wife Sarah Merriman and transportation of one servant.

The Wilson mentioned is likely Henry Wilson who on December 23, 1636, patented 50 acres in Accomack County.

Edward Drew, probably identical with the Drewe of the "Accompts," took out a patent on September 8, 1636, for 300 acres in Accomack County, adjoining the land of Mr. John Howe.

John Lewin, probably the person referred to, patented on May 6, 1634, 500 acres in the County of Upper Norfolk lying on the back side of land lately belonging to Thomas Jordan.

Thomas Seawell on April 20, 1635, patented 400 acres, 350 acres being at the head of the Old Pocoson and 50 acres lying near Benjamin Symms's Marsh.

The Codd mentioned is likely the Thomas Codd who on May 22, 1637, received patent for 300 acres in the Upper County of New Norfolk adjoining Thomas Holt, lying upon the East Branch of Elizabeth River.

Thomas Wray, probably the person called Ray in the text, on May 4, 1636, patented 50 acres in Charles River County upon the back creek of the New Poquoson River adjoining Gilbert Symons due for his personal adventure.

William Parry, probably the Parry noted in the text, on May 22, 1637, patented 350 acres in the Upper County of New Norfolk "at the entering into the narrow of the Easternmost branch of Nansemond River."

The Mason mentioned is almost certainly Francis Mason who came in the *John and Francis* in 1613.

Christopher Boyse on October 23, 1639, patented 300 acres in Charles River County lying north upon the head of the New Poquoson and east upon George Hadderill. This is likely the Hadarell whose bill was left with Robert Lucas.

Gilbert Symonds, Planter, of Elizabeth City County on October 20, 1634, took a 21 year lease on 100 acres lying at the Old Pocoson River.

John Trussell on October 12, 1635, patented 200 acres near the Back River. (It is possible to trace John Trussell from "The Muster of the Inhabitants taken in 1624/25" until he died testate in Northumberland County in 1660.)

In Captain Adam Thoroughgood's patent issued June 24, 1635, for 5350 acres for transportation of 105 persons, Dennis Russell who came in the *Hopewell* in 1628 is a headright.

Presumably "Mr. Ouldis" of the text is Thomas Oldis mentioned as owning land adjoining Captain Francis Hooke, Esq.

On February 9, 1636, Sir John Harvey, then Governor issued a patent to William Tucker, Maurice Tompson, George Tompson, William Harris, Thomas Deacon, James Stone, Cornelius Lloyd of London, Merchants, etc. for 8000 acres in Charles City County known by the name of Berkeley Hundred. Due by deed of sale from the Adventures and Company of Berkeley Hundred etc. This is the James Stone of the text.

This concludes such identifications as have seemed logical to make from the land patents. The writer knows of no other document so clearly revealing the trade in headrights which passed from one person to another like currency.

In conclusion, we would note the "ports of call" of the *Tristram and Jane*. Only five are named, a convenient "etc." hiding the others. The first was Kickhowtan or Kecoughtan, the Indian name for Hampton, which was settled in 1610. The patent to Robert Partin previously quoted shows by as references to "the fort field" and "the church" that this was an established community. Mr. George C. Mason in *Colonial Churches of Tidewater Virginia* states that the Fort Field was the site of Forts Henry and Charles built by Sir Thomas Dale in 1610 on the eastern side of the mouth of Hampton Creek. He locates the churchyard as "at the east end of College Place." This was the church built after 1624 and in use in 1636. Mr. Mason describes it from its foundations as being fifty-three feet six inches long by twenty-three feet wide. Doubtless this was the spot where Daniell Hopkinson wished to be buried "decently."

After selling servants and commodities, the *Tristram and Jane* left Kecoughtan, passed Old Point, entered Chesapeake Bay, and then turned into Back River, which flows into the Bay. This river lies to the northwest of and back of Hampton as its name implies and was in a well settled area. It is formed by the union of two branches now styled Northwest and Southwest. On a British map of the Lower Peninsula, however, made during the Revolution, the Northwest Branch is marked Old Pocoson and the other is unnamed. Some eight or ten miles to the northwest of Old Pocoson lies Poquoson River which in 1636 was known as New Poquoson. It too flows into Chesapeake Bay.

It might be of interest to explain the use of the adjective "new." It was not until 1630 that the Council and Governor issued an order "for the securing and taking in of a tract of land called the forrest, bordering upon the chiefe residence of the Pamunky King, the most dangerous head of the Indian Enemie." The area lying on York River and along the Poquoson River where patents were quickly taken up, was therefore new territory in comparison with Back River, Kecoughtan, and Warwick where land had been cultivated over twenty years. The relative location of the Old and the New Poquoson can be seen in the following patent...to William Bannister for 1000 acres butting upon Footeball Quarter Creek easterly towards Tinkersheire's Neck northerly towards the New Poquoson....

After Back River, the *Tristram and Jane* touched at Old Poquoson and New Poquoson. We can be sure that at both places commodities and servants were sold and hogsheads of tobacco taken on. Turning at New Poquoson the *Tristram and Jane* came down the Bay and headed across to Accomack as the entire Eastern Shore of Virginia was then called.

It seems likely that after leaving Accomack, the boat sailed back through Hampton Roads and across James River into Chuckatuck Creek and Nansemond River. She may also have gone up the James River to its junction with the Appomattox. The basis for this conjecture is the place of residence of the purchasers whom we have been able to identify. They lived mainly in Elizabeth City, Warwick, York, Accomack, Isle of Wight, and Nansemond counties, though a few were of James City and Charles City counties....

We do not know the date of arrival or departure for the *Tristram and Jane*, but we do know that on November 21 Daniell Hopkinson, the merchant, was so ill that he deemed it prudent to make his will [to which the] witnesses were Robert Reeves and Thomas Nant; nothing has been found concerning the latter and it may have been a copyist's error for "Hart." If so, Reeves and Hart were probably mates on the *Tristram and Jane* since each was referred to as "Mister" and each was bequeathed "the fraight of two tunn of goods homeward bound." Reeves appears twice as a headright for William Woolritch of Elizabeth City County in a patent dated June 17, 1635. That would mean two voyages had been made by him prior to that date, suggesting he was employed on a ship trading in Virginia.

Apparently Daniell Hopkinson had married Sarah Clifton whose brother Joseph Clifton had married Daniell's sister Barbara. The bequest of beaver hats reminds us how valuable this fur was then.

Sometimes called castor, which was its trade name, beaver fur was often used as currency.

Joseph Clifton was apparently a faithful executor in discharging his responsibility as this carefully kept accompt book reveals.

R. Sharpe France. "Early Emigrants to America from Liverpool," *The Genealogists' Magazine*, 12 (1955-1958), 234-235 [Lancour No. 220].

The following valuable list of early emigrants to America has been sent to us by Mr. R. Sharpe France, County Archivist for Lancashire. The original manuscript is in the Lancashire Record Office, County Hall, Preston.

QSP 625/2 1686
Quarter Sessions

The names of such persons who voluntarilie came before Oliver Lyme Esquire Maior of Leverpoole, and were examined and bound by Indentures under their hands and seales to serve the severall persons undernamed or their assignes the terme of foure yeares after their arrivall in Virginia or Mariland in America.

1686	Servants to Gilbert Livesley of Leverpoole marriner
10th June	Hugh Owen of Wrexham in the Countie of Denbigh laborer aged 24 yeares
12th June	Elizabeth Jones of the Cittie of Westchester spinster aged 21 yeares
19th June	John Joanes of Wrexham in the Countie of Denbigh laborer aged 21 yeares
29th June	George Walker of Astburie in the Countie of Chester blacksmith aged 27 yeares
ditto	Ann Cooper of Lydiate in the Countie of Lancaster spinster aged 21 yeares
7 Julye	William Evans of the Cittie of Bristol llaborer aged 24 yeares
13 Julye	Alice Jenkinson of Warrington in the Countie of Lancaster spinster aged 21 yeares
	Servants to James Hornbye of Leverpoole marriner
29th Julye	Phillis Ferne of Blurton in the Countie of Stafford spinster aged 21 yeares
	Roger Browne of Llandlehide in Carnarvanshire single person aged 21 yeares
13th August	Ann Johnson of Kinsley in the Countie of Chester spinster aged 21 yeares
	Servants to Edward Tarleton of Leverpoole marriner
6th August	Joan Norres of the Isle of Man spinster aged 26 yeares

ditto	Alice Lacie of the Isle of Man spinster aged 21 yeares
2nd October	Theophilus Basnett of Kelsall in the Countie of Chester single person aged 22 yeares
ditto	Richard Thomas of Clanriott in the Countie of Denbigh butcher aged 30 yeares

Servants to Thomas Sandiford Junior of Leverpoole merchant

1st September	Joseph Low of Ashton in Mackerfeild laborer aged 22 yeares
10th September	Margrett Thomas of Whitchurch in the Countie of Salopp spinster aged 23 yeares
13th September	Thomas Jones of Northopp in the countie of Flint, milner, aged 22 years.
ditto	Sarah Barber of Tamworth in the Countie of Stafford spinster aged 22 yeares

Servants to Edmund Croston of Leverpoole marriner

23rd September	William Alsea of Farnham in Hampshire painter aged 22 yeares
ditto	Samuell Chapman of Brundsley in Derbishire taylor aged 21 yeares
ditto	John Richardson of Mansfeild in Nottinghamshire bricklaier aged 22 yeares
ditto	John Gerrard of Parr in the Countie of Lancaster blacksmith aged 30 yeares
ditto	John Shipabottome of Elton neere Burye in Lancashire husbandman aged 27 yeares
ditto	Samuell Sedwell of Manchester of Lancashire weaver aged 24 yeares
ditto	Amye Pendleton of Manchester aforesaid spinster aged 26 yeares
6 October	Joseph Howard of Broadston in Derbishire joyner aged 36 yeares

Servants to John Banckes of Leverpoole marriner

19th August	Isabell Wilkinson of the Cittie of Carlile spinster aged 22 yeares
10th September	Alice Turner of Goosner in Lancashire widdow aged 30 yeares

Servants to Richard Radcliffe of Leverpoole merchant

27th September	John Naylor sonne of Thomas Naylor of Bowas in the Countie of Stafford aged 28 yeares

Servants to Richard Houghton to Leverpoole merchant

6th October	John Walker of Belfast in the Kingdome of Ireland merchant aged 19 yeares

[6th October, cont.] Judeth Wiresdell of Woolverhampton in Staffordshire widdow aged 19 yeares

---

William Macfarlane Jones, ed. *The Douglas Register, Being a Detailed Record of Birth, Marriages and Deaths together with Other Interesting Notes, as Kept by the Rev. William Douglas, from 1750 to 1797*. Baltimore: Genealogical Publishing Co., Inc., 1977 [Lancour No. 221].

This volume contains the article cited by Lancour, "A List of Ye French Refugees That Are Settled att Mannachin Town...," which was published in the original edition of this volume by J. W. Fergusson & Sons in Richmond (1928), and has also been printed in Lancour No. 224, below. The list, containing 79 names of families or individuals, appears on pages 369-371.

"Communication from Governor Francis Nicholson of Virginia Regarding Huguenot Refugees on Board Ship 'Mary and Ann'," *The Huguenot*, 6 (1933), 82-86 [Lancour No. 222].

Virginia, James City, August 12, 1700.

P. R. O.
Am. & W. Ind. May it please yo'r Lordp.:
No. 638

(Extract)

The 24th of the last month, I had the good Fortune of receiving his Ma'y's Royal Commands of March ye 18th, 1699/1700, sent me by yo'r Lord'p, concerning the Marquis de la Muce, Mons'r de Sailly, and other French Protestant Refugees; and I beg leave to assure yo'r Lord'p, that as I have, so I will endeavor to obey them (they were on board the ship Mary and Ann, of London, George Haws, Commander), who had about 13 weeks passage, and the 23rd of the last month arrived at the mouth of this River), and upon receipt of them, I immediately went down to Kickotan, to give directions in order to their coming hither, some of wh. came on Sunday in the evening, the rest the next day. I wrote to Colo. Byrd and Colo. Harrison to meet them here, w'ch they did, and we concluded that there was no settling them in Norfolk nor thereabouts, because esteemed and unhealthfull place, and no vacant land, except some that is in dispute now betwixt us and No. Carolina: So we thought it would be best for them to go to a place about twenty miles above the Falls of James River, commonly called the Manikin Town. There is a great deal of good Land and unpatented, where they may at present be all together, w'ch we thought would be best for his Ma'ty's Service and Interests, and that they would be astrengthing to the Frontiers, and would quickly make a settlement, not only for themselves, but to receive others when his majesty shall be graciously pleased to send them. They may be prejudicial to his Ma'ty's interest and Service, vizt., by living long together, and using their own language and customs, and by going upon such manufactures, and handicraft Trades, as we are furnished with from England: but according to duty, I shall endeavor to regulate these affairs, and when, please God, the Council meets, I shall lay before them the matters relating to these Refugees. On Tuesday I mustered them, and No. 1 is a copy of the List of them. Colo. Byrd went before them in order to meet them at the Falls of this River, where he formerly lived, to dispose of them thereabouts, till they can gett housses or sheds in the place for their Reception, and he promised to go along with the Marquis and Mons'r de Sailly to show them the Land. The people at present seem to be very well affected towards them, and to commiserate their condition, and some who have seen them have given them money, viz: Colo. Harrison, £5; Mr. Commissary Blair, the like Sum. The Reverend Mr. Stephen Touaie, thereabouts; Mr. Benjamin Harrison, £5; Mr. Attorney General Fowler, something, as likewise Mr. William Edwards, Merchant of this place. I am apt to think that Several Gentlemen and others will be charitable to them. They went from hence yesterday.

It his majesty be graciously pleased to send over more, I humbly propose that Mr. Micajah Perry, merchant of London, may be spoken with about their passage hither, and that they may have their passage on board the Ships which come to the upper parts of James River, w'ch is the nighest place to their settlement, and that there may not above 40 or 50 come in any one Ship: So they may be better accommodated in all respects, for I have observed that when Ships that come into these parts, are crowded with people, 'tis very prejudicial to their health; some getting sicknesses, w'ch not seldom prove catching, some dy on board, and others soon after they come on shore.

Your Lord'ps' dutifull and faithfull humble servant.

FFrs. Nicholson.

(Endorsement). The Gov'r of Virginia.
2 Aug., 1700.
R. 21 Octob.
Accounts of proceedings there, &.

List of ye Refugees

Pierre Delomè, et sa femme.
Marguerite Sene, et sa fille.
Magdalaine Mertle, Jean Vidau.
Tertulien Sehult, et sa femme et deux enfants.
Pierre Lauret, Jean Roger.
Pierre Chastain, a femme et cinq enfants.
Philippe Duvivier.
Pierre Nace, sa femme et Leur deux filles.
Francois Clere, Symon Sardin.
Soubragon, et Jacques Nicolay.

Pierre du Loy, Abraham Nicod.
Pierre Mallet, Francoise Coupet.
Jean Oger, sa femme et trois enfants.
Jean Saye, Elizabet Angeliere.
Jean et Claude Mallefant, avec leur mere.
Isaac Chabanas, sou fils, et Catharine Bomard.
Estienne Chastain, Adam Vignes.
Jean Menager et Jean Lesnard.
Estienne Badouet, Pierre Morriset.
Jedron Chamboux, et sa femme.
Jean Farry et Jerome Dumas.
Joseph Bourgoian, David Bernard.
Jean Chevas, et sa femme.
Jean Tardieu, Jean Moreau.
Jaques Roy, et sa femme.
Abraham Sablet, et des deux enfants.
Quintin Chastatain et Michael Roux.
Jean Quictet, sa femme et un enfant.
Henry Cabanis, sa femme et un enfant.
Jaques Sayte, Jean Boisson.
Francois Bosse, Jean Fouchie.
Francoise Sassin, Andre Cochet.
Jean Gaury, sa femme et un enfant.
Pierre Gaury, sa femme et un enfant.
Jaques Hulyre, sa femme et quatre enfants.
Pierre Perrut, et sa femme.
Isaac Panetier, Jean Parransos sa seur.
Elie Tremson, sa femme, Elizabet Tignac.
Antoine Trouillard, Jean Bourru et Jean Bouchet.
Jaques Voyes, Elizabet Mingot.
Catharine Godwal, Pierre la Courru.
Jean et Michell Cautepie, sa femme et deux enfants.
Jaques Broret, sa femme et deux enfants.
Abraham Moulin et sa femme.
Francois Billot, Pierre Comte (?).
Etienne Guevin, Rene Massoneau.
Francois du Tartre, Isaac Verry.
Jean Parmentier, David Thonitier et sa femme.
Moyse Lewreau, Pierre Tillou.
Marie Levesque, Jean Constantin.
Claud Bardon, sa femme.
Jean Imbert, et sa femme.
Elizabet Fleury, Loys du Pyn.
Jaques Richard, et sa femme.
Adam et Marie Prevost.
Jaques Viras, et sa femme.
Jaques Brousse, sou enfant.
Pierre Cornu, Louiss Bon.
Isaac Fordet, Jean Pepre.
Jean Gaillard, et son fils.

Anthonie Matton, et sa femme.
Jean Lucadou, et sa femme.
Louiss Orange, sa femme et un enfant.
Daniel Taure, et deux enfants.
Pierre Cupper, Daniel Roy, Magdelain Gigou.
Pierre Grelet, Jean Jovany, sa femme, deux enfants.
Pierre Fèrrier, sa femme, un enfant.
La vefve faure et quatre enfants.
Isaac Arnaud, et sa femme.
Pierre Chatanier, sa femme et son pere.
Jean Fonasse, Jaques Bibbeau, Jean March.
Catharine Billot, Marie et Symon Jourdon.
Abraham Menot, Timothy Moul, sa femme, un enfant.
Jean Savin, sa femme, un enfant.
Jean Sargeaton, sa femme, un enfant.
Claude Philipe, et sa femme.
Gabriel Sturter, Pierre de Corne.
Helen Trubyer.

59 femmes ou filles.
38 enfants.
108 hommes. Messrs. De la Muce
.... et de Sailly fout en
205 personnes. tout 207 personnes.

Virginia: James Town, July 31, 1700.
This is a true Copy.

Olivier de la Muce.
Ch. de Sailly.

Received of ye hon'ble Marquis de la Muce and Chas. de la Sailly, ye summe of nine hundred, fourty-five pounds in full for ye passage of two hundred and five people aboord ye ship Mary Ann, bound for Virginia, I say receiv'd this 19th April, 1700.

Geo. Hawes.

£945.
Witness:
Alexander Cleere.

Virginia: James City, July 31, 1700.
This is a true Copy.

Olivier de la Muce.
Ch. de Sailly.

This is a true copy, the original being in the Custody of ———.
(Signed,) FFrs. Nicholson.

Copied from photostat.

(Contributed by Mr. Walter LeSueur Turner, National Treasurer, Roanoke, Virginia.)

Mrs. Grant E. Lilly. "Passengers on the *Peter and Anthony*," *The Huguenot*, 7 (1933-1935), 153-155 [Lancour No. 223].

This list is also printed in Lancour No. 224.

Robert Alonzo Brock. *Huguenot Emigration to Virginia; Documents, Chiefly Unpublished, Relating to the.* Baltimore, 1973 [Lancour No. 224].

This title was originally published as Volume 5 of *Collections of the Virginia Historical Society*, New Series. This edition includes an added eight page supplement. Aside from passenger lists, genealogies of the families of Fontaine, Maury, Dupuy, Trabue, Marye, Chastain, Cocke and others are included.

William Fletcher Boogher. *Gleanings of Virginia History.* Washington, D. C.: W. F. Boogher, 1903 [Lancour No. 225].

The following, "Immigrant List, 1707," is taken from page 8.

The following persons shipped at Bristol, England, with James Gaugh, captain and owner of the ship Joseph and Thomas, and received their wages as boat hands (Liber Z, folio 422, Aug. 2, 1707, Stafford County):

Abraham Loyd,	William Harmous,	William Johnson,
James Ginning,	William Price,	Ellis Giles,
Thomas Jones,	Lewis Johns,	William Roach,
Robert Goalfold,	John Wall,	William Adams,
William Shough,	Arthor Marly,	Thomas Parris,
David Vaughn,	Thomas Calmers,	George Paines.

From the records it is not certain that any of these persons remained in Virginia, but from the similarity of names found in the western portion of Stafford county, and after 1730 in Prince William, it is believed a good portion of them settled in Virginia, whose descendants are now scattered throughout the South and West.

William Macfarlane Jones, ed. *The Douglas Register.* Baltimore: Genealogical Publishing Co., Inc., 1977 [Lancour No. 226].

"Liste Generalle de Tous les Francois Protestants Refugies Establys dans la Paroisse du Roy Guillaume d'Henrico en Virginia, y Compres les Femmes, Enfans, Veuses, et Orphelins" is printed on pages 372-374 of this title as well as in Lancour No. 224.

William Wallace Scott. ["Importations" in] *A History of Orange County Virginia*. Richmond: Everett Waddey Co., 1907 (225-229) [Lancour No. 227].

[The following is headed "Appendix A," and is not indexed with the rest of Scott's book.]

A list of persons who imported themselves, or were imported as servants by others, and who afterwards proved their importation in order to obtain their "head rights" to land in the colony. The date shows the year in which proof of importation was made and recorded. This list was kindly furnished by Mr. Philip H. Fry, for many years clerk of the County and Circuit Courts.

1736 Abel, Joseph
1740 Anderson, John
1740 Anderson, George
1741 Appleby, Robert
1753 Anderson, Hannah
1735 Amburger, Conrade
1735 Bourks, Martin
1736 Butler, John
1735 Bickers, Robert
1740 Brackenridge, Alex.
1740 Bell, James
1740 Brown, Wm.
1739 Blair, Alex.
1739 Butler, John
1740 Black, Thos.
1740 Brawford, Saml.
1740 Baskins, W. M.
1740 Bambridge, Ann
1741 Byrne, Henry
1741 Bradstreet, Francis
1741 Banks, Wm.
1741 Brown, Thos.
1746 Buntine, Wm.
1747 Brown, John
1741 Brady, Wm.
1749 Bird, Saml.
1755 Bailey, Robt.
1755 Beasley, Bennet
1756 Bramham, Francis
1756 Brown, Anne
1735 Burk, Thomas
1735 Bourks, John
1735 Bryan, Dennis
1735 Billingsley, Francis
1736 Cavenaugh, Philemon
1740 Crocket, Robt.
1740 Campbell, Patrick
1740 Caldwell, James
1740 Cardhaut, John
1740 Cole, Wm.
1740 Caldwell, Geo.
1740 Crawford, Patrick
1739 Cathey, James
1739 Camble, John
1739 Cross, Richd.
1740 Carr, John
1740 Christopher, Nicholas
1740 Carr, Jacob
1741 Crawford, John
1745 Crawford, Wm.
1745 Chambers, Elizabeth
1750 Collins, Ann
1751 Carney, Timothy
1752 Carney, Easter
1751 Chaney, Joseph
1744 Coleman, John
1744 Coleman, Margaret
1750 Cook, Geo.
1749 Collins, James
1751 Cole, Edward
1747 Cook, James
1743 Cross, Ellioner
1743 Cooper, Wm.
1738 Cummins, Alex.
1755 Cocke, Chas.
1756 Cussins, Richd.
1746 Campbell, Dugald
1735 Cotton, Joseph
1735 Drake, Samuel
1735 Dealmore, John
1740 Daley, James
1740 Davidson, John

1740 Davis, James
1740 Danning, Elizabeth
1743 Dungan, Margaret
1752 Dooling, Thomas
1749 Durham, John
1751 Drake, Hannah
1755 Davis, John
1746 Duff, Arthur
1746 Duff, Mary
1746 Duling, John
1735 Dyer, James
1735 Dunn, Arthur
1740 Edmiston, David
1745 Edgear, Wm.
1750 Eve, Joseph
1741 Fink, Mark
1745 Frazier, Alex.
1746 Forester, John
1753 Finley, Patrick
1750 Fields, Mary
1740 Fox, James
1749 Ferrell, Honner
1740 Frazer, Robt.
1755 Flanders, Wm.
1746 Frazer, John
1735 Floyd, John
1735 Finlason, John
1735 Floyd, Charles
1736 Grant, John
1740 Gilasby, James
1740 Gelasby, Jesse
1740 Gay, Saml.
1739 Givins, Saml.
1739 Grady, Mary
1740 Gilasby, Margaret
1740 Gilasby, Matthew
1745 Gaines, James
1746 Gibson, Abel
1746 Gibbins, Wm.
1752 Grant, Alex.
1750 Gully, Thos.
1742 Gibson, Margaret
1743 Green, Edward
1747 Gahagan, Thomas
1757 Golder, John
1746 Grace, Ann
1735 Green, Robt.
1735 Gray, Wm.
1740 Hays, John
1740 Hays, Patrick
1740 Hook, Robt.
1740 Harrell, John
1740 Hall, Edward
1740 Hutcheson, Wm.
1740 Henderson, Thomas
1740 Hutcheson, Geo.
1740 Hopkins, Elizabeth
1741 Haney, John
1741 Hart, Henry
1741 Harris, Joseph
1746 Howsin, Thomas
1749 Hussee, Easter
1750 Herrendon, John
1743 Hopkins, James
1755 Henderson, Alex.
1756 Haney, Darby
1735 Home, George
1735 Humphreys, George
1750 Irwin, Anthony
1738 Jones, Thomas
1740 Johnston, Wm.
1740 Johnston, Wm.
1746 Jennings, Edward
1751 Johnson, Peter
1750 Johnson, Peter
1750 Jerman, Thomas
1741 Johnson, Archibald
1746 Jones, Thos.
1735 Johnson, Wm.
1735 Lambotte, Edward
1740 King, Robt.
1740 King, Wm.
1740 Kindle, Thomas
1741 Kines, John
1746 Kelly, Wm.
1752 Kelly, Michael
1737 Kendall, Henry
1755 Kendall, Henry
1735 Kelly, Wm.
1735 Kerchler, Mathias
1740 Logan, David
1740 Long, Wm.
1739 Ledgerwood, Wm.
1739 Lepper, James
1739 Lampart, Edwd.
1740 Leonard, Patrick
1746 Lynch, John
1750 Lyon, Michael
1749 Lamb, Richd.
1746 Lernay, Thomas

1735 Latham, John
1740 McOnnal, Andrew
1740 McDowell, Robt.
1740 McCowin, Francis
1740 McClure, James
1740 Maxwell, John
1739 McCaddan, Patrick
1739 McKay, Agnes
1739 McKay, Wm.
1739 McKay, James
1739 Morphet, John
1739 McDowell, Robt.
1739 Mitchell, David
1739 McDowell, John
1739 McMurrin, Margaret
1739 McDowell, Ephrahim
1739 McAlegant, James
1739 McCanless, Wm.
1739 McCanless, Elizabeth
1739 Mulhalan, John
1739 McLean, Wm.
1739 McLean, Margaret
1739 McDaniel, Wm.
1741 McPherson, Robt.
1741 McPherson, Margaret
1741 McPherson, Alix.
1741 McPherson, Susanna
1741 Mills, James
1745 McNiel, Patrick
1745 McKensey, John
1746 McCullock, Ann
1748 Morris, Wm.
1752 McField, John
1748 Mason, Margaret
1750 Mulholland, Owen
1744 Morgan, John
1744 Morgan, Mary
1735 McCan, John
1735 McMurrin, David
1750 McGinnis, James
1749 Monroe, Wm.
1749 Morris, Jane
1751 Mannen, Andrew
1755 Morgan, Thomas
1755 Mitchell, John
1756 McDonald, John
1735 McCulley, James
1735 McCoy, John
1735 McKenny, John
1735 Mitchell, Wm.
1735 Nicholls, Wm.
1741 Newport, John
1740 Ofrail, Morris
1752 Ogg, John and wife
1750 Onaton, Mary
1735 Parsons, Richard
1736 Parks, John
1740 Patterson, Robert
1740 Poage, Robert
1740 Pickens, John
1746 Page, John
1746 Piner, Thomas
1746 Price, Edward
1746 Parsons, George
1752 Parsons, Mary
1752 Poor, Michael
1754 Phillips, Joseph
1755 Peacock, Thos.
1741 Parks, Thomas
1741 Phillips, Edmund
1735 Pitcher, Thomas
1735 Phillips, Joseph
1736 Ryly, Mical
1741 Ralson, Robert
1740 Ray, Joseph
1740 Reads, Joseph
1736 Rood, James
1740 Reed, Agnes
1740 Robinson, James
1746 Raney, John
1751 Riche, Patrick
1737 Ryan, Solomon
1738 Ramsey, Robt.
1741 Rosse, Alex.
1755 Rakestraw
1755 Rouse, Francis
1756 Rigby, John
1756 Ryan, John
1735 Rouse, Edward
1735 Robinson, Charles
1747 Ross, David
1735 Read, John
1735 Roberson, James
1740 Stevenson, Thos.
1740 Scott, Samuel
1740 Scott, Robert
1740 Steavenson, John
1740 Smith, John
1740 Skillim, Wm.
1739 Steavenson, David

1739 Smith, Wm.
1739 Smith, Elizabeth
1739 Stanton, Elizabeth
1740 Smith, Wm.
1753 Sheets, John
1750 Sims, Joanna
1750 Smith, Owen
1744 Scales, Richard
1749 Sims, Wm.
1749 Scott, James
1742 Sevier, Valentine
1743 Sears, Joseph
1738 Stewart, George
1750 Sleet, James
1750 Smith, Thomas
1755 Smith, Elizabeth
1756 Stokes, Elizabeth
1741 Sutherland, Wm.
1735 Small, Oliver
1735 Stackall, John
1735 Stanton, Matthew
1740 Trimble, John
1740 Thompson, Wm.
1740 Thomason, Moses
1740 Thomason, Alex.
1739 Turk, Robt.
1752 Terret, Nathaniel
1751 Tibbit, Matthew
1743 Thompson, Robt.
1743 Thurston, Sarah
1749 Terrill, Honner
1738 Thomson, John
1755 Thompson, Alexander
1735 Thomas, Joshua
1747 Upton, Henry
1747 Upton, Mary
1735 Vaught, John Paul
1735 Vaught, Mary Catherine, wife,
1735 Vaught, John Andrew, John Casper, sons
1735 Vaught, Catherine, Margaret and Mary Catherine, daughters
1735 Vinyard, John
1735 Warthan, James
1735 Walker, John
1735 Weaver, Peter
1740 Wilson, David
1739 Wilson, Richard
1740 Walsh, Patrick
1740 Williams, Thomas
1740 Wilson, John
1740 Walker, John
1745 Walsh, Joseph
1746 Wood, Thos.
1746 Wallace, Humphrey
1750 Willson, Mary
1738 White, John
1751 Whitman, Wm.
1744 Wheeler, John
1756 Walker, Thomas
1735 Wood, James
1735 Welch, John
1735 Warfin, Richard
1735 Walker, John
1735 Wilhite, Michael
1735 Wilhite, John
1740 Young, Robt.

These importations were almost without exception from "Great Britain," though in many cases Ireland is given specifically as the place whence imported.

The following list is wholly of "German Protestants," the importations have all been proved, and the parties naturalized, January 28, 1743.

Blankenbacker, Zachariah
Bomgardner, Frederick
Christle, Duvald
Fleshman, Peter
Garr, Andrew, John Adam, and Lawrence.
Grays, Lawrence
Thomas, John
Uhld, Christopher
Vallick, Martin
Zimmerman (*alias* Carpenter), John

And on February 24, 1743:

Broyle, Courtney
Manspile, Jacob
Miller, Jacob
Wilhite, John
Wilhite, Tobias

Mrs. W. W. King. "Augusta County Early Settlers, Importations, 1739-1740," *National Genealogical Society Quarterly*, 25 (1937), 46-48 [Lancour No. 228].

This list is from the Orange County Court records and thus the names are included in Lancour No. 227, above.

Vivian Holland [Jewett]. "Abstracts of Naturalization Records, Circuit Court, District of Columbia," *National Genealogical Society Quarterly*, 41 (1953), 41-44, 90-92, 130-131; 42 (1954), 22-24, 68-73, 149-150; 43 (1955), 20-21, 146-147; 44 (1956), 16-19, 109-111, 147-149; 45 (1957) 21-26 [Lancour No. 229].

The article below is apparently incomplete.

Six of the original thirteen states, Delaware, Massachusetts, New York, South Carolina, Virginia and Maryland already had general naturalization laws when the Constitution, providing for Federal naturalization, was adopted....

The Constitution gave Congress the power to "establish an uniform rule of naturalization." The first law required only one year's residence....

There is nothing consistent in the information furnished in these naturalization records. There was no federal supervision and procedures varied widely. Each court administered the law according to its own interpretation and even designed its own form of records. There were considerable differences within the same court, the wealth or dearth of information depending upon the interest and efficiency of the presiding officials.

Old naturalization records, if they still exist, are the property of the court which granted them and are kept within their offices or in some other suitable repository in the community. In the District of Columbia the old naturalization records (1802 to 1926) of the Circuit Court which was abolished in 1911, and of its successor, the District Court, are kept in the National Archives....

A few quick references reveal that George Hadfield, the first to apply for citizenship in the new Federal City, was an architect and designed some of the famous buildings of his adopted city; that Pishie Thompson established a book store on Pennsylvania Avenue; that Thomas Law married Eliza Custis, the granddaughter of Martha Washington; that John Sessford, the printer (who remained nameless in the naturalization records for twenty years) published an annual report on the City of Washington; that Dr. John Logan traveled to Missouri, then to Illinois where he established his home and became the father of John A. Logan, General of the Civil War and later Senator from Illinois. Far from being dry-as-dust statistics, each naturalization record is a potential key to a biography or a link in a family genealogy.

The following are abstracts made from the Naturalization Records of the Circuit Court of the District of Columbia, presumably complete [so far as this article goes - ed.]—petitions received 1802 to 1820. The few discrepancies are listed as they appear.

Andrei, John (William); age 45 in 1817; nativity, Carara, Tuscany, Italy; emigrated from Leghorn, Italy; arrived at Baltimore, Md., 31 Jan. 1806; Declaration of Intention, 6 Dec. 1817; Proof of Residence, June 1820; no witnesses listed; naturalization granted 24 Apr. 1821.

Arney, Joseph; confectioner; age 26 in 1813; nativity, Switzerland; Declaration of Intention, 12 Jan. 1813; Proof of Residence, June 1818; witnesses: Frederick Vieller (?), Frederick D. Tschiffely; naturalization granted June 1818.

Arnott, John; nativity, England; in U. S. since Dec. 1795, 12 years in Virginia; Declaration of Intention, 27 Dec. 1813; Proof of Residence, 27 Dec. 1813; witness, John Sessford; naturalization granted 27 Dec. 1813.

Bachus, John; age 23 in 1813; nativity, England; Declaration of Intention, 7 Jan. 1813; Proof of Residence, 26 Dec. 1815; witness, John McPherson; naturalization granted 26 Dec. 1815.

Barnard, Robert; age 33 in 1819; nativity, Boston, England; emigrated from Liverpool, Eng.; arrived at New York, 18 Oct. 1819; Declaration of Intention, 27 Dec. 1819; Proof of Residence, 28 Dec. 1824; witnesses: Thos. Corcoran, Jr., Jas. Wharton; naturalization granted 28 Dec. 1824.

Blanchard, William; nativity, England; in U. S. since 1 Jan. 1806, Washington, D. C., "upwards of two years"; Declaration of Intention, 13 Jan. 1808; Proof of Residence, 17 Jan. 1811; witness, William Cocking; naturalization granted 17 Jan. 1811.

Bond, Isaac; nativity, Great Britain; in U. S. "about 20 years", in Georgetown "about 15 or 17 yrs.;" Declaration of Intention, 6 June 1811; Proof of Residence, 6 June 1811; witness, Thomas Beall; naturalization granted 6 June 1811.

Bond, Samuel; in U. S. "before 14th day of April 1802;" Proof of Residence, 5 Jan. 1814; witness, Peter Howard; naturalization granted 5 June 1814.

Bopp, Frederick; blacksmith; aged 34 in 1812; nativity, near Frankfort-on-the-Maine, Germany; former allegiance, Prince of Braumfels; emigrated from Hamburg, Germany; arrived at Baltimore, Md., 28 Mar. 1805; Declaration of Intention, 20 June 1812; Proof of Residence, 21 May 1824; witnesses: John Waters, Henry Smith; naturalization granted 21 May 1824.

Brady, Peter; age 26 in 1819; nativity, Longford County, Ireland; emigrated from Liverpool, England; arrived at New York, 9 Nov. 1815; Declaration of Intention, 7 July 1819; Proof of Residence, 8 Jan. 1825; witnesses: John Dumphrey, Thomas Murray; naturalization granted 8 Jan. 1825.

Brannan, John; age 36 in 1820; nativity, city of Exeter, England; emigrated from London, England; arrived at Baltimore, Md., 6 Nov. 1818; Declaration of Intention, 14 Jan. 1820; Proof of Residence, 18 Jan. 1825; witnesses: Thomas Holliday, James Martin; naturalization granted 18 Jan. 1825.

Brerton, Samuel; age 35 in 1819; Former allegiance, Great Britain; emigrated from Liverpool, England; arrived at Alexandria, Va., 29 Aug. 1818; Declaration of Intention, 18 May 1819; Proof of Residence, 28 May 1824; witnesses: John McClelland, Hania (?) Cassaway; another document also dated 28 May 1824, additional signatures only: Wm. Grintor (or Gunter), Wm. Waters, Henry Stoneby, Thos. G. Waters, Moses Poor (?), Charles Fowler, Lowry Griffith Coombe, Truman Tyler, Jacob Noyes, John M. McClelland; naturalization granted 28 May 1824.

Broadback (Brodback), Jacob; age 37 in 1810; former allegiance, Republic of Helvetia; emigrated from Amsterdam, Holland; arrived at Philadelphia, Pa., Nov. 1802; Declaration of Intention, 9 July 1810; Proof of Residence, 11 June 1824; witnesses: Tench Ringgold, Thomas Cook; naturalization granted 11 June 1824.

Brooks, Francis; age 45 in 1820; nativity, Down County, Ireland; emigrated from Nuery; arrived at New York, 14 May 1812; Declaration of Intention, 20 Jan. 1820; Proof of Residence, 3 June 1826; witnesses: George Sweeney, A. T. F. Bill; naturalization granted 3 June 1826.

Brouer, Frederick; in U. S. 18 June 1798; Proof of Residence, 1 Nov. 1819; witnesses: John Knoblock, George Stuiger; naturalization granted 1 Nov. 1819.

Buckley, Christian; age 26 in 1819; nativity Canton Grison, Switzerland; emigrated from Tonniagen; arrived at Philadelphia, Pa., 20 Nov. 1810; Declaration of Intention, 12 June 1819; Proof of Residence, 19 Apr. 1824; witnesses: Benjamin M. Belt, John Duckworth; a second Proof of Residence type document dated 1 June 1824, witnesses: Hezekiah Lenglay, John McLaughlin; naturalization granted 19 Apr. 1824.

Burnes (Burns), Charles; age 28 in 1817; nativity, County of Queens, Ireland; emigrated from Cork, Ireland; arrived at Alexandria, Va., 16 Sept. 1816; Declaration of Intention, 4 Jan. 1817; Proof of Residence, 21 Jan. 1824; witnesses: James Scallion, Nicholas Cassaday; naturalization granted 21 Jan. 1824.

Burns, John; in U. S. since 1800 "inlisted as a seaman in the service of the U. S.," in Washington, D. C. "four years last passed"; Proof of Residence, 21 Jan. 1824; witnesses: James B. Potts; naturalization granted 1 Nov. 1811.

Burton, Charles; artist; aged 36 in 1818; nativity, London, England; emigrated from Liverpool, Eng.; a document dated 16 June

1818 called "Report of ——, an alien made to the Clerk of the Court of Common Pleas called the Mayor's Court of the City of New York"; Declaration of Intention, 16 June 1818; Proof of Residence, 9 May 1825, made in Ablemarle County, Va.; witnesses: Thomas Phoebus, William Young; the Index to the Minutes of the Court state that naturalization was granted 16 June 1818 (but should it be the date of the Proof of Residence document dated 9 May 1825?).

Callan, Nicholas; nativity, Ireland; in U. S. from 18 June 1798; Declaration of Intention undated; Proof of Residence, 6 June 1809; witnesses, Patrick Callan; naturalization granted 6 June 1809.

Campbell, Dan; nativity, Dundee, Scotland; Declaration of Intention, (District of Columbia, County of Alexandria), 25 July 1812; Proof of Residence, 13 June 1817, witnesses, Joseph Huddleston, Greenberry Gaither; naturalization granted 13 June 1817.

Carroll, Daniel, age 38 in 1821; nativity, County of Tipperary, Ireland; emigrated from London, England; arrived at New York, 21 June 1819; Declaration of Intention, - April 1821; Proof of Residence, 8 May 1826; witnesses: Walter Clarke, Edward Berry; naturalization granted 8 May 1826.

Caruso (Carusi), Gaetano; age "51 years and upwards" in 1817; nativity, Naples, Italy; Declaration of Intention, (Court of Common Pleas, Philadelphia), 24 Jan. 1817; Proof of Residence, 30 Dec. 1824; witnesses: Felice Pulizzi, Venenando (Benenando) Pulizzi; naturalization granted 30 Dec. 1824.

Cashell, Randall; age 36 in 1813; nativity, England; Proof of Residence, 19 June 1813, witnesses: Nathl. Bigsby, Archo Lee, Wm. Moore, Jerh. Mudd, Clemt. Newton, Jos. Clarke, Jeremiah Perkins, Tho. Reynolds, James Wharton, Robt. Clarke, George St. Clair, Igna. Boone; naturalization granted 21 June 1813.

Caton, John; nativity, Ireland; in U. S. from 18 June 1798; Proof of Residence, 9 June 1809; witness, Mathias Kyne; naturalization granted 9 June 1809.

Clark, Joseph; in U. S. since 18 June 1798; Proof of Residence, 29 Nov. 1826; witnesses: Richard Spalding, James Birth; naturalization granted 29 Nov. 1826.

Clarke, Francis; former allegiance, Great Britain; Declaration of Intention, undated, made in County Court, Frederick County, Maryland, term beginning "first Monday of Feb. 1803"; Proof of Residence, 17 Apr. 1810; witness: Charles Glover; naturalization granted 18 Apr. 1810.

Clarke, William; nativity, Great Britain; in U. S. "before 14 April 1802"; Proof of Residence, 12 Jan. 1814; witness, James C. King; naturalization granted 12 Jan. 1814.

Connelly, Francis, age 23 in 1819; nativity, Down, Ireland; emigrated from Dublin, Ireland; arrived at Philadelphia, Pa., 16 July 1817; Declaration of Intention, 7 Jan. 1819; Proof of Residence, 5 June 1824; witnesses: Nicholas Callon, William Ottridge; naturalization granted 5 June 1824.

Cook, David; former allegiance, "King of Great Britain and Ireland"; in U. S. "on or about the year 1798," in District of Columbia since 1800; Declaration of Intention, undated; Proof of Residence, 2 documents both dated 4 June 1817; one witnessed by John Wimsett (?), the other by Joseph Johnson; naturalization granted 15 June 1817.

Costigan, Joseph; nativity, Ireland; in U. S. since 1 Dec. 1801; Declaration of Intention undated; Proof of Residence, 20 June 1809, witness, Richard Spalding; naturalization granted 20 June 1809.

Coumba, William; age 26 in 1819; nativity, County of Cornwall, England; emigrated from St. Johns, New Brunswick; arrived at Boston, Mass., 2 June 1818; Declaration of Intention, 2 July 1819; Proof of Residence, 11 Jan. 1825; witnesses: John Hoover, Michael Hoover; naturalization granted 11 Jan. 1825.

Courtenay, John; age 26 in 1820; nativity, Borough of Mitchell, Cornwall, England; emigrated from Plymouth, England; arrived at Boston, Mass., Sept. 1819; Declaration of Intention, 28 March 1820; Proof of Residence, 1 June 1821; witnesses: Robert Keyworth, Solomon Drew; naturalization granted 1 June 1826.

Cropley, George; age 20 in 1819; nativity, City of Norwick, County of Norfolk, England; emigrated from Liverpool, Eng.; arrived at Philadelphia, Pa., 2 Nov. 1819; Declaration of Intention, 24 Dec. 1819, Proof of Residence, 12 May 1825; witnesses: John Lutz, George W. Haller; naturalization granted 12 May 1825.

Cropley, Richard; age 45 in 1819; nativity, County Norfolk, England; emigrated from Liverpool, Eng.; arrived at Philadelphia, Pa., 2 Nov. 1819; Declaration of Intention, 4 Dec. 1819; Proof of Residence, 28 Dec. 1824, witnesses: Thomas Corcoran, Jr., James Wharton; naturalization granted 28 Dec. 1824.

Crowley, Timothy; in U. S. "previous to 14 April 1802"; Proof of Residence, 3 June 1817; witnesses: Benjamin Phiny, John Horner; naturalization granted 3 June 1817.

Cummins, Christopher; age 32 in 1820; nativity, Dublin, Ireland; emigrated from Londonderry, Ireland; arrived at New York 4 July 1819; Declaration of Intention, 3 Aug. 1820; Proof of Residence, 26 Dec. 1825; witnesses: Frederick St—ger (St—ges), Robert Miller; naturalization granted 26 Dec. 1825.

Davis, Edward; nativity, England, in U. S. since Dec. 1806; Declaration of Intention, 30 June 1809; Proof of Residence, 20 June 1812; witness: Thomas C. Wright; naturalization granted 2 Nov. 1813.

Davis, Edward; nativity, Great Britain; Declaration of Intention, 30 June 1809; "Declaration of Naturalization," 30 June 1809; naturalization granted 30 June 1809.

Devlin, John; nativity, Ireland; emigrated from Belfast, Ireland; arrived at Quebec, Canada in 1819, thence to U. S. in same year; Declaration of Intention, dated "first Monday of March, 1821," Rockville, Md., Montgomery Co.; another document similar to the preceding one dated 31 May 1821, Montgomery County Court, State of Maryland; Proof of Residence, 5 May 1825; witnesses: John Waters, Benedict L. Adams; naturalization granted 25 May 1825 (?).

Dix, John; age 29 in 1820; nativity, Staffordshire, England; arrived at Alexandria, Va., 1 Dec. 1810; Declaration of Intention, 12 June 1820; Proof of Residence, 30 May 1825; witnesses: Anthony Holmead, Isaac C. Caske (?); naturalization granted 30 May 1826.

Donoughua, Patrick; nativity, Ireland; in U. S. since 18 June 1798; Proof of Residence, 10 June 1809; witness: John C. Clayton; naturalization granted 10 June 1809.

Dougherty, Joseph; nativity, Ireland; in U. S. since 1 Dec. 1801; Proof of Residence, 29 June 1809; witness: Clotworthy Stephenson; naturalization granted 29 June 1809.

Drew, Solomon; Proof of Residence, 4 June 1825; witnesses: Nicholas Blasdell, Jonathan Wallace; naturalization granted 4 June 1825.

Dufief (Duffief), Cheruibin; in U. S. since 1794; former allegiance, France; a document dated 16 June 1813, at Philadelphia, by Mathew Carey, stating Dufief was "bound apprentice to him about the year 1794 and served him for six years or thereabouts;" another document dated 17 June 1813, Philadelphia, by James Black, stating Dufief "was bound apprentice to him by Mathew Carey in the year 1800;" Declaration of Intention, undated but apparently the same date as the Proof of Residence, judging from the writing and the paper upon which written; Proof of Residence, 24 June 1813; witness, Alexr. L. Joncherez; naturalization granted 24 June 1813.

Dulany, Patrick; nativity, Ireland; emigrated from Dublin, Ireland; arrived at Alexandria "in the District of Columbia," 17 June 1819; Declaration of Intention, 27 June 1820; Proof of Residence, 2 documents; one dated 1 June 1824; witnesses: Grover Miller, Jacob Dixon; and the second, dated 20 Dec. 1825; witnesses: Thomas Robinson, Jesse Fox; naturalization granted 20 Dec. 1825.

Dumph (Dumphey) John; age 30 in 1822; nativity, Kilkenny County, Ireland; emigrated from Dublin, Ireland; arrived at New York, 8 Oct. 1816; Declaration of Intention, 8 June 1822; Proof of Residence, 1 June 1824, witnesses, Thomas Parsons, George P. Maxwell, naturalization granted 1 June 1824.

Ecloff (Eckloff), Christian; age 35 in 1819; former allegiance "King of Prussia"; emigrated from Amsterdam, Holland; arrived at Philadelphia, Pa., 3 July 1817; Declaration of Intention, 10 June 1819; Proof of Residence, 2 documents, the earlier one dated 1 June 1824, witnessed by George Cover is crossed out with a large X, the second one dated 12 June 1824, witnesses, Robert Miller, Henry C. Neals; naturalization granted 12 June 1824.

Elliott (Elliot), Johnathan; printer; age 28 in 1813; nativity, England; Declaration of Intention, 30 Jan. 1813; Proof of Residence, 6 June 1818, witnesses, Richard Wallack, Thomas Dunn; naturalization granted 6 June 1818.

Epinette, Peter (Rev.); in U. S. since 5 Nov. 1806, in Washington, D. C. "more than one year last past"; Proof of Residence, 2 Nov. 1811, witness, Rev'd. Francis Neale, naturalization granted 2 Nov. 1811.

Erskine, John; nativity, Ireland; in U. S. since 18 June 1803, "eight years last past" within the County of Washington; Proof of Residence, 13 June 1814, witness Clotworthy Stephenson; naturalization granted 14 June 1814.

Eschback, John; age 25 in 1825; nativity, Germany; emigrated from Amsterdam, Holland; arrived at Annapolis, Md., Jan. 1817 "being three years and more before he attained the age of twenty-one years."; Declaration of Intention and Proof of Residence, 4 Feb. 1825, witnesses, Henry Bernard, Ernest Guttschride; naturalization granted 4 Feb. 1825.

Fallon, Edward; nativity, Ireland; arrived in Philadelphia, Pa., 1795, to Baltimore in 1777 (1797?), to Washington, D. C., in 1799; Declaration of Intention and Proof of Residence, 11 Jan. 1814, witness, Clotworthy Stephenson; naturalization granted 11 Jan. 1814.

Flinn, Lawrence; age 28 in 1819; nativity, Ireland; emigrated from Newfoundland; arrived at Boston, Mass., 20 April 1818; Declaration of Intention, 1 Jan. 1819; Proof of Residence, 2 June 1824, witnesses, William Joice, George Joice; naturalization granted 2 June 1824.

Gannon, James; nativity, Ireland; in U. S. since 18 June 1798; Proof of Residence, 18 April 1814, witness, Charles Glover; naturalization granted 18 April 1814.

Gerard, William G.; Merchant; in New York 1798; deposition dated 5 March 1813 stating that he had lived in New York since 1798; Proof of Residence, 31 Dec. 1813, witness, Thomas Greeves; naturalization granted 5 Jan. 1814.

Goodall, Thomas; age 26 in 1820; nativity, Ireland; emigrated from Portsmouth, England; arrived at Baltimore, Md., 20 April 1819; Declaration of Intention, 14 Jan. 1820; Proof of Residence, 18 Jan. 1825, witnesses, Thomas Holiday, James Martin; naturalization granted 18 Jan. 1825.

Grace, William; age 28 in 1818; nativity, Capaheaden, Ireland; emigrated from Capaheaden, Ireland; arrived at Alexandria, Va., 20 July 1817; Declaration of Intention, 26 June 1818; Proof of Residence, 8 May 1826, witnesses, George King, John B. Gorman; (Note: "Admitted 9 Aug. 1826") but the Index Book to the Minutes of the Circuit Court says naturalization was granted 8 May 1826.

Grammer, Gottlieb Christopher; age 27 in 1814; nativity, Wertemburgh, Germany; emigrated from Amsterdam, Holland; arrived at Philadelphia, Pa., 2 Dec. 1807; Declaration of Intention, 7 June 1814; Proof of Residence, 10 June 1824, witnesses, Richard Wallach, Esq., Peter Lenox; naturalization 10 June 1824.

Grammer, Gottlieb Christopher; in U. S. since 1809; Proof of Residence undated but enclosed in envelope date 1814, witness, Seth Hayatt; naturalization granted 7 June 1814.

Grassi (Grossi), Rev. John; age 35 in 1810; nativity, Venice, Italy; arrived at Baltimore, Md., 20 Oct. 1810; Declaration of Intention, 20 Dec. 1810; Proof of Residence, 27 Dec. 1815, witness, James Wallace; naturalization granted 27 Dec. 1815.

Greer, James; in U. S. "for five years last past", "one year at least last past in Georgetown"; Proof of Residence, 9 July 1814, witness, Joseph Johnson; naturalization granted 9 July 1814.

Guegan, Louis Henry; age 27 in 1820; nativity, Guemene, France; "he resides in the City of Baltimore"; Declaration of Intention, 2 documents both dated 14 Sept. 1820; Proof of Residence, 17 Jan. 1825, witnesses, Thomas Carbery, Alexander Kerr; naturalization granted 17 Jan. 1826 (?).

Guttslick (Guttschlick), Ernest; age 37 in 1819; nativity, Prussia; emigrated from Amsterdam, Holland; arrived at Annapolis, Md., 2 Feb. 1817; Declaration of Intention, 16 June 1819; Proof of Residence, 27 Jan. 1825, witnesses, A. T. F. Bill, Lewis Magruder; naturalization granted 27 Jan. 1825.

Hadfield (Hatfield), George; architect; age 36 in 1802; former allegiance, Great Britain; in U. S. "upwards of five years" and in "County of Washington upwards of two years"; only one document, without signature, serving, apparently, for both Declaration of Intention and Proof of Residence, dated 14 Aug. 1802; naturalization granted 14 Aug. 1802.

Harper, Walter; age 18 in 1821; nativity, County Wexford, Ireland; emigrated from Dublin, Ireland; arrived at New York month of Sept. 1817; Declaration of Intention, 27 Aug. 1821; Proof of Residence, 27 Dec. 1826. witnesses, William Corme, Samuel Stettinius (sworn 28 Dec. 1826); naturalization granted 27 Dec. 1826.

Harrington, Robert; age 21 in 1819; nativity, County Kerry, Ireland; emigrated from City of Cork, Ireland; arrived at Alexandria, Va., 1 Sept. 1818; Declaration of Intention, 4 Jan. 1819; another document marked "void" lists name of Florence McCarthy as witness; Proof of Residence, 28 Jan. 1825, witnesses, Ambrose Moriarty, Charles Byrne; naturalization granted 28 Jan. 1825.

Hart, John; in U. S. since 18 June 1798 (1794); Proof of Residence, 29 Dec. 1813, witness, Abner Ritchie, who "adds with pleasure that" (torn spot—John Hart?) "was under his command in the Western Reg." (torn spot) "of 1794 and behaved himself well—Col. Carlisles Regt. 2nd Compy of Inty"; naturalization granted 30 Dec. 1813.

Hayre, John; taylor; age 45 in 1812; nativity, Ireland; in U. S. "about 7 years", in District of Columbia "about 6 years"; Declaration of Intention, 2 petitions dated 19 June 1812 and 10 June 1814; Proof of Residence, 15 June 1814, witness, Wm. H. P. Tuckfield; naturalization granted 15 June 1814.

Hollaran, William; age 35 in 1821; nativity, Queens County, Ireland; emigrated from Waterford, Ireland; arrived at New York, 4 Aug. 1816; Declaration of Intention, 23 April 1821; Proof of Residence, 17 May 1826, witnesses, Nicholas Callan, Thomas Murray; naturalization granted 17 May 1826.

Holroyd, Joseph; age 32 in 1820; nativity, Yorkshire, England; emigrated from Liverpool, England; arrived at Alexandria, Va., 8 July 1819; Declaration of Intention, 13 Jan. 1820; Proof of Residence, 18 Jan. 1825; witnesses, Thomas Holiday, James Martin; naturalization granted 18 Jan. 1825.

Hutchinson, Samuel; in U. S. since 18 June 1798; spent seven months abroad on business latter part of 1810 and following spring, family remained here; Proof of Residence, 29 Dec. 1813, witness, Sam Brook; naturalization granted 30 Dec. 1813.

Johnston, James; in U. S. since 18 June 1798, one year within the District of Columbia; Proof of Residence, 25 May 1825, witnesses, Henry Tims, George Thompson; naturalization granted 25 May 1825.

Joyce (Joice), George; age 34 in 1818; nativity, City of Cork, Ireland; emigrated from Cork, Ireland; arrived at Alexandria, Va., 1 Nov. 1817; Declaration of Intention, 20 June 1818; Proof of Residence, 21 May 1824, witnesses, Thomas McIntosh, John Hollihorn; naturalization granted 21 May 1824.

Joyce (Joice), William; age 40 in 1818; nativity Ireland; emigrated from City of Cork, Ireland; arrived at Alexandria, Va., 1 Nov. 1817; Declaration of Intention, 20 June 1818; Proof of Residence, 29 May 1824, witnesses, George Joice, John Hollihan; naturalization granted 29 May 1824.

Keogh, Mathew (Mathias)
(Keogle, Matthias); in U. S. "previous to month of Jan. 1795", in Virginia and Alexandria, "about the month of Jan. 1811" in Washington County; Proof of Residence, 1 Jan. 1814, witness, Sarah McCarthys; naturalization granted 3 Jan. 1814.

Kiernan, Hugh; age 24 in 1818; nativity, Killesandia; emigrated from Liverpool, England; arrived at New York, 22 July 1817; Declaration of Intention, 26 June 1818; naturalization granted 2 June 1828.

Kincaid, James; nativity, Glasgow, Scotland; arrived at Alexandria in the ship William and John, Capt. Woodhouse, in 1807; Declaration of Intention, 30 Apr. 1816; Proof of Residence, 29 Jan. 1820, witnesses, John Laird, John Murdoch; naturalization granted 31 Jan. 1820.

Kinchey, Paul; age 34 in 1819; nativity, Switzerland; emigrated from Haver de Grace; arrived at New York, 10 May 1817; Declaration of Intention, 16 June 1819; Proof of Residence, 12 Jan. 1826, witnesses, Benjamin M. Belt, Solomon Drew; naturalization granted 12 Jan. 1826.

Kneller (Kueller), George; in U. S. "5 years at least", in District of Columbia "1 year at least"; Declaration of Intention, 26 Jan. 1809; Proof of Residence, 1 Feb. 1812, witness, Samuel Stettinius; naturalization granted 12 Feb. 1812.

Kolman, Rev. Anthony; age 37 in 1808; nativity, Kaiserburg, Alsatia; emigrated from Russia; Declaration of Intention, 9 June 1808; Proof of Residence, 3 June 1818, witnesses, Rev. Benedict Fenwick, Joseph Carberry; naturalization granted 3 June 1818.

Kyne, Mathias; nativity, Ireland; in U. S. from 18 June 1798; Proof of Residence, 9 June 1809, witness John Caton; naturalization granted 10 June 1809.

Lake, George; nativity, Great Britain; in U. S. "since 1793", in District of Columbia "since 1804"; Declaration of Intention undated; Proof of Residence, 6 June 1811, witness, Edward Bland; naturalization granted 6 June 1811.

Lambright, George; nativity, Hesse, Germany; in U. S. since 1798; Declaration of Intention, 22 June 1809 (Georgetown); Proof of Residence, 22 June 1809, witnesses, James Calder, James Melvin; naturalization granted 22 June 1809.

Laurie, James; clergyman; age 30 in 1812; nativity, Scotland; in U. S. "since 1802"; Declaration of Intention, 21 July 1812; Proof of Residence undated but enclosed in envelope dated 1813, witness, Joseph Nourse; naturalization granted 28 Dec. 1813.

Law, Thomas, Esqr.; nativity, England; in U. S. since Aug. 1794 (for 15 months, Aug. 1802 to Nov. 1803, in Europe on business), "other occasional absences" but "his domicile is in this district"; Declaration of Intention undated; Proof of Residency, 10 Jan. 1814, witness, James D. Barry; naturalization granted 14 Jan. 1815.

Leidicks (Leidick), Francis; mason; age 44 in 1813; nativity, Darmstedt, Germany; Declaration of Intention, 25 Apr. 1813; Proof of Residence, 8 June 1824, witnesses, Tench Ringgold, Henry Smith; naturalization granted 8 June 1824.

Little, Robert; age 47 in 1819; nativity, London, England; emigrated from Liverpool, England; arrived at Baltimore, Md., 3 Oct. 1819; Declaration of Intention, 27 Dec. 1819; Proof of Residence, 30 Dec. 1824, witnesses, Richard Wallach, Alexdr. McWilliams; naturalization granted 30 Dec. 1824.

Logan, John; age 27 in 1818; nativity, Ayrshire, Scotland; emigrated from Liverpool, England (and Nova Scotia); arrived at Philadelphia, Pa., Dec. 1816; Declaration of Intention, 24 June 1818; Proof of Residence, 5 June 1824, witnesses, Thomas Hughes, David Apples (Applen or Appler); naturalization granted 5 June 1824.

Magnier, Thomas; age 27 in 1818; nativity, County Cork, Ireland; emigrated from Cork, Ireland; arrived at New York, Aug. 1816; Declaration of Intention, 23 Feb. 1818 (note "Report made in Court 30 Jan. 1818") document on back has signatures blotted out; Proof of Residence, 24 May 1824, witnesses, Thomas Parsons, Timothy Bean; naturalization granted 24 May 1824.

Magrath (McGrath), Thomas; nativity, Ireland; in U. S. since 18 June 1798; Declaration of Intention, undated; Proof of Residence, June 1815, witness, John Travers; naturalization granted 8 June 1815.

Mathewson, John Jr.; in U. S. since 18 June 1798; Proof of Residence, 5 Nov. 1813, witness, Abraham Lynch; naturalization granted 5 Nov. 1813.

Mathewson, John Sr.; in U. S. since 18 June 1798; Proof of Residence, 5 Nov. 1813, witness, Thomas Murray; naturalization granted 5 Nov. 1813.

McCormick, Michael; in U. S. "13 years at least", in District of Columbia "7 years last past"; Proof of Residence, 9 July 1814, witness, Joseph Johnson; naturalization granted 9 July 1814.

McDonald, John; painter; nativity, Great Britain; in U. S. "on or before 14 April 1802"; on 20 May 1813, was drafted in the D. C. Militia "and served 3 months in actual service of the U. S."; Proof of Residence, 19 June 1812, witness, Benjamin Bryan; document dated 10 Jan. 1814, called petition for citizenship after Militia Service; Proof of Residence, 10 Jan. 1814, witness, William Prime; naturalization granted 10 Jan. 1814.

McElroy, Rev. John; age 33 in 1816; nativity, Ireland; emigrated from Londonderry, Ireland; arrived at Baltimore, Md., 26 Aug. 1803; Declaration of Intention, 9 Jan. 1816; Proof of Residence, 1 Jan. 1819, witnesses, Charles King, Thomas Mulledy (Mullidy); naturalization granted 11 Jan. 1819.

McIntosh, Thomas; age 30 in 1815; nativity, Scotland; emigrated from "thence"; arrived at Philadelphia, Pa., 23 Aug. 1803; Declaration of Intention, 7 June 1815; Proof of Residence, 20 June 1818, witnesses, George Henderson, George Blagden (Blagsen); naturalization granted 27 June 1818.

Meyer, Henry; in U. S. "at least five years", in Washington "one year at least"; Proof of Residence, 1 Feb. 1812, witness, John F. Keller; naturalization granted 1 Feb. 1812.

Moffet (Moffit), John; mariner; age 22 in 1815; nativity, Ireland; in U. S. "before 18 June 1812"; Declaration of Intention, 22 Nov. 1815 made in Philadelphia, District Court of United States, Eastern District of Pennsylvania; Proof of Residence, 15 June 1819, witnesses, Robert Moffit, Mary Moffit; naturalization granted 15 June 1819.

Moore, James; nativity, Scotland; in U. S. "in the year 1786", resided in Georgetown and Washington; Declaration of Intention, 10 Jan. 1814; Proof of Residence, 10 Jan. 1814, witness, Clotworthy Stephenson; naturalization granted 10 Jan. 1814.

Murphy, Edward; age 33 in 1819; nativity, Ireland; emigrated from Cork, Ireland; arrived at Philadelphia, Pa., 22 Nov. 1816 (?); Declaration of Intention, 26 June 1819; Proof of Residence, 27 May 1826, witnesses, Wm. H. Stewart, Josiah Epex; naturalization granted 27 May 1826.

Murray, Michael; age 30 in 1821; nativity, Roscommon, Ireland; emigrated from Roscommon, Ireland; arrived at New York 19 May 1818; Declaration of Intention, 5 May 1821; Proof of Residence, 25 May 1826, witnesses, Thomas Murray, Patrick Delany; naturalization granted 25 May 1826.

Ogleby, David; stonecutter; age 30 in 1802; nativity, Scotland; in "City of Washington from the year 1793"; Proof of Residence, 14 Aug. 1802, witness, Thomas Machen; naturalization granted 14 Aug. 1802.

Orr, John; nativity, Ireland; in U. S. since 1800; Declaration of Intention, 30 Dec. 1813; Proof of Residence, 30 Dec. 1813, witness, Ambrose Moriatta; naturalization granted 31 Dec. 1813.

Ottridge, William; age 40 in 1819; nativity, Ireland; emigrated from the City of Cork, Ireland; arrived at Norfolk, Va., 10 April

1817; Declaration of Intention, (13) 15 Jan. 1819; Proof of Residence, 4 June 1824, witnesses, Thomas Murray, William Pancoast; naturalization granted 4 June 1824.

Ould, Henry; teacher; age 19 in 1818; nativity, England; arrived at "City Point in Virginia" 12 Nov. 1811; Declaration of Intention, 19 June 1818; Proof of Residence, 20 June 1818, witnesses, James A. Magruder, John Wiley; naturalization granted 20 June 1818.

Pairo, Thomas W.; nativity, Germany; in U. S. "about 8 years", in District of Columbia "about 7 years last past"; Declaration of Intention, 11 June 1811; Proof of Residence, 11 June 1811, witness, Damie Rennoi; naturalization granted 9 Jan. 1816.

Philips, George; age 31 in 1818; nativity, Edinburgh, Scotland; emigrated from Kirkaldie, Scotland; arrived at Norfolk, Va., 20 July 1817; Declaration of Intention, 20 June 1818; Proof of Residence, 21 May 1824, witnesses, Thomas McIntosh, John Hoolhand; naturalization granted 21 May 1824.

Plunkett, Rev'd Robt.; in U. S. since 1790; Proof of Residence, 20 Nov. 1811, witness, Rev'd Francis Neale; naturalization granted 2 Nov. 1811 (?).

Preston, William; age 26 in 1817; nativity, Ireland; emigrated from Sileby, Leicestershire, England; arrived at New York 7 Aug. 1816; Proof of Residence, 27 Dec. 1817, witnesses, John Wiseman, William Rider; naturalization granted 29 May 1824.

Prime, William; nativity, Great Britain; in U. S. "constantly since 28 Nov. 1803" and a note in the Proof of Residence states that he was in the U. S. "before the 14th day of April 1802"; Declaration of Intention, 10 Jan. 1814; Proof of Residence, 11 Jan. 1814, witness, Ziporah Corning; naturalization granted 11 Jan. 1814.

Scallam, James; age 27 in 1812; nativity, Ireland; in U. S. at least 6 or 7 years prior to 1816; Declaration of Intention, 18 June 1812; Proof of Residence, 6 Jan. 1816, witness, Thomas Howard; naturalization granted 6 Jan. 1816.

Scallan (Scallon), Robert; age 21 in 1818; nativity, County Wexford, Ireland; emigrated from Liverpool, England; arrived at Norfolk, Va., 24 Sept. 1817; Declaration of Intention, 11 Nov. 1818; Proof of Residence, 3 June 1824, witnesses, Sam'l Smoot, Wm. Fletcher; naturalization granted 3 June 1824.

Schneller, Joseph; age 21 in 1818; nativity, town of Tyrol, Germany; former allegiance, Emperor of Austria; emigrated from Kiel, Denmark; arrived at Philadelphia, Pa., 3 April 1812; Declaration of Intention, 25 June 1818; Proof of Residence, 20 May 1824, witnesses, Thomas Carbery, Lewis Johnson; naturalization granted 21 May 1824.

Schwarz, Conrad; age 24 in 1818; nativity, Hamburg, Germany; emigrated from Amsterdam, Holland; arrived at Baltimore, Md., Jan. 1803; Declaration of Intention, 4 June 1818; Proof of Residence, 13 April 1824; witnesses, Philip Munro, William Cooper, naturalization granted 13 April 1824.

——— (Sessford), John; printer; age 26 in 1802; former allegiance, Great Britain; arrived in U. S. 5 Dec. 1795, in Washington, D. C., Oct. 1800; document dated "Circuit Court, July term 1802"; document dated 9 July (?) 1826; oath dated 9 June 1826, petitioner states that he is the John ——— of the 1802 document; another oath dated 10 June 1826, witnessed by Wm Cranch (Crauch); naturalization granted (two dates given) 14 Aug. 1802 and 5 June 1826.

Shaeffter (Schaefter – Schaeffter), George Frederich; age 36 in 1819; nativity, Spyeim, Germany; emigrated from Hamburgh, Germany; arrived at Philadelphia, Pa., 26 Sept. 1803; Declaration of Intention, 17 June 1819; Proof of Residence, 13 Jan. 1826, witnesses, John Queen, John Holohan; naturalization granted 13 Jan. 1826.

Siousa, John; age 35 in 1815; nativity, Paris, France; arrived at New York May 1806; Declaration of Intention, 8 June 1815; Proof of Residence, 10 June 1819, witnesses, Worthington Sutherland, Thomas J. Sutherland; naturalization granted 10 June 1819.

Smith, John; age 45 in 1820; nativity, Lincolnshire, England; emigrated from London, England; arrived at Hampton Roads, Va., 13 Sept. 1819; Declaration of Intention, 5 Jan. 1820; Proof of Residence, 1 June 1826; witnesses, Robert Heyworth, Solomon Drew; naturalization granted 1 June 1826.

Spratt, Thomas; age 29 in 1820; nativity, Ireland; emigrated from Waterford, Ireland; arrived at New London, Conn., 1 June 1812; Declaration of Intention, 19 June 1820; Proof of Residence, 27 Dec. 1825, witnesses, James Gettys, John Hollohon; naturalization granted 27 Dec. 1825.

Stephens, Edward; age 32 in 1815; nativity, Ireland; in U. S. since 1809, in Washington "2 years last past"; Declaration of Intention, 7 June 1815; Proof of Residence, 7 June 1815, witness, George Andrews; naturalization granted 7 June 1815.

Sullivan, Jeremiah; age 26 in 1821; nativity, Ireland; emigrated from Cork, Ireland; arrived at Baltimore, Md., 29 July 1817; Declaration of Intention, 16 April 1821; Proof of Residence, 10 May 1826, witnesses, John Hallohan, Danl. Carroll; naturalization granted 10 May 1826.

Tastet (Tastel), Nicholas; age 29 in 1819; nativity, Madrid, Spain; emigrated from St. Sebastian, Spain; arrived at Boston, Mass., 6 Jan. 1814; Declaration of Intention, 23 June 1819; Proof of Residence, 21 Dec. 1824, witnesses, Michael Shaules, Walter Clarke; naturalization granted 20 Dec. 1824.

Thompson, Pishey; age 34 in 1819, nativity, Lincolnshire, England; emigrated from Liverpool, England; arrived at New York 27 Oct. 1819; Declaration of Intention, 27 Dec. 1819; Proof of Residence, 25 May 1825, witnesses, Joseph Gales, Jr., Nathaniel P. Poor; naturalization granted 25 May 1825.

Tschiffely, Frederick D.; nativity, Bern, Switzerland; in U. S. "nearly 9 years last past"; Proof of Residence, 6 June 1814, witness, Joseph Nourse; another document is a letter to the Court from Mr. Tschiffely enclosing the Proof of Residence; naturalization granted 6 June 1814.

Tucker, James; age 33 in 1820; nativity, Plymouth, England; emigrated from Plymouth, England; arrived at Baltimore, Md., 19 July

1819; Declaration of Intention, 11 Jan. 1820; Proof of Residence, 18 Jan. 1825, witnesses, Benjamin King, Andrew Forrest; naturalization granted 18 Jan. 1825.

Tuckfield, Wm H. P.; nativity, Great Britain; in U. S. since April 1801; Declaration of Intention, 29 Jan. 1810; Proof of Residence, 30 Jan. 1810; witness, William Smith; naturalization granted 30 Jan. 1810.

Walker, David; nativity, Ireland; in U. S. "before 14 April 1802"; Proof of Residence, 31 Dec. 1813, witness, Barney Dolan (?); naturalization granted 31 Dec. 1813.

Walker, William; in U. S. 29 Jan. 1795; Proof of Residence, 3 Nov. 1813, witness, Samuel Eliot, Jr.; naturalization granted 4 Nov. 1813.

Wallace, James; note: Rev. Mr. Wallace; age 28 in 1809; nativity, Kilkenny, Ireland; document "Report of ——— an alien" dated 24 July 1809, "Supreme Court, State and City of New York"; affadavit, 2 April 1814, Court of Common Pleas, Mayor's Court of the City of New York, witness, Dewitt Clinton, Esq., mayor of New York; naturalization granted in Circuit Court, District of Columbia, 7 Nov. 1814.

Williams, Thomas; nativity, Ireland; in U. S. 18 June 1798; Proof of Residence, 30 Dec. 1813, witness, Thomas McCutchen; naturalization granted 30 Dec. 1813.

Williams, Thomas Hollaway; age 33 in 1820; nativity, Plymouth, England; emigrated from Plymouth, England; arrived at Philadelphia, Pa., 26 July 1818; Declaration of Intention, 14 Jan. 1820; Proof of Residence, 2 Feb. 1825, witnesses, James Scallun, Philip Crewer; naturalization granted 2 Feb. 1825.

Wilmott (Willmott), Samuel Devonshire; age 53 in 1819; nativity, County of Somerset, England; Declaration of Intention, 8 March 1819 in Court of Common Pleas, Burlington County, New Jersey; note: No papers were to be found showing the date Mr. Wilmott appeared in Court in Washington, D. C. The Index to the Minute Books gives the naturalization date as 8 March 1819 which is obviously erroneous.

Winter, Samuel; nativity, England; in U. S. since 1785; Declaration of Intention, undated; Proof of Residence, 29 Dec. 1814, witness, Ronald Donaldson; naturalization granted 28 Dec. 1814 (?).

Petitions Received, 1821-1850 [Entries by 1825 only]

Abbot, Joseph; age 40 in 1829; nativity, Plymouth, England; emigrated from Plymouth, England; arrived at Norfolk, Va., 21 Sept. 1819; Declaration of Intention, 7 July 1829; Proof of Residence, 4 Dec. 1833, witnesses, Charles W. Boteler and Jonah Bosworth; naturalization granted, 4 Dec. 1833.

Adams, Thomas; nativity, Ireland; in U. S. prior to 14 April 1802; Proof of Residence, 25 May 1832, witnesses, George Sweeny and Thomas Hyde; naturalization granted, 28 May 1832.

Adie, James [arrived 1829]....

Adler, Morris (Moses); age 22 in 1821; nativity, Hesse Cassel; emigrated from Amsterdam; arrived at Philadelphia, 3 Nov. 1816; Declaration of Intention, 11 April 1821; Proof of Residence, 19 May 1827, witnesses, John Baker and Samuel Mickum; naturalization granted, 19 May 1827.

Agg, John; age 39 in 1823; nativity, Evesham, County of Worcester, England; emigrated from Evesham; arrived at Philadelphia, 22 May 1818; Declaration of Intention dated, State of New Jersey, County of Burlington, 25 June 1818; another Declaration of Intention dated Washington, D. C., 13 Dec. 1823; Proof of Residence, 29 Oct. 1827, witnesses, Richard Coxe and Richard Wallack; naturalization granted, 29 Oct. 1827.

Ahmey, Frederick [documents dated from 1844]....

Aigler, Jacob [arrived 1841]....

Ailer, George; age 36 in 1833; nativity, Germany; emigrated from Germany; arrived at Baltimore, 9 Nov. 1816; Declaration of Intention, 26 April 1833; Proof of Residence, 9 Dec. 1836, witnesses, Geo. Lambright and Jonah Essex; naturalization granted, 9 Dec. 1836.

Alexander, Charles P.; age 39 in 1822; nativity, Paris, France; emigrated from Bordeaux, France; arrived at New York, 6 May 1817; Declaration of Intention, 4 June 1822; Proof of Residence, 24 March, 1835, witnesses, Jonas P. Keller and Louis Labrille; naturalization granted, 24 March 1835.

Alexander, William [arrived 1837]....

Archer, William; age about 32 in 1818; nativity, Scotland; emigrated from Greenwich, England; arrived at New York, 25 Sept. 1815; Declaration of Intention, 6 Jan. 1818; Proof of Residence, 3 May 1821, witnesses, Tench Ringgold and Thomas Taylor; naturalization granted, 3 May 1821.

Arteser, John [arrived 1837]....

Baker, Conrad [arrived 1839]....

Barcroft, John; nativity, Ireland; in U. S. prior to 14 April 1802; Proof of Residence, 24 March 1830, witness, Charles Litle; naturalization granted, 26 March 1830.

Barker, Jacob [arrived 1840]....

Barr, Thomas; age 45 in 1845; nativity, Ireland; emigrated from Londonderry, Ireland; arrived at Alexandria, D. C., 12 Aug. 1818; Declaration of Intention 13 Sept. 1845; Proof of Residence 12 April 1848, witness Thomas Plumpsell; naturalization granted, 12 April 1848.

Barry, Francis; nativity, Ireland; in U. S. prior to 14 April 1802; Proof of Residence, 27 May 1836, witnesses, Richard Barry and William Spieden; naturalization granted, 29 May 1836.

Barry, James; age 21 in 1823; nativity Ireland; emigrated from County Cork; arrived at Boston, 18 May 1819; Declaration of Intention, 19 April 1823; Proof of Residence, 22 May 1828, witnesses Jacob Bender and Thos. Magnier (Maguire); naturalization granted, 22 May 1828.

Barry, Richard; age 28 in 1833; nativity, Ireland; emigrated from Dublin, Ireland; arrived at Philadelphia, May 1811; Declaration of Intention, 19 April 1833; Proof of Residence, 19 April 1833, witnesses, William Spieden and Robert T. Barry; naturalization granted, 19 April 1833.

Bates, Thomas; age 39 in 1823; nativity, England; emigrated from Liverpool, England; arrived at Baltimore, 11 Dec. 1818; Declaration of Intention, 25 April 1823; Proof of Residence, 24 June 1829, witnesses, Philip Munro (Manro) and William Nedin; naturalization granted, 24 June 1829.

Baxter, Rev'd Roger; occupation, minister; age about 25 in 1818; nativity, Lancashire, England; emigrated from England; arrived at Baltimore, 5 Jan. 1817; Declaration of Intention, 5 Jan. 1818; Proof of Residence, 7 April 1822, witnesses, Revd. Enoch Fenwick and Stephen H. Gough; naturalization granted, 11 April 1822.

Beardsley, Joseph; age 52 in 1832; nativity, Derbyshire, England; emigrated from Liverpool, England; arrived at Baltimore, 16 June 1819; Declaration of Intention, 29 May 1832; Proof of Residence, 30 May 1835, witnesses, Gregory Ennis and Wm. Service (Serren); naturalization granted, 30 May 1835.

Beardsley, Joseph, Jr.; nativity, England; emigrated from Liverpool, England; arrived at Philadelphia in 1821; Declaration of Intention, 20 May 1835; Proof of Residence, 20 May 1835, witnesses, Richard Wright and Levi Washbourn (Washburn); naturalization granted, 30 May 1835.

Beasley, George [arrived 1841]....

Bede, George; age 50 in 1846; nativity, Ireland; emigrated from Liverpool, England; arrived at New York, 10 March 1818; Declaration of Intention, 15 June 1846; Proof of Residence, 4 June 1849, witness, Charles McNamee; naturalization granted, 4 June 1849.

Bergemann, Henry [arrived 1837]....

Berger, William [documents dated 1850]....

Bergman, J. H. C. [documents dated from 1841]....

Berst, Anthony [arrived 1826 or 1827]....

Bettner, Godfrey [arrived 1833]....

Biondi, Antonio [arrived 1836]....

Bishop, Henry; in U. S. before 12 June 1812, residing in Mass. and N. J. also in District about 10 years; Proof of Residence, Commonwealth of Mass., Essex County, 12 May 1831, witnesses, George W. Raddin and John Hall; Proof of Residence, Washington, D. C., 3 June 1831, witnesses, Thomas Hyde and Edmund J. Brown; Proof of Residence, Washington, D. C., 7 June 1831, witnesses, Daniel Brown and Phebe Brown; naturalization granted, 8 June 1831.

Blackburn, Robt.; occupation, fancy chair maker; age 36 in Feb. 1816; nativity, Rothwell, near Leeds, England; emigrated from Liverpool, England; Declaration of Intention, New York, 19 (28?) Feb. 1816; Proof of Residence, Washington, D. C., 2 May 1823, witnesses, John Espey (Esbey) and John Coussins; naturalization granted, 2 May 1823.

Bohlayer, John C. [arrived 1833]....

Bohleyer, John; age 31 in 1825; nativity, Wirtemburg; emigrated from Rotterdam; arrived at Boston, 22 March 1821; Declaration of

Intention, 19 May 1825; Proof of Residence, 25 May 1830, witnesses, Edward Simms and Morris March; naturalization granted, 25 May 1830.

Borland, Alexander; age 34 in 1823; nativity, Ireland; emigrated from Londonderry, Ireland; arrived at New York, 17 July 1815; Declaration of Intention, 31 Dec. 1823; Proof of Residence, 27 May 1831, witnesses, William Jones and Nicholas Callan; naturalization granted, 27 May 1831.

Boulanger, Jean Joseph Paschale; age 43 in 1831; nativity, Leige; emigrated from Portsmouth, England; arrived at Annapolis, 14 Aug. 1825; Declaration of Intention, 2 April 1831; Proof of Residence, 13 June 1836, witnesses, Charles W. Gouldsborough and Edmund Hanly; naturalization granted, 13 June 1836.

Bouthron, John; age 30 in 1819; nativity, Fifeshire, Scotland; emigrated from Fifeshire; arrived at Philadelphia, 22 (2) April 1817; Declaration of Intention, 13 Jan. 1819; Proof of Residence, 2 June 1828, witnesses, James Ewell and Alexander McCormick; naturalization granted, 2 June 1828.

Boyle, Christopher; age 30 in 1848; nativity, Ireland; emigrated from Dublin, Ireland; arrived at New York, 15 Sept. 1844; Declaration of Intention, 15 Feb. 1848; Proof of Residence, 27 May 1850, witness, John Foy; naturalization granted, 27 May 1850.

Brady, Thomas [documents dated from 1840]....

Breckinridge, William Dunlop [documents dated from 1842]....

Brit, James [arrived 1830]....

Brodbeck, Jacob [arrived 1835]....

Broderick, Thomas; age about 24 in 1818; nativity, Dublin, Ireland; emigrated from Cork, Ireland; arrived at Norfolk, Va., about 4 March 1816; Declaration of Intention, 20 June 1818; Proof of Residence, 2 June 1823, witnesses, Neil McNauty (McNantz) and John H. Downs (?), naturalization granted, 11 June 1823.

Brown, David [arrived 1836]....

Brown, Robert; occupation, stonecutter; age about 32 in 1818; nativity, Scotland; emigrated from Scotland; arrived at New York "latter end Sept. 1810"; Declaration of Intention, 8 Jan. 1818; Proof of Residence, 13 Dec. 1823, witnesses, Peter Lenox and William Archer; naturalization granted, 13 Dec. 1823.

Brown, Thomas [arrived 1830]....

Brown, William [documents dated from 1844]....

Bruning, John H. [arrived 1841]....

Bryan (Brien), Bernard; age 23 in 1821; nativity, Tyrone, Ireland; emigrated from Londonderry, Ireland; arrived at Philadelphia, Pa., 14 August 1816; Declaration of Intention, 18 April 1821; Proof of Residence, 5 May 1829, witnesses, Lewis Carbery and Nicholas Hedges; naturalization granted 5 May 1829.

Buckley, Timothy K. [arrived 1842]....

Buist, David [arrived 1833]....

Buist, William [arrived 1832]....

Bulger, Patrick; age 30 in 1826; nativity, County of Wexford, Ireland; emigrated from Waterford, Ireland; arrived at Baltimore, 20

August 1825; Declaration of Intention, 13 June 1826; Proof of Residence, 28 May 1834, witnesses, Gregory Ennis and James Lawrence; naturalization granted 28 May 1834.

Burrows, John; occupation, mariner; age "born 1791"; nativity, Liverpool, England; arrived at New York, 1807; Declaration of Intention, District Court, Boston, Mass., 2 (or 22) March 1822, while he was residing in Salem, Mass.; Proof of Residence, Alexandria County, District of Columbia, 6 May 1826, witnesses, Oliver Lapham and Thomas Mount; a second Proof of Residence is filed, 11 May 1827, Alexandria County, District of Columbia, witnesses, Daniel Wright and Oliver Lapham; naturalization granted 12 May 1827.

Buthmann, John H.; age 38 in 1844; nativity, Germany; emigrated from Amsterdam; arrived at New York, July 1825; Declaration of Intention, 25 April 1844; Proof of Residence, 22 October 1847, witness, Charles McNamee; naturalization granted 22 October 1847.

Butler, Abraham; age 39 in 1834; nativity, England; emigrated from Liverpool, England; arrived at Alexandria, D. C., 8 July 1819; Declaration of Intention, 4 April 1834; Proof of Resident, 18 May 1837, witnesses Richard Wright and Louis F. Joncherez; naturalization granted 18 May 1837.

Byrne, James [arrived 1840]....

Caden, James; age 44 (or 22) in 1822; nativity, Monaghan County, Ireland; emigrated from Ireland; arrived at Philadelphia, Pa., 3 August 1817; Declaration of Intention, Alexandria, D. C., 14 June 1822; Proof of Residence, 6 June 1831, witnesses, John B. Gormans and Edward Dyer; naturalization granted 6 June 1831.

Callan, Patrick [arrived 1837]....

Calvert, Charles; age 38 in 1832; nativity, England; emigrated from Hull, England; arrived at Whitehall, N. Y., 25 August 1818; Declaration of Intention, 6 June 1832; Proof of Residence, 6 June 1834, witnesses, J. H. Hook (Cook) and Charles G. Wilcox; naturalization granted 6 June 1834.

Carmack (Cammack), Christopher; age 33 in 1830; nativity, England; emigrated from Liverpool, England; arrived at New York, 18 November 1816; Declaration of Intention, 28 December 1830; Proof of Residence, 28 December 1833, witnesses, Nicholas Callan and Edw[d] Dyer; naturalization granted 28 December 1833.

Carmack (Cammack), William; age 38 in 1839; nativity, Lincolnshire, England; emigrated from Liverpool, England; arrived at New York, 17 November 1816; Declaration of Intention, 11 January 1839; Proof of Residence, same, witnesses, Clement T. Coote and Christopher Carmack (Cammack); naturalization granted 11 January 1839.

Carroll, John; age 30 in 1836; nativity, Tipperary, Ireland; emigrated from Waterford, Ireland; arrived at Baltimore, 28 June 1825; Declaration of Intention, 27 June 1836; Proof of Residence, 27 November 1839, witnesses, Henry B. Robertson and Thomas Lloyd; naturalization granted 27 November 1839.

Carter, James; age 23 in 1830; nativity, Plymouth, England; emigrated from Havre; arrived at New York Aug. 1817; Declaration of

Intention, 6 January 1830; Proof of Residence, 6 January 1830, witnesses, Moses Poor and Alfred Elliot; naturalization granted 6 January 1830.

Carusi, Augustus [arrived 1836]....

Casparis, James [arrived 1839]....

Catalano, Salvadore; age "about 48" in 1812; nativity, Island of Sicily (Syracuse); emigrated from Syracuse; arrived at City of Washington, November 1805; Declaration of Intention, 22 June 1812; Proof of Residence, 16 June 1823, witnesses, Richard Spaulding and Tench Ringgold; naturalization granted 16 June 1823.

Choppin, William [arrived 1830]....

Chutkowski, Ignatius [documents dated from 1840; note concerning military service]....

Clark, James A.; nativity, Scotland; lived in Mount Clemens, Michigan, since latter part of 1818 until 1826, in Washington, D. C. since (3) 23 December 1826; Declaration of Intention, Territory of Michigan, County of Macomb, 3 February 1824. Proof of Residence, Territory of Michigan, County of Macomb, 5 February 1826, witnesses, Associate Justices of Macomb County Court, Christian Clemens and Erskine (Ezekiel) Allen; another Proof of Residence, Washington, D. C., 30 March 1829, witnesses, Richard Davis and William Hughes, naturalization granted 29 March 1829.

Clark (Clarke), William [arrived 1843]....

Clarke, John [arrived 1828]....

Clavloux, Mark; age 28 in 1840; nativity, France; emigrated from Havre, France; arrived at Philadelphia, 15 June 1827; Declaration of Intention, 6 June 1840; Proof of Residence, 5 January 1843, witnesses, Thomas Goodal and James O'Neale; naturalization granted 5 January 1843.

Clephane, James; age 25 in 1818; nativity, Scotland; emigrated from Cacalden, Fifeshire, Scotland; arrived at Norfolk, Va., 20 July 1817; Declaration of Intention, 19 January 1818; Proof of Residence, 10 December 1833, witnesses, Richard Wallach and Wm. Redin; naturalization granted 10 December 1833.

Clitsh, Henry Christian Frederick [arrived 1837]....

Coleman, Charles [arrived 1837]....

Collins, George C. [arrived 1832]....

Collins, Thomas; occupation, laborer; birthdate, 6 May 1808; nativity, Castlehyde County, Cork, Ireland; arrived at Boston, Mass., 3 November 1832....

Columbus, Charles; age 40 in 1845; nativity, Leghorn, Italy; emigrated from Leghorn, Italy; arrived at Baltimore, November 1816; Declaration of Intention, 31 May 1845; Proof of Residence 31 May 1845, witness, Leonard Harbaugh; naturalization granted 31 May 1845.

Conlon, Peter [documents dated from 1836]....

Conly (Connelly), Thomas Y.; age 26 in 1835; nativity, County of Armagh, Ireland; emigrated from Belfast, Ireland; arrived at Baltimore, 26 July 1825; Declaration of Intention, 2 May 1835; Proof of Residence, 2 May 1835, witnesses (S) L. M. Wilson and William

Onne (Orme); naturalization granted 2 April (?) 1835.

Connelly, Owen; nativity, Ireland; emigrated from Sligo; arrived at Alexandria, Va., 15 September 1823; Declaration of Intention, Baltimore, Md., 1 October 1830; Proof of Residence, Washington, D. C., 30 December 1836, witnesses, John Ward and Philip H. Minors (Miner, Minor); naturalization granted 30 December 1836.

Conroy, Dominick [arrived 1832]....

Conway, James [documents dated from 1829]....

Cooper, Joseph; age 36 in 1827; nativity, Derbyshire, Eng.; emigrated from Liverpool, Eng.; arrived at Annapolis, Md., 26 September 1819; Declaration of Intention, 31 May 1827; Proof of Residence, 31 May 1832, witnesses, Alexander McIntire and Thomas Woodward; naturalization granted 31 May 1827.

Cooper, William, Jr., age 36 in 1834; nativity, Great Britain; emigrated from London; arrived at Philadelphia 4 June 1805; Declaration of Intention, 29 May 1834; Proof of Residence, 29 May 1834, witnesses, Thomas Munroe and John H. Reily; naturalization granted 29 May 1834.

Coote, Clement T.; age 34 in 1819; nativity, England; emigrated from Cambridgeshire, Eng.; arrived at Philadelphia, 29 August 1817; Declaration of Intention, 15 June 1819; Proof of Residence, 18 October 1822, witnesses, Richard Eno and Thomas Eno; naturalization granted 19 October 1822.

Cowan, Hugh [Declaration of Intention, Chester County, Pa., 1839] ....

Creaser (Creasor), Thomas [arrived 1831]....

Creutzfeldt, William [arrived 1840]....

Croggan (Croggon), Henry B.; age 25 in 1837; nativity, England; emigrated from Plymouth, Eng.; arrived at Alexandria, D. C., 1 July 1818; Declaration of Intention, 20 December 1837; Proof of Residence, 20 December 1837, witnesses, James Mankin and Isaac N. J. Croggan; naturalization granted 20 December 1837.

Cropley, Edward S. [arrived 1827]....

Crotty, Patrick [arrived 1831]....

Cruit, Robert; age 29 in 1824; nativity, Devonshire, Eng.; emigrated from Plymouth, Eng.; arrived at Philadelphia, 15 June 1819; Declaration of Intention, 3 June 1824; Proof of Residence, 27 May 1835, witnesses, Thomas Woodward and Randolph Spalding; naturalization granted 27 May 1835.

Cull, John; age 37 in 1846; nativity, England; emigrated from Guernsey; arrived at Baltimore, 29 June 1818; Declaration of Intention, 27 March 1846; Proof of Residence, 27 March 1846, witness, Andrew Coyle; naturalization granted 27 March 1846.

Cummings, James [arrived 1836]....

Cummings, Patrick [arrived 1837]....

Cunningham, Samuel; age 22 in 1820; nativity, County of Armagh, Ire.; arrived at New York, 12 July 1817; Declaration of Intention, Hagerstown, Md., 20 November 1820; Proof of Residence, Washington, D. C., 1 December 1837, witnesses, Henry B. Robertson, Owen Connelly; naturalization granted 1 December 1837.

Cunnington, Michael; age 28 in 1842; nativity, Ireland; emigrated from Liverpool, Eng.; arrived at New York, 24 July 1832; Declaration of Intention, 1 March 1844; Proof of Residence, 10 December 1844, witnesses, Gregory Ennis and John B. Gray; naturalization granted 10 December 1844.

Curley, James; age 25 in 1822; nativity, County of Roscommon, Ire.; emigrated from Dublin, Ire.; arrived at Philadelphia; Declaration of Intention, Frederick Town, Md., 9 March 1822; Proof of Residence, Washington, D. C., 21 December 1832, witnesses, Thomas Meade and George King; naturalization granted 21 December 1832.

Cuvillier, Joseph; age 33 in 1839; nativity, France; emigrated from Gibralter; arrived at New York, 27 January 1824; Declaration of Intention, 27 May 1839; Proof of Residence, 27 May 1839, witnesses, Edward W. Clarke and Venerando Pulizzi; naturalization granted 27 May 1839.

Daily, John; age 26 in 1836; nativity, Ireland; arrived in this country, 1816; Declaration of Intention, 4 January 1836; Proof of Residence, 4 January 1836, witnesses, Gregory Ennis and Jeremiah Sullivan; naturalization granted 4 June 1836 (?).

Davidson, John [arrived 1827]....

Dawes, Frederick Dawes, (wife, Charlotte Maria); aged 25 in 1819; nativity, England; emigrated from Liverpool, Eng. 1 December 1818; arrived at New York 5 February 1819 with wife, Charlotte Maria Dawes, age 25 years; Declaration of Intention, Montgomery County, Maryland, 13 November 1826; another Declaration of Intention, County of Washington, 16 November 1819; Proof of Residence, Washington, D. C., 2 June 1832, witnesses, Clement T. Coote and Peter Brady; naturalization granted 2 June 1832.

Develin, John S.; age 21 in 1824; nativity, Ireland; emigrated from Montreal; arrived at Plattsburgh, N. Y., 2 April 1820; Declaration of Intention, Washington, D. C., 12 April 1824; Proof of Residence, 26 May 1829, witnesses, V. Pulitizi and Mathew Wright; naturalization granted 26 May 1829.

Deveraux, William [documents dated from 1838]....

Dewdney, John; age 27 in 1832; nativity, Kent County, England; emigrated from Brest, France; arrived at Norfolk, Virginia, 2 August 1823; Declaration of Intention, 2 June 1832; Proof of Residence, 2 June 1832, witnesses, John Barcroft, Leonard Ashton, Thomas Conner; naturalization granted 2 June 1832.

Dickson, John; age 41 in 1838; nativity, Ireland; emigrated from Portiferry; arrived at Newberryport, Massachusetts, May 1818; Declaration of Intention, 29 November 1838; note says, "Admitted—Certificate given 23 March 1841", naturalization granted 23 March 1841.

Dillon, William [arrived 1841]....

Dixon, James [arrived 1827]....

Dodds, James; age 45 in 1824; nativity, Northumberland County, England; emigrated from Port of Leath, Scotland; arrived at New York, 1 September 1816; Declaration of Intention, 9 June 1824; Proof of Residence, 30 June 1836, witnesses, Thomas Magnier and

Archibald Thompson; naturalization granted 30 June 1836.

Doermer, Charles [arrived 1839]....

Donnoghue, John; age 24 in 1825; nativity, County Cork, Ireland; emigrated from Liverpool; arrived at Alexandria, July 1822; Declaration of Intention, 19 December 1825; Proof of Residence, 30 June 1832, witnesses, Thomas Orme and Thomas Hyde; naturalization granted 30 June 1832.

Donovan (Donivan), James [arrived 1834]....

Donovan, John [arrived 1828]....

Donovan (Donavan), Michael [documents dated from 1844]....

Dooley, Michael [arrived 1832]....

Douglass, John; age 29 in 1828; nativity, Scotland; emigrated from Island Jamacia (?) (Jamorcia?); arrived at Boston, November 1816; Declaration of Intention, 11 December 1828; Proof of Residence, 11 December 1828, witnesses, Cadwallader Evans and Thomas M. Abbott; naturalization granted 11 December 1828.

Dowling, William; age 37 in 1824; nativity, Ireland; emigrated from Dublin; arrived at Baltimore, 17 October 1817; Declaration of Intention, 5 June 1824; Proof of Residence, (7) 17 May 1830, witnesses, George Miller and Patrick Delaney; naturalization granted 17 May 1830.

Doyle, John [documents dated from 1835]....

Doyle, Michael [arrived 1839]....

Draine, Charles; age 30 in 1829; nativity, Ireland; emigrated from Belfast; arrived at Eastport, Maine, 7 September 1822; Declaration of Intention, 25 March 1846; Proof of Residence, 24 June 1834, witnesses, John Simon and Samuel Rumy (Rury); naturalization granted 24 June 1834.

Dreisch, Michael [documents dated from 1840]....

Dubant, Marc; age 48 in 1841; nativity, France; emigrated from Bordeaux; arrived at Philadelphia, 15 April 1816; Declaration of Intention, 23 March 1841; Proof of Residence, 2 June 1845, witness, James F. Holliday (Halliday); naturalization granted 2 June 1845.

Dubuisson (Duboisson), Revd. Stephen Langaudelle; occupation, minister; age about 29 in 1816; nativity, France; emigrated from France; arrived at New York, 21 November 1815; Declaration of Intention, 17 June 1816; a paper dated Leonardtown, Md., 22 April 1822, mentions a Proof of Residence, but does not include an enclosure, signed W. J. Brooke; naturalization granted 29 April 1822.

Duffey, James [arrived 1842]....

Drumphey, Thomas; age 26 in 1842; nativity, Ireland; emigrated from Waterford; arrived at Baltimore, July 1820; Declaration of Intention, March Term 1842; Proof of Residence, March Term 1842, witnesses, John A. Donlin and Robert Ball; naturalization granted March Term 1842.

Dunn, John; Proof of Residence, 17 December 1823, witnesses, James Scallon and Nicholas Cassidy; naturalization granted 17 December 1823.

Dzierozynski, Francis; age 43 in 1822; nativity, Orsani, Poland; emigrated from Orsani, Poland, 12 November 1821; Declaration of Intention, County of Alexandria, District of Columbia, 14 June 1822; Proof of Residence, Washington, D. C., 12 May 1828, witnesses, Joohue Millard and James Neale; naturalization granted 12 May 1828.

Earl, Robert; age 37 in 1837; nativity, Cambridgeshire, England; emigrated from Liverpool; arrived at Alexandria, Virginia, 9 August 1820; Declaration of Intention, 13 April 1837; Proof of Residence, 10 December 1839, witnesses, James Williams and John Dove; naturalization granted 10 December 1839.

Ebeleng, Henry [arrived 1839]....

Ebeleng, Frederick [documents dated 1850]....

Eberback, Henry [arrived 1832]....

Eckardt, Henry; age 39 in 1825; nativity, Wirtemberg; emigrated from Amsterdam; arrived at Baltimore, 19 February 1820; Declaration of Intention, 10 May 1825; Proof of Residence, 18 May 1830, witnesses, David Appler and Frederick Stringer; naturalization granted 18 May 1830.

Eckloff, Godfrey; age 39 in 1823 (born 14 January 1784); nativity, Prussia; emigrated from Amsterdam; arrived at Philadelphia, 2 August 1817; Declaration of Intention, Philadelphia, 11 October 1823; Proof of Residence, Washington, D. C., 3 May 1836, witnesses, Christian Eckloff and Lewis Beelers; naturalization granted 3 May 1836.

Egan, William; age 45 in 1838; nativity, Ireland; emigrated from Scotland; arrived at New York, March 1818; Declaration of Intention, 5 December 1838; Proof of Residence, 10 December 1840, witnesses, Joseph S. Clarke and Anthony Holmeade; naturalization granted 10 December 1840.

Eigler, Jacob (filed under Aigler in Index to Naturalization) [arrived 1841]....

Einbroet, John David [arrived 1837]....

Ellis, Henry [documents dated from 1836]....

Elvans, Richard; age 41 in 1821; nativity, England; emigrated from Guernsey; arrived at Baltimore, 20 October 1818; Declaration of Intention, 16 April 1821; Proof of Residence, 23 June 1829, witnesses, Robert Barnard and Morris Adler; naturalization granted 23 June 1829.

Emmerick, John [arrived 1833]....

Emmert, Henry [arrived 1839]....

Emmert, William [arrived 1832]....

Ennis, Gregory; age 30 in 1822; nativity, Ireland; emigrated from Newfoundland; arrived at Boston, 4 May 1816; Declaration of Intention, 3 June 1822; Proof of Residence, 29 May 1832, witnesses, Jeremiah Sullivan and Mich^{l} Connelly; naturalization granted 30 May 1832.

Ennis, Philip; age 36 in 1824; nativity, Ireland; emigrated from County of Wexford; arrived at Baltimore, 9 April 1819; Declaration of Intention, 15 January 1824; Proof of Residence, 6 July

1829, witnesses, Joseph S. Clark and George Sweeny; naturalization granted 6 July 1829.

Erb, Charles [arrived 1831]....

Evans, Evan [arrived 1832]....

Farrar, John Morgan; age 35 in 1825; nativity, County of Dublin, Ireland; emigrated from London; arrived at Baltimore, 21 October 1817; Declaration of Intention, 8 January 1825; Proof of Residence, 25 May 1830, witnesses, Edward Simmes (Semmes) and Morris March; naturalization granted 25 May 1830.

Feeney, William [arrived 1828]....

Feiner, William; age 29 in 1822; nativity, Munster; emigrated from Munster 22 May 1812; Declaration of Intention dated Alexandria, District of Columbia, 14 June 1822; Proof of Residence dated Washington, D. C., 12 May 1828, witnesses, Joshua Millard and James Neale; naturalization granted 12 May 1828.

Ferguson, William [arrived 1837]....

Ferrity, Nicholas [arrived 1828]....

Fill, John [arrived 1832]....

Finkman, Conrad [arrived 1839]....

Fischer, George Andrew [arrived 1840]....

Fister, John; age 30 in 1837; nativity, Switzerland; emigrated from Amsterdam; arrived at Philadelphia, 15 October 1816; Declaration of Intention, 18 May 1837; Proof of Residence, 22 April 1841, witnesses, Robert Connell and Jacob Kengla; naturalization granted 22 April 1841.

Fitzgerald, David [arrived 1841]....

Fitzgerald, James; age 34 in 1833; nativity, County of Waterford, Ireland; emigrated from Town of Waterford, Ireland; arrived at New York, November 1825; Declaration of Intention, 27 November 1833; Proof of Residence, 30 March 1836, witnesses, John H. Baker and Michael McCarty; naturalization granted 23 May 1836.

Fitzgerald, John [arrived 1826]....

Fitzgerald, John [arrived 1842]....

Fitzpatrick, James [arrived 1827]....

Flaherty, John; age 31 in 1848; nativity, Ireland; emigrated from Galway; arrived at Baltimore, June 1818; Declaration of Intention, District Court, 5 June 1848; Proof of Residence, same, witness, William Flaherty; naturalization granted 5 June 1848.

Flaherty, William [arrived 1836]....

Flannigan, Michael; age 39 in 1824; nativity, Ireland; emigrated from Cork, Ireland; arrived at Baltimore, 29 September 1818; Declaration of Intention, 2 June 1824; Proof of Residence, 5 April 1830, witnesses, Thomas Magnier and Francis Conly, naturalization granted 5 April 1830.

Fleming, John; age 29 in 1823; nativity, County of Cork, Ireland; emigrated from Quebec; arrived at Alexandria, 1 November 1818; Declaration of Intention, 17 April 1823; Proof of Residence, 16 May 1828, witnesses, George McCormick and Martin Larner; naturalization granted 16 May 1828.

Forrestil (Forrestel), James; age 35 in 1844; nativity, Ireland;

emigrated from Dublin; arrived at New York, 10 May 1842....

Foy, John; occupation, gardener; nativity, United Kingdom; in U. S. "many years before the 18th day of June 1812"; Declaration of Intention, June Term 1817 Fayette County Court, Kentucky; Proof of Residence, Washington, D. C., 11 May 1821, witnesses, Alex McWilliams and Thomas Claxton; naturalization granted 12 May 1821.

Foy, John [arrived 1829]....

Foy, Mordecai [arrived 1827]....

Francis, John; birthdate, 10 June 1806; nativity, County Kerry, Ireland; emigrated from County Kerry, 12 June 1825; arrived at Albany, N. Y., 13 August 1825; Declaration of Intention, Cambria County, Pennsylvania, 3 October 1832; Proof of Residence, Washington, D. C., 12 December 1840, witnesses, Philip Ennis and Owen Connelly; naturalization granted 14 December 1840.

Francis, Richard [arrived 1841]....

Franklin, William [Declaration of Intention dated 1834]....

Fraser, James; age 42 in 1824; nativity, England; emigrated from Liverpool; arrived at Alexandria, 24 May 1817; Declaration of Intention dated Supreme Court, County of Fairfax, 25 May 1818; a second Declaration of Intention is dated Washington, D. C., 3 June 1824; Proof of Residence, Washington, D. C., 3 June 1824, witness, Cornelius Wells; there is, also, a second Proof of Residence dated Dist. of Columbia, 4 June 1827, witnesses, Cornelius Wells and Robert G. Lanphier; naturalization granted 4 June 1827.

Frere, Barrow [arrived 1832]....

Frere, James B.; age 43 in 1825; nativity, Hereford County, England; emigrated from Cadiz, Spain; arrived at Boston, June 1815; Declaration of Intention, 16 April 1825; Proof of Residence, 29 November 1837, witnesses, James Gettys and Henry B. Robertson; naturalization granted 30 November 1837.

Fullalove, James; age 42 in 1832; nativity, England; emigrated from Liverpool; arrived at Baltimore, October 1817; Declaration of Intention, 25 June 1832; Proof of Residence, 21 April 1841, witnesses, James Gettys and Francis Goss (?); naturalization granted 21 April 1841.

Gaddis, Adam; age 25 in 1822; nativity, Ireland; emigrated from New Brunswick; arrived at Alexandria, 21 August 1820; Declaration of Intention, 29 October 1822; Proof of Residence, 5 June 1831, witnesses, Morris D. C. Marsh and John Judge; naturalization granted 6 June 1831.

Gahan, William; age 51 in 1833; nativity, Ireland; emigrated from Engcorthy (?), Ireland; arrived at Boston, 8 June 1818; Declaration of Intention, 27 May 1833; Proof of Residence, 21 May 1836, witnesses, Gregory Ennis and John F. Callan; naturalization granted 31 May 1836.

Galabrun (Gallibrun), Louis Jean; age 35 in 1937; nativity, France; emigrated from Havre; arrived at New York, January 1834; Declaration of Intention, 9 January 1837; Proof of Residence, 20 May 1845, witness, Jonas P. Keller; naturalization granted 20 May 1845.

Gallant, William; in U. S. prior to 1802; Proof of Residence, 31 May 1830, witnesses, David Glenn and Thomas Connolly; naturalization granted 31 May 1830.
Gautier, Charles [arrived 1838]....
Gerdes, Ferdinand H. [arrived 1836]....
Geffers, William Joseph [arrived 1841]....
Gillott, Joseph [arrived 1830]....
Giveny, Bernard; age 41 in 1831; nativity, County of Cavan, Ireland; emigrated from Dublin; arrived at Philadelphia, 19 October 1819; Declaration of Intention, 11 October 1831; Proof of Residence, 2 May 1835, witnesses, William Dowling and John Goinor; naturalization granted 2 May 1835.
Gonzalez, Ambrozio I. [arrived 1828]....
Gordon, James; age 63 in 1845; nativity, Ireland; emigrated from Liverpool; arrived at Boston, 23 May 1809; Declaration of Intention, 1 July 1845; Proof of Residence, Dist. Court, 5 June 1848, witness, Gustavus A. Clarke; naturalization granted 5 June 1848.
Gormlay, Philip [arrived 1827]....
Gould, John; age 48 in 1848; nativity, England; emigrated from London; arrived in U. S. 1816; Declaration of Intention, 1 November 1848; Proof of Residence, same, witness, Gustavus A. Clarke; naturalization granted 1 November 1848.
Greason, William [arrived 1837]....
Green, James [documents dated from 1845]....
Green, Owen [documents dated from 1845]....
Green, Patrick; age 54 in 1848; nativity, Ireland; emigrated from Dublin; arrived at Alexandria, D. C., 1 June 1819; Declaration of Intention, 3 June 1848; Proof of Residence, 3 June 1850, witness, Charles Kiernan; naturalization granted 3 June 1850.
Grey, Cyril Vernon [arrived 1842]....
Grimes, Guy; age 46 in 1837; nativity, County Down, Ireland; emigrated from Belfast; arrived at Baltimore, 12 July 1818; Declaration of Intention, 17 January 1837; Proof of Residence, 9 December 1840, witnesses, Robert Cunningham and William Douglass; naturalization granted 9 December 1840.
Grupe, William [arrived 1841]....
Gunton, Thomas, Junior; age about 33 in 1817; nativity, County of Norfolk, England; emigrated from England; arrived at Baltimore about last of June 1816; Declaration of Intention, 7 November 1817; Proof of Residence, 9 November 1822, witnesses, Richard Wallach and William Gunton; naturalization granted 9 November 1822.
Guttensohn, John [arrived 1841]....
Hagarty, William [documents dated from 1835]....
Hager, Christopher [arrived 1828]....
Hager, Frederick [arrived 1829]....
Hager, Godfrey (Gottfried) [arrived 1837]....
Hammont, James [arrived 1834]....
Hanagan, Peter B. O. [arrived 1833]....
Handley, James; age 23 in 1827; nativity, County of Galway, Ire-

land; emigrated from Galway; arrived at Baltimore year of 1817; Declaration of Intention, 24 December 1827; Proof of Residence, 24 December 1827, witnesses, John Dowling and Arthur Thompson; naturalization granted 24 December 1834 [*sic*].

Haney, Hugh [arrived 1828]....

Hanna, Francis; age 26 in 1831; nativity, Ireland; emigrated from Ireland; arrived at New York in 1816; Declaration of Intention, 15 October 1831; the Proof of Residence is undated but apparently was same date as the Declaration of Intention, witnesses, George Phillips and Daniel Homans; naturalization granted 15 October 1831.

Hardy, Henry [arrived 1834]....

Harlihy (Horlihy), Daniel [arrived 1827]....

Harper, Andrew; age 26 in 1822; nativity, Ireland; emigrated from Londonderry; arrived at Ogdensburg, N. Y., 16 July 1821; Declaration of Intention, 22 December 1822; Proof of Residence, 24 December 1827, witnesses, Thomas Magnier and Thomas Murray; naturalization granted 24 December 1827.

Harrison, Richard; age 28 in 1826; nativity, County of Thorn, England; emigrated from London; arrived at Norfolk, Virginia, 1818; Declaration of Intention, 27 May 1826; Proof of Residence, 2 April 1839, witnesses, Samuel H. Taylor and Ignatius N. Clements; naturalization granted 2 April 1839.

Harvey, William; age 45 in 1823; nativity, England; emigrated from Island of Guernsey; arrived at Baltimore, 30 September 1818; Declaration of Intention, 16 September 1823; Proof of Residence, 1 June 1824, witnesses, Joriah Bonooitte (Bonooith) and Charles Bill; naturalization granted 1 June 1829.

Heider, John Frederick [arrived 1841]....

Hefferen, Patrick; age 30 in 1824; nativity, Ireland; emigrated from City of Cork; arrived at Alexandria, District of Columbia, 1 November 1817; Declaration of Intention, 4 June 1824; Proof of Residence, 13 July 1829, witnesses, Patrick Delaney and James Sweeney; naturalization granted 13 July 1829.

Heill, Joseph [arrived 1837]....

Hein, Samuel [documents dated from 1841]....

Heitmuller, Alfred [arrived 1837]....

Heitmuller, Charles A. T. [arrived 1840]....

Helfrick, John [arrived 1834]....

Henry, Christian Frederick [arrived 1841]....

Henry, John [arrived 1829]....

Hercus, George; age 30 in 1822; nativity, Haddington, Scotland; emigrated from Leith; arrived at Philadelphia, 12 September 1817; Declaration of Intention, 3 June 1822; Proof of Residence, 26 May 1828, witnesses, William Fitzhugh and J. F. Caldwell; naturalization granted 26 May 1828.

Hess, Jacob [arrived 1832]....

Hess, William [documents dated 1850]....

Hibbs, Charles [arrived 1830]....

Higgins, Patrick [arrived 1834]....

Hine, William [documents dated 1850]....
Hitz, Florian [arrived 1835]....
Hitz, John [arrived 1831]....
Hitz, John, Jr. [arrived 1831]....
Hoffman, George [arrived 1833]....
Hoffman, George [arrived 1832]....
Hollidge, James (John) [arrived 1833]....
Holohan, John; age "about" 28 in 1818; nativity, Ireland; emigrated from Dublin; arrived at Boston, 18 June 1812; Declaration of Intention, 28 December 1818; Proof of Residence, 9 November 1822, witnesses, Joshua Couch and Asa L. Bassett; naturalization granted 9 November 1822.
Hopp, Nicholas [arrived 1838]....
Horning, John [arrived 1827]....
Hughes, Hugh [arrived 1829]....
Hughes, John; nativity, Monaghan, Ireland; emigrated from Dublin; arrived at Philadelphia, 15 September 18--; Declaration of Intention, 27 May 1837 (?); Proof of Residence, 30 May 1840, witnesses, James ——ity and John Leach; naturalization granted 1 June 1840. (Only two fragments, the left half of a printed Declaration of Intention were in the envelope.)
Hurstcamp, Henry [arrived 1836]....
Iddins, Frederick [arrived 1837]....
Iddins, Samuel [arrived 1840]....
Indermaur, Jeremiah; nativity, Switzerland; emigrated from Amsterdam; arrived at Philadelphia, November 1817; Declaration of Intention, 13 January 1830; Proof of Residence, 6 April 1835 (?), witnesses, Andrew Noer and Godfrey Eckloff; naturalization granted 6 May 1835.
Iost, Benedict [arrived 1837]....
Ivey, William Henry [arrived 1834]....
Jacobi, William [arrived 1832]....
Jaeger, Benedict [emigrated from Hamburg, 1827; arrived New York, 1831]....
Jirdinston, Peter William [documents dated 1837]....
Joice, Richard; age 26 in 1824; nativity, County Cork, Ireland; emigrated from Cork; arrived at Norfolk, Va., July 1818; Declaration of Intention, 2 June 1824; Proof of Residence, 29 May 1832, witnesses, Jeremiah Sullivan and John C. Remely; naturalization granted 29 May 1832.
Jordan, Thomas; merchant; "late of Great Britain and Ireland"; Declaration of Intention, New York, 20 December 1817; Proof of Residence, Washington, D. C., 2 July 1836, witnesses, James Gooch and Thomas Harrison; naturalization granted 2 July 1836.
Jost, Benedict [arrived 1837]....
Joyce, John J.; age 30 in 1848; nativity, Ireland; emigrated from Cork; arrived at Norfolk, Va., May 1820; Declaration of Intention, District Court, 5 June 1848; Proof of Residence, same, witness, Michael Joyce; naturalization granted 5 June 1848.
Joyce, Michael; age 28 in 1844; nativity, Ireland; emigrated from Cork; arrived at New York, 28 August 1825; Declaration of Inten-

tion, 10 September 1844; Proof of Residence, same, witnesses, Patrick Byrne and Charles McNamee; naturalization granted 10 September; naturalization granted 10 September 1844.

Judge, John; age "about" 28 in 1818; nativity, County of Mayo, Ireland; emigrated from Portsmouth, England; arrived at Alexandria, 5 November 1817; Declaration of Intention, 29 December 1818; Proof of Residence, 16 April 1823, witnesses, John B. Forrest and Edward Semmes; naturalization granted 16 April 1823.

Kohling (Kahling), John Michael [arrived 1839]....

Kaisser, Herm [arrived 1839]....

Kane, Patrick [arrived 1842]....

Kaufmann, George [arrived 1832]....

Kavanaugh, John; age 35 in 1834; nativity, Ireland; emigrated from Liverpool; arrived at New York, July 1819; Declaration of Intention, 19 April 1834; Proof of Residence, same, witnesses Wm. C. Easton and Charles G. Wilcox; naturalization granted 19 April 1834.

Keane, John Stephen; age 28 in 1824; nativity, Ireland; emigrated from Limerick; arrived at New York, May 1816; Declaration of Intention, 21 May 1824; Proof of Residence, 2 June 1834, witnesses, Gregory Ennis and Thomas Magnier; naturalization granted 2 June 1834.

Kearnan, Patrick; age "about" 26 in 1816; nativity, County Kerry, Ireland; emigrated from Ireland; arrived at New York, 26 September 1812; Declaration of Intention, 4 April 1817; Proof of Residence, 4 June 1827, witnesses, Joseph Etter and Nicholas Callan; naturalization granted 4 June 1822. (?)

Kedglie, John; age in 1821; nativity, East Lothian, Scotland; emigrated from Liverpool; arrived at New York, 17 December 1807; Declaration of Intention, 23 April 1821; Proof of Residence, 26 April 1839, witnesses, George Creniella (?) and George Lowry; naturalization granted 26 April 1839.

Kehl, John V. [arrived 1842]....

Keily, Rev. Jeremiah; occupation, Minister; age "about" 20 in 1818; nativity, County Cork, Ireland; emigrated from Cork; arrived at Boston, 24 May 1818; Declaration of Intention, 26 June 1818; Proof of Residence, 5 December 1823, witnesses, Hezekiah Langley and Samuel Newton, and for reference, Rev. John Smith; naturalization granted 5 December 1823.

Keiser, Henry [documents dated from 1841]....

Keith (Keitch), John; age 25 in 1820; nativity, England; emigrated from London; arrived at New York, October 1817; Declaration of Intention, 10 June 1820; Proof of Residence, 11 June 1832, witnesses, John H. Houston and John Williams; naturalization granted 11 June 1832.

Keleher, James [arrived 1832]....

Keller, Jonas; age 55 in 1824; nativity, Switzerland; emigrated from Bordeaux; arrived at New York, 6 May 1816; Declaration of Intention, 11 June 1824; Proof of Residence, 23 June 1829; naturalization granted 23 June 1829.

Keller, Jonas P.; age 23 in 1831; nativity, France; emigrated from Bordeaux; arrived at New York, August 1816; Declaration of Intention, 1 June 1831; Proof of Residence, same witnesses, William Stewart and Jacob Hilbus; naturalization granted 1 June 1831.
Keller, Michael [arrived 1831]....
Kelly, Bernard; age 25 in 1824; nativity, County Donegal, Ireland; emigrated from Liverpool; arrived at Alexandria, D. C., 15 July 1819; Declaration of Intention, 10 August 1824; Proof of Residence, 15 April 1840, witnesses, John H. Goddard (?) and James C. Deasale (?); naturalization granted 15 April 1840.
Keobel, Jacob [arrived 1832]....
Keppler, Henry [arrived 1832]....
Kiernan, Charles [arrived 1830]....
Kinney, Jeremiah [arrived 1842]....
Kinsley, Benjamin; age 33 in 1822; nativity, Lincolnshire, England; emigrated from Liverpool; arrived at Philadelphia, 19 July 1817; Declaration of Intention, 18 April 1822; Proof of Residence, 27 May 1828, witnesses, Charly Vanable and Jeremiah Perkins; naturalization granted 27 May 1828.
Kirkwood, Jonathan [arrived 1834]....
Kleindienst, John P. [documents dated 1850]....
Kleindienst, Sebastian [arrived 1832]....
Klotz, George [arrived 1833]....
Korff, John [documents dated from 1838]....
Krafft, George; age 27 in 1832; nativity, Germany; emigrated from London; arrived at New York, July 1825; Declaration of Intention, 17 May 1832; Proof of Residence, 16 June 1836, witnesses, William Waters and John Bohleyer (Bohleger); naturalization granted 16 June 1836.
Krafft, John; age 31 in 1824; nativity, Württemburg; emigrated from London; arrived at Baltimore, 26 October 1818; Declaration of Intention, 3 June 1824; Proof of Residence, 21 December 1829, witnesses, Frederick C. DeKrafft and Thomas Taylor; naturalization granted 21 December 1829.
Kraft (Kroft), Christopher [arrived 1832]....
Krebs, Charles I. [arrived 1832]....
Kroes, Peter Paul [arrived 1832]....
Kuhl, Henry [arrived 1832]....
Lakemeyer, Frederick [arrived 1843]....
Lamby, William [arrived 1829]....
Lauchrey (Laukney), Hugh [arrived 1831]....
Law, John George; age 36 in 1832; nativity, England; emigrated from Spalding, England; arrived at Philadelphia, 19 July 1817; Declaration of Intention, 6 July 1832; Proof of Residence, 5 June 1834, witnesses, Richard Wright and Nicholas Callan; naturalization granted 5 June 1834.

[At this point the article ceases to be continued.—Ed.]

Rev. William J. Gammon. "Emigrants to Bath County, North Carolina, 1695-1702," *National Genealogical Society Quarterly*, 25 (1937), 28-30 [Lancour No. 230].

Mr. D. L. Corbitt, Office of Secretary N. C. Historical Commission, March 30, '37, writes:

"Bath County was formed from the territory south of Albemarle and north of the Pamtecough (now Tar and Pamlico rivers), in 1696.

This county was set up by authority of the Governor and his council, and it was allowed two representatives in the General Assembly of Albemarle.

It was not a county with the status of Albemarle County, which had administrative, legislative and judicial functions. Bath County was accorded only judicial functions except, of course the local administrative duties performed by its Justices of the Pleas and Quarter sessions.

In 1705 Bath County was divided into Pantecough, Wickham and Archdale precincts, which were allowed two representatives each to the General Assembly of Albemarle.

About 1712 Archdale was changed to Craven, Wickham was changed to Hyde, and Pamlico was changed to Beaufort. These three counties are still in existence.

In 1870 a county by the name of Pamlico was erected from parts of Bath and Craven counties.

Bath County, so far as I have been able to ascertain, never was abolished. Its territory was included in the three precincts formed in 1705, and even though there are instances where this section was referred to as Bath County as late as 1733, the county did not function as such."

The following lists of immigrants and claimants who received land were copied in 1916 from an old deed book in Craven Co., N. C. by Rev. Wm. J. Gammon, then of Louisville, Ky.:

"List of Emmigrants, brought to Bath County, North Carolina, for which land was granted to the person bringing them, or inducing them to come."

June, 1695. By Thomas Blount:

Wm. Hancock, wife Elizabeth Hancock.

February 10, 1696. By Wm. Glover:

Fenox, James
Fenox, Ann
Fenox, Robert
Bartlett, Wm.
Bartlett, Thomas
Bartlett, Edward
Batchelor, Edward
Willson, An
Willson, Jona
Willson, Jno.

October 18, 1701. By Jno. White:

White, John, Sr.
White, John, Jr.
White, George
White, Sarah
White, Abigall
Nash, Prudence
White, Francis
White, Mary
White, Luck
White, Media
Reed, Charles
Reed, Mary
Starborough, Sampson
Jenkins, Jones
Jenkins, Dorman
Tarmigan, Isaiah

September 1701. By Farnifould Green:

Leeds, Abraham
Leeds, Elizabeth
Leeds, Elizabeth Jane Jr.
Leeds, Sarah
Leeds, Martha
Hall, Nat-
Garrett, Mary
Hosea, Wm.
Grimes, John

May, 1701. By Wm. Barrow.

Neuman, Thomas
Neuman, Elizabeth
Neuman, Jane
Collins, Wm.
Batson, Abraham
Batson, Elizabeth
Batson, Rose
Read, Mary
Bush, Wm.
Bush, Martha, Wm's. wife
Bush, Martha, dau. of Wm.
Bush, Wm. Jr.
Bush, Sarah
Bush, Elloner
Hopkins, John
Morrison, Hannah
Morrison, Rich'd
Morrison, Susanna

December, 1701. By Joseph Ming:

Bosur, Abraham
Stokes, Samuel
Porter, John
Porter, John, Jr.
Porter, Edward
Porter, Joseph
Ming, Thomas

March, 1701/2. By Nathaniel Chevin:

Smith, John
Smith, Jane
Allen, James
Horning, Elizabeth
Pidgin, Jane
Huggin, George

March, 1702. By Richard Smith:

Willson, Wm.
Willson, Ann, Sr.
Willson, Ann, Jr.
Willson, Mary
Willson, James
Willson, Richard

March, 1702. By James Nevill:

Tylor, Nicholas
Nevill, Richard
Gorganus, Francis
Nevill, James, Jr.

April 13, 1702. By Thomas Dearham:

Tummelton, Obadiah Benj.
Bellensby, John
Hoodson, Wm.
Lee, Thomas
Nasebitt, Wm.
Webb, Thomas
Tellown, Peter
Clark, Honnery
French, Philip
Hall, Job
Jopp, Jona-

No date. By Thomas Jones:

Jones, Nicholas
Benington, Thomas Cornelius
Baley, Richard
Miles, Sarah
Miles, Betty
Barnett, Thomas
Ming, Jos
Thomas, Edmund wife of above
Watson, John
Howes, Thomas
Bonaway, Peter
Falkoner, John
Lyle, Henry
Wm. a negro
Huchison, Wm.
Betty, an Indian
Scott, Ellenor
Lucas, John
Barker, Wm.
Quary, Robert
Shelton, James
Masey, George
Yeamens, Benjamin
Shallown, James

September, 1701. By Nathaniel Chevin:

Davis, Edward
Davis, Susanna
Brown, Wm.
Fulton, Samuel
Early, Thomas
Wiggins, Wm.
Hanley, Wm.
Edwards, Thomas
Hardee, John
Brown, John
Ellis, Wm.

September 9, 1701. By Peter Godfrey:

Hardy, John
Brown, Wm.
Ellerlee, Thomas
Widgen, Wm.

December 19, 1701. By Thomas Worsley:

Martin, Francis	Martin, Wm.
Martin, Elizabeth Jr.	Martin, Ann

July 22, 1702. By Henry Lockey:

Lockey, Henry	Lockey, Thomas	Lockey, George
Lockey, Ann	Lockey, Fraser	

October 28, 1702. By Thomas Lepper:

John Read

October 28, 1702. By John Nellson, Jr.:

Nellson, John, Sr.	two passages:	Nelson, Joan
Nelson, Elizabeth	Capps, Wm.	Woodis, Judith
John, Nelson, Sr.	Nelson, Mary	

June 22, 1702. By Wm. Brice:

Brice, Wm.	Linfield, Francis	Depee, Elizabeth
Brice, Ann	Linfield, John	Depee, David."

Adelaide L. Fries. *Records of the Moravians in North Carolina.* Raleigh: Edwards & Broughman Printing Co., 1922 [Lancour No. 231].

[The following list, from Volume 1, pages 68-69, gives the names of twenty-six Moravian immigrants to North Carolina, 1753-1759, made up from certificates of land grants in the Herrnhut (Saxony) archives.—after Lancour]

1. 1753. Johann Christoph Sack, Koenigsberg, Germany.
2. 1753. Reinhold Gerhard Georgi, Koenigsberg, Germany.
3/1. 1754. Georg Gottfried Gambs, Strassburg, France. (1000 acres).
3/2. 1754. Johann Leonard Roederer, Strassburg, France. (1000 acres).
4. 1754. Hans Ernst von Zezschwiz, Herrnhut, Saxony.
5. 1754. Johann Steinhauer, Riga, Russia.
6/1. 1754. Traugott Bagge, Gottenberg, Sweden. (1000 acres).
6/2. 1754. Benjamin Bagge, Gottenberg, Sweden. (1000 acres).
7. 1754. Cornelius van Laer, Zeist, Holland.
8. 1754. Abraham Duerninger & Co., Herrnhut, Saxony.
9. 1754. Johanna Sophia von Schweinitz, Herrnhut, Saxony.
10. 1754. Johann Casper Rosenbaum, Dantzig, Prussia.
11. 1754. Heinrich Giller, Herrnhut, Saxony.
12. 1754. Madtz Jensen Klein, Drammen, Norway.
13. 1754. Johann Steinhauer, Riga, Russia.
14. 1754. C. F. Martens (for Single Brethren's Diacony), Herrnhut, Saxony.
15. 1754. Johann Hartmann, Hirschberg, Silesia.
16. 1754. Jean Jacque de Schwarz, Coire, Switzerland.
17. 1754. Christian Schmidt, Stettin, Prussia.
18. 1754. Jean Henri de Planta de Wildenberg, Coire, Switzerland.

19/1. 1754. Michael Zellich, Riga, Russia (1000 acres)
19/2. 1754. Johannes Andreas Schmutz, Strassburg, France. (1000 acres).
20. 1754. Friedrich von Wiedebach, Herrnhut, Saxony.
21. 1754. Gottfried Clemens, Barby, Saxony.
22. 1754. Johann Christoph Sack, Koenigsberg, Germany.
23. 1754. Johann Erhardt Dehio, Herrnhut, Saxony.
24. 1754. Friedrich Justin von Bruiningk, Livonia, Russia.
25/1. 1754. Hans Hermann von Damnitz, Guettau, Saxony. (1000 acres).
25/2. 1755. Johann Gustav Frey, Errestfer, Russia. (1000 acres).
26. 1759. Friedrich Heinrich von Bibra, Modlau, Silesia.

A map of Der Nord Carolina Land und Colonie Etablissement, dated 1754, shows the Wachau as divided into "Societaets Land," (for the Land Company) and "Unitaets Land," (for the Unity). For the time being it was considered that each Certificate carried with it the lot bearing the corresponding number, though an actual award of the lots was not made until 1767, by which time the map had been a couple of times redrawn to secure a more convenient partition of the land.

As soon as the purchase of the Wachau had been arranged in London instructions were sent to Bethlehem for the selection of the first colonists, and for the beginning of the settlement on the North Carolina tract.

Most of the men chosen were at the time resident in Christiansbrunn, an agricultural center on the Nazareth Land [Christian's Spring, one and one-half miles from Nazareth, Pa.]. The place, originally known as Albrecht's Brunn, had been re-named in 1749, in honor of Christian Renatus von Zinzendorf, and in December of that year a company of Single Brethren had settled there, to conduct a farm, dairy, mill, etc. From this group of unmarried men the first colonists were now selected, special care being taken to send men whose talents and professions fitted them for the needs of pioneer work. Their names, places of birth, age, and qualifications, the latter taken from the memorandum book of Frederick William Marshall [who was in England in 1753, a member of Zinzendorf's household in London; the comments are not his but are copied from a report made by someone in Pennsylvania], preserved in the Salem Archives, which gives the most interesting comment of the various lists extant, are as follows:

1. Bernhard Adam Grube, a German by birth, aged 37 years, Ordinarius, Pfleger, and upon occasion cook and gardener.
2. Jacob Loesch, born in New York, aged 31, their Vorsteher, as in Christiansbrunn.
3. Hans Martin Kalberlahn, born in Norway, aged 31, their surgeon.
4. Friedrich Jacob Pfeil, born in Germany, aged 28, shoe-maker, sick-nurse, and moreover willing and skillful in many things.

5. Erich Ingebretsen, born in Norway, aged 31, mill-wright and carpenter.
6. Henrich Feldhausen, born in Holstein, aged 38, shoe-maker, carpenter, mill-wright, cooper, sieve-maker, turner, and also Pennsylvania farmer.
7. Jacob Lung, born in Germany, aged 40, gardener, washer, and skillful in many things not mentioned. A man whom all animals love.
8. Hans Petersen, born in Danish Holstein, aged 28, tailor, grubber, wood-cutter, skillful in many things and willing in all.
9. Johannes Beroth, born in Germany, aged 28, a Pennsylvania farmer.
10. Christopher Merkly, born in Germany, aged 39, baker, and good, true, dependable farmer, a soldier Brother, whom we are sorry to lose in Christiansbrunn.
11. Hermannus Loesch, born in Pennsylvania, who must go this time on account of this knowledge, but whom we will recall in the spring [a member of the Spangenberg surveying party in 1752, he did not return to Pennsylvania until some years later].
12. Johannes Lischer, who shall study the road, the country, etc., and make himself known, so that in future, according to custom, he can be our messenger to North Carolina.
13. Our dear Nathaniel Seidel, who will conduct them to the place, and the latter part of December bring us a report, with Br. Lischer.
14. Gottlob Königsdorfer, Chor Jünger of the Single Brethren.
15. Joseph Haberland.

Of these the last two named intended to accompany the party only to the Susquehanna, but there decided to go all the way, later returning to Pennsylvania with Seidel and Lischer, leaving the eleven others to form the nucleus of the colony.

The Christiansbrunn members of the party left home on Oct. 2nd for Bethlehem, where they remained a few days and from there the formal start was made.

A. R. Newsome, ed. *Records of Emigrants from England and Scotland to North Carolina, 1774-1775*. Raleigh: State Department of Archives and History, 1962 [Lancour No. 232].

Reprinted from Lancour No. 232A, the text is given below.

A. R. Newsome, ed. "Records of Emigrants from England and Scotland to North Carolina, 1774-1775," *The North Carolina Historical Review*, 11 (Jan. 1934), 39-54 [Lancour No. 232A].

Pursuant to a letter from John Robinson, secretary of the Treasury, December 8, 1773, customs officials in England and Scotland supplied lists of persons who took passage on ships leaving Great Britain during the years 1773-1776, giving names, ages, quality, occupation, employment, former residence, reasons for emigrating, and the name of the vessel and master. These records, somewhat incomplete as now preserved in the Public Record Office of Great Britain under the classification Treasury Class 47, Bundles 9-12, contain many thousands of names and important information on a remarkable population movement which was of great significance to America and of arresting attention to the landed and manufacturing interests and the government of Great Britain [footnotes here and following omitted]. They have been printed in part in *The New England Historical and Genealogical Register* (1908-1911).

The largest group consisted of indented servants bound for New York, Pennsylvania, Maryland, and Virginia; and the next largest, of emigrants sailing from ports in northern England to Nova Scotia, Virginia, and New York. The emigration practically ceased after September, 1775. The movement from Scotland was due chiefly to the oppressive rent policy of the Highland proprietors and middlemen of the region extending from Ayr County to the Shetland Islands. A traveler on an emigrant ship in 1774 wrote: "It is needless to make any comment on the conduct of our Highland and Island proprietors. It is self-evident what consequences must be produced in time from such numbers of subjects being driven from the country. Should levies again be necessary, the recruiting drum may long be at a loss to procure such soldiers as are now aboard this vessel." However, in the war which began a year later between England and the American colonies, many of the Highlanders were loyal to England and from them was recruited the Royal Highland Regiment. Economic conditions were of paramount importance in driving the emigrants from England and Scotland and in luring them to the New World.

With less attractive economic conditions, North Carolina did not receive so large a share of the new settlers, particularly those from England, as did Virginia, Maryland, Pennsylvania, or New York. The mass movement to North Carolina was more pronounced among the Scotch Highlanders, due partly to the fact that since about 1739 many of their kinsmen had already settled on the Cape Fear in the counties of Cumberland, Bladen, and Anson. In 1770 the General Assembly, in behalf of about sixteen hundred Highlanders who had landed in the province during the past three years, passed an act exempting settlers who came direct from Europe from the payment of all taxes for a term of four years. At the outbreak of the Revolution, the estimated number of Scotch Highlanders in North Carolina was 15,000.

The compilation here printed is from transcripts in the North Carolina Historical Commission of the selected records of those emigrants whose destination was North Carolina.

The list of emigrants from England to North Carolina contains about one hundred names. There are nearly three times as many males as females, and the average recorded age of the entire group is twenty-five years. Twenty-three are listed as indented servants, of whom three are women, nine are indented for four years, and two for two years. The group consists of artisans from the cities of England. Several pleasure-seekers and six family groups are noted.

Nearly five hundred names are in the lists from Scotland. There are nearly one hundred family groups. The males exceed the females in the ratio of about three to two, and there are seventy children without sex designation. The average recorded age is twenty-five years. The majority consists of farmers and laborers from the Highland counties of Argyle, Sutherland, and Caithness. Low wages, high rents, low prices of cattle, high prices of bread due to distilling, the conversion of farm lands into sheep pastures, and the exactions of landlords at home, added to the reputation of Carolina for high wages, cheap land, and plentiful provisions, account largely for the emigration.

RECORDS OF EMIGRANTS FROM ENGLAND

An account of all Persons who have taken their passage on Board any Ship or Vessel, to go out of this Kingdom from any Port in England, with a description of their Age, Quality, Occupation or Employment, former residence, to what Port, or place they propose to go, & on what Account, & for what purposes they leave the Country

From January 15 to January 23, 1774

Embarked from the Port of London

William Wilson, 38, Planter, London, Carolina, Carolina, Jno. Besnard, as a planter.

Benjamin Blackburn, 28, Clergyman, London, Carolina, Carolina, Jno. Besnard, to settle there.

Robert Rose, 20, Planter, London, Carolina, Carolina, Jno. Besnard, as a planter.

George Ogier, 15, Planter, London, Carolina, Carolina, Jno. Besnard, as a planter.

Robt. Knight, 26, Planter, London, Carolina, Carolina, Jno. Besnard, as a planter.

Henry Chapman, 30, Jeweller, London, Carolina, Carolina, Jno. Besnard, to work at his Business.

Henry Maskal, 19, Clerk, London, Carolina, Carolina, Jno. Besnard, as a Clerk.

John Williams, 30, Cabinet Maker, London, Carolina, Carolina, Jno. Besnard, for Employment.

Thomas Vernan, 22, Silk Throwster, London, Carolina, Carolina, Jno. Besnard, for Employment.

Embarked from the Port of Falmouth [Cornwall]
Colin Campbell, -----, -----, Carolina, Le De Spencer (Packet Boat), Capt. Pond, no further Account.
Custom House London, 15th February 1774. Exd Jno. Tomkyns.
From February 20 to February 27, 1774
Embarked from the Port of London
William Scott, 21, Malster, Scotland, North Carolina, Margaret & Mary, Saml. Tzatt, for Employment.
Margaret Scott, 16, Spinster, Scotland, North Carolina, Margaret & Mary, Saml. Tzatt, for Employment.
William Sim, 24, Husbandman, Scotland, North Carolina, Margaret & Mary, Saml. Tzatt, for Employment.
Jane Sim, 24, Wife to William Sim, Scotland, North Carolina, Margaret & Mary, Saml. Tzatt, for Employment.
David Marshal, 24, Clerk, Scotland, North Carolina, Margaret & Mary, Saml. Tzatt, as a Clerk.
James Blakswik, 21, Clerk, Scotland, North Carolina, Margaret & Mary, Saml. Tzatt, as a Clerk.
David Wilson, 38, Merchant, London, Carolina, Union, Wm. Combs, on Business.
John Macklin, 24, Gentleman, Oxford, Carolina, Union, Wm. Combs, to Settle.
Mary Macklin, 23, Wife to John Macklin, Oxford, Carolina, Union, Wm. Combs, to Settle.
Lewis Ogier, 47, Weaver, London, Carolina, Union, Wm. Combs, to Settle.
Catherine Ogier, 40, Wife to the above, London, Carolina, Union, Wm. Combs, to Settle.
Thomas Ogier, 20, Silk Throwster, London, Carolina, Union, Wm. Combs, to Settle.
Lewis Ogier, 19, Silk Throwster, London, Carolina, Union, Wm. Combs, to Settle.
Catherine Ogier, 16, Spinster, London, Carolina, Union, Wm. Combs, to Settle.
Lucy Ogier, 13, Spinster, London, Carolina, Union, Wm. Combs, to Settle.
Charlotte Ogier, 9, Spinster, London, Carolina, Union, Wm. Combs, to Settle.
John Ogier, 8, School Boy, London, Carolina, Union, Wm. Combs, to Settle.
Mary Ogier, 6, Spinster, London, Carolina, Union, Wm. Combs, to Settle.
Peter Ogier, 5, School Boy, London, Carolina, Union, Wm. Combs, to Settle.
Custom House London, 22d April 1774. Exd. Jno. Tomkyns.
From March 21 to March 28, 1774
Embarked from the Port of Liverpool
John Edward, 26, Farmer, Cheshire, South Carolina, Polly, -----, To Farm.
Jane Edward, 27, his Wife, Cheshire, South Carolina, Polly, -----, going with her Husband.

William Simpson, 43, Cooper, B Lincolnshire, South Carolina, Polly, -----, To Trade.
James Wilson, 18, Sadler, Bedfordshire, South Carolina, Polly, -----, To Trade.
James Clark, 42, Butcher, Middlesex, South Carolina, Polly, -----, To Trade.
William Walker, 37, Merchant, Yorkshire, South Carolina, Polly, -----, To Trade.
Custom Ho: London, 28th May 1774. Ex^{d}. Jno. Tomkyns.

From April 19 to April 26, 1774

Embarked from the Port of London

Janet Belton, 20, Spinster, London, Carolina, Magna Charta, R^{d}. Maitland, going to her Friends.
Tobiah Blackett, 25, Spinster, London, Carolina, Magna Charta, R^{d}. Maitland, going to her Friends.
Custom H. London, 22^{d}. June 1774. Ex^{d}. Jno. Tomkyns.

From May 10 to May 17, 1774

Embarked from the Port of London

John Grafton, 25, Drawing Master, London, Carolina, Briton, Alex^{r}. Urquhart, on Business.
Nathaniel Worker, 25, Gentleman, London, Carolina, Briton, Alex^{r}. Urquhart, on Pleasure.
Custom H^{o}. London, 5th July 1774. Ex^{d}. Jno. Tomkyns.

From May 17 to May 24, 1774

Embarked from the Port of London

Mary Bands, 35, Widow, Herts, North Carolina, Friendship, John Smith, Indented Servant for Four Years.
Mary Kenneday, 21, Spinster, Scotland, North Carolina, Friendship, John Smith, Indented Servant for Four Years.
John Brown, 21, Book keeper, Birmingham, North Carolina, Friendship, John Smith, Indented Servant for Four Years.
George Taverner, 21, Groom, Southwark, North Carolina, Friendship, John Smith, Indented Servant for Four Years.
Edward Gilks, 22, Leather dresser, Coventry, North Carolina, Friendship, John Smith, Indented Servant for Four Years.
John Forster, 24, Printer, London, North Carolina, Friendship, John Smith, Indented Servant for Four Years.
Thomas Winship, 26, Clockmaker, Reading, North Carolina, Friendship, John Smith, Indented Servant for Four Years.
John Darby, 40, Baker, London, North Carolina, Friendship, John Smith, Indented Servant for Four Years.
William Andrews, 31, Carpenter, Surry, North Carolina, Friendship, John Smith, Indented Servant for Four Years.
Custom H^{o}. London, 13 July 1774. Ex^{d}. Jno. Tomkyns.

From May 24 to May 31, 1774

Embarked from the Port of London

Miss Tong, 16, Spinster, London, Carolina, Pallas, J. Turner, going on Pleasure.
M^{r}. Ginnings, 25, Clerk, London, Carolina, Pallas, J. Turner, as Clerk to a Merchant.

Mrs. Molley, 30, -----, London, Carolina, Pallas, J. Turner, going to her Husband.

Custom Ho. London, 13th. July 1774. Exd. Jno. Tomkyns.

From July 10 to July 17, 1774

Embarked from the Port of London

Sarah White, 56, Merchant, London, Carolina, Carolina, Jno. Besnard, going on Business.

John Detlaf, 30, Taylor, London, Carolina, Carolina, Jno. Besnard, going to Settle.

Sarah Detlaf, 25, Wife of John Detlaf, London, Carolina, Carolina, Jno. Besnard, going to Settle.

Custom Ho. London, 15 August 1774. Exd. Jno. Tomkyns.

From July 31 to August 7, 1774

Embarked from the Port of London

John Butler, 25, Gentleman, London, Carolina, Carolina Packet, John White, going to Settle.

Ann Butler, 25, Wife of John Butler, London, Carolina, Carolina Packet, John White, going to Settle.

Thomas Andrews, 35, Potter, London, Carolina, Carolina Packet, John White, going to Settle.

William Templeman, 28, Jeweller, London, Carolina, Carolina Packet, John White, going to Settle.

John Smith, 22, Cabinet Maker, London, Carolina, Carolina Packet, John White, going to Settle.

Custom Ho. London, 31st. August 1774. Exd. Jno. Tomkyns, Assist: Inspr. Genl.

From August 14 to August 21, 1774

Embarked from the Port of London

David Adkins, 22, Cooper, Lincoln, Carolina, William, Philip Wescott, Indented Servant.

James Nichols, 24, Silver Caster, London, Carolina, William, Philip Wescott, Indented Servant.

Thomas Winter, 21, Husbandman, Leicester, Carolina, William, Philip Wescott, Indented Servant.

John Rixon, 22, Brazier & Copper Smith, Birmingham, Carolina, William, Philip Wescott, Indented Servant.

Benjamin Evans, 22, Sail Cloth Weaver, Cornwall, Carolina, William, Philip Wescott, Indented Servant.

John Anthony, 21, Baker, Middlesex, Carolina, William, Philip Wescott, Indented Servant.

James Smith, 21, Painter & Glazier, Nottingham, Carolina, William, Philip Wescott, Indented Servant.

Michael Delancy, 21, Husbandman, Ireland, Carolina, William, Philip Wescott, Indented Servant.

Custom House London, 24th Octob- 1774. Exd. Jno. Tomkyns Assist: Inspr. Genl.

From October 3 to October 10, 1774

Embarked from the Port of London

Rachael L'Fabuere, 40, Lady, London, ----- Curling, going for Pleasure.

Jane Bignell, 47, Servant of Rachael L'Fabuere, London, Carolina, London, ----- Curling, going with M[rs] L'Fabeure [*sic*].

Ann Bowie, 36, Servant of Rachael L'Fabeure, London, Carolina, London, ----- Curling, going with M[rs] L'Fabeure.

Eliz[a]. Batty, 16, a native of Carolina, London, Carolina, London, ----- Curling, going home.

Ann Weston, 30, Lady, London, Carolina, London, ----- Curling, going for pleasure.

John West, 28, Gentleman, London, Carolina, London, ----- Curling, going for pleasure.

John Auldjo, 15, Gentleman, London, Carolina, London, ----- Curling, going for pleasure.

Alex[r]. Auldjo, 16, Gentleman, London, Carolina, London, ----- Curling, going for pleasure.

Robert Dee, 33, Gentleman, London, Carolina, London, ----- Curling, going for pleasure.

Henry Houseman, 35, Gentleman, London, Carolina, London, ----- Curling, going for pleasure.

Embarked from the Port of Newcastle

Thomas Stead, 17, Butcher, Hull, Cape Fear, Rockingham, Richard Hopper, going to his Father, who lives there.

Custom H[o]. London, 10th Novemb. 1774. Ex[d]. Jn[o]. Tomkyns Assist: Insp[r]. Gen[l].

From October 17 to October 24, 1774

Embarked from the Port of London

Stephen Eglin, 25, Draper, London, Carolina, Newmarket, Gilbert Wilson, going to settle.

Jasper Scouler, 30, Carpenter, London, Carolina, Newmarket, Gilbert Wilson, going to settle.

Rob[t]. Maxwell, 18, Clerk, Scotland, Carolina, James, Isaac Thompson, going to settle.

Willson Dabzall, 25, Jeweller, Scotland, Carolina, James, Isaac Thompson, going to settle.

Bezabeer Forsyth, 22, Gentleman, Scotland, Carolina, James, Isaac Thompson, going to settle.

Sarah Eastwood, 16, Spinster, London, South Carolina, Lowther, Tho[s]. Cowman, Indented Servant.

Joseph Dyer, 21, Waiter, London, South Carolina, Lowther, Tho[s]. Cowman, Indented Servant.

William Kenneday, 25, Peruke Maker, London, South Carolina, Lowther, Tho[s]. Cowman, Indented Servant.

Ralph Richardson, 35, Gardener, Surry, South Carolina, Lowther, Tho[s]. Cowman, Indented Servant.

Custom H[o]. London, 5th Decemb. 1774. Ex[d]. Jn[o]. Tomkyns, Assist: Insp[r]. Gen[l].

From November 7 to November 14, 1774

Embarked from the Port of London

William Ripley, 22, Farmer, York, Carolina, Mary & Hannah, Henry Dixon, going to Settle.

John Sanderson, 45, Farmer, York, Carolina, Mary & Hannah, Henry Dixon, going to Settle.

John Blythe, 32, Gentleman, London, Carolina, Mary & Hannah, Henry Dixon, on Pleasure.

James Flatt, 25, Taylor, London, Carolina, Mary & Hannah, Henry Dixon, Indented Servant for two years.

James Trenham, 22, Butcher, York, Carolina, Mary & Hannah, Henry Dixon, Indented Servant for two years.

Custom H^o^. London, 5th December 1774. Ex^d^. Jno. Tomkyns Assist: Insp^r^. Genl.

From November 28 to December 6, 1774

Embarked from the Port of London

John Mackenzie, 16, Clerk & Bookkeeper, Scotland, Carolina, Briton, Alex^r^. Urquhart, going to settle.

Alexander Douglas, 22, Husbandman, Scotland, Carolina, Briton, Alex^r^. Urquhart, going to settle.

Christopher Smith, 49, Husbandman, Switzerland, Carolina, Briton, Alex^r^. Urquhart, going to settle.

Esther Smith, 35, Wife to the above, Switzerland, Carolina, Briton, Alex^r^. Urquhart, going to settle.

Andrew Milborn, 7, Child, Switzerland, Carolina, Briton, Alex^r^. Urquhart, going to settle.

Christopher Milborn, 2, Child, Switzerland, Carolina, Briton, Alex^r^. Urquhart, going to settle.

Custom H^o^. London, 13th Janry 1775. Ex^d^. Jno. Tomkyns Assist: Insp^r^. Genl.

RECORDS OF EMIGRANTS FROM SCOTLAND

R. E. Philips to John Robinson

Sir

In obedience to your Letter of the 8th. of December 1773, I am directed to enclose to You, Lists of Persons, who have taken their Passage from the Ports of Port Glasgow and Kirkaldy, for North America on board the Ships Commerce and Jamaica Packet, for the Information of the Right Honorable the Lords Commissioners of His Majesty's Treasury.

Customhouse Edinburgh
20th. June 1775 R. E. Philips

Port Kirkaldy [in Fife County across the Firth of Forth from Edinburgh] An Account of Emigration from this Port and precinct to America or other Foreign Ports from the 5th. of June 1775, to the 11th. d^o^. both inclusive.

Emigrants on board the Jamaica Packet of Burntisland [near Kirkaldy] Thomas Smith master for Brunswick North Carolina.

Miss Elizabeth Mills & her servant going to reside in S^o^. Carolina from Dundee.

John Durmmond & John Marshall Coopers from Leith, goes out because they get Wages than in their own Country.

John Douglas Labourer from Dundee, goes out for the above Occasion John Mills and Thomas Hill Joiners from D^{o}. go to settle in S^{o}. Carolina.

Andrew Williamson, James Jamaison & William Mitchell Farmers & Fishermen from Schetland with their Wives & seven Children.

Farmers and Fishermen go abroad because the Landholders in Schetland have raised their rents so high that they could not live without sinking the little matter they had left. Total 20 Passengers.

N. B. no other Emigration from this Port or precinct in the Course of this week.

Signed Robert Whyt Coll^{r}:
Philip Paton Comp^{r}:

Port Stranraer, An Account of Emigrants shipped at Stranraer the 31st May 1775 on board the Jackie of Glasgow James Morris Master for New York in North America, with a Description of their Age, Quality, Occupation, Employment, Former Residence, On what Account and for what purposes they leave the Country.

25, Ja^{s}. Matheson, 38, Labourer, New Luce [near Stranraer], North Carolina, In hopes of good Employment.
26, Jean McQuiston, 27, ---, New Luce, North Carolina, ---.
27, Marg^{t}. Matheson, 4, ---, New Luce, North Carolina, ---.
28, Jno. McQuiston, 46, Labourer, Inch [near Stranraer], North Carolina, In hopes of better Employm^{t}.
29, Cathr: Walker, 46, ---, New Luce, North Carolina, For a better way of doing.
36, Ja^{s}. McBride, 38, Farmer, New Luce, North Carolina, The High rent of Land.
37, Janet McMiken, 39, ---, New Luce, North Carolina, ---.
38, Arch^{d}. McBride, 7, ---, New Luce, North Carolina, ---.
39, Eliz: McBride, 5, ---, New Luce, North Carolina, ---.
40, Jenny McBride, 4, ---, New Luce, North Carolina, ---.
61, Ja^{s}. Steven, 27, Farmer, Inch, N^{o}. Carolina, In hopes of better Bread.
62, Chr^{n}. Steven, 23, ---, Inch, N^{o}. Carolina, with her Brother.
63, Sarah Steven, 16, ---, Inch, N^{o}. Carolina, with her Brother.
64, Thos. Steven, 11, ---, Inch, N^{o}. Carolina, with his Brother.
65, Jno. Dalrymple, 40, Farmer, New Luce, N^{o}. Carolina, The High Rent of Land.
66, Marg. Gordon, 39, ---, New Luce, N^{o}. Carolina, ---.
67, Mary Dalrymple, 19, ---, New Luce, N^{o}. Carolina, ---.
68, Jn. Dalrymple, 17, ---, New Luce, N^{o}. Carolina, ---.
69, Arch^{d}. Dalrymple, 15, ---, New Luce, N^{o}. Carolina, ---.
70, Ja^{s}. Dalrymple, 11, ---, New Luce, N^{o}. Carolina, ---.
71, Ann Dalrymple, 9, ---, New Luce, N^{o}. Carolina, ---.
72, Janet Dalrymple, 7, ---, New Luce, N^{o}. Carolina, ---.
73, Jean Dalrymple, 5, ---, New Luce, N^{o}. Carolina, ---.

74, W^{m}. Dalrymple, 2, ---, New Luce, N^{o}. Carolina, ---.
75, Alex^{r}. McBride, 22, Labourer, New Luce, N^{o}. Carolina, In hopes of better Employment.
78, John Duff, 20, A Herdsman, New Luce, N^{o}. Carolina, In hopes of good Employ^{t}.
79, Wm Eckles, 40, Shoemaker, Inch, N^{o}. Carolina, In hopes of good Business.
80, Martha McKenzie, 45, ---, Inch, N^{o}. Carolina, ---.
81, John Eckles, 12, ---, Inch, N^{o}. Carolina, ---.

Customh^{o}. Stranraer 5 June 1775.

N. B. As all the Married Women follow their Husbands and the Children their parents, We have inserted no Reason, for their leaving the Country, after their Names.

John Clugston Collr.
Polk McIntire
Comp.

R. E. Philips to John Robinson

Sir,

In obedience to your Letter of the 8th. of December 1773, I am directed to inclose to you, a List of Persons who have taken their Passage from the Port of Greenock, for North America, on board the Ship Christy Hugh Rellie Master bound to New York, and Georgia, and the Ship Ulysses James Wilson Master bound for North Carolina, for the Information of the Right Honorable the Lords Commissioners of His Majestys Treasury.

Customhouse Edinburgh, 8th May 1775. R. E. Philips

Port Greenock List of Passengers from the 28th April 1775, Incl. to the 5 May 1775 Exclusive, [by the Ulysses James Wilson Master for North Carolina].

Math. Lyon, 49, Weaver, Glasgow, Want of Employ.
Mary Lyon, his spouse, 50, ---, Glasgow, ---.
James Lyon, 21, Weaver, Glasgow, Want of employ.
John Kennburgh, 24, Labourer, Glasgow, Want of employ.
James Kennburgh, 27, Labourer, Glasgow, Want of employ.
John McNabb, 24, Labourer, Argyleshire, Want of employ.
Jean Campbell his Spouse, 19, ---, Argyleshire, ---.
Tebby McNabb, 20, to get a husband, Argyleshire, ---.
Doug. McVey, 30, Labourer, Argyleshire, Want of employ.
James Buges, 27, Merchant, Edinb., to follow his business.
Marg. Hog his spouse, 25, to comfort her husband, Edinb., ---.

Ed. Penman D Coll^{r}
John McVicar D Comp

R. E. Philips to John Robinson

Sir

In obedience to your Letter of the 8th of December 1773, I am directed to inclose to you, a List of Persons who have taken their Passage from the Port of Greenock, for North America, on board the

Ship Monimia Edward Morrison Master, bound for New York, and the Ajax Robert Cunningham Master for North Carolina, for the Information of the Right Honorable the Lords Commissioners of His Majestys Treasury.

Custom house Edinburgh R. E. Philips
8th June 1775

List of Passengers from the 26th of May 1775 Inclusive to the 2d June 1775 Exclusive.

Walter Mcfarlane, 20, Gentleman, To be a Merchant, North Carolina, In the Ajax Robert Cunningham Master.

Mary Menzies, 25, Lady, Going to her Husband, ---, In the Ajax Robert Cunningham Master.

Edward Penman D. Collector
Signed John McVicar D. Compr
John Dunlop Tide Surveyor

Commissioners of the Customs in Scotland to John Robinson

Sir,

The inclosed Paper is a List of Persons lately sailed as Emigrants, to Wilmington in North Carolina, from the Port of Greenock, which We transmit to you Sir, for the Information of the Right Honorable the Lords Commissioners of the Treasury.

Archd Menzies
Charterhouse Edinburgh, 22 August 1774. George Clerk Maxwell
Basil Cochrane

List of Passengers on board the Ship Ulysses James Chalmers Masr for Wilmington in North Carolina.

Robet McNicol, 30, Glenurcha [Argyleshire], Gentn, High Rents and oppression.
Jean Campbell, 24, Glenurcha, his wife, ---.
Annapel McNicol their Daug., 8, Glenurcha, ---.
Abram Hunter, 28, Greenock, Shipmas., To Build.
Thomas Young, 21, Glasgow, Surgeon, To follow his Trade.
John McNicol, 24, Glenurcha, Workman, High rents & oppression.
Angus Galbreath, 30, Glenurcha, Workman, Poverty Occasioned by want of work.
Katrine Brown his wife, 26, ---, ---, Poverty Occasioned by want of work.
Angus Fletcher, 40, Glenurcha, Farmer, High rents & Oppression.
Katrine McIntyre his wife, 40, Glenurcha, ---, High rents & Oppression.
Euphame Fletcher, 10, Glenurcha, their child, High rents & Oppression.
Mary Fletcher, 6, Glenurcha, their child, High rents & Oppression.
Nancy Fletcher, 3, their child, High rents & Oppression.
John McIntyre, 45, Glenurcha, Farmer, High rents & Oppression.
Mary Downie, 35, Glenurcha, his wife, High rents & Oppression.

Nancy McIntyre, 11, Glenurcha, their child, High rents & Oppression.

Don[d] McIntyre, 8, Glenurcha, their child, High rents & Oppression.

Christy McIntyre, 5, Glenurcha, their child, High rents & Oppression.

John McIntyre, 4, Glenurcha, their child, High rents & Oppression.

Duncan McIntyre, 40, Glenurcha, Farmer, High rents & Oppression.

Katrine McIntyre, 28, Glenurcha, his wife, High rents & Oppression.

John Sinclair, 32, Glenurcha, Farmer, High rents & Oppression.

Mary Sinclair, 32, Glenurcha, his wife, High rents & Oppression.

Donald McIntyre, 28, Glenurcha, Farmer, High rents & Oppression.

Mary McIntyre, 25, Glenurcha, his wife, High rents & Oppression.

Don[d] McFarlane, 26, Glenurcha, Farmer, High rents & Oppression.

Don[d] McFarlane, 6, Glenurcha, his son, High rents & Oppression.

Duncan Sinclair, 24, Glenurcha, Farmer, High rents & Oppression.

Isobel McIntyre, 24, Glenurcha, his wife, High rents & Oppression.

John McIntyre, 35, Glenurcha, Farmer, High rents & Oppression.

Marg[t]. McIntyre, 30, Glenurcha, his wife, High rents & Oppression.

Malcolm McPherson, 40, Glenurcha, Farmer, High rents & Oppression.

Christ[n] Downie, 30, Glenurcha, his wife, High rents & Oppression.

Janet McPherson, 10, Glenurcha, their child, High rents & Oppression.

Will[m]. McPherson, 9, Glenurcha, their child, High rents & Oppression.

Will[m]. Picken, 32, Glenurcha, Farmer, High rents & Oppression.

Martha Huie, 26, Glenurcha, his wife, High rents & Oppression.

Rob[t] Howie, 18, Glenurcha, Workman, Poverty Occasion'd by want of work.

Arc[d] McMillan, 58, Glenurcha, Farmer, High rents & Oppression.

Mary Taylor, 40, Glenurcha, his wife, High rents & Oppression.

Barbra McMillan, 20, Glenurcha, their Daug[r], High rents & Oppression.

John Greenlees, 25, Kintyre [Argyleshire], Farmer, High rents & Oppression.

Mary Howie, 25, Kintyre, his wife, High rents & Oppression.

Peter McArthur, 58, Kintyre, Farmer, High rents & Oppression.

Chirs[t] Bride, 52, Kintyre, his wife, High rents & Oppression.

John McArthur, 16, Kintyre, their child, ---.

Ann McArthur, 38, Kintyre, their child, ---.

Jean McArthur, 20, Kintyre, their child, ---.

John McArthur, 28, Kintyre, their child, ---

Dan[l] Calewell, 18, Kintyre, Shoemaker, Poverty Occasion'd by want of work.

Robt Mitchell, 26, Kintyre, Taylor, Poverty Ocasion'd by want of work.
Ann Campbell, 19, Kintyre, his wife, Poverty Ocasion'd by want of work.
Alex^{r} Allan, 22, Kintyre, Workman, Poverty Ocasion'd by want of work.
Iver McMillan, 26, Kintyre, Farmer, High rents & Opression.
Jean Huie, 23, Kintyre, his wife, High rents & Opression.
John Ferguson, 19, Kintyre, Workman, Poverty Occasiond by by want of work.
Rob McKichan, 32, Kintyre, Farmer, High rents & Opression.
Janet McKendrick, 24, Kintyre, his wife, High rents & Opression.
Neil McKichan, 5, Kintyre, their son, High rents & Opression.
Mal^{m} McMullan, 58, Kintyre, Farmer, High rents & Opression.
Cath^{n} McArthur, 58, ---, his wife, ---.
Daniel McMillan, 24, ---, Farmer their child, High rents & Opression.
Arch^{d} McMillan, 16, ---, their child, High rents & Opression.
Gelb^{t} McMillan, 8, ---, their child, ---.
Don^{d} McKay, 20, ---, Taylor, High rents & Opression.
Danl Campbell, 25, ---, Farmer, High rents & Opression.
And^{w} Hyndman, 46, ---, Farmer, High rents & Opression.
Cath^{n} Campbell, 46, ---, his wife, High rents & Opression.
Mary Hindman, 18, ---, their child, High rents & Opression.
Marg^{t} Hyndman, 14, ---, their child, High rents & Opression.
Angus Gilchrist, 25, ---, their child, High rents & Opression.
Mal^{m} Smith, 64, ---, Farmer, High rents & Opression.
Mary McAlester, 64, ---, his wife, High rents & Opression.
Peter Smith, 23, ---, their child, High rents & Opression.
Mary Smith, 19, ---, their child, High rents & Opression.
Duncan McAllum, 22, ---, Shoemaker, High rents & Opression.
Cath^{n} McAlester, 30, ---, his wife, High rents & Opression.
Neil Thomson, 23, ---, Farmer, High rents & Opression.
David Beaton, 28, ---, Farmer, High rents & Opression.
Flora Bride, 29, ---, his Wife, High rents & Opression.
John Gilchrist, 25, ---, Cooper, High rents & Opression.
Marion Taylor, 21, ---, his wife, High rents & Opression.
Neil McNeil, 64, ---, Farmer, High rents & Opression.
Isobel Simpson, 64, ---, his wife, High rents & Opression.
Danl McNeil, 28, ---, their child, High rents & Opression.
Hector McNeil, 24, ---, their child, High rents & Opression.
Peter McNeil, 22, ---, their child, High rents & Opression.
Neil McNeil, 18, ---, their child, High rents & Opression.
Willm McNeil, 15, ---, their child, ---.
Mary McNeil, 9, ---, their child, ---.
Allan Cameron, 28, ---, Farmer, High rents & Opression.
Angus Cameron, 18, ---, Farmer, High rents & Opression.
Katrine Cameron, 21, ---, his wife, High rents & Opression.

Alex Campbell D Com^{r} Jo Clerk D. Coll^{r}
P^{t} Greenock John Dunlop T S

The above List of Passengers is from the 12th August 1774 Incl. to the 18th Augt 1774 Incl.

Commissioners of the Customs in Scotland to John Robinson

Sir

We have herewith transmitted a Copy of a Letter from the principal Officers of the Customs at Campbelton [near Kintyre], giving an Account of a Ship touching there, from Greenock, with Emigrants taken on board in the Island of Isla [Islay], which, if judged requisite, you will be pleased to lay before the Lords Commissioners of His Majestys Treasury.

Customho. Edinbg
3d. Jany 1775

M Cardonnel
George Clerk Maxwell
Basil Cochrane

Ronald Campbell and Archibald Buchanan to Commissioners of Customs in Scotland

Customhouse Campbelton
12th December 1774

Honourable Sirs,

In obedience to your Letter of the 15th of December 1773, We beg leave to acquaint your Honours that the Brigantine Carolina Packet Malcolm McNeil Master, with Goods from Greenock for Cape Fair in North Carolina, was put into this Harbour by a contrary wind on the 2d. and sailed on the 7th. instant, having on board sixty two Passengers, of whom thirty were men, fifteen Women, and seventeen Children; This Ship after sailing from Greenock, called at Lochindale in Isla, where the Passengers were taken on board, part of whom belonged to the Island of Isla, and part to the Island of Mull [north of Islay] who had come to Isla, to take their Passage.

By the best accounts we could get, only five of these Passengers were People of any consequence the rest were of a lower class, Servants of these Gentlemen, or Labourers who could pay for their Passage. We are &ca.

Signed Ronald Campbell
Archd Buchanan

Commissioners of the Customs in Scotland to John Robinson

Sir

The Officers of the Customs in the Islands of Schetland in consequence of the Instructions received from hence, having particularly examined sundry Emigrants for America, put into Schetland by Distress of Weather; We have inclosed the said Examinations, (Copies of them) as containing apparently the genuine Causes of many persons leaving the Country, and going to America, desiring you will lay the same before the Lords Commissioners of the Treasury for their Information.

Customho. Eding., 30th May 1774.

Archd Menzies
George Clerk Maxwell
Basil Cochrane

Port Lerwick [Shetland Islands]
Report of the Examination of the Emigrants from the Counties of Caithness and Sutherland on board the Ship Bachelor of Leith bound to Wilmington in North Carolina.

William Gordon saith that he is aged sixty and upwards, by Trade a Farmer, married, hath six children, who Emigrate with him, with the Wives and Children of his two sons John & Alexander Gordon. Resided last at Wymore in the Parish of Clyne in the County of Sutherland, upon Lands belonging to William Baillie of Rosehall. That having two sons already settled in Carolina, who wrote him encouraging him to come there, and finding the Rents of Lands raised in so much that a Possession for which his Grandfather paid only Eight Merks Scots he himself at last paid Sixty, he was induced to emigrate for the greater benefit of his children being himself and Old Man and lame so that it was indifferent to him in what Country he died. That his Circumstances were greatly reduced not only by the rise of Rents but by the loss of Cattle, particularly in the severe Winter 1771. That the lands on which he lived have often changed Masters, and that the Rents have been raised on every Change; and when Mr Baillie bought them they were farmed with the rest of his purchase to one Tacksman [a middleman who leased large areas and sublet small farms] at a very high Rent, who must also have his profits out of them. All these things concurring induced him to leave his own country in hopes that his Children would earn their Bread more comfortably elsewhere. That one of his sons is a Weaver and another a Shoe Maker, and he hopes they may get bread for themselves and be a help to support him.

William McKay, aged Thirty, by Trade a Farmer, married, hath three children from Eight to two years Old, besides one dead since he left his own country, resided last at ——— in the Parish of Farr in the County of Strathnaver upon the Estate of the Countess of Sutherland. Intends to go to Wilmington in North Carolina, because his stock being small, Crops failing, and bread excessively dear, and the price of Cattle low, he found he could not have bread for his Family at home, and was encouraged to emigrate by the Accounts received from his Countrymen who had gone to America before him, assuring him that he might procure a Comfortable Subsistence in that country. That the land he possessed was a Wadset of the Family of Sutherland to Mr Charles Gordon of Skelpick, lying in the height of the country of Strathnaver, the Rents were not raised.

W^m^. Sutherland, aged Forty, a Farmer, married, hath five children from 19 to 9 years old, lived last at Strathalidale in the Parish of Rea, in the County of Caithness, upon the Estate of the late Colonel McKay of Bighouse; Intends to go to North Carolina; left his own country because the Rents were raised, as Soldiers returning upon the peace with a little money had offered higher Rents; and longer Fines or Grassums [a premium paid to a feudal superior on entering upon the holding], besides the Services were oppressive in the highest degree. That from his farm which paid 60 Merks

Scots, he was obliged to find two Horses and two Servants from the middle of July to the end of Harvest solely at his own Expense, besides plowing, Cutting Turf, making middings [manure heaps], mixing Dung and leading it out in Seed time, and besides cutting, winning, leading and stacking 10 Fathoms of Peats yearly, all done without so much as a bit of bread or a drink to his Servants.

John Catanoch, aged Fifty Years, by Trade a Farmer, married, hath 4 Children from 19 to 7 years old; resided last at Chabster in the Parish of Rae, in the County of Caithness, upon the Estate of Mr. Alexr. Nicolson, Minister at Thurso, Intends to go to Wilmington North Carolina; left his own Country because crops failed, Bread became dear, the Rents of his Possession were raised from Two to Five Pounds Sterling, besides his Pasture or Common Grounds were taken up by placing new Tennants thereon, especially the grounds adjacent to his Farm, which were the only grounds on which his Cattle pastured. That this method of parking and placing Tenants on the pasture Grounds rendered his Farm useless, his Cattle died for want of Grass, and his Corn Farm was unfit to support his Family, after paying the Extravagant Tack duty. That beside the rise of Rents of Scarcity of bread, the Landlord exacted arbitrary and oppressive Services, such as obliging the Declarant to labour up his ground, cart, win, lead and stack his Peats, Mow, win and lead his Hay, and cut his Corn and lead it in the yard which took up about 30 or 40 days of his servants and Horses each year, without the least Acknowledgement for it, and without Victuals, save the men that mowed the Hay who got their Dinner only. That he was induced to Emigrate by Advices received from his Friends in America, that Provisions are extremely plenty & cheap, and the price of labour very high, so that People who are temperate and laborious have every Chance of bettering their circumstances- Adds that the price of Bread in the Country he hath left is greatly Enhanced by distilling, that being for so long a time so scarce and dear, and the price of Cattle at the same time reduced full one half while the Rents of lands have been raised nearly in the same proportion, all the smaller Farms must inevitably be ruined.

Eliz: McDonald, Aged 29, unmarried, servant to James Duncan in Mointle in the Parish of Farr in the County of Sutherland, Intends to go to Wilmington in North Carolina; left her own country because several of her Friends having gone to Carolina before her, had assured her that she would get much better service and greater Encouragement in Carolina than in her own Country.

Donald McDonald, Aged 29 years, by Trade a Farmer and Taylor, married, hath One Child six years Old. Resided last at Chapter in the Parish of Rae in the County of Caithness upon the Estate of Mr Alexr Nicolson Minister at Thurso, intends to go to Carolina; left his own Country for the reasons assigned by John Catanoch, as he resided in the same Town and was subjected to the same Hardships with the other. Complains as he doth of the advanced price of Corn, owing in a great measure to the consumption of it in Distilling.

John McBeath Aged 37, by Trade a Farmer and Shoe maker, Married, hath 5 children from 13 years to 9 months old. Resided last in Mault in the Parish of Kildonnan in the County of Sutherland, upon the Estate of Sutherland. Intends to go to Wilmington in North Carolina; left his own country because Crops failed, he lost his Cattle, the Rent of his Possession was raised, and bread had been long dear; he could get no Employment at home, whereby he could support himself and Family, being unable to buy Bread at the prices the Factors on the Estate of Sutherland & neighboring Estates exacted from him. That he was Encouraged to emigrate by the Accounts received from his own and his Wife's Friends already in America, assuring him that he would procure comfortable subsistence in that country for his Wife and Children, and that the price of labour was very high. He also assigns for the Cause of Bread being dear in his country that it is owing to the great quantities of Corn consumed in brewing Risquebah.

James Duncan, Aged twenty seven years, by Trade a Farmer, married, hath two Children, one five years the other 9 Months old. Resided last at Mondle in the Parish of Farr in the Shire of Sutherland, upon the Estate of Sutherland, Intends to go to Wilmington in North Carolina; left his own Country because Crops failed him for several years, and among the last years of his labouring he scarce reaped any Crop; Bread became dear and the price of Cattle so much reduced that One Cows price could only buy a Boll [a measure of 6 bushels generally in Scotland] of Meal. That the People on the Estate of Sutherland were often supplied with meal from Caithness, but the Farmers there had of late stopt the sale of their Meal, because it rendered them a much greater Profit by Distilling. That he could find no Employment at home whereby he could support his Family. That he has very promising Prospects by the Advices from his Friends in Carolina, as they have bettered their circumstances greatly since they went there by their labours. Lands being cheap and good Provisions plenty, and the price of Labour very encouraging.

Hector Mcdonald, Aged 75, Married, a Farmer, hath three sons who emigrate with him, John Alexander & George from 27 to 22 years old, also two Grand Children Hector Campbell aged 16, and Alex^{r} Campbell aged 12, who go to their Mother already in Carolina. Resided last at Langwall in the Parish of Rogart in the County of Sutherland, upon the Estate of Sutherland. Intends to go to North Carolina, Left his own Country because the Rents of his possession had been raised from One pound seven shillings to Four pounds, while the price of the Cattle raised upon it fell more than One half, and not being in a Corn Country the price of Bread was so far advanced, that a Cow formerly worth from 50sh. to £ 3 - could only purchase a Boll of Meal. He suffered much by the death of Cattle, and still more by oppressive Services exacted by the factor, being obliged to work with his People & Cattle for 40 days and more Each year, without a bit of Bread. That falling into reduced Circumstances he was assured by some of his children already in America that his Family might subsist more comfortably there, and in all events they can scarce be worse. Ascribes the excessive price of corn to the consumption of it in distilling.

William McDonald, Aged 71, by Trade a Farmer married hath 3 children from 7 to 5 years Old, who emigrate with him. Resided last at little Savall in the Parish of Lairg in the county of Sutherland, upon the Estate of Hugh Monro of Achanny. Intends to go to Wilmington in North Carolina; left his own Country because Crops failed, Bread became dear, the Rents of his possession were raised, but not so high as the Lands belonging to the neighboring Heritors, by which and the excessive price of Meal, the lowness of the price of Cattle, and still further by a Cautionary [personal security] by which he lost 30 £ Sterling, his Circumstances were much straightened, so that he could no longer support his Family at Home, tho' Mr. Monro used him with great humanity. That his Friends already in Carolina, have given him assurance of bettering his condition, as the price of labour is high and Provisions very cheap. Ascribes the high price of Corn to the Consumption of it in Distilling.

Hugh Matheson, Aged 32, married, hath 3 children from 8 to 2 years Old, also a Sister Kathrine Matheson aged 16, who emigrate with him, was a Farmer last at Rimsdale in the Parish of Kildonan in the County of Sutherland, Leaves his Country and goes to Carolina, because upon the rise of the price of Cattle some years ago the Rent of his Possession was raised from £2.16.0 to £5.10.0. But the price of Cattle has been of late so low, and that of Bread so high, that the Factor who was also a Drover would give no more than a Boll of Meal for a Cow, which was formerly worth from 50 sh to 3 £ and obliged the Tenants to give him their Cattle at his own price. That in these grassing Counties little Corn can be raised, and for some years past the little they had was in a great measure blighted and rendered useless by the frost which is common in the beginning of Autumn in the Inland parts of the Country. That in such Circumstances it seems impossible for Farmers to avoid Ruin, and their distresses heighten'd by the consumption of corn in distilling in a Grassing Country where little can be raised. That encouraged by his Friends already in America, he hath good hopes of bettering his Condition in that Country.

Willm. McKay, Aged 26, Married, a Farmer last at Craigie in the Parish of Rae and County of Caithness, upon the Estate of George McRay Island handy [Handa Island]; Goes to Carolina because the Rent of his Possession was raised to double at the same time that the price of Cattle was reduced one half, and even lower as he was obliged to sell them to the Factor at what price he pleased; at the same time his Crope was destroyed by bad Harvests, and Bread became excessively dear, owing in a great measure to the Consumption by distilling. That the Services were oppressive, being unlimited and arbitrary, at the pleasure of the Factor, and when by reason of sickness the Declarant could not perform them he was charged at the rate of one shilling p day. He had Assurances from his Friends in

America that the high price of labour and cheapness of Provisions would enable him to support himself in that Country.

Alex. Sinclair, Aged 36, Married, hath 3 children from 18 to 2 years Old, a Farmer last at Dollochcagy in the Parish of Rae and County of Caithness, upon the Estate of Sir John Sinclair of Murkle. Left his own Country and goes to Carolina, because the Tacksman of Sr John Sinclair's Estate, demanded an advanced Rent and Arbitrary Services, which in the present Distresses of the Country could not be complied with without ruin. That he is encouraged by his Friends in America to hope to better his Circumstances there.

George Grant, Aged twenty, Married, a Farmer last at Aschog in the Parish of Kildonan in the County of Sutherland on the Estate of ——————— Intends to go to North Carolina, because Crops failed so that he was obliged to buy four months Provisions in a year, and at the same time the price of Cattle was reduced more than One half. That his Brothers in Law, already in America have assured him that from the Cheapness of Provisions, and the high price of labour, he may better his Circumstances in that Country.

William Bain, Aged 37, a Widower, by Trade a Shopkeeper, resided last in Wick in the County of Caithness. Intends to go to Carolina. Left his own Country because he could not get bread in his Employment, the Poverty of the Common People with whom he dealt disabling them to pay their debts. Hopes to better his Condition in America, but in what business he cannot determine till he comes there.

George Morgan, Aged 37, Married, hath two children. One 7 the other One year Old, a Farmer last at Chabster in the Parish of Rae, and County of Caithness, upon lands belonging to M^{r}. Alex^{r}. Nicolson Minister at Thurso. Goes to Carolina leaving his country for the same reasons and upon the same Motives assigned by John Catanoch, who was his Neighbour. See Pages 3^{d} & 4th of this Report.

Willm Monro, Aged thirty four, Married, Emigrates with his Wife, a servant maid, and a servant boy, by Trade a Shoemaker, resided last at Borgymore in the Parish of Tongue, and County of Sutherland. Left his own Country as his Employment was little and he had no hopes of bettering his Circumstances in it, which he expects to do in America.

Patrick Ross, Aged thirty five Unmarried, lately Schoolmaster in the Parish of Farr, in the County of Sutherland. Goes to America on the Assurance of some of his Friends already in that Country of procuring a more profitable School for him.

Alex^{r}. Morison, Aged Sixty, Married, hath One Son and a Servant Maid, who emigrate with him; resided last at Kinside in the Parish of Tongue and County of Sutherland, on the Estate of Sutherland, by Occupation a Farmer. Left his Country as the Rents of his Possession were near doubled, the price of Cattle low, and little being raised in that Country, what they bought was excessive dear, beside the Tenans were in various ways opprest by Lord Raes Factors; and by the Reports from America he is in hopes of bettering his Circumstances in that Country.

George McKay, Aged 40, Married, hath one Child, a year old, by Trade a Taylor and Farmer, last at Strathoolie in the Parish of Kildonan and County of Sutherland, upon that part of the Estate of Sutherland set in Tack to George Gordon by whom his rent was augmented, and great Services demanded, vizt 12 days work yearly over and above what he paid to the Family of Sutherland. That the price of Cattle on which he chiefly depended was greatly reduced, and the little Corn raised in the Country almost totally blighted by Frost for two years past, by which the Farmers in general were brought into great distress. In these Circumstances he had no resource but to follow his Countrymen to America as the condition can scarce be worse.

Donald Gun, Aged thirty three, married, hath three Children from 8 years to 5 weeks old, by Trade a Taylor, resided last at Achinnaris in the Parish of Halerick in the County of Caithness. Finding he cannot make bread in his own Country, intends to go to America in hopes of doing it better there.

John Ross, Aged 47, a Widower hath six Children, from 20 to 5 years Old, who emigrate with him, by Trade a Farmer, last at Kabel in the Parish of Farr and County of Sutherland, upon the Estate of Sutherland. Goes to Carolina, because the rent of his Possession was greatly Advanced the price of Cattle which must pay that Rent reduced more than one half, and bread which they must always buy excessively dear. The evil is the greater that the Estate being parcelled out to different Factors and Tacksmen, these must oppress the subtenants, in order to raise a profit to themselves, particularly on the Article of Cattle, which they never fail to take at their own prices, lately at 20/- or 20 Merks, and seldom or never higher than 30/ tho' the same Cattle have been sold in the Country from 50 to 55 sh. By these means reduced in his circumstances, And encouraged by his Friends already in America, he hopes to live more comfortably in that Country.

James Sinclair, Aged twenty one years, a Farmer, married, hath no Children, resided last at Forsenain in the Parish of Rea, and County of Caithness, upon the Estate of Bighouse now possest by George McRay of Islandhanda, upon a Farm, paying 8 £ Sterling Rent, that he left his own Country because Crops of Corn had, and Bread was very dear; he had lost great part of his Cattle two years ago, the rearing Cattle being his principal business, the prices of Cattle were reduced on half while the Rents were nevertheless kept up and in many places advanced. In such Circumstances it was not possible for people of small stock to evite ruin. His Father, Mother and Sisters and some other Friends go along with him to Carolina, where he is informed land and Provisions are cheap, labour dear, and Crops seldom fail. What employment he shall follow there he hath not yet determined, but thinks it will be Husbandry.

Aeneas McLeod, Aged sixty, a Farmer, married, hath one Daughter 15 years Old. Resided last in the Parish of Tongue in the County of Sutherland upon the Estate of Lord Rae. Goes to Wilmington in North Carolina, where he proposes to live by day labour, being informed that one days Wages will support him a week. Left his own Country because upon the rise of the price of Cattle some years ago, the Rent of his Possession was raised from 28/ to 38/ a year, but thereafter when the price of Cattle was reduced one half the Rent was nevertheless still kept up. Moreover being near the house of Tongue, He was harrassed and oppressed with arbitrary Services daily called for without Wages or Maintenance.

Aeneas Mackay, Aged twenty, single, resided last with his Father in the Parish of Tongue and county of Sutherland; hath been taught to read, write and cypher, and goes to Carolina in hopes of being employed either as a Teacher or as a Clerk; He has several Relations and Acquaintances there already, who inform him he may get from 60 to 70 £ a year in this way, which is much better than he had any reason to expect at home.

Donald Campbell, Aged 50, a Farmer, married, has one Son 12 years Old, resided last in the Parish of Adrahoolish, in the County of Sutherland on the Estate of Rea. Intends to go to Carolina because the small Farm he possest could not keep a Plough, and he could not raise so much Corn by delving as maintain his Family and pay his Rent, which was advanced from 21/ to 30/. Has hopes of meeting an Uncle in America who will be able to put him in a way of gaining his Bread.

W^m^ McRay, Aged 37, a Farmer, married, has four Children from 8 years to 18 Months old; and one man Servant, who emigrate with him; resided last at Shathaledale in the Parish of Rea, and County of Caithness upon the Estate of George McRay of Bighouse. Left his Country because the Rent of his Possession was raised from 30 to 80 £ Scots, while at the same time the price of Cattle upon which his subsistence and the payment of his Rent chiefly depended had fallen in the last Seven years at least one half. In the year 1772 he lost of the little Crop his Farm produced and in Cattle to the value of 40 £ Sterling - under these loses and discouragements, he had assurances from a Brother and Sister already in Carolina, that a sober industrious man could not fail of living comfortably, Lands could be rented cheap, and Grounds not cleared purchased for 6^d^. an Acre, that the soil was fertile, and if a man could bring a small Sum of Money with him he might make rich very fast. He proposes to follow Agriculture but has not yet determined, whether he will purchase or rent a Possession.

Willm McLeod, Aged twenty six, a Farmer, married, has one Son two years old; resided last in the Parish of Adrachoolish, in the County of Sutherland, upon the Estate of Bighouse; intends to go to Wilmington in North Carolina, where he has a Brother settled who wrote him to come out assuring him that he would find a better Farm for him than he possest at home (the rent of which was considerably raised upon him) for One fourth of the Money, and that he will live more comfortably in every respect.

Hugh Monro, Aged twenty-six, a Shoemaker, married, hath no children. Resided last in the Parish of Tongue and County of Sutherland. Goes to Carolina upon assurance that Tradesmen of all kinds will find large Encouragement.

Willm. Sutherland Aged twenty four, married, left an only Child at home. Resided last in the Parish of Latheron and County of Caithness, upon the Estate of John Sutherland of Forse. Goes to Carolina because he lost his Cattle in 1772, and for a farm of 40/ Rent, was obliged to perform with his Family and his Horses so many and so arbitrary services to his Landlord at all times of the year, but especially in Seed time & Harvest, that he could not in two years he possest it, raise as much Corn as serve his Family for six months That his little Stock daily decreasing, he was encouraged to go to Carolina, by the Assurances of the fertility of the land, which yields three Crops a year, by which means Provisions are extremely cheap, Wheat being sold at 3 shills. a Boll, Potatoes at 1 Sh so that one Mans labour will maintain a Family of Twenty Persons. He has no Money, therefore proposes to employ himself as a Day labourer, his Wife can spin & Sew, and he has heard of many going out in the same way who are now substantial Farmers. At any rate he comforts himself in the hopes that he cannot be worse than he has been at home.

James McKay, Aged 60, a shoemaker, married, has one child, Resided last on Lord Raes Estate in Strathnaver. Left his own country, being exceeding poor, and assured by his Friends who contributed among them the money required to pay for his Passage, that he would find better employment in Carolina.

This and the 20 preceding Pages contain the Examination of the Emigrants on board the Ship Batchelor of Leith, Alexr Ramage Master, taken by the officers at the Port of Lerwick.

15th April 1774.

A List of Passengers or Emigrants on Board the Ship Jupiter of Larne Samuel Brown Master for Wilmington in North Carolina, their Names, Ages, Occupations or Employments and former Residence.

1, John Stewart, 48, Clothier, Glenurchy.
2, Elizabeth, 46, his wife, Glenurchy.
3, John Stewart, 15, their son, Glenurchy.
4, Margaret, 13, their Daughter, Glenurchy.
5, Janet, 12, their Daughter, Glenurchy.
6, Patrick Stewart, 6, their son, Glenurchy.
7, Elizabeth, 3, their Daughter, Glenurchy.
8, Donald MacIntire, 54, Labourer, Glenurchy.
9, Katherine, 41, His Wife, Glenurchy.
10, Mary, 12, their Daughter, Glenurchy.
11, Margaret, 9, their Daughter, Glenurchy.
12, John McIntire, 6, their son, Glenurchy.
13, Duncan McIntire, 5, their son, Glenurchy.
14, William Campbell, 28, Labourer, Glenurchy.
15, Katherine, 32, His Wife, Glenurchy.
16, Robert Campbell, 2, His Son, Glenurchy.
17, Duncan Campbell, ——, His Son an Infant, Glenurchy.

18, Donald Mac Nichol, 40, Labourer, Glenurchy.
19, Katherine, 33, His Wife, Glenurchy.
20, John McNicol, 6, their son, Glenurchy.
21, Nicol McNicol, 4, their son, Glenurchy.
22, Archibald McNicol, 2, their son, Glenurchy.
23, Mary, ——, their daughter an Infant, Glenurchy.
24, John McIntire, 35, Labourer, Glenurchy.
25, Ann, 32, His Wife, Glenurchy.
26, Margaret, 6, their Daughter, Glenurchy.
27, Archibald McIntire, 4, their Son, Glenurchy.
28, John McIntire, ——, their Son an Infant, Glenurchy.
29, Archibald Stewart, 30, Shoemaker, Glenurchy.
30, Ann Sinclair, 65, Spinster, Glenurchy.
31, Margarit her Daugh[r]., 25, Spinster, Glenurchy.
32, Ann McIntire, 60, Spinster, Glennurchy.
33, Christian Downy, 25, Spinster, Glennurchy.
34, Katherine McVane, 30, Spinster, Glennurchy.
35, Mary Downie, 4, her daughter, Glennurchy.
36, Joseph Downie an Infant, ——, her son, Glennurchy.
37, Dugal McCole, 38, Labourer, Glennurchy.
38, Ann, 38, his Wife, Glennurchy.
39, Marget, 10, their Daughter, Glennurchy.
40, Mary, 8, their Daughter, Glennurchy.
41, Sarah, 2, their Daughter, Glennurchy.
42, An Infant, ——, ——, Glennurchy.
43, Angus McNicol, 30, Labourer, Glennurchy.
44, Ann, 20, His Wife, Glennurchy.
45, Dougald Stewart, 40, Labourer, Glenurchy.
46, His Wife, 40, Labourer, Glenurchy.
47, John Stewart, 16, their son, Glenurchy.
48, James Stewart, 10, their son, Glenurchy.
49, Thomas Stewart, 6, their son, Glenurchy.
50, Alexander Stewart, 4, their son, Glenurchy.
51, Allan Stewart, 44, Late Lieut[t]. in Frasers Regiment, Apine.
52, Donald Carmichail, 22, His Servant, Apine [Argyle County].
53, Lilly Stewart, 7, his natural Daugh[r]., Apine.
54, Alexander Stewart, 35, Gentleman Farmer, Apine.
55, Charles Stewart, 15, His Son, Apine.
56, John McCole, 49, Labourer, Apine.
57, Mildred McCole, 40, His Wife, Apine.
58, John McCole, 16, their son, Apine.
59, Samuel McCole, 15, their son, Apine.
60, Donald McCole, 12, their son, Apine.
61, Dougald McCole, 8, their son, Apine.
62, Alexander McCole, 4, their son, Apine.
63, Katherine, 2, their Daughter, Apine.
64, Evan Carmichael, 40, Labourer, Apine.
65, Margaret, 38, His Wife, Apine.
66, Archibald Carmichael, 14, their Son, Apine.
67, Allan Carmichael, 12, their Son, Apine.

68, Katherine, 3, their Daughter, Apine.
69, Duncan McCole, 35, Farmer, Apine.
70, Christian, 35, His Wife, Apine.
71, Dugald McCole, 20, Their son, Apine.
72, Christian, 2, their Daughter, Apine.
73, Katherine, 3, their Daughter, Apine.
74, Malcolm McInish, 40, Labourer, Apine.
75, Jannet, 36, His Wife, Apine.
76, John McInish, 20, Their son, Apine.
77, Ann, 15, Their Daughter, Apine.
78, Catherine, 11, Their Daughter, Apine.
79, Donald McInish, 8, their Son, Apine.
80, Archibald McInish, 4, their Son, Apine.
81, Kenneth Stewart, 40, late Ship Master, Apine.
82, Isobel, 30, His Wife, Apine.
83, Alexander Stewart, 14, their Son, Apine.
84, John Stewart, 5, their Son, Apine.
85, Banco Stewart, 3, their Son, Apine.
86, Christian, 3, their Daughter, Apine.
87, William an Infant, ——, their son, Apine.
88, Mary Black, 16, their Servant, Apine.
89, Christian Carmichael, 14, their Servant, Apine.
90, John Black, 14, their Servant, Apine.
91, Dugald Carmichael, 55, Farmer, Apine.
92, Mary, 55, His Wife, Apine.
93, Archibald Colquhoun, 22, her Son, Apine.
94, Ann Colquhoun, 20, her Daughter, Apine.
95, Donald McCole, 34, Labourer, Apine.
96, Katherine, 40, his Wife, Apine.
97, Evan McCole, 6, their son, Apine.
98, John McIntire, 32, Taylor, Alpine.
99, Katherine, 30, his Wife, Alpine.
100, Donald McIntire, 3, their son, Alpine.
101, John McIntire, 1, their son, Alpine.
102, Gilbert McIntire, 34, Taylor, Alpine.
103, Ann, 36, his Wife, Alpine.
104, Charles McIntire, 11, their Son, Alpine.
105, Margaret, 9, their Daughter, Alpine.
106, Evan McIntyre, 5, their Son, Alpine.
107, Malcolm McIntire, 1, their Son, Alpine.
108, Duncan McCole, 45, Farmer, Alpine.
109, Christian, 40, His Wife, Alpine.
110, Duncan McCole, 21, His son, Alpine.
111, Mary, 18, their Daughter, Alpine.
112, Sarah, 15, their Daughter, Alpine.
113, Christian, 10, their Daughter, Alpine.
114, Mildred, 6, their Daughter, Alpine.
115, Ann, 3, their Daughter, Alpine.
116, Donald Black, 45, Labourer, Lismore [Argyle County].
117, Jannet, 34, His Wife, Lismore.

118, Christian, 8, his Daughter, Lismore.
119, Ann, 4, his Daughter, Lismore.
120, Ewen, 4, their Son, Lismore.
121, Duncan, 1-3/4, their Son, Lismore.
122, Archibald Carmichael, 26, Labourer, Lismore.
123, Mary, 26, His Wife, Lismore.
124, Catherine, 7, their Daughter, Lismore.
125, Lachlan McLaren, 25, Labourer, Apine.
126, Lawrine McLarine, 20, Joiner, Apine.
127, Donald McLaren, 12, Labourer, Apine.
128, Duncan McLaren, 30, Labourer, Apine.
129, David McCole, 30, Labourer, Apine.
130, Duncan McIntire, 55, Labourer, Apine.
131, Katherine, 55, His Wife, Apine.
132, May, 24, Their Daughter, Apine.
133, Katherine, 17, Their Daughter, Apine.
134, Elizabeth, 14, Their Daughter, Apine.
135, Miss Christy McDonald, 25, Symstress, Apine.
136, Duncan McCallum, 30, Labourer, Apine.

Reasons assigned by the Persons named on this and y[e] three preceeding Pages of this List for their Emigrating follows Viz[t]. The Farmers and Labourers who are taking their Passage in this Ship Unanimously declare that they never would have thought of leaving their native Country, could they have Supplied their Families in it. But such of them as were Farmers were obliged to quit their Lands either on account of the advanced Rent or to make room for Sheepherds. Those in particular from Apine say that out of one hundred Mark Land that formerly was occupied by Tennants who made their Rents by rearing Cattle and raising Grain, Thirty three Mark Land of it is now turned into Sheep Walks and they seem to think in a few years more, Two thirds of that Country, at least will be in the same State so of course the greatest part of the Inhabitants will be obliged to leave it. The Labourers Declare they could not Support their families on the Wages they earned and that it is not from any other motive but the dread of want that they quit a Country which above all others they would wish to live in. Captain Allan Stewart formerly a Lieutenant in Frasers Regiment goes with an Intention of settling in the Lands granted him by the Government at the End of last War. But should the Troubles continue in America he is Determined to make the Best of his way to Boston and Offer his Services to General Gage.

The Tradesmen have a prospect of getting better Wages but their principal reason seems to be that their relations are going and rather than part with them they chuse to go along.

Signed Duncan Campbell Collector
Neil Campbell Comptroller

September 4th. 1775.

Port Greenock List of Passengers from this Port from the 8th September 1774 inclusive, to the 15th September 1774 exclusive, [in the Diana, Dugald Ruthven for North Carolina].

William McDonald, Kintyre, Farmer, 40, Wilmington North Carolina, For High Rents & better Encouragement.

Isobel Wright, Kintyre, ——, 36, Wilmington North Carolina, For High Rents & better Encouragement.

Mary McDonald, Kintyre, ——, 4, Wilmington North Carolina, For High Rents & better Encouragement.

Jessy McDonald, Kintyre, ——, 2, Wilmington North Carolina, For High Rents & better Encouragement.

Archibald Campbell, Kintyre, Farmer, 38, Wilmington North Carolina, For High Rents & better Encouragement.

Jean McNeil, Kintyre, ——, 32, Wilmington North Carolina, For High Rents & better Encouragement.

Mary Campbell, Kintyre, ——, 7, Wilmington North Carolina, For High Rents & better Encouragement.

Lachlan Campbell, Kintyre, ——, 2, Wilmington North Carolina, For High Rents & better Encouragement.

Girzie Campbell, Kintyre, ——, 6, Wilmington North Carolina, For High Rents & better Encouragement.

Finlay Murchie, Kintyre, Farmer, 45, Wilmington North Carolina, For High Rents & better Encouragement.

Catherine Hendry, Kintyre, ——, 35, Wilmington North Carolina, For High Rents & better Encouragement.

Arch[d] McMurchy, Kintyre, ——, 10, Wilmington North Carolina, For High Rents & better Encouragement.

Charles McMurchy, Kintyre, ——, 5, Wilmington North Carolina, For High Rents & better Encouragement.

Neil McMurchy, Kintyre, ——, 3, Wilmington North Carolina, For High Rents & better Encouragement.

Barbara McMurchy, Kintyre, ——, 1/2, Wilmington North Carolina, For High Rents & better Encouragement.

Duncan McRob, Kintyre, Taylor, 26, Wilmington North Carolina, For High Rents & better Encouragement.

Elizabeth McMurchy, Kintyre, ——, 8, Wilmington North Carolina, For High Rents & better Encouragement.

Hugh Sillar, Kintyre, Farmer, 55, Wilmington, North Carolina, For High Rents & better Encouragement.

Catharine Currie, Kintyre, ——, 62, Wilmington North Carolina, For High Rents & better Encouragement.

Mary Sillar, Kintyre, ——, 27, Wilmington North Carolina, For High Rents & better Encouragement.

Catharine Sillar, Kintyre, ——, 23, Wilmington North Carolina, For High Rents & better Encouragement.

Gilbert McKenzie, Kintyre, Farmer, 34, Wilmington North Carolina, For High Rents & better Encouragement.

Mary McKenzie, Kintyre, ——, 27, Wilmington North Carolina, For High Rents & better Encouragement.

Arch[d]. McMillan, Kintyre, Farmer, —, Wilmington North Carolina, For High Rents & better Encouragement.

Patrick McMurchie, Kintyre, Farmer, 17, Wilmington North Carolina, For High Rents & better Encouragement.

Elizabeth Kelso, Kintyre, ——, 50, Wilmington North Carolina, For High Rents & better Encouragement.

Hugh McMurchie, Kintyre, Farmer, 46, Wilmington North Carolina, For High Rents & better Encouragement.

Arch[d] McMurchie, Kintyre, Farmer, 21, Wilmington North Carolina, For High Rents & better Encouragement.

Mary McMurchie, Kintyre, ——, 17, Wilmington North Carolina, For High Rents & better Encouragement.

Elizabeth McMurchie, Kintyre, ——, 14, Wilmington North Carolina, For High Rents & better Encouragement.

Robert McMurchie, Kintyre, ——, 9, Wilmington North Carolina, For High Rents & better Encouragement.

Neil Hendry, Kintyre, Taylor, 27, Wilmington North Carolina, For High Rents & better Encouragement.

Coll McAlester, Kintyre, Taylor, 24, Wilmington North Carolina, For High Rents & better Encouragement.

Mary McAlester, Kintyre, ——, 31, Wilmington North Carolina, For High Rents & better Encouragement.

John McVicar, Glasgow, Taylor, 36, Wilmington North Carolina, For High Rents & better Encouragement.

Alexander Speir, Glasgow, Clerk, 19, Wilmington North Carolina, For High Rents & better Encouragement.

Signed Jo Clerk D Coll[r]
Alex[r]. Campbell D Compt[r]

"Foreign Protestants for Carolina in 1679," *Proceedings of the Huguenot Society of London*, 10 (1912-1914), 187-189 [Lancour No. 233].

The two papers following are among the records of the Admiralty now preserved at the Public Record Office.

	hoes. Men.	fem. Woom.	enf. Child.
Mr. de Rousserie	1		
Mr. his friend	1		
Mr. alsoe his friend	1		
Mr. Crozar	2	2	
Mr. his friend	1		
Mr. Olivier	1		
Mr. Forestier	2		
Mr. Serré	1	1	2
Mr. Rousseau	1	1	6
Mr. Thibou	2	1	4

Mr. le Riche	1	2	
Mr. Varin	1	1	1
Mr. Fourré	1	1	6
Mr. Prevost	2	1	
Mr. Baston	1	1	1
Mr. Garder	1	1	
Mr. Guerard Junior	1		
Mr. Guerard one of ye undertakers .	7	3	4

rec[d] & read ye 15 Oct. 79 [1679].
Endorsed:—
Names of 18 Fr: Protestants
going to Carolina in the Richmond.
Adm. Navy Board, Miscellanea, 3537.
(*Miscellaneous Papers*, 1650-1680).

A List of ye Forraign Protestant Famillies which are willing to be transported for Carolina.

Wee whose names are underwritten doe hereby ingage & promise every one for himselfe to embarke our Selves & famillies on board of the Richemont or other his Ma[ties] Frigot as soone as wee become acquainted with her being ready to receive us, to be transported for Athley River or other part of Carolina lying more Southerly than the 34 Degrees of North lattitude, for to settle there ye manufactures of Silke, oyle, Wines &c, which many of us are skilled and practised in: Beeing all of us Forraign Protestant come from beyond ye Seas or having made our stopp in England upon ye account of this Voyage: during which we are to be maintained by Mr. René Petit & Mr. Jacob Guerard, Soe as his Ma[ty] shall be att noe farther Charges than to maintaine the Shipps Company and Such as shall be under his Maties pay.

Number of Famillies.	Number of persons.
Noé Serres of Brïe with his famillie composed of 6 persons	6
P. Roulleau (?) of Orleans with his Famillie . . .	8
Louis Thibou of Orleans with his Famillie	8
P. Guerard of Normandy with his Famillie	2
Samuel Conire (?) of Xaintonge with his Famillie . .	2
S. Siocart of Bordeaux with his Famillie	5
De Rousieryé of Languedoc with his Famillie . . .	3
...Jesue Dedayounnare of Normandy with her Famillie . .	4
Demas Depomar of Normandy with his Famillye . . .	3
[A] la marque de Jean Le Riche of ye Palatinat . . .	5
Expietienne Cazin of Paris with his famillie . . .	2
Jacque Varien &c of Rouen of Normandy with his famillie .	2
Triquiau of Allençon	3
Frere Foure of Paris with his Famillie	8
Piere Cofe (?) of Geneva	2
A. Prevost of Dieppe	3
Olivier of Dauphiné	3

Isaac Caton of picardy	3
Samuel Jermain of Diepe	2
Jean Garder of picardy	2
Forestier minster wth	6
Martin with his famillie of	5
In all 20 Famillies besides one of ye Undertakers composed of	14
[*sic*]	90

On the other side:—

We under written doe humbly Certifye that most of the Subscribers In the list mentioned on the other Syde being all forrain protestants have come to Us, And Promised Us, that they will be Ready to performe punctually the Conditions there In mentionned on their parte to be performed. Dated london the 8th of novembr 1679.

Peter Bar
Francis Tyssen.

Adm. Class 1, *No.* 5139 (*Orders in Council*, 1679-1688).
(*Communicated by Miss E. H. Fairbrother.*)

Daniel Ravenel. *"Liste des François et Suisses" from an Old Manuscript List of French and Swiss Protestants Settled in Charleston, on the Santee and at the Orange Quarter in Carolina Who Desired Naturalization. Prepared Probably about 1695-6*, 2nd ed. Baltimore [reprint], 1968 [Lancour No. 234].

This seventy-seven page work with a folding map contains a list of 154 French and Swiss refugees, with origins, who were anticipating naturalization in 1696.

Theodore D. Jervey. "The White Indentured Servants of South Carolina," *The South Carolina Historical and Genealogical Magazine*, 12 (1911), 163-171 [Lancour No. 235].

Mr. Lancour made reference to the list, from page 171, which is printed below.

List of Convicts Imported from Bristol to the province of So. Carolina on board the Ship called the Expedition John McKenzie was.

Edward Bond, Convicted 4th. October 1726 Com. Wilts Felony 7 Years.

Mary Walter,	Convicted
Henry Cooper,	16th. March 1727.
Eliz: Ends,	Com Wilts
Solomon Grar,	Felony
John Moore,	7 Years.

Wm. Purnell Eod. Die Com Wilts petty Larceny.

John Dudson,	Convicted 16 March 1727 Worcester
Thos. Oliver,	Felony 7 Years.
W^{m}. Thompson,	Convicted
Thos. Smith,	24 Augst
Mary Deeley,	Worcester
Jane Lewis,	Felony 7 Years.
Mary Robertson,	Convicted
W^{m}. Vaughn,	14 Sep^{t}. 1728
Sam: Foster,	at Bristol
Robt. Kates,	Felony
W^{m}. Fitchut,	7 Years.
W^{m}. Richardson,	Convicted 8 Janry 1728 at Bristol Felony 7 Years.
John Evans,	Convicted 22^{d} July 1728
Joseph Ashton,	at Gloucester
Ralph Phillips,	Felony 14 Years.
Caleb Stowell,	D^{o}
Mary Hillier,	Felony 7 Years.

Henry A. M. Smith. "Purrysburgh," *The South Carolina Historical and Genealogical Magazine*, 10 (1909), 187-219 [Lancour No. 236].

Pages 208-210 contain "A List of the Germains and Switz Protestants under the Command of Coll^{o} Purry qualified before his Excellency Robert Johnson Esquire Governour of this Province on the 22 and 23 days of December 1732," giving the names of ninety-three aliens naturalized at that time, with their ages only.

David Huguenin agé de	60
Susanne Jacot sa femme	47
Danl Huguenin son fils	14
David son fils	8
Abraham son fils	10
Marguerite sa fille	12
Josué Robert	56
Josué Robert son fils	21
Marie Madeleine sa fille	29
Anne Valleton Veuve de Pierre Jeanneret	49
Henry son fils	19
Jacques Abram son fils	17
Jean Pierre son fils	14
Marie sa fille age de	21
Rose Marie sa fille	9
François Buche	46
Margarette sa femme	50
Jean Pierre son fils	4
Danl Henry son fils	1
Abram son fils	2
Susanne sa fille	8

Henry Girardin	32
Marguerite sa femme	32
David son fils	7
Henry son fils	4
Anne sa fille	2
Francois Bachelois	46
Madeleine sa femme	36
Batiste son fils	6
Francois sa fille	3-1/2
Marie sa fille	1-1/2
La veuve Breton	53
Jean Pierre breton son fils agé de	17
Ulric bac age de	50
Jacob Calame age de	56
Abram Marte age de	60
David Giroud age de	18
Jacob Henry Meuron age de	19
Madame Varnod	
Abram Varnod son fils	
Francois son fils	
Frantions sa fille	
Mariane La fille	
Andriane Richard	
Monsieur Purry	
Monsieur buttal	
Monsieur Flar	

Names of the Germains

Jaque Winkler 15 de Lage	
Anna Catarina Winkler	43
Jaque Winkler	19
Nicholas Winkler	16
Son Jaque Winkler	9
Luis Winkler	6
Frederick Winkler	3
Eve Elizabeth	12
Theobald Küffer	49
Anna Margarita	40
Jaque Küffer	16
Theobald Küffer	13
Margaritt	14
Elissabeht Margaritt	11
Elizabeht Catarina	9
Maria Ottillia	4
Barbara	2
Luis Kohl	45
Anna Barbara	40
Son Nicolas	11
Son Jaquer	5
Nicolas	3

Margaritha	13
Anna Marill	8
Maria Margaritha	1
Nicolas Riger	46
Anna Barbara	36
Son Michael Riger	13
Janett Ottallia	18
Catarina Barbara	4
Henrich Cronenberger	40
Elizabeht	35
Nicolas Cronenberger	15
Gertrues	5
Anna Catharina	2
Sorg Mengersdorff	28
Anna Sibilla	26
Son Hendrick Mengersdorff	3
Elizabeht	2
Andrew Winckler	23
Anna Susan	23
Leonhards Franck	50
Anna Susana	48
Danl Franck	8
Christian Fuus	32
La Sama	45

Gilbert P. Voigt. "The German and German-Swiss Element in South Carolina, 1732-1752," *Bulletin of the University of South Carolina*, 103 (1922), 60 pages [Lancour No. 237].

The following list is copied, in modified format, from pages 56-60 of this title.

Some Saxe-Gothan Settlers.

The following list of German and German Swiss settlers at Saxe-Gotha, or Congaree, is only a partial one. In some instances the origin of the settler is given. There were two distinct elements, the German-Swiss (Reformed) and the German (Lutheran).

Date of Grant	Name	(Origin)
June 3, 1742.	Jno. Theyler	(Switzer)
" " "	Jac. Theiler	(Switzer)
" " "	Jac. Remensperger (Riemensperger)	(Switzer)
" " "	Ulrich Shillig	
" " "	Jno. Liver (Lever)	
" " "	Chas. Kansler (or Kanster)	
" " "	Hans Buss	
" " "	Henry Weiber	
" " "	Abram Giger (Geiger)	
" " "	Herman Gyger (Geiger)	

June	3,	1742.	Hans Jac. Gyger (Geiger)
"	"	"	Jno. Landriker (?)
"	"	"	Henry Boume
"	"	"	Casper Frey (Fry) (Switzer)
"	"	"	Julius Credy
"	"	"	John Gallasper
"	"	"	Martin Fridig (Friday)
"	"	"	Gasper Hanstear
Sept.	7,	1742.	John Frasher
March	2,	1743.	Jac. Spenler
June	8,	1743.	Jacob Young (Jung)
April	14,	1744.	Jno. Wessingher
Oct.	5,	1744.	Philip Pool
Nov.	29,	1744.	John Mathys (Mathias?) (near Saxe-Gotha)
Nov.	30,	1744.	Rudolph Buchter
Dec.	8,	1744.	Hanna Maria Stolea
"	"	"	Jno. Shillig
"	"	"	Michael Long (Berne)
Jan.	18,	1745.	Andrew Buck
"	"	"	Melchior Sower (Sauer)
Jan.	31,	1745.	Ulrick Bachman (Additional Grant)
Mar.	14,	1745.	J. J. Fridig (opposite SaxeGotha. Additional grant.)
Mar.	16,	1745.	Jacob Drafts
Mar.	18,	1745.	Mich'l Craft (Croft) (Wuerttemberg)
Mar.	19,	1745.	John Rester (Wuerttemberg)
Apr.	22,	1745.	Jno. Christian Hauser
June	6,	1747.	Godfrey Trayor (Dreher?)
Aug.	14,	1747.	Solomon Ade (Addy) (from Georgia)
Nov.	6,	1747.	Christian Kotiler (via Philadelphia)
"	"	"	Lawrence Wetzel
"	"	"	Jac. Stackley (opposite Saxe-Gotha)
"	"	"	Antony Cottler (Kotiler?)
"	"	"	Jno. Blewer (via Havana)
Nov.	10,	1747.	Jno. Abraham Schwerdafeger (Prussia)
Nov.	12,	1747.	Hans Eric Scheffer (German Protestant)
Nov.	18,	1747.	Jno. Teller (Switzer?)
Nov.	20,	1747.	Henry Ton (had arrived about 1737)
Jan.	13,	1748.	Conrad Scheis
"	"	"	David Amstutz (Berne. Had previous grant in Orangeburg)
Jan.	22,	1748.	Casper Fry (had arrived in 1737)
Jan.	28,	1748.	Catherine Croft (Kraft)
"	"	"	Abraham Eichler
Mar.	4,	1748.	Geo. Ackerman
Mar.	9,	1748.	Jacob Weaver. Arrived some time before.
"	"	"	Jno. Geger (near Saxe-Gotha. Arrived some years before).
Apr.	30,	1748.	Henry Fiesler
"	"	"	Conrad Scheis

Apr. 30, 1748.	John Friday
" " "	Anna Baumgart
May 19, 1748.	Mich'l Reais (From Georgia)
July 19, 1748.	Barbary Appeal (?)
" " "	Martin Hassemager
" " "	Christian Kohla (Kotiler?) (Near Saxe-Gotha)
" " "	Magdalen Appeal
" " "	Jacob Burchland
" " "	Barbary Husar
" " "	Henry Metz (Near Saxe-Gotha)
Dec. 20, 1748.	Conrade Myer (Meyer) (Switzer)
" " "	Jacob Warle
" " "	Mary Magdalen Millner
Jan. 6, 1749.	Christian Bendeker (Congrees or Waterees. Captured en route.)
Jan. 12, 1749.	Valentine Door
Jan. 19, 1749.	Geo. Hind
" " "	Maria Reyn
" " "	Jno. Bokman
" " "	Henry Crody
" " "	Jno. Hendrich Hillman
Jan. 24, 1749.	Margaret Swart (From Pennsylvania)
Feb. 2, 1749.	Gilbert Guilder
" " "	John Gable
Feb. 3, 1749.	Mary Ann Seaman (?)
" " "	Jno. Walder
Aug. 2, 1749.	Hans Bother (or Bothen)
" " "	John Struck
" " "	John Struck, Jr.
" " "	Christian Rottlesperger (Rodelsperger)
Sept. 6, 1749.	Baletis Affray

[The following are dated Oct. 17, 1749 and marked "Palatines."]

Joh. Kuller	Andreas Cranmer	Geo. Gottlieb
Mich'l Calfiel	Jno. Geo. Watchter	Jno. Adam Epting
Geo. Ludovick Finch	Jno. Geo. Buckheart	Nich. Prester
Geo. Hipp	Andreas Schwachler-	Nich. Dirr
Hans Mich'l Swagert	Conrad Beck [back	Chris'r Ramenstein
Joh. Rich	Jno. Titerly	Marg't Burkmayer
Joh. Circus	Conrad Burkmeier	Jos. Vorsner
Joh. Jac Leitzeit	Joh. Curner	Chris'r Henry Hoppold
Chris'r Saltzer	Verner Ulmer	Andreas Rift
Joh. Freyer	Jno. Geo. Lapp	Clemens Fromm
Fred'k Mack	Mich'l Looser	Evea Knoll
Andreas Emmesk		

[The following is transcribed exactly from page 60.]

Nov. 24, 1749.	Jno. David Mercle	(German.	Arrived	"lately")
" " "	Jos. Meyer	"	"	"
" " "	Joh. Herman	"	"	"
" " "	Jac. Hoffner	"	"	"
" " "	Peter Herr	"	"	"

Nov. 24, 1749.	Peter Hummel	(German. Arrived "lately")
" " "	Conrad Shirer	" " "
" " "	Michael Bucks	" " "
" " "	Jacob Bollmann	" " "
Dec. 17, 1749.	Frederick Schmebile..	(Above Saxe-Gotha)
Dec. 15, 1749.	Abraham Pflining	" " "
" " "	Hans Geo. Franz	" " (Switzer)
" " "	Hans Jacob Hogheim	" " (German)
" " "	Phil. Jac. Schuller	" " "
" " "	Anna Maria Ruffin (Ruff)	" " [*sic*]

Janie Revill. *A Compilation of the Original Lists of Protestant Immigrants to South Carolina, 1763-1773.* Columbia, S. C.: The State Co., 1939 [Lancour No. 238].

This 163 page work is a list, transcribed from the Journals of the Council of the Colony of South Carolina, giving the names of immigrants with the number of acres of land allotted under the Bounty Act of 1761.

A reprint of this work, dated 1974, is available from the Genealogical Publishing Company, Baltimore.

E. Merton Coulter, ed. "A List of the First Shipload of Georgia Settlers," *Georgia Historical Quarterly*, 31 (1947), 282-288 [Lancour No. 239].

This list by Captain Thomas of the *Anne* of persons sent to Georgia in November 1732, for the purpose of establishing the colony, has been reprinted together with Lancour No. 240 [see note below]. The 118 names are carefully annotated as to the subsequent careers of the settlers.

E. Merton Coulter and Albert B. Saye, eds. *A List of the Early Settlers of Georgia.* Athens, Ga.: The University of Georgia Press, 1949 [Lancour No. 240].

This work contains the names of approximately 2,800 emigrants to Georgia between June 1732 and June 1742, listed in two sections according to whether or not they paid their own way, with age, occupation, date of embarkation and date of arrival. No ships are mentioned.

A 1967 Athens reprint is available from the Genealogical Book Company. This reprint includes Lancour No. 239.

Adelaide L. Fries. *The Moravians in Georgia, 1735-1740*. Raleigh, N. C., 1905 [Lancour No. 240-1].

The following list of arrivals in Georgia is taken from pages 236 to 238.

April	6th,	1735.	August Gottlieb Spangenberg	From Germany.
"	"	"	John Töltschig	" "
"	7th,	"	Peter Rose	" "
"	"	"	Gotthard Demuth	" "
"	"	"	Gottfried Haberecht	" "
"	"	"	Anton Seifert	" "
"	"	"	Michael Haberland	" "
"	"	"	George Haberland	" "
"	"	"	George Waschke	" "
"	"	"	Friedrich Riedel	" "
Oct.	11th,	"	John Regnier	From Pennsylvania.
Feb.	17th,	1736.	David Nitschmann, (the Bishop)	From Germany.
"	23rd	"	Christian Adolph von Hermsdorf	" "
"	"	"	Henry Roscher	" "
"	"	"	John Andrew Dober	" "
"	"	"	Maria Catharine Dober, (wife of Andrew D.)	" "
"	"	"	George Neisser	" "
"	"	"	Augustin Neisser	" "
"	"	"	David Zeisberger	" "
"	"	"	Rosina Zeisberger, (wife of David Z.)	" "
"	"	"	David Tanneberger	" "
"	"	"	John Tanneberger, (son of David T.)	" "
"	"	"	David Jag	" "
"	"	"	John Michael Meyer	" "
"	"	"	Jacob Frank	" "
"	"	"	John Martin Mack	" "
"	"	"	Matthias Seybold	" "
"	"	"	Gottlieb Demuth	" "
"	"	"	John Böhner	" "
"	"	"	Matthias Böhnisch	" "
"	"	"	Regina Demuth, (wife of Gotthard D.)	" "
"	"	"	Judith Töltschig, (wife of John T.	" "
"	"	"	Catharine Riedel, (wife of Friedrich R.)	" "
"	"	"	Anna Waschke, (mother of George W.)	" "
"	"	"	Juliana Jäschke	" "
"	"	"	Rosina Haberecht, (wife of Gottfried H.)	" "

Sept. 16th, 1737.	Anna Catherina Rose, (daughters of Peter R.)	
" " "	Maria Magdalena Rose,	
Jan. 28th, 1738.	David Zeisberger, Jr.	From Holland.
" " "	John Michael Schober	" "
Oct. 16th, "	Peter Böhler, (missionary to negroes)	From Germany.
" " "	George Schulius, (assistant missionary)	[From Germany.]
" " "	Simon Peter Harper	From England.
May 18th, 1740.	John Hagen	From Germany.
Autumn, 1774.	Ludwig Müller	" "
" "	John George Wagner	" "
March 5th, 1775.	Andrew Brösing	From North Carolina.

Spain. Archivo General de Indias, Seville. *Catálogo de Pasajeros a Indias durante los Siglos XVI, XVII y XVIII Redactado por el Personal Facultativo del Archivo General de Indias bajo la Dirección del Director del Mismo Don Cristóbal Bermúdez Plata*, 3 vols. Sevilla: Imprenta Editorial de la Gavidia, 1940-1946 [Lancour No. 241].

The following lists were constructed from pages 233-285 of volume two of the Catalogue, which is carefully indexed by place. Lancour suggests that this work contains lists from 1538 to 1559, to Florida and Louisiana, while in fact "Louisiana" is a place name used in a later period, and all of the names given for Florida are from the year 1538. The Catalogue contains an index of ship masters which was not used in the compilation below.

Año 1538.

26 Enero [January].

3899. Pedro de Míguez, hijo de Pedro de Míguez y de Isabel de Morillo, vecino de Jaén, a la Florida [destination omitted hereafter]. V-62

3907. Francisco de Llera, hijo de Diego de Llera y de Catalina de Tejada, vecino de la villa de Rabanera... Presentó una información hecha en Baeza ante el escribano Juan Merlín, en 19 de Noviembre de 1537. V-62 v.

3908. Juan de Barrionuevo, hijo del Licenciado Marcos de Barrionuevo y de Ana de Henao, vecino de Avila... V-62 v.

En la cabecera del folio 271 figura, en letra de la época, la indicación siguiente: "La gente que pasa a la Florida con el adelantado don Hernando de Soto".

3914. Pedro de Gámez, hijo de Pedro de Gámez y de Isabel de Bovillo, vecino de Jaén... V-271

3915. Juan de Gámez, hijo de Hernando de Gámez y de Isabel de Pancorbo... V-271

3916. Luis de Gámez, hijo de Pedro de Gámez y de Isabel de Gormaz, natural de Jaén... V-271
3917. Juan Gómez, hijo de Tomás Çamarrón y de María del Salto, vecino de Jaén... V-271
3918. El Capitán Pedro Calderón, hijo de Rodrigo Calderón y de Beatriz de Hoces, vecino de Badajoz, con sus hijos: Isabel Sayaga, Rodrigo Calderón y Gonzalo de Hoces... V-271
3919. Luis Bravo, hijo de Baltasar Bravo y de Leonor Rodríguez, vecino de Badajoz... V-271
3920. Francisco Tarascón, hijo de Diego de Segovia y de Isabel Docano, vecino de Badajoz... V-271
3921. Diego de Castro, hijo de Pedro de Castro y de Mari Sánchez, vecino de Badajoz... V-271
3922. Juan Suárez, hijo de Pedro de Santamaría y de Juana Suárez, vecino de Cáceres... V-271 v.
3923. Juan Periáñez, hijo de Cristobal Periáñez y de María González, vecino de Alcantara... V-271 v.
3924. Andrés Hernández, hijo de Martín Hernández y de Beatriz Mora, vecino de Badajoz... V-271 v.
3925. Esteban de Vega, hijo de Juan de Vega y Mari Miguela, vecinos de Vega... V-271 v.
3926. Juan de Cieza, hijo de Hernando de Cieza y de Beatriz Alvarez, vecinos de Valladolid... V-271 v.
3927. Francisco de la Rocha, hijo de Vasco de Medina y de Isabel González de la Rocha, vecino de Badajoz... V-271 v.
3928. Baltasar Maldonado, hijo de Blas Maldonado y de Beatriz Méndez, vecino de Salvatierra... V-271 v.
3929. Juan del Nieto, hijo de Pedro Nieto y de Catalina Hernández, vecino de Saldaña... V-271 v.
3930. Baltasar Hernández, hijo de Francisco Hernández y de Catalina Martín, vecinos de Badajoz... V-272
3931. Alonso Gutiérrez, hijo de Diego Macías y de Isabel Gutiérrez, vecino de Mérida... V-272
3932. Diego Vázquez, hijo de Lope Vázquez y de Constanza Margarida, vecino de Villar del Rey... V-272
3933. Juaz Díaz, hijo de Rodrigo Díaz y de Catalina Vázquez, vecinos de Badajoz... V-272
3934. Bernal García y Hernand Sánchez, hijos de Toribio Sánchez y de Mari Gómez, vecinos de Badajoz... V-272
3935. El Capitan Alvaro Nieto, hijo de Pedro Martín Nieto y de Mari Sánchez de Torrejena, vecino de Alburquerque, y sus hermanos Esteban de Torrejena y Juan Nieto... V-272
3936. Juan Hernández, [hijo] de Francisco Pérez Pentiero y de Catalina Martín, vecino de Alburquerque... V-272
3937. Juan García Pachudo, hijo de Gonzalo García Pachudo y de María Rodríguez la Pachuda... V-272
3938. Blas de Vargas, hijo del Maestre Bartolomé y de María de Vargas, vecinos de Alburquerque... V-272 v.
3939. Juan Rodríguez Terrón, hijo de Francisco Hernández Terrón y de Leonor Rodríguez del Valle, vecinos de Alburquerque... V-272 v.

3940. Juan Landro, hijo de Alonso Ramos y de Beatriz Rodríguez Landro, vecino de Alburquerque... V-272 v.

3941. Alvaro Preciado, hijo de Juan Preciado y de Catalina González, vecino de Alburquerque... V-272 v.

3942. Pedro Martín, hijo de Pascual Sánchez y de Clara Martín, vecinos de Alburquerque... V-272 v.

3943. Bartolome Rodríguez Landero, hijo de Alonso Rodríguez Landero y de Isabel Pérez, vecinos de Alburquerque... V-272 v.

3944. Diego Sánchez, hijo de Juan Lorenzo y de Leonor Sánchez, vecinos de Alburquerque... V-272 v.

30 Enero.

4048. Pedro Pérez, hijo de Alonso Pérez y de Inés Hernández, vecino de Alburquerque... V-279 v.

4049. Francisco Bragado, hijo de Juan Rodríguez Bragado y de Catalina Pérez, vecinos de Alburquerque... V-279 v.

4050. Domingos Hernandez, hijo de Juan Vázquez y de Constanza Hernández, vecinos de San Vicente... V-280

4051. Francisco de Robles, hijo de Juan de Robles y de María Fernández, vecino de Oropesa... V-280

4052. Bartolomé de Oropesa, hijo de Fernando de Sandoval y de Catalina Sánchez, vecinos de Oropesa... V-280

4053. Andrés de Basconcelos, hijo de Gómez de Silva y de doña Guiomar Pacheca, vecinos de Badajoz... V-280

4054. Antón Martín, hijo de Baco [*sic*] Martín y de Catalina Margallas, vecinos de Badajoz... V-280

4055. Gonzalo Alonso, hijo de Alonso García y de Inés Pérez, vecino de Badajoz... V-280

4056. Antón Rodríguez, hijo de Andrés López y de Beatriz Rodríguez, vecinos de Badajoz... V-280

4057. Alvaro de Coto, hijo de Andrés López y de Beatriz Alvaro, vecinos de Badajoz...

4058. Pedro Alonso, hijo de Juan Fernández y de Catalina Fernández, vecinos de Badajoz... V-280 v.

4059. Rodrigo Sánchez, hijo de Alvaro Rodríguez y de Isabel de Rivera, vecino de Montijo... V-280 v.

4060. Domingo Sardina, hijo de Bartolomé Vázquez y de Isabel Rodrígeuz... V-280 v.

4061. Manuel López, hijo de Pedro López y de Catalina López... V-280 v.

31 Enero.

4064. Francisco de Guzmán, hijo de Benito Rodríguez y de Francisca Hernández, vecinos de Sevilla... V-281

4065. Jerónimo de Herrera, hijo de Juan López y de María Herrera, vecinos de Cheles, cerca de Badajoz... V-281

1 Febrero.

4071. Leonardo de Angulo, hijo de Juan de Angulo y de Catalina Rodríguez, vecino de Villalar, cabe Tordesillas... V-281

4072. Alvaro Pérez, hijo de Alvaro Pérez y de Elvira Alonso, vecino de Almendralejo... V-281

4073. Alonso Hernández de Sevilla, hijo de Alonso Hernández de Sevilla y de Juana García, vecino de la Fuente del Maestre... V-281

4074. Gómez Hernández, hijo de Gómez Hernández y de Leonor Lavada, vecino de Almendralejo... V-281

4075. García Martín, hijo de Bartolomé Pérez y de Catalina Alonso, vecino de la Fuente del Maestre... V-281 v.

4076. Hernando de Miruena, hijo de Juan de Miruena y de Mari González, vecino de Talavera... V-281

4077. Cosme de Salamanca, hijo de Pedro de Pascua y de Ursula Martínez, vecino de Salamanca... V-281 v.

4078. Mateo Gómez, hijo de Alonso Gómez y de Giomar Alonso, vecino de Alburquerque... [*Este asiento tiene la indicación "nihil" V. n.° 4066*]. V-281 v.

4079. Pedro Mexía, hijo de Pedro Martín, vecino de la villa de Alcuexcar, y de Juan García... V-281 v.

4080. Pedro de Godoy, hijo de Pedro Cornejo y de María Pantoja, vecinos de Mérida... V-281 v.

4081. Andrés Serrano, hijo de Andrés Serrano y de Juana Hernández, vecino de la Aceña de Lara... V-281 v.

4082. Alonso Rodríguez, hijo de Asencio García y de María Rodríguez, vecinos de la villa de Zafra [*Este asiento tiene la indicación "nihil" V. n.° 4067*]... V-281 v.

4083. Pedro Moreno, hijo de Pedro Moreno y de Constanza López de Miranda, vecinos de Puentedehume... V-282

4084. Alonso de Raya, hijo de Juan de Raya y de Catalina de Cazorla, vecino de Ubeda... V-282

4 Febrero.

4085. Francisco Hernández, hijo de Martin Hernández y de Juana Hernández, vecinos de Navarrete... V-282

4086. Juan de Ortuño, hijo de Pedro Ortuño y de Juana, vecino de Arançana... V-282

4087. Pero Díaz, hijo de Juan García Colchero y de Beatriz García, vecinos de Llerena... V-282 v.

5 Febrero.

4088. Juan Bautista, hijo del Licenciado Diego Alonso y de Isabel de Castilla, vecino de Toledo... V-282 v.

5 Mayo.

4089. Alonso de Villalobos, hijo de Francisco de Villalobos y de Catalina de Peñalosa, vecinos de Jaén... V-282 v.

6 Febrero.

4093. Ximón Báez, hijo de Gonzalo Báez y de Catalina Alonso, vecino de la Nava del Membrillo, tierra de Mérida... V-282 v.

4094. Alonso Macías, hijo de Bartolomé Macías y de Ana Sánchez, vecino de la Nava del Membrillo, tierra de Mérida... V-282 v.

4095. Andrés Marín, hijo de Alonso Sánchez, cepillero, y de Catalina Marín, vecino de la Nava del Membrillo, tierra de Mérida... V-283

4096. Alonso Pacheco, hijo de Diego Pacheco y de Juana Martín, vecinos de la Nava del Membrillo, tierra de Mérida... V-283

4097. Martín Dorel, hijo de Francisco Dorel y de María Fernández, vecinos de Arenillas, tierra de Campos... V-283

4098. Pedro Alonso, hijo de Pedro Alonso y de Isabel González, vecino de la villa de Usagre... V-283

4099. Pedro Grajero, hijo de Alonso Grajero y de Catalina Márquez, vecino de Llerena... V-283

4100. Juan Villegas, hijo de García Hernández y de Teresa Villegas, vecino de Valencia de la Torre... V-282

4101. Juan de Aguilar, hijo de Juan Sánchez y de Catalina Sánchez, vecinos de Valencia de la Torre... V-283

4102. Alonso Cornejo, hijo de Francisco Cornejo y de Leonor González, vecino de Valencia de la Torre... V-283 v.

4103. Juan Gutiérrez, hijo de Francisco Gómez Montero y de Isabel Gutiérrez, vecino de Usagre... V-283 v.

4104. Juan García Xena, hijo de Juan García Xena y de Teresa González, vecino de Usagre... V-283 v.

4105. Vasco Martín, hijo de Juan Vásquez y de Violante Alonso, vecino de Usagre... V-283 v.

4106. Francisco Gómez, hijo de Francisco Gómez y de Isabel Gutiérrez, vecinos de Usagre... V-283 v.

4107. Alonso Sánchez Holgado, hijo de Alonso Sánchez Holgado y de Constanza Alonso, vecino de Usagre... V-283 v.

4108. Juan Martín, hijo de Andrés García y de Inés García, vecino de Usagre... V-283 v.

4109. Juan Martín, hijo de Juan Virgino y de Mari García, vecinos de Usagre... V-283 v.

4110. Juan Domínguez, hijo de Hernan Domínguez y de Catalina Martín, vecinos de Usagre... V-283 v.

4111. Alonso de Pereda, de color loro, hijo de Alonso de Pereda y de Margarita, natural de Talavera, a la Florida. Presentó una carta de ahorría, por la cual parece ser libre, que pasó ante Felipe Rodríguez escribano público de la villa de Talavera en 11 de Octubre 1537... V-283 v.

4112. Juan González, hijo de Alonso Miguel y de Mencía Gutiérrez, vecinos de Usagre... V-284

4113. Rodrigo de Soto, hijo de Juan García de Monasterio y de Mari Guirao, vecino de Usagre... V-284

4114. Francisco Muñoz, hijo de Diego Muñoz y de Leonor González, vecino de Usagre... V-284

8 Febrero.

4115. Toribio Sánchez, hijo de Toribio Sánchez y de Mari Sánchez, vecino de tierra de Béjar... V-284

7 Febrero.

4116. Alonso Moreno, hijo de Juan Moreno y de Mencía Sánchez, vecinos de Badajoz... V-284

4117. Alonso Hernández, hijo de Diego Hernández Bejarano y de Juana Fernández, vecinos de Juciana... V-284 v.

8 Febrero.

4122. Martín de Murga, hijo de Martín de Murga y de María Ochoa, vecinos de Murga... V-284 v.

4123. Juan de Çarate, hijo de Juan de Çarate y de María de Tejada, vecino de Ordua... V-284 v.
4124. Diego Pérez, herrador, hijo de Francisco Fernández y de Beatriz, vecino de Sevilla, a Florida, con su hijo Bartolomé Ruiz, calcetero... V-284 v.

9 Febrero.

4125. Pedro Hernandez de Rivera, hijo de Pedro de Ribera y de Teresa Rodríguez, vecinos de Mondoñedo... V-285
4126. Juan Ruiz de Çaras, hijo de Alonso de Arévalo y de Mari Alvarez del Canto... V-285
4127. Cristóbal García de Salamanca, hijo de Cristóbal García y de María Fernández, vecino de Salamanca... V-285
4128. Juan Hernández, hijo de Alonso Hernández y de Catalina Hernández, vecino de Castrojeriz... V-285

11 Febrero.

4129. Bernabé Manjón, hijo de Alonso García y de Mari González, vecino de Iznatorafe... V-285
4130. Andrés García, hijo de Pedro García y de Mari García, vecinos de León... V-285 v.
4131. Arias de Vinanbres, hijo de Rodrigo de Vinanbres y de Inés García, vecinos de Astorga... V-285 v.

12 Febrero.

4132. Luis Moreno, de color loro, vecino de Ubeda, a la Florida, en compañía del factor Luis Hernández Biedma. Presentó una carta de ahorría, por la cual parece ser libre, fecha en Ubeda ante Martín Hernández de Montiel, escribano público, en 25 de Enero de 1538... V-285 v.
4133. Juan de Barrutia, hijo de Pedro de Barrutia y de Mari Martínez de Mendía, vecinos de Mondragón... V-285 v.
4134. Diego García de León, hijo de Diego de León, Alcalde de Villanueva de Barcarrota, y de Mayor García, vecinos de la dicha villa... V-285 v.
4135. Pedro Blasco, hijo de Diego Vázquez y de María Vázquez, vecino de Villanueva de Barcarrota... V-286
4136. Juan de Acosta, hijo de Hernando de Acosta y de Juana Rodríguez, vecino de Villanueva de Barcarrota... V-286
4137. Francisco Vázquez, hijo de Antón Vázquez y de Catalina Pérez, vecinos de Villanueva de Barcarrota... V-286
4138. Manuel Castaño, hijo de Juan Castaño y de María Rodríguez, vecinos de Villanueva de Barcarrota... V-286
4139. Francisco de Cisnero, hijo de Pedro de Cisnero y de María López, vecinos de Fregenal, a la Florida. Lleva consigo a Diego de Cisnero, su hijo y a Inés Rodríguez, su mujer... V-286
4140. Juan Méndez Solís, hijo de Pero González y de Catalina Sánchez, vecinos de Susona... V-286

13 Febrero.

4148. Toribio Hernández, hijo de Juan Rodríguez y de Juana Hernández, vecinos de Viego... V-286 v.
4149. Juan de Vargas y Vasco Núñez de Vargas, hijos de Hernando de Vargas y de Inés Alvarez de Balboa, vecinos de Burguillos, tierra del Duque de Béjar... V-286 v.

4150. Francisco Méndez, hijo de Francisco de Sotomayor y de Leonor Rodríguez, vecinos de Burguillos... V-286 v.
4151. Juan Gómez, hijo de Juan Gómez y de Juana Gómez, vecino de Llemaya, que es del Duque de Alba... V-286 v.
4152. Luis de Fuentes, hijo de García de Fuente y de Beatriz de Escobar, vecino de Sevilla... V-286 v.
4153. Pedro de Soria, hijo de Juan de Soria y de Ana, vecino de Oropesa... V-287
4154. Pedro de Torres, hijo de Alonso Martín y de Elvira de Torres, vecinos de Medina del Campo... V-287
4155. Santiago Descobar, hijo de Diego Martínez Pimienta y de María de Ponte, vecino de Becerril del Campo... V-287
4156. Pedro Hernández, hijo de Sebastián Gómez y de Juana Sánchez, vecino de Horcajo de la Rivera... V-287
4157. Francisco Pérez, hijo de Juan Pérez y de María Sanchez, vecino de Horcajo de la Rivera... V-287
4158. Juan de Lobera, gallego, hijo de [*Está imcompleto este asiento*]... V-287
4159. Diego de Paz, hijo de Francisco de Paz y de Agueda de Gaona, vecino de Segovia... V-287 v.

14 Febrero.

4160. Alonso Caro, hijo de Juan García Caro y de María Hernández, vecinos de Medellín... V-287 v.
4161. Juan Calderón, hijo de Alvaro García Calderón y de Teresa Alvarez, vecino de Medellín... V-287 v.
4162. Lope de Escobar, hijo de Alonso de Escobar y de María de Herrera, vecinos de Medellín... V-287 v.
4163. García de Godoy, hijo de Hernando de Xerez y de Elvira de Godoy, vecinos de Medellín... V-287 v.
4164. Alvaro de la Cadena, hijo de Lope de la Cadena y de Elvira Núñez de la Parada, vecinos de Medellín... V-288
4165. Gonzalo Martín, hijo de Tome Sánchez y de Catalina Rodríguez, vecinos de Medellín... V-288
4166. Alonso Mendano, hijo de Rodrigo Mendano y de Catalina García, vecinos de Medellín... V-288
4167. Manuel Hernández, hijo de Alvaro Pérez y de Isabel Hernández, vecinos de Badajoz... V-288
4168. Pedro Delgado, hijo de Esteban Delgado y de Catalina Rodríguez, vecino de Medellín... V-288 v.
4169. Alonso Sánchez de Medina, hijo de Diego de Medina y de Catalina Sánchez, vecino de Medellín... V-288 v.
4170. Francisco Cumplido, hijo de Antón Cumplido y de Francisca Vellosa... V-288 v.
4171. Esteban Pérez Conejo, hijo de Hernán Pérez Conejo y de Juana Sánchez, vecino de Llerena... V-288 v.
4172. Juan Clemente, hijo de Hernando Alonso Tarrabajano y de Francisca Sánchez, vecinos de Sevilla, a la Florida, con su mujer Isabel de Herrera y su hija Inés de Herrera... V-288 v.
4173. Pedro Valenciano, hijo de Juan Valenciano y de Catalina García, vecino de Valencia... V-289

4174. Pedro Arias, hijo de Diego Arias y de Isabel de Sedano, vecino de Astorga... V-289

4175. Alonso Çapata, hijo de Cristóbal López y de Juana Sánchez, vecinos de Sevilla... V-289

4176. Pedro de Angulo, hijo de Pedro de Angulo y de Isabel de Tamayo, vecinos de los Barrios de Gureba... V-289

4177. Juan de Leiba, hijo de Diego de Leiba y de Juana de la Ventana, vecinos de Leiva... V-289

4178. Alonso de Angulo, hijo de Juan de Angulo y de Beatriz de Palacios, vecinos de Arçiniega... V-289

4179. Martín de Frías, hijo de Diego de Valderrama y de Isabel de Frías, vecinos de Frías... V-289

4180. Diego de Meneses, hijo de Juan de Meneses y de Mari Gutiérrez, vecinos de Talavera de la Reina... V-289 v.

15 Febrero.

4182. Pedro de Arévalo, hijo de Pedro de Arévalo y de Ana Calderón... V-289 v.

4183. Juan Flores, hijo de Alonso Flores y de Catalina Alonso, vecinos de Badajoz... V-289 v.

4184. Gonzalo Hernández Barreto, hijo de Juan Barreto y de Catalina González, vecinos de Badajoz... V-289 v.

4185. Juan Carrón, hijo de Juan Esteban y de Isabel Hernández, vecino de Badajoz... V-289 v.

4186. Hernando Muñoz, hijo de Juan Muñoz y de María González, vecinos de Celleros... V-289 v.

4187. Bartolomé Guisado, hijo de Lorenzo Guisado y de Inés García, vecinos de Cabril (?)... V-290

4188. Lucas de Paredes, hijo de Andrés de Paredes ye de Leonor Torquemada, vecino de Paredes... V-290

4189. Juan de Paredes, hijo de Juan de Paredes y de Francisca López, vecino de Paredes... V-290

4190. Francisco Galochero, hijo de Antonio Calochero [*sic*] y de Juana la Guerrera, vecino de Paredes... V-290

4191. Juan de Pravia, hijo de Juan Hernández, escribano, y de Mencía Hernández de Grado, vecino de Pravia... V-290

4192. Domingo Ramos, hijo de Alonso Ramos y de Beatriz Rodríguez Landera, vecinos de Alburquerque... V-290

4193. Juan de Anguis, hijo de Diego de Anguis y de Catalina de Mesa, vecino de Ubeda... V-290

4194. Rodrigo Çaydino, hijo de Rodrigo Alonso Çaydino y de Constanza Díaz, vecino de Alburquerque... V-290

4195. Juan Rodríguez, hijo de Ginés Rodríguez y de Isabel Gómez, vecino de Fregenal... V-290 v.

4196. Alonso Pérez, hijo de Cristóbal Pérez de Rivadeneyra y de Francisca de Nava, vecinos de Maqueda... V-290 v.

4197. Gonzalo de Villegas, hijo de Juan de Villegas y de Beatriz de la Cueva, vecino de Palencia... V-290 v.

16 Febrero.

4211. Juan de la Peña, hijo de Iñigo de Villán y de Catalina Díaz de la Peña, vecino de Salinas de Ruyseco... V-290 v.

4212. Sancho de Torres, hijo de Sancho Martínez de Torres y de Elvira Sánchez Guerra, vecinos de Quintanilla de Pienço... V-290 v.

4213. Juan de Retes, hijo de Juan Iñiguez y de María López de Retes... V-290 v.

4214. Juan de Vega, hijo de Gonzalo Téllez de Vega y de Juana Téllez de Vega, vecinos de Badajoz... V-291

4215. Hernando de Vega, hijo de Juan de Vega y de doña Catalina Pinel, vecino de Jerez, cerca de Badajoz... V-291

4216. Pedro Núñez de Prado, hijo de Juan Núñez de Prado y de doña María de Solís, vecinos de Fuente de Arco... V-291

4217. Manuel de Torres, hijo de Francisco de Torres y de Catalina García, vecinos de Badajoz... V-291

4218. Juan de Molina, hijo de Bartolomé Ximénez y de Teresa de Vera, vecino de Ubeda... V-291

4219. Hernand Herrero, hijo de Juan García Herrero y de Juana Matheos, vecinos de Fuente de Arco... V-291

4220. Juan González, hijo de Juan García Hernández y de Mayor Hernández, vecinos de Badajoz... V-291

4221. Pedro de Valtierra, hijo de Gonzalo Martínez y de Catalina de Valtierra, vecinos de León... V-291

4222. Diego de Sanabria, hijo de Juan de Sanabria y de Cecilia Vázquez, vecinos de Medellín... V-291 v.

4223. Hernán González, hijo de Alonso González y de Mari Gómez, vecino de Medellín... V-291 v.

4224. Francisco Redondo, hijo de Juan Redondo y de Isabel de Carmona, vecino de Medellín... V-291 v.

4225. Juan de Amor, hijo de Juan de Amor y Marina de Quemada, vecino de Sevilla... V-291 v.

4227. Juan de Volaños, hijo de Francisco Loçano y de Elvira Cambran, vecinos de la Fuente el Maestre... V-291 v.

4228. Pedro de Consuegra, hijo de Bartolomé de Consuegra y de Juana Ramírez, vecinos de Arahal... V-292

4229. Juan de Soto, hijo de Juan de Soto y de Leonor Gutiérrez, vecino de Villanueva de la Serena... V-292

4230. Aparicio Gómez, hijo de Alonso Desteban y de Mari Ortego, vecino de Toledo, a la Florida con su mujer Mariana... V-292

4231. Juan Guerrero, hijo de Alonso Guerrero y de Antona Romana, vecino de la Fuente el Maestre... V-292

4232. Alvaro Ortiz, hijo de Francisco Ortiz y de María de Toro, vecino de la Fuente el Maestre... V-292

4233. Hernando Masuelas, hijo de Hernando Masuelas y de Inés de Valgrande, vecino de Villanueva de la Serena... V-292

18 Febrero.

4236. Alonso Corbalan, hijo de Francisco Corbalan y de Catalina Izquierdo, vecinos de Medina de Ríoseco... V-68

4237. Antonio de Cordoba, hijo de Anton de Cordoba y de María Anríquez, vecino de Medina de Ríoseco... V-68

4240. Francisco de Calvente, hijo de Juan Serrano de Calvente y de María Hernández, vecinos de Jaén... V-292 v.

4241. Juan González, hijo de Pedro González y de Juana González, vecino de Alba de Tormes, a la Florida. Presentó ante nos una información de testigos que pasó ante Pedro Hernández, escribano público de la villa de Alba, y ante el bachiller Diego Ximénez, corregidor de la dicha villa en 12 de Febrero de 1536. 18 Febrero. V-292 v.

4242. Francisco González, hijo de Francisco González y de María Hernández, vecino de Ocaña... V-292 v.

4243. Cristóbal del Orden, hijo de Gómez del Orden y de Teresa Díez, vecino de Roa... V-292 v.

4244. Juan de Castro, hijo de Pedro de Castro y de Isabel de Turreñas, vecino de Benavente... V-293

4245. Francisco de Salazar, hijo de Diego de Salazar y de María de la Cruz, vecino de Burgos... V-293

4246. Diego del Aguila, hijo del Comendador Diego del Aguila y de doña María, vecino de Avila... V-293

4247. Pedro Rodríguez, hijo de Pedro Rodríguez de Agre y de Beatriz de Soria, vecino de Almazán... V-293

4248. Pedro Alonso, hijo de Juan Macías y de Elvira García, vecino del Azanchal... V-293

4249. Benito Martín Albarrán, hijo de Juan Martín Albarrán, vecino de Usagre... V-293 v.

4250. Juan de Gamez, hijo de Diego de Gamez y de María García, vecino de Vitoria... V-293 v.

4251. Francisco de Aguilera, hijo de Francisco de Aguilera y de Aldonça de Salinas, vecinos de Alcalá de Henares... V-293

4252. Juan de Cuebas, hijo de Juan de Cuevas y de Beatriz López, vecinos de Medellín... V-293 v.

4253. Favián Calderón, hijo de Favián Calderón y de María de Castro, vecinos de Medellín... V-293 v.

4254. Juan de Amarilla, hijo de Juan de Amarilla y de María González, vecinos de Medellín... V-293 v.

4255. Martín de Vera, hijo de Juan Bázquez y de Barbola Bázquez, vecino de Aroche... V-294

4256. Francisco Xuárez, hijo de Juan Xuárez y de María del Castillo, vecinos de Toledo... V-294

4257. Pero Pérez, hijo de Hernando de Villanueva y de Catalina Rodríguez, vecinos de Húbeda... V-294

4258. Hernando Morzillo, hijo de Alonso Morcillo y de Isabel Rodríguez, vecinos de Villanueva de la Serena... V-294

4259. Alonso Gómez, hijo de Alonso Gómez y de Marina Alonso, vecinos de Villanueva de la Serena... V-294

19 Febrero.

4261. Alonso de Raya, hijo de Juan de Raya y de Catalina de Caçorla, vecinos de Húbeda... V-294 v.

4262. Juan Martín, hijo de Lorenzo Martín y de Isabel Martín, vecino de la Morera, a la Florida. Presentó ante nos una fé, fecha en Castilleja de la Cuesta, de ciertos testigos ante Bartolomé Hernández, alcalde ordinario de la dicha villa y ante

Cristóbal Martínez de Alcázar, clérigo, notario apostólico [*V. n.° siguiente*].—19 Febrero. V-294 v.

4263. Andrés Pérez, hijo de Juan Hernández, carretero, y de Mari Hernández, vecino de la Morera, a la Florida. Se le da licencia en virtud del testimonio citado en el asiento anterior.—19 Febrero. V-294 v.

4264. Gómez Martín y Juan Blanco, hijos de Diego Gómez y de Marina Alonso, vecino de Almendralejo... V-294 v.

4265. Juan Domínguez y Alonso Gallego, hijos de Francisco Domínguez y de Elvira García, vecinos de Alconera... V-294 v.

4266. Juan Dorgas, hijo de Lope de Babia y de Elvira Fernández, vecinos del Azanchal... V-294 v.

4267. Juan Martín, hijo de Bartolome Martín y de Catalina González, vecinos del Azanchal... V-295

4268. Francisco de Aguillar, hijo de Blas Galisteo y de Elvira de Aguillar, vecinos de Salvatierra, del condado de Feria... V-295

4269. Pedro de la Torre, hijo de Bartolomé González, clérigo, y de Isabel González, de color loro, natural de la Torre, a la Florida. Mostró una carta de ahorría que pasó ante Esteban Çambrano, escribano público de la villa de la Torre en 20 de Enero de 1538.—19 Febrero. V-295

4270. Julián López, hijo de Juan López de Deredia [*sic por* Heredia?] y de Ozenda, vecinos de Axpuru [*sic*]... V-295

4271. Hernando de Figueroa, hijo del alcalde Rodrigo Alvarez y de Isabel Rodríguez, vecinos de Zafra... V-295

4272. Alonso Bázquez, hijo de Andrés Bázquez y de Leonor Rodríguez, vecinos de Zafra... V-295 v.

4273. Gonzalo Cuadrado, hijo de Gonzalo Cuadrado y de Mari González, vecinos de Zafra... V-295 v.

4274. Diego Sánchez, hijo de Hernán Alvarez y de Isabel Sánchez, vecino de Zafra... V-295 v.

4275. Pedro de Lazarte, hijo de Pedro de Lazarte y de María de la Torre, vecino de la Torre... V-295 v.

4276. Alonso de Oviedo, hijo de Francisco de Oviedo y de Francisca Rodríguez, vecino de Zafra... V-295 v.

4277. Juan Salvador, hijo de Francisco Hernández de Hernán Núñez y de Mencía Rodríguez, natural de Hernán Núñez...V-295 v.

4279. Juan Sánchez de Cantos, hijo de Bartolomé Sánchez de Cantos y de Lucía López, vecino de Guadix... V-296

4280. Gonzalo Rodríguez, hijo de Alonso Sánchez y de Ana Rodríguez, vecino de Mingabriel... V-296

4281. Juan del Campo, hijo de Pedro García del Campo y de Ana Rodríguez, vecino de Medellín... V-296

4282. Bartolomé Ximénez, hijo de Bartolomé Ximénez y de Lucía Gómez, vecinos de Consuegra... V-296

4283. Francisco Ruyz de Ocampo, hijo de Francisco Rodríguez y de Mari Blas García, vecinos de Salamanca... V-296

4284. Francisco López, hijo de Martín López y de Isabel Dominguez, vecinos de Plasencia... V-296

4285. Yvan Fuertes, hijo de Juan de Ortega y de Inés Fuertes, vecinos de Palençuela... V-296 v.

4286. Juan Fernández, hijo de Pedro Márquez Hernández y de Elvira Fernández, vecinos de Alaejos... V-296 v.

4287. Agustín Carrión, hijo de Pedro Martínez Carrión y de Mari González, vecino de Melgarejo... V-296 v.

4288. Diego de Mosquera, hijo de Galaor Mosquera y de Juana Rodríguez, vecinos de Castro Nuño... V-296 v.

21 Febrero.

4298. Rodrigo Alvarez, hijo de Andrés Vázquez y de Leonor Rodríguez, vecinos de Zafra... V-301

4299. Pedro de Venero, hijo de Juan de Venero y de Elvira Sánchez de Venero, vecino de la villa de Escalante, que es en la merindad de Trasmiera, a la Florida.—21 Febrero. V-301

4300. Gonzalo Sánchez Mexía, hijo de Alonso Sánchez Mexía y de Leonor de Volaños, vecinos de Burguillos, y doña Isabel de Mexía y Mendo Mexía, hijos del dicho Alonso Sánchez y de Leonor de Volaños, a la Florida con su hermano [*V. n.° siguiente*].—21 Febrero. V-301

4301. Leonor de Volaños, madre de Gonzalo Sánchez Mexía, de doña Isabel de Mexía y de Mendo Mexía, a la Florida, con sus hijos [*V. n.° anterior*]—21 Febrero. V-301

4302. Pedro de Bargas, hijo de Rodrigo de Bargas y de Isabel Adame, vecinos de Frexenal... V-301 v.

4303. Diego García del Pozo, hijo de Pero García del Pozo y de Juana García del Pozo, vecinos del Villarejo de Salvanes, a la Florida.—21 Febrero. V-301 v.

4304. Juan Núñez, hijo de Luis Núñez y de Constanza Núñez, vecino de Sevilla, collación de Santiago del Viejo... V-301 v.

22 Febrero.

4314. Alonso Caro, hijo de Hernan Caro y de Elvira López, vecinos de Valencia de la Torre... V-301 v.

4315. Gonzalo Mateos, hijo de Hernán Mateos y de Catalina González, vecino de Valencia de la Torre... V-301 v.

4316. Bartolomé Rodríguez, hijo de Bartolomé Rodríguez y de María Rodríguez, vecino de Valencia [de la Torres?]... V-301 v.

4317. Alonso Muñoz, hijo de Juan Muñoz y de Mari Sánchez de la Iguera... V-302

4318. Lorenzo Martín, hijo de Gonzalo Martín Ferrezuelo y de Mari Gutiérrez, vecino de Usagre... V-302

4319. Bartolomé de Sagredo, hijo de Alonso de Sagredo y de Francisca Zerrato... V-302

4320. Cristóbal de Palacio, hijo de Francisco de Medina y de María de Gijón... V-302

4321. Juan de Arroyo, hijo de Rodrigo de Arroyo y de Isabel García, vecinos de Medellín... V-302

4322. Juan de Basarte, hijo de Hernando de Termanda y de Mari Ortiz, vecino de Basaurti... V-302

4323. Gaspar de Valencia, hijo de Hernando de Llerena y de Juana Díez, vecino de Málaga... V-302 v.

4324. Lázaro de Valdivieso, hijo de Andrés Martínez de Valdivieso y de Juana Martínez, vecino de Villorado... V-302 v.
4325. Miguel Bautista, hijo de Maestre Pedro, tonelero, genovés, y de Catalina Hernández, vecino de Jerez... V-302 v.
4326. Martín Xuárez, hijo de Martín Xuárez y de Catalina de Caytán, vecinos de Salamanca... V-302 v.
4327. Alonso de Tordesillas, hijo de Pedro de Tordesillas y de Catalina Sánchez, vecinos de Fuente el Saúco, y él vecino de Sevilla... V-302 v.

23 Febrero.

4328. Juan de Azevedo, hijo de Juan de Azebedo y de Isabel Rodríguez, vecinos de Villanueva de la Serena... V-303
4329. Diego de Rivera, hijo de Francisco de Rivera y de Mari Alonso Guerrera, vecino de la Fuente del Maestre... V-303
4330. Alonso García Espino, hijo de Sebastián García del Espino y de Isabel Sanchez Conquera... V-303
4331. Juan Páez, hijo de Cristóbal Páez y de Beatriz Alonso, vecinos de Villanueva de Barcarrota... V-303
4332. Francisco Sabastián, hijo de Alonso Sabastián y de Juana Macías, vecinos de Villanueva de Barcarrota... V-303
4333. Juan Galbán, hijo de Francisco Galván y de María Esteban, vecinos de Valverde... V-303
4334. Juan Bázquez, hijo de Gonzalo Bázquez y de Catalina Bázquez, vecinos de Villanueva de Barcarrota... V-303
4335. Pedro Mudo, hijo de Juan López y de Catalina, vecinos de Llerena... V-303 v.
4336. Pedro Hernández, hijo de Hernando Alonso y de P. (?) Hernández, vecinos de Badajoz... V-303 v.
4337. Alexos Martín, hijo de Pedro Martín y de Mencía Hernández, vecinos de Badajoz... V-303 v.
4338. Hernando Idalgo, hijo de Juan Idalgo y de Catalina Hernández, vecinos de Medellín... V-303 v.
4339. Cristóbal Cía, hijo de Ruy González y de Francisca Rodríguez, vecinos de Fregenal... V-303 v.
4340. Francisco de Tapia, hijo de Alonso Malaber y de Inés de Tapia, vecinos de Zafra... V-303 v.
4341. Andrés de Çeçeyl, hijo de Juan de Çeçeyl y de Clara de Yrue, vecino de Eíbar... V-304
4342. Diego López Márquez, hijo de Diego López Márquez y de Isabel Ramírez, vecino de Segura... V-304
4343. Melchor de Arroyal, hijo de Gutiérrez García de Arroyal y de Francisca Alvarez de San Bicente, vecinos de Toledo... V-304
4344. Francisco de Salazar, hijo de Francisco de Salazar y de doña Bernardina de Cartagena... V-304
4345. Alonso Sánchez Morales, hijo de Diego Sánchez Morales, y de Mari Franca, vecino de Sevilla... V-304
4346. Melchor de Consuegra, hijo de Juan García Merino y de Catalina Hernández, vecino de Abenoja... V-304
4347. Francisco González, hijo de Luis González y de Isabel Rodríguez, vecino de Aracena... V-304

4348. Domingo de la Cavex, hijo de Iñigo de Marcoleta y de María Ruiz de Ibarra, vecino del valle de Salcedo... V-304 v.

25 Febrero.

4356. Juan García, hijo de Francisco García y de Mari Sanchez, vecino de Valverde de Badajoz... V-304 v.

4357. Rodrigo de Bocanegra, hijo de Juan de Bocanegra y de Juana Sánchez, vecinos de Villalba... V-304 v.

4358. Francisco Bellaz, hijo de Pedro Bellaz y de... vecino de Fuente el Saúco... V-304 v.

4359. Pedro de Çalduendo, hijo de Juan Ochoa de Çalduendo y de Sancha de Ocadiz, vecino de Çalduendo... V-304 v.

4360. Rodrigo Corona, hijo de Pedro de Olías y de Juana López, vecino de Torrejón de Velasco... V-304 v.

4361. Francisco de Yelbes, hijo de Gonzalo de Yelbes y de Catalina Hernández, vecino de Guadalcanal... V-304 v.

4362. Flores de Otañes, hijo de Flores de Otañes y de Teresa de Terreros, vecino del valle de Troncoso... V-305

4363. Francisco Muñoz, hijo de Hernando de Orellana y de Catalina Pizarro, vecino de Trujillo... V-305

4364. Juan Rodríguez, hijo de Juan Martín de la Cámara y de Isabel Sánchez, vecino de Cáceres... V-305

4365. Luis Medina, hijo de Alonso González y de Mari Sánchez, vecino de León... V-305

4366. Cristóbal de Salazar, hijo de Benito Rodríguez y de María de Salazar, vecino de Tordesilla de la Orden... V-305

4367. Antonio Hernández, hijo de Diego Hernández y de Teresa de Castro, vecino de Ubeda... V-305

26 Febrero.

4393. Francisco Pacheco, hijo de Diego Pacheco y de Juana Martín, vecino de la Nava del Membrillo, tierra de Mérida... V-305 v.

4394. Pascual García, hijo de Hernando Caballero y de Ana Martín, vecino de tierra de Galisteo... V-305 v.

4395. Bartolomé Hernández, hijo de Juan Montaño y de María Alonso, vecino de Zafra... V-305 v.

4396. Juan Sayago, hijo de Alonso Martín y de Juana Sayaga, vecino de Zafra... V-305 v.

4397. Pedro Díaz de Herrera, hijo de Juan Díaz de Herrera y de Marina García, vecino de Ocaña... V-305 v.

4398. Juan Garrido, hijo de Matheo Garrido y de Catalina Martín, vecino de Beçeda... V-305 v.

4399. Francisco de Meneses, hijo de Francisco de Meneses y de Leonor Vázquez, vecinos de Usagre... V-305 v.

4400. Gonzalo Alonso, hijo de Gonzalo Gómez y de Mari Núñez, vecino de Usagre... V-305 v.

4401. Hernán Sánchez de la Fuente, hijo de García González de la Bera y de Juana Martín, vecino de Valencia de la Torre, a la Florida [*V. n.° 4404*].—26 Febrero. V-305 v.

4402. Cristóbal Martín, hijo de Juan Martín y de Isabel Zambrano, vecino de Rivera... V-306

4403. Gonzalo Martín, hijo de Sabastián González y de Teresa Sánchez, vecino de Azuaga... V-306

4404. Pedro Hernández de la Bera, hijo de García González de la Bera y de Toribia Hernández, vecino de Valencia de la Torre, a la Florida [*V. n.° 4401*].—26 Febrero. V-306

4405. Alonso Díaz, hijo de Juan Alonso y de Catalina Díaz, vecino de Valencia de la Torre... V-306

4406. Cristóbal Gutiérrez, hijo de Alvaro Gutiérrez y de Catalina Blanca, vecinos de Nozeda... V-306

4407. Juan Díez [*entre renglones* hijo] de Juan Díez y de Isabel Martínez, vecino de Arcos, y Juan Díez, vecino del dicho lugar [*sic*]... V-306

4408. Andrés Rodríguez, hijo de Andrés Rodríguez y de Catalina Rodríguez, vecino de Villanueva de Barcarrota... V-306

4409. Francisco Pérez, hijo de Diego Pérez y de Mari Hernández, vecino de Villanueva de Barcarrota... V-306

4410. Pedro de Bustamante, hijo de García Hernández y de Inés Díaz, vecino de Burguillos... V-306 v.

4411. Diego Enríquez, hijo de Pedro Lopez de Calatayud y de doña María Enríquez, vecino de Valladolid... V-306 v.

4412. Pedro de Sotomayor, hijo de Antonio de Ribera y de doña Isabel de Sotomayor, vecino de Soria... V-306 v.

4413. Bartolomé García, hijo de Alonso García y de Beatriz Méndez, vecinos de Talavera... V-306 v.

4414. Andrés Guisado, hijo de Juan Hernández y de Juana Guisada, vecino de Talavera... V-306 v.

4415. Diego Hernández, hijo de Antón Hernández y de Isabel Ximénez, vecino de Sevilla... V-306 v.

4416. Francisco Vázquez, hijo de Luis Vázquez y de Mari Vázquez, vecino de Salamanca... V-306 v.

4417. Francisco Rodríguez, hijo de Alvar Rodríguez y de Leonor Çamora, vecino de Villavicencio de los Caballeros... V-306 v.

4418. Pedro Hernández, hijo de Juan Rodríguez de Grados y de Catalina Hernández, vecino de Sevilla... V-307

4419. Pedro de Villalobos, hijo de Alonso de Villalobos y de Inés de Rojas, vecino de Toledo... V-307

4420. Cristóbal de Oliva, hijo de Francisco Domínguez, latonero, y de Francisca Hernández, vecino de Córdoba... V-307

4421. Salvador Rodríguez, hijo de Alonso Rodríguez y de Juana González, vecino de Trujillo... V-307

4422. Gonzalo de Bustamente, hijo de Miguel Sánchez y de Leonor López, vecinos de Sevilla... V-307

4423. Alonso Muñoz, hijo de Martín Marcos y de Catalina Ruiz, vecino de Sevilla... V-307

4424. Francisco de Villanueva, hijo de Hernando de Villanueva y de Isabel Fernández, vecino de Badajoz... V-307

4425. Andrés Ximénez, hijo de Andrés Martín Ximénez y de María Alonso, vecino de Badajoz... V-307 v.

4426. Bartolomé Sánchez Rendón, hijo de Bartolomé Sánchez Rendón y de Ana Martín, vecinos de la Algaba... V-307 v.

4427. Hernán Gómez, hijo de Bartolomé de Guerrera y de Isabel Gómez, vecinos de Sevilla... V-307 v.
4428. Pedro de Salas, hijo de Lope de Salas y de Francisca Fernández, vecinos de Talavera... V-307 v.
4429. Alonso del Andrada, hijo de Rodrigo Alonso y de Francisca Fernández, vecinos de Talavera... V-307 v.
4430. Juan Vélez, hijo de Pedro Vélez y de Antona de Ortega, vecino de Tordesillas... V-307 v.
4431. Juan Núñez, hijo de Fernán Núñez y de Isabela Alvarez, vecinos de Curiel... V-308
4432. Alonso Salván, hijo de Juan de la Fuente y de Isabel Sánchez, vecino de Aldeanueva del Arzobispo... V-308
4433. Antonio Velázquez, hijo de Juan Velázquez de Robledo y de dona María Espes, vecino de Valladolid... V-308
4434. Martín González de Molina, hijo de Alonso González y de Catalina González, vecinos de Molina... V-308
4435. Diego de Prado, hijo de Juan Rodríguez, gallego, y de Isabel de Morales, vecino de Molina... V-308
4436. Juan Muñoz, hijo de Martín Marcos y de María García, vecino de la villa Cidaler... V-308
4437. Juan Gómez, hijo de Hernán Martín y de Catalina Sánchez, vecinos de Ciudad Real [*Este asiento está tachado*]... V-308 v.
4438. Pedro Verdugo, hijo de Alvaro Verdugo y de Catalina Alvarez, vecino de Canizal... V-308 v.
4439. Pedro Morán, hijo de Francisco Morán de Valderas y de Inés García, vecino de Villanueva de Valrroz... V-308 v.
4440. Juan Alvarez, hijo de Alonso Yáñez y de Leonor Fernández, vecino de Badajoz... V-308 v.
4441. Alonso de Madrigal, hijo de Juan de Madrigal y de María Gorda, vecino de Molezuelas... V-308 v.
4442. Juan de Calzada, hijo de Antón de Calçada y de María Santiago, vecino de Oña... V-308 v.
4443. Diego de Bracamonte, hijo de Diego de Bracamonte y de Inés de Benavides, vecino de Villanueva de Valdexamus... V-308 v.
4444. Gerónimo de Rojas, hijo de Francisco Ruiz y de Ana de Rojas, vecino de Alcalá de Henares... V-309
4445. Gerónimo de Dueñas, hijo de Pedro Hernández Fandiño y de Beatriz Ferrera, vecino de Galicia... V-309

27 Febrero.

4446. Hernán Bravo, hijo de Fernando de Villarreal y de Marina Brava, vecino de Lepe... V-309
4447. Bartolomé Muñoz, hijo de Juan Núñez y Nicolasa Salcedo, vecinos de Cádiz... V-309
4448. Benito Sánchez, hijo de Antón Sánchez y de María López, vecinos de Talavera... V-309 v.
4449. Andrés Martínez, hijo de García Martínez y de Elvira Hernández, vecino de Pino... V-309 v.
4450. Alonso Cacho, hijo de Pedro García y de Juana García, vecinos de Talavera... V-309 v.

4451. Baltasar de Trujillo, hijo de Miguel de Trujillo y de María de Villalobos, vecino de Sevilla... V-309 v.
4452. Francisco de Castejón, hijo de Antonio de Castejón y de Francisca de Lizardo, vecino de Soria... V-309 v.
4453. Cristóbal Ortiz, hijo del Licenciado Ortiz y de Elvira de la Puebla, vecino de Sevilla... V-309 v.
4454. Juan García, hijo de Juan García y de Isabel Rodríguez, vecino de Badajoz... V-310
4455. Pedro de Perena, hijo de Francisco Martín y de María Hernández, vecinos de Perena... V-310
4456. Luis García, hijo de Pedro Sánchez y de Clara Martín, vecino de Badajoz... V-310
4457. Diego Hernández, hijo de Francisco Martín y de Juana Martínez de Zambrana... V-310
4458. Bartolomé Bázquez, hijo de Juan García y de Beatriz Rodríguez, vecinos de Badajoz... V-310
4459. Francisco Martínez, hijo de Francisco Martín y de Mari Martín, vecinos de Salamanca... V-310
4460. Francisco Despinosa, hijo de don Pedro Despinosa y de Teresa de Molina, vecino de Andújar... V-310 v.
4461. Luis de Hinistrosa, hijo de Juan Hernández de Hinistrosa y de doña Guiomar de Torres, vecino de Sevillo... V-310 v.
4462. Andrés Martín, hijo de Jorge Ruiz Quiebrabrazos y de Marina Ruiz, vecinos de Andújar... V-310 v.
4463. Diego García, hijo de Martín García y de Constanza de Pareja, vecinos de Almería... V-310 v.
4464. Bartolomé Ruiz, hijo de Francisco Ruiz Barragán y de Elvira Ximénez, vecinos de Andújar... V-310 v.
4465. Jorge Hernández, hijo de Alonso Hernández y de Aldonza Báez, vecinos de Valverde... V-311
4466. Juan Llorente, hijo de don Francés Lançón y de doña Isabel Aynes, vecinos de Valencia... V-311
4467. Alonso Rodríguez, hijo de Alonso Rodríguez y de Isabel López, vecinos de Peñafiel... V-311
4468. Juan González, hijo de Alonso Vázquez y de Catalina Alvarez... V-311
4469. Gonzalo Méndez, hijo del Bachiller Cristóbal Méndez y de Leonor Bázquez, vecino de Villanueva de Barcarrota... V-311
4470. Hernán Pérez, hijo de Diego Pérez y de María Hernández, vecino de Villanueva de Barcarrota... V-311
4471. Fabián Rodríguez, hijo de Alvar García, vecinos de Yebahernando... V-311 v.
4472. Francisco Alonso, hijo de Bernardino de Grañón y de Ana Martín, vecino de Nájera... V-311 v.
4473. Hernán Vázquez, hijo de Antona Martín y de Pedro Domínguez, vecino de Aroche... V-311 v.
4474. Miguel de Tiedra, hijo de Gabriel de Tiedra y de Ana Martín, vecino de Salamanca... V-311 v.
4475. Pedro Bacorero, hijo de Antonio Váez Bacorero y de Juana de Lara, vecino de Herrera... V-311 v.

4476. Gonzalo Silvestre, hijo de Gonzalo Silvestre y de Isabel Morena, vecino de Herrera... V-311 v.
4477. Alonso de la Puente, hijo de Francisco de la Puente y de Juana de Sosa, vecino de Zafra... V-311 v.
4478. Hernando Alonso Hidalgo, hijo de Pedro Martín y de Leonor Alonso, vecino de Montánchez... V-312
4479. Alvaro González, hijo de García Hernández y de Constanza Alvarez, vecino de Montánchez... V-312
4480. Pedro Yáñez, hijo de Alonso Yáñez y de Teresa Fuertes, vecino de Madrigal... V-312
4481. Bernardo, loro, criado del capitán Pedro Calderón, a la Florida. Prensentó carta de ahorria del dicho Pedro Calderón, cuyo esclavo era, en que parece es horro y libre, la cual pasó ante Iñigo López, escribano público de Sevilla en 25 de Febrero de 1538.—27 Febrero. V-312

28 Febrero.

4482. Juan Gómez de Bega, hijo de Diego de Mesa y de Francisca de Vega, vecino de Sevilla... V-312
4483. Bartolomé Gómez, hijo de Alvar Gómez y de Ana Gómez, vecino de Mérida... V-312
4484. Francisco de Valverde, hijo de Hernando de Valverde y de Isabel de Velasco... V-312 v.
4485. Diego Rodríguez, hijo de Antonio Rodríguez y de Elvira Gómez, vecinos de Coria de Galisteo... V-312 v.
4486. Francisco de Guzmán, hijo de Diego López de Guzmán y de Teresa Alvarez, vecinos de Toledo... V-312 v.
4487. Sabastián de Sampedro, hijo de Luis Alvarez y de Beatriz de Sampedro, vecino de Tordesillas... V-312 v.
4488. Rodrigo de Osorio, hijo de García de la Milla y de Juana Hernández de Osorio, vecinos de Sevilla... V-312 v.
4489. Bernabé Ortiz, hijo de Diego Rengel y de Elvira Ortiz, vecinos de Almendralejo... V-312 v.

1 Marzo.

4490. Don Lorenzo, hijo de don Juan de Cárdenas y de Leonor Hernández, vecino de Sevilla... V-313
4491. Jorge Ortiz, hijo de Pedro Santiago y de Beatriz Velasco... V-313
4492. Leonos [*sic*] de Temiño, hijo del jurado Hernando Barniellos y de doña Isabel de Alcoçer, vecinos de Sevilla... V-313
4493. Francisco Alvarez, hijo de Juan Francés y de Isabel Alvarez, vecino de Milla... V-313
4494. Francisco Ortiz, hijo de Diego Ortiz y de Juana de Vellosillo, vecino de Roa... V-313
4495. Gaspar de Monterde, hijo de Pedro Monterde y de Catalina Caminos, vecino de Mosqueruela... V-313
4496. Vicente Martín, hijo de Juan Martínez de Maceguilla y de María Sánchez de Almodóvar, vecinos de Ciudad Real... V-313 v.

2 Marzo.

4497. Pedro de Medenilla, hijo de Lope Martínez de Medenilla y de Isabel Romero, vecinos de Salinas... V-313 v.

4498. Pablos Hernández, hijo de Pablos Hernández y de Catalina Angas, vecino de Zafra... V-313 v.
4499. Alonso García, hijo de Ruy Gómez el de Ronquilla y de Isabel de Ronquillo, vecinos de Olivas... V-313 v.
4500. Hernando de Castañeda, hijo de Diego González y de Juana González, vecinos de Yeara... V-313 v.
4501. Diego de Soto, hijo de García Hernández Soto y de María Hernández, vecinos de Soto... V-313 v.
4502. Salvador de Mendano, hijo de Rodrigo de Mendano y de Catalina García, vecinos de Medellín... V-313 v.
4503. Alvaro Alonso, hijo de García Hernandez y de María Hernandez, vecinos de los Santos... V-314
4504. Francisco Rodríguez, hijo de Juan Rodríguez y de Ana González, vecinos de los Santos... V-314
4505. Diego López de Bustamante, hijo de García López de Bustamante y de María González de Bustamante, vecino de Villasuso... V-314
4506. Juan Ruiz, hijo de Pedro Ruiz y de Bárbara Martínez, vecinos de Arroyuelo... V-314
4507. Gómez Gutiérrez, hijo de Francisco de Campos y de Elvira López, vecinos de Villanueva de Barcarrota... V-314
4508. Juan de Herrera, hijo de Francisco de Herrera y de Beatriz González, vecinos del Almendral... V-314
4509. Juan de Obregón, hijo de Alonso Martín y de María Gutiérrez, vecino de Villamiel, en el Obispado de Ciudad Rodrigo... V-314
4510. Juan Coles, hijo de Juan Coles y de Luisa Rodríguez, vecino de Zafra... V-314
4511. Juan de Sarabia, hijo de Francisco de Sarabia y de Catalina Hernández, vecino de Plasencia... V-314 v.
4512. Juan Díaz Bermejo, hijo de Alonso Yáñez y de Beatriz González, vecino de Oliva, y Alonso y Diego, hijos del susodicho y de Isabel Rodríguez... V-314 v.
4513. Francisco Grande, hijo de Miguel Grande y de María Hernández, vecino de Villanueva del Fresno... V-314 v.
4514. Juan de Villafaña, hijo de Pedro de Villafaña y de María de Otaça, vecinos de Valladolid... V-314 v.
4515. Cristóbal de Villafaña, hijo de Francisco de Torres y de Teresa de Villafaña, vecino de Sevilla... V-314 v.
4516. Juan Gallego, hijo de Juan Martín Bermejo y de Beatriz Velázquez, vecino de Oliva... V-314 v.
4517. Juan Carrasco, hijo de Martín Hernández y de Leonor Díez, vecinos de Oliva... V-314 v.
4518. Francisco Rodríguez, hijo de Gómez Rodríguez y de Catalina García, vecinos de Oliva... V-314 v.
4519. Alonso Díez, hijo de Lope Díez y de Isabel Hernández, vecinos de Oliva... V-315
4520. Diego de Santa María y Pedro de Santa María, hijos de Sancho Ortiz de Santamaría y de doña Elvira de Santamaría, vecinos de Orrantia, que es en el valle de Mena... V-315

4521. Hernán Guisado, hijo de Francisco Sánchez y de María Guisado, vecino de Villanueva de la Serena... V-315

4522. Martín Sánchez, hijo de Pedro González Açedo y de María Sánchez, vecino de Villanueva de la Serena... V-315

4523. Pedro Guisado, hijo de Pedro Guisado y de Isabel Gómez, vecino de Almedina... V-315

4524. Francisco Ortiz, hijo de Pedro Ortiz, hijo de Pedro Ortiz y de María de Lezcano, vecino de Segovia... V-315

4525. Rodrigo Mulero, hijo de Francisco Sánchez Morón y de María Vázquez, vecino de Badajoz... V-315

4546. Lope Alonso Vacamorena, hijo de Francisco Hernández, herrador, y de María Alonso, vecino de Zafra... V-315

6 Marzo.

4537. García de la Rocha, hijo del comendador Francisco de la Ronce [*sic*] y de Isabel Sánchez de la Rocha, vecino de Badajoz ... V-315 v.

4538. Juan Núñez de Herrera, hijo de Juan Núñez y de Leonor Herrera, vecinos de Badajoz... V-315 v.

4539. Juan de la Calle, hijo de Andrés Miguel y de Leonor de Caçuera, vecino de Sanfrontes, arrabal de Zamora... V-315 v.

4540. Hernán Arias de Saavedra, hijo de Hernán Carrillo y de doña Juana Saavedra, vecino de Sevilla... V-315 v.

4541. Bartolomé de Morales, hijo de Micer Marcos de Morales y de Catalina de Puncarreda, vecino de Sevilla... V-315 v.

4542. Gregorio Salazar, hijo de Juan de Salazar y de Mari Sánchez, vecino de Becerril del Campo... V-315 v.

4543. Gregorio Vizcaíno, hijo de Gregorio Vizcaíno y de Pascuala de Tovalín, vecino de Pedraza de Campos... V-315 v.

4544. Gutierre de Bustillo, hijo de Rodrigo Goala y de doña María de Cavallos, vecinos de Villasedil... V-316

4545. Andrés de Vega, hijo de Juan de Vega y de Isabel Gutiérrez, vecino de Cáceres... V-316

4546. Diego de Vega, hijo de Pedro de Tapia y de Isabel Díaz, vecino de Peroluengo, tierra de Salamanca... V-316

4547. Hernán Pérez, hijo de Hernán Pérez y de Catalina de la Vega, vecino de Santerbas... V-316

4548. Diego de Monrroy, digo de Diego de Monrroy y de doña Isabel, vecinos del Almendral, a la Florida [*V. n.° siguiente*].—6 Marzo. V-316

4549. Lope de Tordoya, hijo de Diego de Monrroy y de doña Isabel, vecinos de Almendral, hermano de Diego de Monrroy, a la Florida [*V. n.° anterior*].—6 Marzo. V-316

4550. Pedro López, hijo de Gómez Tejedor y de Catalina López, vecinos de Quiroga... V-316

4551. Diego Velázquez, hijo de Hernando Velázquez y de Mari Alonso, vecino de Oropesa... V-316

8 Marzo,

4565. Don Antonio Osorio, hijo del Marqués de Astorga y de Isabel Pérez, natural de Astorga... V-316 v.

4566. Diego de Cisneros, hijo de Bartolomé de Cisneros y de Lucía Alonso, natural de Astorga... V-316 v.
4567. Juan López, hijo de Basco López y de Inés Vázquez, natural Astorga... V-316 v.
4568. Arias Díaz de Losala, hijo de Ximón Díez y de Mari Alvarez de Losala, natural de Astorga... V-316 v.
4569. Pedro Sánchez, hijo de Alonso Sánchez y de Beatriz de Artezón, natural de Astorga... V-316 v.
4570. Hernando de Catroverde, hijo de Pero Alvarez y de Mari Fuerte, natural de Astorga... V-316 v.
4571. Hernando de Briones, hijo de Esteban de Briones y de Juana de Medina, vecino de Astorga... V-316 v.
4572. Juan Martínez, hijo de Juan Daça y de Elvira Hernández, vecino de Astorga... V-316 v.
4573. Andrés Alonso, hijo de Juan Martínez y de Isabel Alonso, vecino de Astorga... V-316 v.
4574. Lorenzo de Cacavelos, hijo de Juan Ruiz y de Mari García, vecino de Astorga... V-316 v.
4575. Giraldo Pérez, hijo de Juan Pérez y de Catalina Alonso, vecino de Astorga... V-316 v.
4576. Francisco de Reinoso, hijo de Gonzalo de Reinoso y de Isabel Escobar, vecino de Bovadilla... V-317
4577. Gómez Hernández, hijo de Bartolomé Román y de Mari García, vecino del Almendral... V-317
4579. Toribio de Calvarrasa, hijo de Bartolomé de San Martín y de Francisca Sánchez, vecino de Salamanca... V-317
4580. Don Diego de Mendoza y Lope de Acuña, hijos del Comendador Antón Ruiz de Contreras y de doña Leonor de Acuña, vecinos de Illescas... V-317
4581. Hernan Mexía, hijo de Diego López de Villalobos y de Beatriz de Orosco, vecinos de Illescas... V-317
4582. Gutierre Dorado, hijo de Gómez Dorado y de María Sánchez, vecinos de San Martín de Mondoñedo... V-317
4583. Bernaldo de Quirós, hijo de Diego Bernaldo de Quirós y de Ana Brial, vecino de Sevilla... V-317 v.
4584. Francisco de Casillas, hijo de Rafael de Casillas y de Isabel de Segura, vecinos de Antequera... V-317 v.
4585. Diego de Tobar, hijo de Rodrigo de Tobar y de Beatriz de Segura, vecinos de Marchena... V-317 v.
4586. Juan de Porres, hijo de Rodrigo Darze y de doña María de Rosales, vecinos de Medina de Pomar... V-317 v.
4587. Tristán de Lozano, hijo de Tristán de Lozano y de doña María, vecinos de Marchena... V-317 v.

9 Marzo.

4595. Pedro de Poço, hijo de Alonso del Pozo y María del Pozo, vecino de Salmerón... V-317 v.
4596. Luis de Salcedo, hijo de Antonio de Caravaca y de María de Lluba, vecina de Salmerón... V-317 v.
4597. Francisco Martín Galindo, hijo de Alonso Sánchez Galindo y de Leonor Martín, vecino de Bollullos... V-318

4598. Pedro de Pedraza, hijo de Diego de Pedraza y de María de Salamanca, natural de Salamanca... V-318
4599. Bartolomé Calderón, hijo de Alonso Calderón y de Beatriz Rodríguez, vecino de Zamora... V-318
4600. Juan González, hijo de Pedro Alvarez y de Isabel González, vecino de Pontevedra... V-318
4601. Pedro Hernández, hijo de Juan Fernández y de Alzonza Fernández, vecino de León... V-318
4602. Diego Fernández, hijo de Diego de Ordaz y de Inés de Barra, vecino de Castroverde... V-318
4603. Rodrigo de Gallegos, hijo de Juan de Escobar y de Beatriz de Gallegos, natural de Sevilla... V-318
4604. Pedro de Caravajal, hijo de Hernando de Narbáez y de Isabel de Caravajal, vecino de Antequera... V-318 v.
4605. Gonzalo de Malpaso, hijo de Antonio de Malpaso, vecino de Segovia... V-318
4606. Melchor de Isla, hijo de Antonio de Isla y de Catalina Paniagua, vecino de Medina de Ríoseco... V-318 v.
4607. Luis de Moscoso, hijo del comendador Alonso Hernández de Diosdado y de doña Isabel de Albarado, vecinos de Zafra, a la Florida, con sus hermanos Juan de Albarado y Cristóbal de Mosquera.—9 Marzo. V-318 v.
4608. Martín de Penãlosa, hijo de Martín Peñalosa y de Leonor González, vecino de Zafra... V-318 v.
4609. Juan López, hijo de Alvar López y de Isabel Gómez de Cuebas, vecino de Sevilla... V-318 v.
4610. Juan de Otaço, hijo de Cristóbal de Gamarra y de...[*roto*] Rivera, natural de Pedrosa... V-319

11 Marzo.

4611. Bueso [*sic*] Marbán, hijo de García Marbán y de María de Benavides, natural de Villanueva de Valdepeñas... V-319
4612. Esteban Marbán, hijo de Juan Marbán y de María Sánchez, vecino de la Baniz (?)... V-319
4613. Gregorio de Medina, hijo de Juan de Medina y de Guiomar de Carrión, vecinos de la Vaniz (?)... V-319
4631. Francisco de Bañuelos, hijo de Bañuelos y de Juana de Frías, vecino de Briviesca... V-319
4632. Juan de Herrera, hijo de Andrés de Granada y de María López, vecino de Herrera... V-319 v.
4633. Francisco Alonso, hijo de Antón Alonso y de Francisca Ruiz, vecinos de Pedroca... V-319 v.
4634. Alonso Cornejo, hijo de Antón Cornejo y de Isabel Guerra, vecinos de Castrocalbón... V-319 v.
4635. Diego de Ovieta, hijo de Pedro Sánchez de Ovieta y de María de Llanos, vecinos del valle de Salcedo, a la Florida [*V. n.° 4617*].—11 Marzo. V-319 v.
4636. Pedro Ponce de León, hijo de Guillén de Casaus y de doña Inés Ponce de León... V-319 v.
4637. Alonso de Sygura, hijo de Pedro de Segura y de Elvira de Rojas, vecinos de Sevilla, a la Florida con su hijo Juan, y de Leonor Guillén.—11 Marzo. V-319 v.

4638. Cristóbal de Salas, hijo de Gabriel de Salas y de María de Zamora, vecino de Sevilla... V-319 v.
4639. Juan de Castro, hijo de Pedro de Castro y de Isabel de Torienzo, vecinos de Benavente, a la Florida [*Este asiento está tachado*].—11 Marzo. V-320
4640. Alonso Vázquez, hijo de Juan Vázquez y de Elvira Ponce, vecinos de Valladolid... V-320
4641. Antonio Sedeño, hijo de Francisco Sedeño y de María Alonso, vecinos de Valladolid... V-320
4642. Francisco Gómez, hijo de Juan Rubio y de Isabel García, vecinos de Oliva... V-320
4643. Antón García, hijo de Gómez Rodríguez y de Catalina García, vecinos de Oliva... V-320
4644. Diego de Zevedo [*sic por* Acevedo?], hijo de Rodrigo Maldonado y de Isabel de Zevedo, vecino de Salamanca... V-320
4645. Miguel Ambila, hijo de Juan Ambila y de María Ambila, vecinos de Jaca... V-320
4646. Francisco de Villafranca, hijo de Diego de Villafranca y de Catalina de las Marinas, vecinos de Laguna... V-320
4647. Francisco Moreno, hijo de Francisco Moreno y de Catalina Hernández, vecino del Villarejo de Salabazán... V-320
4648. Antonio de Troche, hijo de Pedro de Arévalo y María Troche, vecino de Olmedo... V-320 v.
4649. Alonso de Argote, hijo de Francisco González de Argote y de Florencia Morano, vecino de Astorga... V-320 v.
4650. Antonio de Benabides, hijo de Francisco de Benabides y de Isabel de Argote, vecino de Astorga... V-320 v.
4651. Alonso Díaz, hijo de Toribio Díaz y de Isabel Gómez, vecino de Pedrosa... V-320 v.
4652. Juan González de Alor, hijo de Alonso Vázquez de Alor y de Catalica Alvarez, vecinos de Villanueva de Barcarrota... V-320 v.
4653. Juan Botello, hijo de Rodrigo Botello y de Marina Rodríguez, vecinos de Villanueva de Barcarrota... V-320 v.
4654. Alonso de la Parra, hijo de Bartolomé Parra, clérigo, y de Catalina Pérez, vecinos de Villanueva de Barcarrota... V-320 v.
4655. Juan Vázquez, hijo de Francisco Pérez y de María Vázquez, vecinos de Villanueva de Barcarrota... V-320 v.
4656. Esteban Yáñez, hijo de Juan Lucas y de Francisca Bázquez, vecinos de Villanueva de Barcarrota... V-320 v.
4657. Gonzalo Bázquez, hijo de Gonzalo Bázquez y de Catalina Bázquez, vecino de Villanueva de Barcarrota... V-321
4658. Alonso de Botello, hijo de Diego Gill [*sic*] y de Isabel Votella [*sic*], vecinos de Villanueva de Barcarrota... V-321
4659. Francisco Bázquez Caballedo, hijo de Alonso Bázquez Caballero y de Catalina Botella, vecinos de Villanueva de Barcarrota... V-321
4660. Pedro Blasco, hijo de Alonso Blasco Milano y de Isabel García, vecinos de Villanueva de Barcarrota... V-321

4661. Lope de Saavedra, hijo de Hernando de Torres y de Francisca Sánchez, vecino de la Puebla de Montalván... V-321

4662. Pedro de Santa Marta, hijo de Alonso de Santamarta y de Gracia Ortiz, vecinos de Astorga, a la Florida [*Otro asiento del mismo tenor aparece tachado al folio 77 v.*]... V-321

13 Marzo.

4693. Alonso Esteban Majarón, hijo de Pedro Martín Majarón y de Leonor González, vecinos de Usagre... V-321 v.

4694. Juan de Saldáñez, hijo de Juan Gutiérrez Castellanos y de Elena de Saldáñez, vecinos de Usagre... V-321 v.

4695. Pedro Martín, hijo de Benito Martín y de Leonor González, vecino de Usagre... V-321 v.

4696. Juan Martín, de color loro, a la Florida. Presento una escritura de alhorría, que pasó ante Pedro Ruiz de Porras, escribano público de Sevilla en 29 de Marzo de 1538 [*sic*]... V-321 v.

4697. Francisco de Lerena, hijo de Pedro de Lerena y de María González, vecinos de Arcos... V-321 v.

4698. Salvador, hijo de Hernando Fortes y de Olaria, vecinos de Valles... V-321 v.

4699. Francisco Rodríguez del Manzano, hijo de Gonzalo Rodríguez el Manzano y de doña Francisca de Villafuertes, vecinos de Salamanca... V-322

4700. Francisco Maldonado, hijo Rodrigo Maldonado y de doña Beatriz Ordóñez, vecino de Salamanca... V-322

4701. Esteban Zembrano, hijo de Alvar Rodríguez Zembrano y de Elvira García, vecino de Fuentes del Maestre... V-322

4702. Diego García, hijo de Juan Hernández y de María Alonso, vecino de la Fuente del Maestre... V-322

15 Marzo.

4709. Juan Martín, hijo de Sebastián Martínez y de María de Vidanes... V-322

4710. Cristóbal Lechuga, hijo de Luis Forcer y de Catalina Lechuga, vecino de Baeza... V-322

4711. Pedro de Briviesca, hijo de Pedro de Briviesca y de María de Quintana... V-322 v.

4712. Juan Romero, hijo de Florestán de Fuentes y de Elvira González, vecinos de Cazorla... V-322 v.

4713. Bartolomé de Herrada, hijo de Juan Gómez de Ribera y de María de Herrada, vecinos de Herrada... V-322

4714. García de Fuertes, hijo de Pedro Rodríguez de Buenaño y de Luciana de Fuertes, vecinos de Cazorla... V-322 v.

4715. Juan de la Corredera, hijo de Juan Delgado y de María Sánchez de la Corredera, vecinos de Vitigudino... V-322 v.

4716. Sebastián Medrano, hijo de Luis Fernández y de Leonor de las Haves, vecino de Sevilla... V-322 v.

4717. Francisco Guiñi, hijo de Francisco Guiñi y de María Gutiérrez, vecino de Valladolid... V-322 v.

25 Marzo.
4774. Pedro de Cabrera, hijo de Manuel López de Cabrera y de Mencía Alonso, vecinos de Curiel... V-85
4775. Miguel de Basaras, hijo de Pedro de Basaras y de Mari Velázquez, vecinos de Peñaranda... V-85
4777. Hernán González de la Hosa, hijo de Hernán González de la Hosa y de Inés Martínez, vecinos de Aracena... V-85

"Ship Lists of Passengers Leaving France for Louisiana, 1718-1724," *The Louisiana Historical Quarterly*, 14 (1931), 516-520; (1932), 68-77, 453-467; 21 (1938), 965-978 [Lancour No. 242].

The ship *The Count de Toulouse*

1718

Rolle des Passagers embarquez sur le vaisseau le Comte de Toulouze commandé par Monsieur le Chavalier de Grieu pour aller à la Louisianne.

Sçavoir

1. Monsieur Larcebault, Directeur General de la Compagnie
2. Les Srs Gordon, Capitane de'Infanterie
3. " " Simon, Commis de la compie.
4. " " Ferrarois, id
5. " " Renaudière
6. La femme du Sr Renaudière
7. Le Sr Loustaud, Commis de la Compie.

Mineurs

Le Sr Letoile, Brigadier
" " Ollivier, Sous Brigadier
La femme du Sr. Ollivier
Marc, Sergent
La Plume, Caporal

Gerard	Chevalier	La Grandeur
Saint Jean	Francoeur	La Branche
La Sonde	Va de bon coeur	Lepine

Quatre femmes de mineurs Trois enfans de mineurs
Jean Ponletet, garçon servant les mineurs
Total 22 personnes

Soldats

Saint Sauveur	Jean Rinaud	Pierre Ramée
Saint Julien	Saint Martin	Bellavoine
Balcon	Saint Martin	Yvon Troissard
Malo	Sa femme	Du Plessix
Sociodon	La Pensèe	La Farge
La Girardière	Ollivier Damiel	Jean Renoud
La femme du dit La Girardière	Saint Louis	Deslois
	Sa femme	Pierre Nerisson
Jean Larragonois	Sa fille	Jean Grandjean

Andre Beaudoin
Blondelet Cadet
Antoine Darnaud
Jacques Darnaud
Beaulieu
Cagnerel
Joseph Guery
Saint Martin
Nicolas Le Preaux
François Le Crosnier
Saint Jean
Sa femme
Jean Simon
La Fontaine
Edme Cheret
François Farcine
Laurens Manduisson
Jean François Le Crosnier
Deshamps
Crosnier
Jacques Moreau
Joseph de St. Georges
Augustine le Grand
Jean Etienne Philipe
Bernard Surge
Pierre Chevenet
Nicolas Gods
Nicolas Locar

Total 53 personnes

Amanville
Jacques Tanson
Domestiques de M. M. Larcebault et Gordon

Total 2 personnes

Ouvriers en Tabac

Mr. de Montplaisir, Inspector
Le Sr. Banjou, Conductor des ouvriers
Antoine Descarail
Pierre Ricard
Pierre Talu
Bertrand Besse
Pierre Gibert
Abraham Sisac
Jean Du Michel
Pierre Chaudruc
Pierre Andibert
Jean Fouillouse
Pierre Oisou
Jean Guirand
Jean Pourcharesse
Jacques La Rogue
Pierre Capdu
Jean Fegas
Pierre Laval
Jean Brouguet

Total 20 personnes

Concessionaires de la Societe des Sr. de Lair

Le Sr. Dufour de Courcelles
Tanns, brasseur
Michel Du buc, serruier

Total 3 personnes

Concession de M. de Baulne
Procureur du Roi

Le Sr. de Baulne
Madame de Baulne
M. le Chevalier
Melle. Boiron
Le Sr. Boiron
Le S. Demony fils ainé
Melle. Demony
Le S. de la Verge
Le S. Morel, Sécrétaire de M. de Baulne
Le S. Sigy, Commis
Louis Bouvalet, cuisinnier
Jean Bouvalet
Cristine Allard
Poires, arquebusier
Sonnis, tonnellier
Sabureau, cordonnier

Total 17 personnes

Concession de M. Pellerin

Le S. Pellerin
Me. Pellerin
Son fils
Pierre Guezo, son neveu
Noël Soileau, idem
Louis Bourbon, dit Ossement
Le femme du dit Bourbon
Annette Guillett, servante

Marie, servante negresse libre
Marguerite Argière, servante

Total 17 personnes

Concession des Srs. Lantheaume et Dubreuil

Le Sr. Lantheaume
Le Sr. Dubreuil
Me. Dubreuil
Deux de leurs enfans
Marie Gomband, servante de la Rochelle
Francoise, idem
Dauphin Cottive, charpentier de Paris
Jacques Ravaux de Mezieres, menuzier
Jacques Dioré, tonnelier de la Salle
Jacob David, cordonnier de La Rochefoucault
Jacques Francois Moreau, menuzier de Paris
Romain David, tailleur de La Rochefoucault
Bernard Caudelon, labourer de Tonzac
Pierre Lefebvre, idem, de Corbie pres Amiens
Francois Couronnay, idem, pres Lizieux
Jacques de Gaule, idem, de Chaalons
Jean Pinam, idem, pres Poitiers

Total 18 personnes

Récapitulation

Officers et Employes de la Compagnie d'Occident	7
Mineurs, leurs femmes et leurs enfans	22
Soldats, leurs femmes et leurs enfans	53
Domestiques de M. M. Gordon et Larcebault	2
Ouvriers en tabac	20
Concessionnaires de la Société de M. M. de Laire	3
Mr. de Baulne et ses gens	17
Mr. Pellerin et ses gens	10
M. M. Lantheaume et Dubreuil et leurs gens	18
Total des passagers	152

Il est permis au sus-dit Capitaine de passer dans son vaisseau le Comte de Toulouze les cent cinquente-deux personnes desnommés au présent estat, aux conditions qu'il observera les ordonnances du Roy.

Fait au bureau des Classes de la Marine à la Rochelle le quinziéme Novembre mil sept cent dix huit.

Hurlot

Nota—Le Sieur Edmond Sauvage officer s'est embarqué sur ce vaisseau quoy qu'il ne soit point sur le présent rolle.

Et Tanns de la concession de Mr. Delaire a dézerté.

Le Vaisseau *Le Philippe*

Rolle des Passagers Embarqués sur le Vaisseau Le Phillippes de la Compagnie D'Occident Capitaine Sr. Pipourse pour estres mis à terre à la Louisianne.

Premièrement.

Resté à terre et est débarqué dan *La Dauphine*:
Le Sieur Patrice Sauvage, Enseigne d'Infanterie.
Le Sr. De Beaulieu, Enseigne Reformé.

Concession des Srs. de Semonville et Canet
Habitans

Le Sr. de Semonville
Made. de Semonville
Le Sr. Canet
Made. Canet
Le Sr. de Bellegarde
François Girard, de Mezières sur Meuse
François Presson de Verdun
Henry Tremon de Mezières
Martin Dauvergne de Champeau en Brie
Louis de Flande de Corbie
Olne la Force, sa femme
Antoine Gaget de Verdun
Firmin de Flandre de Corbie
Jean Giros de Chabannes en Poictou
Francois Gallas de Paris
Guy Samson d'Houville en Beauce
Louis Estienne Leve de Paris
Pierre le Comte, de Dorton en Franche Comté
François Lupé de Paris
Claude Chevalier de Lion
François Payen de Peronne en Picardie
Nicolas Marcelles d'Arras
Jean La Fontaine de Fougere en Bretagne
Nicolas Lhomme de Chartres en Beauce
Jean Autrusseau de la Rochelle
Pierre Mauduisson de Beaugency
Marie Lemoine Dubourg d'Alvert en Saintonge

Concession du Sr. Olivier Labitant

Le Sr. Olivier
Louis de Bru de Paris, son commis
Marie Rousseau de St. Jean d'Angely, sa gouvernante
Pierre Lemoine de St. Mexant Évêché du Mans
Jean Menard de Bouteville près Angoulême
Pierre Brutier de Ruffé près Angoulême
Charles Antoine de Cannes de Paris
Jean Jolivet de Paris
Guillaume Damiens de Paris, Chirurgien
Jean Morin de Chateaubriand en Bretagne
Martin Alay de Chezeau en Touraine
Jacques Munier de Paris
Marc Boyer de la Rochelle
Pierre Bonu de la Rochelle

Concession de Beaucoudré

Le Sr. de Beaucoudré, concessionnaire
Marianne le Clerk de Paris sa gouvernante
Louis Pierre Dubois de Paris son commis, deserté
Jacques le Compte de Poictiers, idem
Maturin Masse de Mareuil en Poictou
Pierre Bidas de Francoeur Dumans, deserté
Antoine Barrait de Nantes, idem
Jean du Rieux de Saurnur, idem
Jean Milain de Augers, renvoyé

Martin Siguinos de Sts. Marie évêché de Nantes
Pierre Vaunier dt. Sans Soucy de Lavale, renvoyé
Jean Leval d'Angers, Renvoyé
Gabriel Demoins de Bouilles Laurens
Philippe Daniau
Le femme du dt. Daniau
Michel Lugué
Gabriel Milain

Concession de Sr. Brossard

Le Sr. Brossard de Lion
Mathieu Brossard son neveu
Made. Brossard sa belle soeur
Le Sr. Machou de Paris
Made. Grandin de Paris
Made. Faucon d'idem
Noël de Prevon de Lion
François Riviere d'idem
Louis Bernoldy
Catherine Chagneau de Rompsay
Marie Chagneau d'id.
Jean Chagneau d'id.
Marie Tachon d'id.
Jean Laboureau de Dompierre
Estienne Chagneau
Claude Doirier de Beaugency
François Chagneau
Marie Chatessin de Lion
Michel Bessac de Saintes
Jean Bouchard
Jean Tachon de Saintes
Louis Tachon

Concession de Sr. Mazy

Le Sr. Mazy
Le Sr. le Maistre
Louis Martinot de Tours
La femme du dt. Martinot
Louis Martinot leur fils
Therese Chailloux de la Rochelle
Louis Brisard de Tours
François Lamouveaux de Paris
François Allevin de Corbeil
Jacques Herisse de Tours
Jacques du Bois de Metz
François Allain de Tours
Antoine Denis de Paris
Antoine de la Goublaye de Fontainebleau
Gregoire Farrias
Rene Farrias
Jean Lhospital
Mathurin Dreux

Soldats

Silvestres, sergent
Boutier dit de Langle
DuVernay, cadet
DuRouvroy, cadet
Protest, cadet
Cezille L'aîné, Cadet
Cezille Le Cadet, cadet
Craft Alorge
Roussel L'aîné
Durand La Roche
sa femme
Benjamin Simon
Estienne Brassard d. Limage
Jean Baptiste Emery
Jean Thomas le Compte
Charles Compagnon
Paul Mazaye
Roussel Le Cadet
La Vasseur L'aîné
Le Vasseur Le Cadet
Duverger
sa femme
Hiacinthe Marchand
sa femme
Louis Fagot
sa femme
Ponce Merault
sa femme
St. Prix
Guerdon
Henry La Ville
Pierre Langevin
La Lancette
sa femme

Soldats Embarqués à Bayonne par Ordre de la Cour

Jean Pierre de Vaux
Pierre Fillatreau
Joseph Chola
Antoine Misère
Pierre Henry Devos
Louis Theodore Brisebois
Claude Bertel
Martin Bardel
Antoine Joseph Deur
Antoine Guerie
Charles Merier
Jean Baptiste Beauveau
Lenneur Guibert

Concession.	78
f. et filles	23
P. Part.	4
Offers. et soldats	30
déserteurs	13
	148

Passagers Libres.

Le Sr. Dumont
Batteon
Marselat, menuisier, de la concession de Mrs. de Laire
Catenat, tailleur de pierres, de la concession de Mrs. de Laire
Pierre Le Bel de la Concession de Mr. Massy

Je soussigné Directeur de la Compagnie D'occident certiffe le présent Rolle véritable pour le nombre de cent quarante-huict personnes à La Rochelle.
le 25 Janvier 1719 Lestobec

Il est permis au sus-dit Capitaine de Passer dans son Vaisseau le Philippe les cent quarante-huict personnes Desnommées au present Estat, aux conditions qu'il observera les ordonnances du Roy. Fait a la Rochelle le 26 Janvier 1719.

Hurlot

1719

Le Vaisseau *Le St. Louis*

Rôle des personnes embarqués pour la Louisianne sur le vaisseau le St. Louis commandé par le sieur Du Coulombier party de la rade de la Palisse pour la dittee Colonie le 21 du mois de Mars de la presente année 1719.

Concessionnaires

Concession du Sr. Cantillon	hommes	femmes et filles	Enfans	Nombre
La Sr. Cantillon	1			
Pierre Ruau	1			
Pierre Texier	1			
Denys Souloone	1			
Guillaume Leyne	1			
Thomas Hussy	1			
Jeanne Broat		1		

Guillame Jordan	1			
Jean Mathieu la Hosse	1			
Jean Courcy	1			
Simon Courbier	1			
Louis Courcel	1			
Jean Cornelly	1			
Anne Barault		1		
Jean Owen	1			
Jean Smith	1			
	14	2	.. [*sic*]	16
de l'autre part	14	2	..	16
Jonathan Darby, commis	1			
Jean Darling, idem	1			
Robert Cook, Irlandois	1			
Jean Bidet, Charon	1			
Estienne Bonnet, Menuisier	1			
Jean Jullien, Boulanger	1			
Elie Bertin, Boulanger et Cuiser	1			
Nicolas Crozimier, Labourer	1			
Michel Foret, Tonnelier	1			
Jacques Courtableau, idem	1			
Jacques Garant, Labourer	1			
Charles Lesné, valet	1			
Pierre Mongon, Raffineur	1			
Christophle Batteton, Mineur	1			
Ollivier Paronneau, Maréchal	1			
Charles Dupain, Laboureur	1			
Honoré Rotureau, Meunier	1			
Pierre Sebastien Lartout, Tailleur	1			
Jean Dessans, Perruquier	1			
Marie Bertin, Servante		1		
Jacques Autraseau, Charpentier	1			
Jean Rancon, Tailleur	1			
Jacques Barbier, Charpentier	1			
Simon Le Gas, Laboureur	1			
	37	3	..	40
de l'autre part	37	3	..	40
Concession de François Caussepain				
François Caussepain	1			
Charlotte Vendul, sa femme		1		
Pierre Caussepain	1			
Marie Caussepain		1		
Madelaine Fontaine, servante		1		
Passagers particuliers				
Madame Couturier		1		
Marie Martin sa servante		1		

Troupes				
Cadets				
Vincent Michel Rousselet	1			
Joseph Rousselet	1			
Sergents				
Du Rouvroy	1			
Soldats				
Simon Le Gendre	1			
Andre Jonneau	1			
Simon Fouguet de Bellecourt	1			
Jean Micheau	1			
Philippe Fouguerolle	1			
sa femme		1		
Jean Hubert	1			
Exilez par lettre de Cachet				
Le St. Ballay, chirurgien	1			
Déserteurs et autres gens envoyez par ordre de la Cour				
Albert dit Rencontre	1			
Paul Andre dit la Soye	1			
Pierre Fresines dit Chateauneuf	1			
Picard ~	1			
Jean Bary dit laGrandeur	1			
	54	9	..	63
de l'autre part	54	9	..	63
Pierre Camusat dit Champagne	1			
François Poupart dit Rencontre	1			
Charles Areus dit Beausoleil	1			
Jean Louis Achard dt. St. Paul	1			
Joseph Pomart dt. St. Laurent	1			
Joseph Jouvens dt. St. Joseph	1			
François Catinois	1			
Claude Nicolas	1			
Jean Baptiste Eurard	1			
Lavigne	1			
Tranche Montagne	1			
Primptems	1			
La Navette	1			
	67	9	..	76

Je soussigné Directeur de la Compagnie d'Occident certiffie le présent Rôle véritable pour le nombre de soixante-seize personnes embarquées sur le vaisseau le St. Louis pour la Louisianne sous le commandement du Sr. Du Coulombier à la Rochelle le 17 Mars 1719

Lestobec

Il est permis au susdit Capitaine de passer dans son vaisseau Le St. Louis les soixante-seize personnes dénommées dans le present Rolle aux conditions qu'il observera les ordonnances du Roy.

Fait a la Rochelle les jour et an que dessue

Hurlot

Rôle des personnes embarquées pour la Louisianne sud la Flute la Marie commandée par Mr. Tapic party de la rade Chef de Baye pour la ditte Colonie le vingt huite May, 1719.

Premièrement Concession du Sr Case	hommes	femmes et filles	Enfans	Nombre
Le Sr François Nicolas Caze	1			
Le Sr Jacques Caze de Guisy	1			
Ouvriers ou domestiques				
Pierre Mascavy	1			
François Bechet	1			
Marie Bechet		1		
Guillaume Bechet	1			
sa femme		1		
Jean Bechet age de 4 ans			1	
Genevieve Bechet		1		
Antoine Caupin	1			
Concession de Mr Valdetere				
François Marechal	1			
Pierre Verié	1			
Louis Bergé	1			
Louis de la Haye	1			
Marie Fret		1		
Laurens Boyneau	1			
François Tezé	1			
de l'autre part	12	4	1	17
Concession de Mr. de Laire				
Jean Brulé	1			
Robert Jacob	1			
Gennevieve Poulin sa femme		1		
Passagers Particuliers				
La Demoiselle Duval		1		
La Dlle Charlotte Duval, sa fille			1	
Marie Louise Elizabeth Lepiner		1		
Marie Charlotte, petite, sa fille			1	
Jacques Pigeaud Me Cordier	1			
Pierre Pigeaud]				
François Pigeaud]			3	
Louis Pigeaud]				
Rene Etienne Meroq de Saumier	1			
Louis Monville	1			

Le Sr Boutard	1			
Antoine Falcon	1			
Gens engagez au service de la Cie pour la Louisiane				
Claude Bordier, Masson	1			
Louis de la Soeur, matelot	1			
Thoynoud Filatreau sa femme		1		
Andre Magon	1			
Mauthurin Bonnet sa femme		1		
Louis Courtez	1			
Jean Baptiste Frebourg	1			
Samuel St. Quentin	1			
	25	9	6	40
de l'autre part	25	9	6	40
Troupes				
Mr. Le Valdeterre, Capitaine	1			
Mr. de Saintray de Birague, Lieutenant	1			
Mr. Marchand de Courcel, Lieutenant	1			
Le Sr. Dumont de Montygny, sous lieutenant	1			
Lr Sr. Malouet, idem	1			
Le Sr. Andriot, idem	1			
Le Sr. Flaming, Enseigne	1			
Cadets				
Le Sr. François Soyez	1			
Sergents				
Garnier	1			
Giberty	1			
Guerin	1			
Soldats				
Vincent	1			
Jean Gentil	1			
Edme Vitard	1			
Benoise Temin sa femme		1		
Jean Buffy	1			
Charles Diette	1			
Jean Beauvois	1			
Charles Vollard	1			
Michel Mechin	1			
Francois Le De	1			
Barthélemy de La Haye	1			
Pierre La Motte	1			
Pierre Sozet	1			
Jean Marquet	1			
François Balet	1			
Nicolas Belleret	1			

Rogues Michel	1			
	52	10	6	68
de l'autre part	52	10	6	68
Louis Damont	1			
Jean Clautier	1			
Christophe Maninard	1			
Louis Dupain	1			
Pierre Parils	1			
Nicolas Florieux	1			
Pierre Le Roy	1			
Robert de la Haye	1			
Jean Follin	1			
Jean Marchand	1			
Claude Benoist	1			
François Dumont	1			
Jacques Michel Biberon	1			
Jacques Guerin	1			
Louis La Marche	1			
Déserteurs et autres envoyage par ordre du roy				
Michel Beau	1			
François Charpentier	1			
Pierre Laurendicq	1			
Marie Françoise Coquerelle, sa femme		1		
Françoise Laurendicq sa fille			1	
Jean Pierre Bonger	1			
George Clarasky	1			
Benoist Monder St. Amant	1			
Pierre Le Tourneur	1			
Philippe Sterling	1			
Jean B^te^ Breau	1			
Jacques Begon	1			
Pierre Pasquier	1			
Passerasse Hobreman	1			
Thomas Hoorwegh du Hoost	1			
Jean Boyd mort en route de Maladie	1			
François Longchamp	1			
	82	11	7	100
de l'autre part	82	11	7	100
Jean Françoise Vigneron	1			
Daniel Liguet	1			
Marguerite de Larbre sa femme		1		

Catherine Ligny sa fille		1	1	
Jean Bte Jarry	1			
Jean Janson de Lagrange	1			
Marie Ferdinande Cotet sa femme		1		
Isabelle Jansot sa fille			1	
Ambroise Moreau	1			
Jeanne Paul sa femme		1		
Nicolas Le Breton	1			
Jacques Le Bourgeois	1			
Gabriel Maindet	1			
Jean François de la Gaubertiére	1			
Jacques Salmon	1			
Pierre Masson	1			
Michel Gaultier	1			
Jean Housset dit Ringal	1			
Jeanne Partois sa femme		1		
Louis Galle	1			
Catherine Nicole sa femme		1		
Dominique Reges ou Lamotte fraudeur de tabac sa femme est à Cognac en prison	1			
Vandre Cuttin de Gembry	1			
Ignace de Bolle	1			
Antoine Gerre de Lavillette	1			
François Bufet	1			
Simon Stelly	1			
Albert de St. Frouly	1			
Jacques Callay	1			
Marie Boyer fille agé de 20 ans				
Aristian Ladner Luisse	1			
Pierre Bargan	1			
Pierre François Petrouchy	1			
	107	17	9	133
de l'autre part	107	17	9	133
Gens venus depuis les Rolles arrêtez				
Le Sr. Coutte de la Concession de Mrs. de Laire	1			
Le Sr. de Chavannes par Lettre de Cachet	1			
Le Sr. Jullien Sansor, fradeur de tabac	1			
Louis Raymond Boildieu, soldat	1			
Jean Bte Boquet, id.	1			
Milan Denis, id.	1			
Charles Bontems, Cadet	1			
Louis Telbo de Luçon de la Concession de Mr. Valdeterre	1			
Rene Gautier, Soldat de la Compagnie	1			

François Gentil, id.	1			
Monsr. de Rouvere, sous Lieutenant d'Infanterie	1			
Marie Landrot fe. d'un soldat		1		
	119	18	9	145

Je soussigné Directeur de la Compagnie d'Occident certiffie le présent Rôle véritable pour le nombre de cent quarante six personnes embarquées sur le vaisseau Le Marie sous le Commandement du Sr. Tapye a La Rochelle le 27 May 1719.

Lestobec

Il est permis au sus-dit Capitaine de passer dans sons vaisseau La Marie les cent quarante six personnes denommez dans le present Rôle aux conditions qu'il observera Les ordonances du Roy.

Fait à la Rochelle Le 27, May, 1719.

Hurlot

Jacques Renaud envoyé de Rouën par Lettre de Cachet arrivé depuis le present Rolle arreté ce que je certiffie véritable venfoy pour le d. Renaud.

Lestobec

HURLOT

Le Vaisseau *l'Union*

Rôle des personnes embarquées pour la Louisianne sur le vaisseau L'Union commandé par Mr. de la Mancelière Grané party de la rade de Chef de Baye pour la ditte Colonie le 28e. May de la presente année 1719.

Concession du Sr Caze	Premièrement hommes	femmes et filles	Enfans	Nombre
Monsieur de Villardeau, Directeur Général de la Colonie de la Louisianne	1			
Le Sr. Marlot, teneur de livre de Villardeau	1			
Jean Bard de Paris, valet de Mr. Villardeau	1			
Concessionaires				
Mr. Renaud	1			
Catton	1			
Les Srs. Ozias	1			
Durendy	1			
de La Brosse	1			
Pugeol	1			
Lallemand	1			

Bernard Toré	1			
La femme du dit Sr. Toré		1		
sa fille			1	
Ignace Roerou	1			
Ouvriers de la Concession de Monsr. Renaud				
François Bastin	1			
Joseph Pepin	1			
Pierre Troquelet	1			
	15	1	1	17
de l'autre part	15	1	1	17
Antoine Denis	1			
Simon Jacquemin	1			
Joseph Chartier	1			
Gregoire Stin	1			
Jean Jacques Petrard	1			
Pierre de la Plante	1			
Jean Lamontagne	1			
Jean B^te^ Le Feure	1			
Nicholas Dumont	1			
Jean Pouillard	1			
Hubert Fine	1			
Joseph Gautier	1			
Laurens Rocroix	1			
Lievains Frogneux	1			
François Beguet	1			
Nicolas Baudeson	1			
Philippe Manur	1			
Leonard Blampin	1			
Joseph Catherine	1			
Nicolas Darmuseau	1			
Hubert de Tierse	1			
Barthelemy Renier	1			
Joseph Faussier	1			
Louis Legrand	1			
Remis Bisseret	1			
Joseph Boissieux	1			
Joseph Morage	1			
Guillaume Britel	1			
Jacques Coquillard	1			
Pierre Tisson	1			
Jean de la Garde	1			
Antoine Prevost	1			
Jeanne Prevost sa femme		1		
Elizabeth Prevost sa fille			1	
Annette Prevost idem			1	
Gabriel Le Doux fille			1	
Jean Jacques de Manaye	1			
	48	2	4	54

de l'autre part	48	2	4	54
Concession de Mrs. de Ponival				
Le Sr. Jacques de Ponival	1			
Le Sr. Claude de Ponival	1			
Ouvriers				
Joseph de Trusquelay	1			
Jean de Trusquelay	1			
Jean Lavenant			1	
Marin Saumon			1	
Thomas Martin			1	
René Gaudin	1			
Jean Le Gallay	1			
François Chevalier	1			
Jean Gerard			1	
Passagers particuliers				
Le Sr. Couturier	1			
Jeanne Gaudin sa femme		1		
Jeanne Gouturier leur fille		1		
Pierre Desjean adressé à Mr. Diron Capitaine à la Louisianne	1			
Le Sr. Renaud	1			
Le Sr. François de Verteuil de Beaumasson	1			
Jean Verteuil son fils			1	
Le Sr. Descreuset	1			
Troupes				
Le Sr. Carrier de Mancray, cape.	1			
Le Sr. De Beauchamp, Lieutenant	1			
Le Sr. Degua, id	1			
Le Sr. Le Sorteval, id	1			
Made. De Sorteval son epouse		1		
Le Sr. de Kgoet sous lieutenant	1			
Le Sr. Deysautier, idem	1			
Le Sr. de Coustillan id	1			
	67	4	10	81

de l'autre part	67	4	10	81
Cadets				
Le Sr. Moguet	1			
Sandra	1			
Michel	1			
Darbonne	1			
Dufour	1			
Mauricet	1			
Deysautier	1			
Reneux	1			
Sergent				
Jacques Livet	1			

Soldats				
Pierre Charles Sainton	1			
François Augustin Sainton	1			
Pierre Heroulx	1			
Vincent François Annet	1			
Pierre Jamin	1			
Nicholas Bringuan	1			
Robert Cheron	1			
Jean Lavergne	1			
George Ysquain	1			
Jean Louis Lousy	1			
Louis Salomon	1			
Adrien le Capitaine	1			
Jacques Paquet	1			
Guillaume Barbeau	1			
Jacques Chevrié	1			
Pierre Gobet	1			
Philippi Marteau	1			
François Perichon	1			
Charles Croliés	1			
Nicholas Robin	1			
François Patreu dt. Beaulieu	1			
Claude Gouin	1			
	98	4	10	109
de l'autre part	98	4	10	109
Gens engagez pour le service de la Compe à la Louisiane				
Antoine le Breteche Me. Canonier	1			
Le Sr. Boiriou earluer patron de Felougue	1			
Le due Boiriou son épouse		1		
Jean Viens dt Carpantra Charper	1			
Exillez par ordre du Roy				
Le. Sr. Praromand Suisse	1			
Le Sr. Nolland Irlandois	1			
Le Sr. De Baliguand de St. Quentin	1			
Le Sr. Tourdan de Paris	1			
Nicolas Joussaint dt. La Bonté	1			
Jean George dt. Bataillard	1			
Claude Duval dit San Soucy	1			
Hyacinthe Geoffray dit Provinçal	1			
Déserteurs des troupes du Roy				
Jean Duval dit St. Jean	1			
Joachim Claude dit San Façon	1			
Gaspard Stichy de Suisse	1			
Joseph Augustin Bobles	1			
Gaspard Engler de Suisse	1			

Nicolas Jardinier	1			
François Pozat	1			
Pierre Bideau dt. St. Jacques	1			
Marice Chesy	1			
Pierre Leonard dt. St. Michel	1			
Jean de la Creuse dit Comtois	1			
Jacques Lorin dit Tarascon	1			
	121	5	10	136
de l'autre part	121	5	10	136
Louis Vincent Terasse dit Poitevin	1			
Claude Antoine dit Vaudray	1			
Vaudray	1			
Paquet de Guisse dit Sançoucy	1			
Barthelemy Grandrin dit St. Louis	1			
Jean Despace dit Beausejoir	1			
Jean Almene dit Langlois	1			
Antoine Medieu dit Bellefleurs	1			
Jacques Jeune dit Baguette	1			
Mathieu Salouin	1			
Vincelle Starusquy	1			
Zaccarie Beaurepas	1			
Jean Guillaume Beuret	1			
Antoine Gabriel dt. la Forest	1			
Gaspart Silar	1			
Gerouilt Vattre	1			
Martin Raspasser	1			
François Antoine dt. Tosse	1			
Claude Fortier dt. sans regret	1			
Noel Aubert	1			
Andre Pasquier	1			
François Tibaud dt. San Quartier	1			
Louis Dange dt. La Sonde	1			
Simon Laine	1			
François de Salle	1			
Michel Grandin dt. St. Amant	1			
Rene Brindonneau	1			
Jean Renaud	1			
	148	5	10	163
de l'autre part	148	5	10	163
Fraudeurs de tabac				
Pierre Voisin dit Montreuil	1			
Pierre Bouteau	1			
Faussonniers				
Claude Guillaume de Loan	1			
Jean Guillaume id.	1			
Pierre Magny	1			

Vagabons envoyés de Paris et autrés de Rennes				
Jean Chechery	1			
Charles Bellamy	1			
Germain Casse dt. Godain	1			
Jean Launay Dumans	1			
Urbain Paquiot	1			
Rene Autain de la Meilleraye	1			
François Soussié	1			
Jean Chesnay de la Flèche	1			
Pierre Arreau	1			
Thomas des Mars	1			
Pierre Guerard de Grand Camp	1			
Nicolas Valet	1			
Jean Charles	1			
Jean Guilloy	1			
Jean B^{te} Ferrand dt. de Melcoeur	1			
Jean Verrier	1			
Robert Teusse	1			
Charles La Cour	1			
Simon Menard	1			
Jacques Larmeron	1			
Jean Vernoy dt. Le Compte	1			
	174	5	10	189
de l'autre part	174	5	10	189
Etienne Toussiger	1			
Louis Blav	1			
Pierre Senouche	1			
Guillaume Dempierre	1			
	178	5	10	193

Je soussigné Directeur de la Compagnie d'Occident Certiffie Le present Role véritable pour Le nombre de Cent quatre vingttreize personnes embarquées sur le vaisseau L'Union sous le Commandement de Mr. de La Manceliere Grané. Fait a La Rochelle le 27 May 1719.

Lestobec

Il est permis au sus-dit Capitaine de passer dans son vaisseau L'Union les cent quatre-vingt-treis personnes denommées dans le présent Rôle aux conditions qu'il observera Les ordonnances du Roy. Fait à La Rochelle le 27 May 1719. Hurlot

[Prior to this point, which is the beginning of the fourth installment, the source material was given in French, with some appropriate translations in English given in brackets, which were omitted above. From this point on only the English translation is given. The conclusion of the article was never published.]

1719

Roll of the passengers embarked on the vessels of the Company of the Indies for Louisiana since July 1, 1719.

List of the concessionaries (or grantees), private passengers, infantry officers, cadets, soldiers, exiles by order of the King and all others who have been embarked at La Rochelle to pass to Louisiana from July 1, 1719, to this very day. Namely:

On the ship *The Two Brothers*, sailed August 19, 1719

Concession of the Chevalier de Tourneuille

Mr. Le Chev'er de Tourneuille

Workmen

Adrien Pigeon
Charles Robin
Jacques Millet
Jean B'te Cesar, negro
Jean Moras
Jacques Pesson
Marie Audebran, servant

Concession of Mr. Villemont

Mr. de Villemont
Made. de Villemont, his wife
M'lle Jean de Villemont] their children
M'lle Marie Anne de Villemont]

Workmen

Jean Tabarre
Eustache de Lignaule
Alphonse Ninger
Mathurin Charvau
Charles Antoine Morisset
Jacques Chaigneau
Marie Girarde
Anne Broutier
Tudick Manie
Anne Vrignault
Jean B'te David
Henry Gedeon

Concession of Mr. Chantreau de Beaumont

M. Chantreau de Beaumont
Catherine Aubry, his wife
Madeleine Chantreau]
Francois Chantreau] their children
Marie Michel Chantreau]
Antoine Chantreau]
Charles Hurau, his son-in-law

Valets

Pierre Namblard
Pierre de Nantes
Nicolas Crochet

Private Passengers

Pierre Dumans, tailor
Marie Anne Dumans, his wife
Le Sr. St. Olivier
Le Sr. Love
Marie Fermignac, wife of Sergeant Guerin who left on the Flute "La Marie"
Jean La Rieux] her children
Marie La Rieux]

Persons engaged in the service of the Company

Mathurin Bonnet, master-carpenter of artillery

Francois Bonnet] his children
Nicholas Bonnet]

Officers

Le Sr. de Reclot, officer in expectation

Le Sr. Lafon ditto

Names	*Place of birth*	*Age*	*Height ft.in.*	*Hair*	*Trades*
Pierre Delmas, sergeant	Rodez in Languedoc	25	5.5	chestnut	
	Cadets				
Bonnere Francois Langlois	Paris	19	4.9	ditto	
Le Sr. de St. Just	ditto	24	5.2	blond	
Richard Masson	ditto	31	4.8	black	
Le Sr. de la Commerie	ditto	20	4.8	chestnut	
Le Sr. Hugot	Troys in Champagne	17	4.8	black	
Le Sr. Baudouin	Paris	13	4.5	blond	
	Soldiers				
Alexandre Aufret	Paris for N. O.	18	5.	black	carver
Pierre Paillard	Abbeville	15	4.½	chestnut	
Jacques Philippe Pezé	Betune in Artois	22	5.	ditto	wig-maker
Nicolas Poyer	Paris	31	4.10	ditto	
Jean B'te de Condamine	Nimes	19	5.	ditto	
Jean B'te Lemaitre	Caen	32	4.8	ditto	baker
Jacques Contant	Angers	16	4.7	ditto	laborer
Jacques Normandin	La Rochelle	18	5.	black	baker
Guillaume Rolland	Paris	16	4.	chestnut	
Martial Simon	Nantes	14	4.6	ditto	
Charles Marchand	St. Gervais near Alencon	23	5.	ditto	laborer
Alain Brian	Ponscore in Brittany	22	5.	ditto	ditto
Pierre Tostain	St. Pierre Lizieux	23	4.8	ditto	ditto
Pierre Paysant	St. Jean of Angely	30	4.8	black	hatter
Joseph Houssaye	Port Louis	33	5.	ditto	sailor
Pierre Ponan	Metz	27	4.8	chestnut	
Jacques Joseph Barbotte	Dol in Brittany	40	5.2	black	laborer
Jacques Lenaud	Xaintes	22	5.1	chestnut	mason
Jean Paren	Rouen	20	4.8	black	rope-maker
Francois Roy	Montigny	30	4.10	ditto	laborer
Francois Losserandes	Savoy	40	5.	ditto	gardener
Jacques Guignard	Croizie in Brittany	18	4.8	chestnut	
Pierre Achard	Bordeaux	30	4.5	ditto	laborer
Laurent Monier	Marinande in Guiène	14	4.6	black	lock-smith
Pierre Peltier	Nantes	21	4.8	ditto	weaver
Pierre Dominique Bayard	Valencienne	32	4.10	chestnut	
Jacques Harnault	Saintonge	22	4.8	ditto	weaver
Mathieu Courtineau	Charente	36	5.2	black	

	Tobacco Smugglers				
Pierre Ducret	Mans	40	5.	black	weaver
Louis Malbos	Saussignargue	40	5.2	light	shoe-maker
Louis Marsseau	Bersuire	24	5.	ditto	weaver
Marguerite Cartier, wife of Malbos					
Claude Liepart	Monchetlaby	65	5.3	gray	baker
Francois Momieur	Brenneville	25	5.2	chestnut	weaver
Jean Ste. Brissy	Chassigny	24	5.3	ditto	stone-cutter
Andre Langlois	Faucour in Normandy	55	5.3	ditto	laborer
	Dealers in contraband salt				
Claude Chetivot	Soissons	45	5.3	gray	
Claude Chapelle	Ste. Marie of Bois	37	5.3	black	
Claude Manez	Berry	35	5.4	light	able seaman
Charles Druin	Biron Sorce	36	5.3	ditto	ditto
Charles Demarty	City of Andoussy	38	5.3	ditto	weaver
Pierre Morin, called Claire Fontaine	Sette	35	5.3	ditto	
Jean Jerboz	Sernion	32	5.4	ditto	
Jean B'te Minozet	L'Ossosigny	30	5.1	ditto	
Jean Lefebre	Angers	49	5.1	gray	
Jean Royon	Breneuil	18	5.2	blond	
Jean Savouret, called Canville	Canville	60	5.1	gray	
Jean Bigord	Longueil	20	5.4	black	shoe-maker
Jean Dumoulin	Origny	30	5.	ditto	brewer
Jacques Dertin	Abbeville	28	5.1	light	laborer
Jacques Debzet	St. Amand	55	5.4	ditto	shoe-maker
Jacques Cary	Picardy	40	5.1½	ditto	able seaman
Jacques Vasseur	Candot	20	5.	black	weaver
Nicolas Francois Batalle	Busigny	20	5.	light	
Nicolas Moncel	Sommeville in Champagne	37	5.	ditto	able seaman
Nicolas Bileux	Anger-on-Saône	22	5.	ashy	life-saver
Andre Cabulot	Abbeville	23	5.5	chestnut	able seaman
Andre Lenoir	St. Amand	37	5.1	black	
Andre Mianez	Angers	20	5.3	light	laborer
Antoine Camus	Paris	41	5.	black	
Antoine Dusaussoir	Cury	38	5.	ditto	
Michel Tellier	Vervin	50	5.5	chestnut	brewer
Michel Treguenot	Plomion	47	5.	black	able seaman

Francois Condot	Eauteville	23	5.5	light	
Francois Botel	Ronsoy	17	4.9	black	
Francois Amand	Cuerieux	35	5.1	black	
Pierre Bouvard	Sologne	17	5.1	light	
Pierre Hypin, called Hubert	Chogueux	18	5.2	blond	laborer
Pierre Seillier	Chognet Bristet	40	5.5	ashy	flax-dresser
Pierre Connyot	Gremier	19	5.2	chestnut	
Louis Devochet, called Petitjean	Amiens	29	5.	black	
Louis Laloix	Berneuil	26	5.2	light	weaver
Louis Despagne	Rontoir	21	5.3	light	
Thomas Bouclet	Geante	40	4.8	black	wooden shoe-maker
Urbain Caret	Ansilvieux	30	4.8	ditto	
Guillaume Dieu	Veunan	45	5.2	blond	able seaman
Germain Boulle	Comté	35	5.3	light	ditto
Nicolas Ouaillier	Irson	35	5.3	ditto	ditto
Roland Duru	Any	40	5.2	black	shoe-maker
Jeanne Letrillard, his wife					
Antoine De Roy	St. Pierre	30	5.1	chestnut	
Jean Fresson	Irson in Thieras	36	5.3	light	
Jean Merle	Savoy	36	5.4	ditto	
Jean Trolet	Vilars l'Hopital	38	5.4	black	
Francois Court	Savoy	30	5.2	chestnut	
Antoine Trolet	Crunont	40	5.3	ditto	
Francois Bertin	Bourguenville	26	5.2	ditto	
Francois Hautois	Beneuil	38	5.4	black	weaver
Etienne Valet	Angers	32	5.3	ditto	
Jean Le Roy	Freret	21	5.3	light	
Vagabonds coming from Orleans					
Jean Valencie	Combreu near Orleans	29	5.	light	
Denis Brouere	Angerville	24	5.2	black	
Jacques Denis	Paris	40	4.6	blond	wig-maker
Benoist Dufeu	Toussien in Bresse	19	5.	black	
Louis Toussard	Blois	15	4.	chestnut	
Nicolas Touzet, called Richard	Versailles	18	5.1	ashy	baker
Ditto coming from Lyon					
Francois Fouteur	St. Colombe in Dauphiné	39	5.3	chestnut	sailor
Marguerite Michon, his wife					
Etienne Falguet	Savoy	40	4.8	light	
Etienne Hodieu	Lyon	21	4.7	black	
Charles, called Metz	Lisle in Flanders	15	5.	blond	

Julien Descomptez	Lyon	45	5.4	light	paper-maker
Jean Riviere	Marty-on-Ance	50	5.	black	vine-dresser
Family children					
Jean Fouquet	Orleans	30	5.	black	
Pierre Maillard	Versailles	22	5.	light	joiner
Blancard, called St. Blaise, deserter	Toulon	29	5.1	chestnut	

Women and girls taken for fraud

Nicole Le Doux	Madeleine Brisson	Marie Jeanne Goguet
Marie Auril	Marie Michel	Marie Ficlou Herode
Marie Grillon	Marie Ceinturier	Marie Claire Annot
Jeanne Tacy	Francoise Bagnelot	Marie Anne Grize
Louise Durand	Anne Namond	Francoise Fressin
Jeanne Lenfant	Francoise Ferret	Jeanne Arnandé
Marie Bordeau	Blanche Vigneron	

Women and girls coming from Rochefort by order of the Council

Marie Anne Porche	Orleans	30
Jeanne Le Feure	Paris	38
Marie La Fontaine	ditto	38
Catherine Haby	ditto	21
Catherine Oudart	ditto	33
Babet La Fleur	ditto	34
Marie Louise Brunette, called Valentin	ditto	28
Marie Paris	Orleans	30
Marie Igonnet	Auvergne	22
Marguerite Vallet	St. Quentin	25
Marie Francoise de Coutelier, called Perty	Sens in Burgundy	18
Tiennette Gennet	ditto	33
Jeanne Vigneron	Langres	49
Genevieve Chanuallon	Melun	30
Marie Duclaud	Soissons	23
Marie Jeanne d'Aigremont	Abbeville	21

On the ship *Le Marechal d'Estrées*, sailed August 19, 1719

Officers

Le Sr. Courbette, Lieutenant of Infantry
Le Sr. Simarre, Ensign
Le Sr. Legendre, ditto
Le Sr. Habains, Officer in expectation
Le Sr. Duclos, ditto

Cadets

Les Sr. Chabert	Paris	22	4.8	black	
Antoine Frizon	ditto	14	4.5	chestnut	
Francois Gillot	ditto	13	4.5	ditto	

Soldiers

Jean Bte Mallet	Rouen	20	5.2	ditto	founder

Michel Micouin	Villedieu	24	4.8	ditto	goldsmith
Noel Perault	Paris, St. Paul	17	4.6	black	silkworker
Claude Gaudray	Metz	48	5.	ditto	gardener
Ouerre Henault	Angers	29	5.	chestnut	upholsterer
Jean Bte. Charles Baillard	Amiens	17½	5.	ditto	
Nicolas Courbec	Trépagny-on-Vexin	39	5.	ditto	
Andre Martin	Chatillon in Bery	28	5.	ditto	tailor
Jean Bte. Hus	Eloye, Bishopric of Avranche	17	5.2	blond	
Francois Cadiou	Auray	17	4.8	black	
Hurbain Rochereau	Saumur	22	4.8	ditto	laborer
Simon Nedelec	Landerneau in Brittany	24	5.	ditto	
Jean Hurault	Mélun in Brie	28	5.	brown	
Amedee Gaston Baillet	Brest	21	4.8	black	
Natalis Bertrand	Gerandan	29	5.	chestnut	gardener
Charles Robin	Légère in Marche	24	5.	ditto	
George Taluar	Dol in Brittany	18	5.4	ditto	
Francois Jolly	Nantes	28	4.6	black	
	Tobacco Smugglers				
Jean Claude LeCoint	Le Font, Franche Comté	15	4.1	brown	
Jacques Spegrand, called La Franchise	Quet in Dauphiné	36	5.1	chestnut	
Antoine Pussin	Lisle in Flanders	30	5.2	light	
Rene Chapon	Autun	18	4.5	black	
Pierre Maurin	Marsominge in Bresse	28	5.	ditto	
Nicolas Martel	Dijon	15	4.2	light	
Etienne Laporte	Bourg in Bresse	35	4.5	chestnut	
Pierre Comté	Lyon	26	5.3	light	maker of gold and silver cloth
Jacques Villet	Lyon	21	5.1	ditto	
Jacques Bertrand	St. Pierre of Mans	40	5.1	black	
Francois Bruneteau	Sables of Aonne	35	4.9	ditto	laborer
Jacques Vialet	Begorre	34	4.6	light	hemp-comber
Joachim Rossel	Beaumont	56	4.6	gray	
Pierre Paillard	Vestal	30	5.2	light	tailor
André Bouchet	La Botière	36	5.3	black	ditto
Michel Gaondet	Gamertre	35	5.	ditto	hemp-comber

Alexandre Corresux	Autragne	22	4.4	light	paper-maker
Jacques Biot	Begorre	55	4.6	black	
Joseph Raymond	Poilin	27	5.2	ditto	surgeon
Pierre Gay	Chaleau Roux	20	4.5	ditto	
Jean Payen	Granot	58	5.	ditto	
Pierre Carpentier	Poulerville	12	4.5	ditto	
Paul Fournier	St. Neux	12	4.5	blond	
Thomas Hyvalle	Corbey	10	4.3	ditto	
Paul Bardet	Vieux Rouin	30	5.	chestnut	
Jacques Rolland	Vubay in Artois	18	5.	ashy	
Jean Ouailly	Belquin in Artois	70	5.2	gray	
Jean Naudin	Paris	45	4.9	black	
Rennes Raquin, his wife					
Antoine Pacot	Dijon	35	4.9	black	
Francoise Pacot, his sister					
Barthelemy Berlemon	Port	42	5.6	ditto	
Marguerite Morice, his wife					
Margte. Berlemon, their child					
Jean Padot	Dain	18	4.6	ditto	
Denis Dalavier	Capin	17	4.6	ditto	
Louis Minard	Dauphin	15	4.6	blond	
Louis Danel	Daupin in Artois	16	5.2	light	
Paguette	Ferriere				
Pierre Launois	Remy	38	5.3	black	
Simon Lucas, called Lamontagne	Thomas, Normandy	50	5.	gray	cook
Antoine Derville, called Lacroix	Mantigny in Picardy	28	5.1	red	
Jean Delmaz	Dalby Cange, (Normandy)	40	5.	ashy	
Jean Durand	Landisatz in Normandy	34	5.2	black	
Marie Charpentier, his wife					
Blaise Cheminet	St. Agnal deux	40	5.	ditto	laborer
Henry Petit	Belame	50	5.1	light	mason
Denis Verdun	Châlon in Farne	40	5.1	chestnut	laborer
Joseph Vallet	Champlieux	30	5.1	ditto	ditto
Jacques Rivet	St. Nizier below Charlieux	24	5.2	ditto	ditto
Jean Ste. Forsine, called Romain	Rome	40	5.	black	tailor
Claude Anselme	Roma in Bresse	40	5.	light	laborer
Claude Darsin	Mont Louet	20	5.	chestnut	ditto
Philbert Gouard	Villefranche	19½	4.7	black	ditto
Jean Bte. Monet	Bourg St. Christophle	40	5.	ditto	ditto
Jean Nimond, called Granger	Pout in Beaujolais	29	5.	light	ditto

Claude Tiers	Port Anton in Dauphiné	35	4.8	black	ditto
Jean Pierre Lustier	Velin	28	4.8	ditto	ditto
Michel Dubois	St. Bonnet in Dauphiné	30	4.6	ditto	ditto
Jean Chanat	Autragne in Languedoc	24	5.1	ditto	ditto
Pierre Feratier	Jensinet Luchon	26	4.5	ditto	ditto
Francois Varenne	Valence	40	5.	ditto	ditto
Pierre Moulin	Ginodan	35	5.4	chestnut	d'to
Claude Rioux	Gennister	22	5.1	blond	ditto
Mathieu de Cour	St. Frod	35	4.5	black	ditto
Vidalle Brion	Retourno	35	5.2	ditto	ditto
Vincent Barnier	Chabrillan	25	4.6	ditto	ditto
Jean Gussis, called Philbert	Tellier	42	4.7	light	ditto
Philbert Baudot	St. Quin near Paris	42	4.8	black	ditto
Antoine Courtine					
Jean Lyonnard					
	Dealers in contraband salt				
Jullien Cretien	Lisle in Flanders	22	5.4	black	thatcher
Francoise Gaguet, his wife					
Adrien Prevost	Honnecourt	24	5.3	ditto	laborer
Charles Mariez	Jean Court	17	5.5	blond	ditto
Martin Montulet	Sousman Lemoine in Liège	36	5.5	black	nail-maker
Adrien Le Bay	Plomion	30	5.2	blond	laborer
Claude Mornon	La Roully	45	5.5	light	ditto
Mathias Ponchon	Licourt	35	4.8	black	ditto
Philippe Ouarnier	Izengerenelle	40	5.2	light	ditto
Victor Le Roy	Licourt	19	5.2	ditto	ditto
Francois Moy	Izon in Bèry	36	5.2	black	ditto
Louis Vullier	St. Jean d'Angely	27	5.1	chestnut	mason
Claude Senechal	Couin	35	5.3	light	tailor
Elizabeth Collas, his wife					
Marie Jeanne, ditto, their child					
	Vagabonds coming from Lyon				
Francois Lafon	Sencier	33	5.3	chestnut	shoemaker
Jean Miquel	ditto	21	5.4	light	silkworker
Aime Pichon	Lyon	17	5.1	ditto	ditto
Jean Raymond	ditto	40	5.1	ditto	blacksmith
Jacques Seyby	ditto	16	4.3	black	shoemaker
Nicolas Radeau	ditto	40	5.2	light	
Pierre Courson	Bordeaux	17	5.2	ditto	buttonmaker

Family children					
Sebastien Moreau	Paris	20	5.1	blond	tailor
Charbonnier, called La Feuillade	ditto	28	5.3	light	surgeon
Jacques Deslande	Versailles	29	5.2	black	
Nicolas Regnault	Corbeille	30	5.2	ditto	
Francois Alot	Chartres in Besse	20	5.3	chestnut	
Jean Bte. Faiquy	Paris	20	5.	ashy	upholsterer

Exiled persons coming from Bayonne by order of M. de Berwick

Jean Le Clerc	Paris	27	5.	chestnut	
Thomas de Route	Tronne in Espagne	63	5.	black	
Antoine Beroude	ditto	60	5. $\frac{1}{2}$	ditto	
Antoine Glatigny	Plomion	25	5.1	black	pit-sawyer
Nicolas Legrand	L'Écaille	26	5.	red	laborer
Jacques Rivet	Grigny	24	5.1	black	laborer
Nicolas Fauble	Picardy	38	5.2	light	tile-maker
Charles Boulanger	Vonyeville	30	5.	black	butcher
Jean Pierre, called Petitjean	Paris	20	4.7	ditto	mason
Martin Esloir	Troville	20	5.2	ashy	laborer
Pierre Aubert	Crisse	55	5.2	gray	mason
Gabriel Besoin, called Le Chat	Boussel near Pailly	44	5.	black	laborer
Jacques Vollet	La Chapelle Blanche	35	4.7	ditto	tile-maker

Deserters

Pierre Doet, called Granville	Callais	24	5.	chestnut	
Romain Roman, called St. Germain	Toar	26	5.2	ditto	
Jean Renault, called Sans Regret	Lyon	28	5.3	ditto	

Vagabonds coming from Orleans

Nicolas Berenger	St. Laurent de Lin in Anjou	47	5.5	gray	
Martial Morin					
Claude Emanuel Batisier, called Dumenil	Paris	20	5.3	light	surgeon

Vagabonds coming from Rennes

Pierre Menoux	Sens	33	5.1	black	
George Mercier	Valence	36	5.	ditto	
Jean Fleury, his wife					
Jean Mercier]					
Madeleine Mercier] their children					
Jeanne Mercier					

On the ship *The Duke de Noailles*, sailed September 16, 1719

Concession of M. Dartaguiette

Le Srs. Babaqui, Sorvate, D'hospital, (and) Tessendier, surgeon
Pierre Degrat

Concession of Mr. Bail de Beaupré

Mr. Bail de Beaupré
Made. de Beaupré, his wife
Marie Marchand, chamber-maid
Anne, called Laport, ditto

Workmen

Jean Devigne
Jean Devigne, his wife
Pierre Devigne] their
Jean Devigne] children
Nicolas Ansiot
Jacques Quertems
Jean Fosse
Jean Parabert
Jean Brevier
Nicolas Laveine
Mathieu Dorange
Antoine Langlois
Simon Montais
Marie Montais, his wife
Joseph Montais] their
Jacob Montais] children
Jeanne Montais]
Louis Le Mire
Michel Gambier
Jean Brunel
Gilles Hanry

Private Passengers

Le Sr. Pinon Tours
Marguerite Tout-douce

Officers

Le Sr. Caron, Captain of Infantry
Le Sr. Detcheparre, Lieutenant of Infantry
Le Sr. de Longueval, ditto
Le Sr. de Brassee, ditto
Le Sr. Courten, Sub-lieutenant
Le Sr. de Villecourt, ditto
Le Sr. Charreau, ditto
Le Sr. Chevalier Lambert, ditto
Le Sr. Duguartier, ensign
Le Sr. Franchomme, ditto
Le Sr. de St. Esteban, ditto

Names	*Place of birth*	*Age*	*Height ft.in.*	*Hair*	*Trades*
	Cadets				
Le Srs. Claude Tilloy	Paris	21	5.	blond	
Claude Jordan	Valence	19	5.2	ditto	
Jean Bte. Malter	Paris	18	4.8	black	
	Sergeant				
Jacques La Roche	Châlons in Champagne	43	4.8	ditto	tailor
	Soldiers				
Pierre Antoine Duflos	Tournay in Flanders	30	5.	brown	wig-maker

Guy Le Guerre	Carhaix in Brittany	24	5.4	black	
Claude Mercier	Paris	17	4.6	blond	tailor
Elzear Felix de Crèvecoeur	St. Omer	36	4.1	brown	
Luc Druet	Nancy	17	4.	blond	
Claude Roussel	Corby in Picardy	44	5.	chestnut	laborer
Francois Moreau	Chateau Signon in Ivernois	33	5.	black	silk-worker
Francois Billecault	Auxerre in Burgundy	37	5.2	ditto	surgeon
Jacques Gouet	Clermont in Auvergne	26	5.2	chestnut	weaver
Rene du Rocher	Poitiers	16	4.8	black	wig-maker
Florent Lemoine	Saumur	18	4.10	ditto	ditto
Charles Duval	Villedieu l'Espoil, Basse Normandy	24	5.	chestnut	surgeon
Agatte Ange Perdon	Saumur	45	5.2	blond	ditto
Francois Maingueneau	Paris	21	5.	brown	
Jean Maillard	Brest	22	5.	chestnut	
Jean La Marzelle	Libourne	40	5.	black	wig-maker
Nicolas Brau	Nevers	26	5.2	ditto	farrier
Denis Gouet engaged by the Company					butcher
Pierre Voysin engaged by the Company	Paris				pavier
Pierre Betuchet engaged by the Company		17	5.	ditto	
Francois Dubois					
Louis Ozanne					
Jean Dupré					
Jean Francois Frementier	Rennes	45	5.2	blond	
Etienne Le Roy	La Flèche in Anjou	30	5.2	black	joiner
	Dealers in contraband salt				
Jean Brunet	Angers-on-Saône	19	5.	light	miller
Charles Calet	Vergon	35	5.	brown	miller
Francois Girault, called Bonnemar	Rilly	30	5.	black	dresser
Rene Linger	Martizet	45	5.1	chestnut	edge-toolmaker
Jacques Gentil	ditto	41	5.1	black	laborer
Louis Perin	Neont in Poitou	42	5.1	ditto	ditto
Alexis Dujardin	Bagnolet	21	5.1	light	gardener
Guillaume Chapelle	Ste. Marie du Bois	48	5.7	black	laborer
Pierre Malsieu	Charbont	42	5.	ashy	sailor
Louis de Roche	Neuilly in Normandy	26	5.1	chestnut	laborer
Claude Ridel	Paris	33	5.5	black	joiner
Jean Trocour	Amiens	40	5.4	ditto	weaver
Joseph Deschamps, called La Roze	Lambry	45	5.3	ditto	rope-maker

Claudine Guenée, his wife					
Claude Glaine	Roman in Dauphiné	24	5.2	light	carpenter
Jean Dupré	Senerpon	13	4.	ashy	shoemaker
Louis Nicolas Famechon	Dingue	15	4.	blond	
Louis Massuel	Hotion	30	5.3	chestnut	puppetmaker (?)
Jacques Bouchet	La Selle in Tourenne	45	5.1	gray	laborer
Francois Dauphin	Neont in Poitou	32	5.	black	
Nicolas Pallier	Sere in Tourenne	45	5.	chestnut	
Francois Baudet, called Bastillon	La Chapelle Blanche	48	5.1	gray	
Louis Blanchard	Arleu	15	4.	ashy	
Adrien Verdure	Cette Outre	50	5.	ashy	
Jean Gottefrin	ditto	55	5.	gray	
Louis Assay, called Manchet	Montrichard in Tourenne	50	5.	black	laborer
Pierre Aubert	Crisse	55	5.2	black	mason
Vincent Froger, called Pied-de-Chat	Marsilly	38	5.	black	
Jean Demarty	City of Landousy	43	5.1	ditto	weaver
Louis Blochet	Verluy	33	5.3	chestnut	
Jean Ste. Tringuar	Caneillan	15	4.8	light	
Thomas Dupré	Senerpon	14	5.	black	shoemaker
Thomas Ansau	ditto	40	5.	ditto	
Bernard, called Van	Paris	17	5.1	chestnut	turner
Antoine Alard	Montreuil	20	4.9	black	
George Tesson	Tombière in Gennevois	34	5.	chestnut	
Jacques Lambert	St. Neulisse in Savoy	24	5.	black	
Jacques Noiron	Barentin on Seine	48	4.½	ditto	
Michel Pinchard	Rinsart	32	5.5	light	carter
Jean Demarty	Sury-on-Oise	35	5.2	ditto	weaver
Philippe Lehaut, called St. Olive	Corby	30	5.1	ditto	
Jean Dauvin	Neuilly	37	5.2	black	weaver
Jean Ste. Nottard, called Montal	Paris	31	5.2	light	joiner
Marie Durisse, his wife					
Francois Couttant	Tiviers	38	5.3	black	able seaman
	Tobacco Smugglers				
Etienne Malezieux	Dampierre in Champagne	40	4.5	chestnut	laborer
Nicolas D'Estel	Metz	24	5.	light	baker
Jean Collain	Coublanc	30	5.4	ditto	ropemaker
Jean Biat	Elbet	28	4.6	black	coppersmith

Marie Vasseur, his wife					
Pierre Cussin	Sarmelieux	33	5.1	black	vine-dresser
Jeanne Fremy, his wife					
Claude Nicolas Cussin, their child					
Pierre Passerat	St. Arban	36	5.2	ditto	gardener
Louis Guemel	Verton	18	4.6	light	mason
Jean Gottard	St. Genis Lavar in Lyonnais	27	5.	black	weaver
Ennemond Berson	Lyon	50	4.5	light	laborer
Pierre Maurix	Marsonning in Bresse	50	5.	black	
Joseph Joumas	Ventadour road	58	5.3	ditto	baker
Francois Cheron					
Laurent Ferrand					
Louis Roussel	Chalaindray	15	4.2	chestnut	laborer
Benoist Etienne Veillon	St. Arban	47	5.1	gray	ditto
Claude Dutartre	Dermois, Franche Comté	25	5.1	light	joiner
Jean Soubaygné					
Catherine Detrouillet, his wife					
Catherine Soubaygné] Anne Soubaygné] their children					
Claude Bernard, called Chambery					
Marie Giraude, his wife					
Francois Berthelot, called Marais	Talent	48	4.8	black	able seaman
Joseph Raffin	Cursia in Bresse	40	5.6	chestnut	miller
Antoine Fleury	Bourg in Bresse	32	5.6	ditto	
Catherine Fenerolle, wife of Damel					

Vagabonds taken at Orleans

Silvain Thomas	Meule	35	4.7	black	laborer
Pierre Fausset	Sussy in Béry	23	4.7	ditto	ditto
Michel Branchet	St. Benoist-on-Loire	54	5.2	gray	ditto
Andre Pepin	La Trinite in Normandy	25	5.	black	ditto
Rene Jean	Paris	52	5.	gray	goldsmith
Marguerite Pepie, his wife					
Pierre Barbier	St. Germain Lavelle	19	5.2	chestnut	

Deserters coming from Bayonne by order of M. the Marshall of Berwick

Nicolas Girard   Joachim La Rogue

Exiled Women

Francoise Gaffer   Marie Hardy

Copy of the Lists of passengers for Louisiana who have been embarked at La Rochelle since July 1, 1719.

Done at La Rochelle, April 11, 1720.   Lestobec

[At this point the article, which was marked "to be continued," ceased, thus leaving the period 1719 to 1724 undone.]

L. Perez. "French Immigrants to Louisiana 1796-1800," *Publications of the Southern History Association*, 11 (1907), 106-112 [Lancour No. 242-1].

[With the subheading, "Settlements of Bastrop and Morehouse in the District of Ouachita. Condensed Documentary History," the first two and one-half pages of this piece are nothing but a list of documents.]

Etat des Familles arrivées par Mr. le Baron de Bastrop le 19e. Avril 1797.—en vertu de Son Contract

Samüel Curswel,	age de 35 ans	
Sa Femme,	34	
Jeanne Sa Fille,	10	5 têttes
Robert Son Fils,	5	
Mathiew, do.,	3	
Jean de Hart	43 ans	
Sa Femme,	43	
Abraham Son Fils,	14	
Jean, Idem,	12	7 têttes
Winton, Idem,	10	
Jeannette Sa Fille,	7	
Jacob Son Fils,	2	
Samuel Brown,	31 ans	
Sa Femme,	31	
Charles Son Fils,	4	
Sali Sa Fille,	6	7 têttes
Charles Son Fille,	4	
Elisabeth Sa Fille,	3	
Rachel ditto,	2	
Charles Gim,	27 ans	
Sa Femme,	25	4 têttes
Jean Son Fils,	1	
Henriette Hardy, Opheline,	9	
Jacques MacCalester,	32 ans	
Sa Femme,	25	4 têttes
Elisabeth Sa Fille,	9	
Jacques Son Fils,	5	

Jean Kurter,		36 ans	6 têttes
Sa Femme,		32	
William, Son Fils,		7	
Mathieu, ditto,		6	
Hamilton, do.,		4	
Jeannette, Sa Fille,		1	
Joseph Seggers,		46 ans	8 têttes
Sa Femme,		36	
Jean, Son Fils,		12	
Sali, Sa Fille,		11	
Joseph, Son Fils,		10	
Faderie, Idem,		8	
Marie, Sa Fille,		4	
Elisabeth, do.,		2	
Jacques MacMahan,		25 ans	4 têttes
Sa Femme,		23	
Elisabeth, Sa Fille,		4	
Maria, ditto,		2	
Jean Kugel,		22 ans	4 têttes
Sa Femme,		19	
Elisie, Son Fils [sic],		3	
Marthe, Idem,		1	
Guillaume Stuart,		53 ans	8 têttes
Sa Femme,		37	
George, Son Fils,		18	
Michel, ditto,		12	
Salli, Sa Fille,		10	
David, Son Fils,		8	
Rachel, Sa Fille,		6	
Mary, ditto,		2	
Joseph Boëñ,	Garcon,	23 ans	7 têttes
Isaac Och,	do.,	21	
Bernard Jochs,	do.,	19	
George Cimbers,	do.,	24	
Silvain Baskem,	do.,	22	
Michel Rotscher,	do.,	23	
André Wilne,	do.,	22	
Total des Individus,			64 têttes

Au Fort Miro le 8e, May 1797 ./.
.... Fithiol.

Etat des familles arrivées á ce Poste, des Etats Unis, le 7e, May 1797—par la voye de la Nlle Madrid et de le Natchés, sous la conduite du Mr. de Bréard en Vertu du contract passé avec Mr. le Baron de Bastrop.

William Burney, age de	58 ans	
Sa Femme,	46	4 têttes
Elisabeth Arrie, Ophéline,	1	
Datis Négrisse *da dit* Burney,	11	
William Burney, Fils,	28 ans	
Sa Femme,	25	
Jean, Son Fils,	8	5 têttes
Jacques, Idem,	6	
Gillaume, Idem,	1	
Latrie Power,	43 ans	
Sa Femme,	30	
Catherine, Sa Fille,	10	
Nancy, ditto,	8	8 têttes
Thomas, Son Fils,	7	
Folli, Sa Fille,	5	
Margareite, do.,	4	
Martha, do.,	2-1/2	
Henry Kurter,	28 ans	
Sa Femme,	26	4 têttes
Catherine Sa Fille,	5	
Joseph, Son Fils,	3-1/2	
Abraham Kurter Frere *da sus dit?*	22 ans	2 têttes
Joseph Kurter, Idem,	21	
Christoffer Offen,	49 ans	
Sa Femme,	50	
Jean, Son Fils,	20	6 têttes
Joseph, Idem,	18	
Maria, Sa Fille,	14	
Margareite, do.,	8	
Yve Qacharie, Champagne,	50 ans	2 têttes
[or Vve] Nice, Sa Negrisse,	15	
Charles Onil,	35 ans	
Michel Silvain,	35	4 têttes
Caleb Husted [?]	21	
Guill. Miller,	21	
En tout,		35 têttes

Au Fort Miro le 10 May, 1797 ./.

.... Fithiol.

Mrs. F. O. James. "Passenger Lists Taken from Manifests of the Customs Service, Port of New Orleans, 1813-1837," *New Orleans Genesis*, 1 (1962), 23-28 [Lancour No. 243].

[Only the first instalment of this article, covering the period to 1821, was published, although it was to be continued. Subsequent issues of the *Genesis* have been checked carefully. The arrangement of the original article has been modified to allow the avoidance of repeating the name of the ship and the date for each passenger.]

January-December, 1813 Book 1, Page 1.

Sch. *Louisa*, March 22

Charles Nun
A. Benetio
Sam Black
Francisco Allice
Mark Barn

Sch. *Paula*, March 29

Augustine Ancona
Jose Servillies
Bernardo LeFan
Jacques A. Coste
Francisco Contret
Francisco Mendez
Francisco Dunan

Sch. *Creole*, March 30

Mme. Borron

Sch. *Susette*, March 30

Batiste Roman

Sch. *Conception*, April 22

J. B. Rivarde

Sch. *Ceceilia*, April 26 [also *Cecilia*]

Catalina Basneve
Mr. St. Jago
Jos. McCuillin
Mrs. Felicity Salande
John W. Summonton

Sch. *Susette*, April 29

Michael Roache

Sch. *Expedition*, May 5

Capt. H. Holmes
M. Dufour
M. Lavignac
M. Lecond

Sch. *Louisa*, May 13

John Rendon

Sch. *Two Friends*, May 17

L. Penson
C. Connor

Sch. *Industry*, May 18

Savage

Sch. *Lady of the Lake*, May 21

I. Ellis
T. Willis
S. Davenport

Sloop *New York of Providence*, May 21

James Larence
Andrew Allen
Ronald Dombrowsky
Major Hayden Edwards
Patrick Gilmour
John Gaston

Book 1, Page 2.

Sch. *Paula*, May 21

Esedro Zains

Sch. *Creole*, May 22

Joseph Lacoste
John Rouse

Sch. *Henriquita*, May 22

Mr. Smith
Madam Movant
Mr. Monternant
Mrs. S. James

Sch. *Felicity*, May 24

Vincent Ramo
Jos. Redando

Sch. *Flying Fish*, May 24

Francis Armaud

Sch. *Nuestra Ira*, May 24

Domingo Rodriques

Sch. *Dell Carmen*, May 28

Maria Montanet

Sch. *Susette*, May 29

Sophia Destrahan
Celeste Pastor

Ship *Caroline*, May 29

Gertrude Pigott
Betty Pigott
Frances Pigott
William Pigott

Sloop *Nancy*, June 4

Hannah Hah
Daniel Hah
Gabriel Hah
Philis Hah

Sch. *Florentine*, June 4

M. Mitchell

Sch. *Cecilia*, June 9

P. H. Delay

Sch. *Paula*, June 14

Mme. Cathrine Asree (Wife of Capt.)

Sch. *Louisa*, June 21

Sefroy D'Celive

Sch. *Diligence*, June 22

Thomas Holden

Sch. *Susette*, June 25

Jos. Dutrieul

Sch. *Susette*, June 26

Seriaco Newola

Sch. *Diligence*, July 14

Pedro Golba
John Fraga

Sch. *Felicity*, July 15

Pedro Limos
Maria Prados

Sch. *Flying Fish*, July 15

John LaCoste

Sch. *Cecilia*, July 21

Jos. Perez
Francisco Mendez
Servando Goetier

Book 1, Page 3.

Sch. *Rosalie*, July 31

Capt. Ignatius Fowler
Manuel Androi
Robt. Mitchell
Philma Pero

Sch. *Flying Fish*, Aug. 21

Felix Salvador
M. Mathews
Lee White
Joseph Suiveyor

Sch. *Rosalie*, Sept. 4

Dr. Murphy
John Smith

Andre Westalot	A. H. Rivaide	
John Miller		

Sch. *Cecilia*, Sept. 7

M. Maquez	M. Sandie	Juan Antonia
M. Paul	Manuel Cred	

Sch. *Rose in Bloom*, Sept. 29

Firmin Henry	Jean Henry	

Sch. *Jealous*, Oct. 2

Mrs. Garraye & 2 children	J. B. Dulusse	Emile Sarmet
	A. Moran	Jos. Ledet

Sch. *Flying Fish*, Oct. 4

L. Armaud

Sch. *Cecilia*, Oct. 6

Lorenzo Comins	Joseph Rufeil	Pedro Sanchez

Sch. *Magdalena*, Oct. 18

Lee White	John E. Smith	

Sch. *Susette*, Oct. 23

M. Heytas	M. Perez	

Sch. *Celeste*, Nov. 13

M. Salvadore	M. Jean	

Sch. *Rosalie*, Nov. 14

P. Anoy

Sch. *Felicity*, Dec. 4

Pedro Simons

Sch. *Magdalena*, Dec. 5

Samuel Harrison	Marshell Smith	

Book 1, Page 1A.

Sch. *Susette*, Jan. 14

George Faire	John Dawson	
John Fon	Lewis Monant	

Brig. *Bourbon*, Jan. 16

Miguel Elloustardo

Sch. *Caridao*, Jan. 19

Domingo Garcia

Sch. *Magdalena*, Feb. 15

Mme. Larnagan & Son	Jose Huber	
Mme. Vaughn	Samuel L. Reeder	

Sch. *Louisa*, Feb. 15

Wm. H. Robinson

Sch. *Bolodore*, Feb. 16

Peter Alba	John H. Hudson	Mary (african woman of color)
Antonia Marin	Chas. Baron	
	Joaquin Baran	

Sch. *Creole*, Feb. 18

John Smith	Mme. Garcia	Mamsell Sevey
Robert Criswell	Mme. Morant & Servant girl	Mme. Dumo
Abel Terriell		John Dumo

Sch. *Susette*, Feb. 23

Wm. Roseblaque	Mme. Connise	Joseph Portas
Mme. Ramos	Mr. Mulsin	

Sch. *Paula*, Feb. 24
Raymond Castile
Sch. *Creole*, Mar. 19
Mme. Garcia | Mr. Ballazan | Francisco Manuveb
Sch. *Cecilia*, Mar. 19
Wm. Simonton

Book 1, Page 5.

Sch. *Magdalena*, Dec. 4
M. Bernard | G. Mallerin | Lorenzo Roman
Miguel Fowiner | Juan Moretti | Jose Groda
Pedro Oliver | Pedro Garand
Sch. *Creole*, Dec. 6
Aug Dow | Juan White | M. Cooper
Allen Gorham | M. Peraco
Sch. *Celeste*, Dec. 7
Jno. F. Miller | F. Holland | Solomon Gorham
I. Dobson | John B. Goulson
Sch. *Susette*, Dec. 9
Jules Caesar | Julian Ybario | Francisco Braun
I. B. Hern | Mamie Heytas | Juan Montaner
Sch. *Marguerite*, Dec. 14
P. Fernandez
Sch. *Dauphine*, Dec. 20
F. Brunetti | Juan Pinlats | A. Caperdaino
Sch. *Pearl*, Dec. 27
Sapier | Gerard | Fourfundle
Winego | Fourman

March-April, 1815. Book 1, Page 6.

Sch. *Susanna*, Mar. 7
P. Fernandez
Sch. *Nesesidad*, Mar. 13
I. Morant | G. Moore | F. A. Bernardo
I. Carbonear | Bernardo Valle | V. Ramos
Ivan Osida | Angee Dour | M. Saranet
Sch. *Felicity*, Mar. 25
Richard Harrison | John Lynch
Wm. Dooley | Mrs. Martel
Sch. *Dos Amingos*, Apr. 8
Edmond Forestal | W. M. Robertson | H. Hesse
M. Detreau | M. Boras | P. Rivier
Sch. *Creole*, Apr. 14
Mme. Hervia | Mme. Rhamsey

January-December, 1821 Book 1, Page 7.

British Brig *Liberality*, Jan. 3
J. Gordon | Chas. Roberts | Geo. McGillam
Samuel Adamson | Jas. Roberts | Thos. McFadson

Sch. *Athenian*, Jan. 4

J. Battalter
H. Patterson
R. Blane
Wm. Henry & 3 children
M. Garcia

Sloop *New York*, Jan. 10

James Lawrence
Major Hayden Edwards
Andrew Allen
Patrick Gilmore
Rynald Dombrowsky
John Gaston
Enoch Earl

Brig. *Alexandria*, Jan. 12

John LeGanta
Balada Lopox

Sch. *Victoria*, Jan. 17

M. Delusle
M. Larick
M. Sacie
Miss Walkins
Miss Mairgin
Miss Rosalie Vilie
Miss Zino

Sch. *Sunflower*, Jan. 18

Walter Byrnes
David Wilson

Brig. *Monai*, Jan. 19

James Briton
John Hetten

Brig. *Laura Townes*, Jan. 19

Silvester Blanc
Victor Borris
Louis A. Buchet
John Figowido

Book 1, Page 8.

Brig. *Margaret*, Jan. 20

Mrs. Barbarts

Brig. *Silk Worm*, Jan. 20

Joseph Allegu
Bartholomew Benny

Brig. *Stativa*, Jan. 23

Mrs. Mary Johnson

Brig. *Mary Ann*, Jan. 23

Dudley Bale
John Patterson
Jacob Grusitive

Sch. *Bee*, Jan. 28

Andrew Anderson

Sch. *Experiment*, Feb. 1

Thos. Ferry
Chris. Yates Fonda
Wm. Brown
R. Skates
James Green
Joseph Green
Joseph Smith
Samuel Brown

Brig. *Clarissa Ann*, Feb. 2

Mrs. L. Harris

Ship *Elbe*, Feb. 2

Capt. Teasdale

Sch. *Baraco*, Feb. 3

John Harhly
Geo. Wallin

Sch. *W. B.*, Feb. 6

Francis Magamas
Francis Dott

Brig. *Washington*, Feb. 7

Chas. Cushing
Peter Hogenor
John Baptist

Brig. *Columbus*, Feb. 9

T. Schroeder

Brig. *Penelope*, Feb. 9

Louis Simon (Fils Mulatto man, Cabin passenger)

Book 1, Page 9.

Sch. *Louisa*, Feb. 12

I. Alies (with two female slaves)
F. Sabia
J. DeBann
Lewis Arno
Francis Montoro
M. Ouasil (with one free mulatto boy)

Brig. *William & James*, Feb. 13

Capt. Gad Peck

Ship *Anna Maria*, Feb. 14

Gibbons
LeRoy
Chas. Haron & son

Ship *Mary Maria*, Feb. 15

Dr. Isaac Newton
Chapelle

Schooner *Comet*, Feb. 15

William Bager

Ship *General Hamilton*, Feb. 15

George Miller

Sch. *St. Antonie*, Feb. 20

Morgan Jones

Sch. *Cygnet*, Feb. 23

Viz. A. G. Aldrich
Viz. Joseph Baranard

Sch. *Margaret*, Feb. 23

Benjamin Young

Sloop *New York*, Feb. 23

Lewis Jarre
J. R. Blood
J. Alsie
Walter C. Hayes
Elihu Smith
James McDonald
John Ungerwater
John Brame

Book 1, Page 10.

Brig. *Margaretto*, Feb. 23

Miss Roberts

Brig. *Friendship*, Feb. 25

Nathaniel Hart

Brig. *Catherine*, Feb. 25

William Whitehest
A. Hacket

Ship *Edw. Downes*, Feb. 26

Wm. Jas. McClean
Richard Beck
A. R. Kenna
Matt. Burns

Sch. *Victoire*, Feb. 28

Martin Talas
E. Riggio
E. Danney
A. Fanagette

Ship *Margiana*, Feb. 28

John Sherman

INDEX OF SHIP NAMES

INDEX OF PLACE NAMES

America / United States of America

Foreign Nations

England (cont.)
Cheshire 84 132
Christchurch 69 71
Cornwall 99 132 134
Coventry 133
Derbyshire 85 110 114
Devonshire 114
Dowton 70
Elton 85
Ely 69
Evesham 109
Exeter 97
Falmouth 132
Farnham 85
Flint 85
Gloucester 158
Goosner 85
Gravesend 10
Greenwich 109
Hampshire 68 69 85
Harfield 69
Hereford County 119
Hertfordshire 133
Howes 69
Howton 70
Howton Conquest 69
Hull 112 135
Isle of Wight 68
Kelsall 85
Kent County 115
Kinsley 84
Lancashire 69 84 110
Langport 70
Leeds 110
Leicester 134
Leicestershire 69 106
Lincolnshire 107 112 124 133
Liverpool 14 84 85 96 97 99 103 104 106 107 110 112 114-117 119 120 123 124 132
London 10 69-74 76 82 86 87 97 98 104 107 118 120 121 123 124 128 131-136
Longworth 70
Lydiate 84
Mackerfield 85
Malden 70
Manchester 85

England (cont.)
Mansfield 85
Milden 69
Mitchell 99
Newcastle 135
Newgate 15 18
Newport 68
Norfolk 99
Norfolk County 120
North Allerton 69
Northopp 85
Northumberland 115
Nottingham 134
Nottinghamshire 85
Norwich 69 71
Norwick 99
Oxford 69 71 132
Parr 85
Plymouth 107 108 112 114
Poorchmouth 69
Porbery 69
Portsmouth 101 111 123
Preston 14 84
Preston in Andernesse 69
Raschiffe 69
Rothwell 110
St. Martins in the Fields 69
Salop 85
Sileby 106
Somersetshire 69 70 108
Southwark 133
Spalding 124
Staffordshire 84-86 100
Staple Inn 69
Surrey 69
Surry 133
Sutton 69
Tamworth 85
Thorn Co. 121
Warrington 84
Westchester 84
Whitchurch 85
Wiltshire 70 157
Witley 69
Woolverhampton 86
Worcester 69 158
Worcestershire 109
York 69 135 136

England (cont.)
Yorkshire 69 103
France 21 100 113 115 189
Abbeville 208 209 211
Alsace 103
Alençon 156 208
Alvert 192
Amiens 191 210 212 217
Andoussy 209
Angers 192 193 208-210 212
Angers-sur-Saône 209 217
Angerville 210
Angoulême 192
Anjou 215 217
Ansilvieux 210
Any 210
Arleu 218
Arras 192
Artois 208 213
Auray 212
Autragne 213 214
Autun 212
Auvergne 211 217
Auxerre-en-Burg 217
Avranche 212
Bagnolet 217
Barentin-sur-Seine 218
Basse Normandy 217
Bayonne 194 215 219
Beauce 192
Beaugency 192 193
Beaumasson 203
Beaumont 207 212
Begorre 212 213
Belame 213
Belquin in Artois 213
Beneuil/Berneuil 210
Berry 209
Bersuire 209
Bèry 212 214
Betune 208
Birague 198
Biron Sorce 209
Blois 210
Bordeaux 109 116 123 124 208 214
Bouilles Laurens 193
France (cont.)
Bourg-en-Bresse 212 219
Bourg St. Christophe 213
Bourguenville 210
Boussel 215
Bouteville 192
Breneuil 209
Brenneville 209
Bresse 210 212
Brest 115 212 217
Bretagne 192 208 212 217
Brie 156 192 212
Brittany 192 208 212 217
Burgundy 211 217
Busigny 209
Caen 208
Calais 215
Candot 209
Caneillan 218
Canville 209
Capin 213
Carhaix 217
Cette Outre 218
Chabannes 192
Chabrillan 214
Chalaindray 219
Chaleau Roux 213
Châlon in Farne 213
Chalons 191
Châlons in Champagne 216
Champagne 208 209 222
Champeau 192
Champlieux 213
La Chapelle Blanche 215
Charbont 217
Charente 208
Charlieux 213
Chartres 192
Chartres in Besse 215
Chassigny 209
Chateaubriand 192
Chateau Signon in Ivernois 217
Chatillon in Bery 212
Chezeau 192
Chognet Bristet 210
Chogueux 210
Clermont 217

France (cont.)
Combreu 210
Comté 210
Corbeil/Corbeille/Corbey/ Corbie/Corby 191-193 213 215 217 218
Coublanc 218
Couin 214
Courcel 198
Courcelles 190
Crisse 215 218
Croizie 208
Crunont 210
Cuerieux 210
Cursia in Bresse 219
Cury 209
Dain 213
Dalby Cange 213
Dampierre in Champagne 218
Dauphine 156 212-214
Daupin 213
Dermois 219
Dieppe 156 157
Dijon 212 213
Dingue 218
Dol 208 212
Dompierre 193
Dorton 192
Eauteville 210
Eloye 212
Faucour 209
Felougue 204
Ferriere 213
Flanders 210 212 214
Fontainebleau 193
Fougere 192
Franche Comté 192 212 219
Francoeur Dumans 192
Freret 210
Gamertre 212
Geante 210
Gembry 200
Gennister 214
Gerandan 212
Ginodan 214
Granot 213
Gremier 210
Grigny 215

France (cont.)
Guemene 102
Guiène 208
Guisy 197
Haver de Grace 103
Havre 112 119
Honnecourt 214
Hotion 218
Houville 192
Irson 210
Irson in Thieras 210
Izengerenelle 214
Izon in Bèry 214
Jean Court 214
Jensinet Luchon 214
Kaiserberg 103
La Botière 212
La Chapelle Blanche 215 218
La Flèche 217
Lambry 217
Landerneau 212
Landisatz 213
Landousy 218
Langres 211
Languedoc 156 208 214
La Rochefoucault 191
La Rochelle 191-194 196 197 201 206-208 219
La Roully 214
La Salle 191
La Selle in Tourenne 218
La Trinite in Normandy 219
Lavale 193
L'Écaille 215
Le Font 212
Légère 212
Le Mans 192
Libourne 217
Licourt 214
Liège 214
Lille 210
Limage 193
Lion 192 193
Lisle 210 212 214
Lizieux 191
Loan 205
Longueil 209
L'Ossosigny 209

France (cont.)
Lyon 210-212 214 215 219
Mans 209
Mantigny in Picardy 213
Marinande in Guiène 208
Marche 212
Mareuil 192
Marsilly 218
Marsominge 212
Marsonning in Bresse 219
Martizet 217
Marty-on-Ance 211
Melun 211 212
Metz 193 208 212 218
Meule 219
Meuse 192
Mezieres 191 192
Monchetlaby 209
Montigny/Montygny 198 208
Mont Louet 213
Montreuil 218
Montrichard in Tourenne 218
Nancy 217
Nantes 192 193 208 212
Neont in Poitou 217 218
Neuilly in Normandy 217 218
Nevers 217
Nimes 208
Normandy 156 209 213 217
Origny 209
Orleans 156 210 211 215
Pailly 215
Paris 107 109 156 192 193 201 204 206 208-219
Peronne 192
Picardy 157 192 209 213 215 217
Plomion 209 214 215
Poilin 213
Poitiers/Poictiers 191 192 217
Poitou/Pictou/Poictou 192 217
Ponscore 208
Port 213
Port Anton 214
Port Louis 208
Poulerville 213

France (cont.)
Pout in Beaujolais 213
Quet in Dauphine 212
Remy 213
Rennes 206 215 217
Retourno 214
Rilly 217
Rinsart 218
Rochefort 211
Rodez 208
Roma in Bresse 213
Roman in Dauphine 218
Rome 213
Rompsay 193
Ronsoy 210
Rontoir 210
Rouen 156 201 208 211
Ruffé 192
Sables of Aonne 212
St. Agnal deux 213
St. Amand 209
St. Arban 219
St. Benoist-sur-Loire 219
St. Bonnet 214
St. Colombe 210
Ste. Marie du Bois 209 217
Saintes/Xaintes 193 208
Sts. Marie Évêché 193
St. Frod 214
St. Genis Lavar in Lyonnais 219
St. Germain Lavelle 219
St. Gervais 208
St. Jean d'Angely 192 208 214
St. Laurent de Lin 215
St. Mexant Évêché 192
St. Neulisse in Savoy 218
St. Neux 213
St. Nizier 213
St. Omer 217
Saintonge/Xaintonge 156 192 208
St. Paul 212
St. Pierre 210
St. Pierre Lizieux 208
St. Pierre of Mans 212
St. Quentin 211
St. Quin 214

Scotland (cont.)
Latheron 150
Leith/Leath 115 121 136 143 150
Lerwick 143 150
Lismore 152 153
Lochindale 142
Mault 145
Mointle 144
Mondle 145
Mull 142
Murkle 147
New Luce 137 138
Rea 143 144 146-149
Rimsdale 146
Rogart 145
Rosehall 143
Savall 146
Schetland 137 142
Shathaledale 143 149
Shetland Islands 130 143
Skelpick 143
Stranraer 137 138
Strathnaver 143 150
Strathoolie 148
Sutherland 131 143-150
Thurso 144 147
Tongue 147-149
Wick 147
Wymore 143
States of Jersey
Guernsey 114 117 121
Spain, Abenoja 177
Alaejos 176
Alba 171
Albade Tormes 174
Albuquerque/Alburquerque 166-168 172
Alcalá de Henares 174 180
Alcantara 166
Alconera 175
Alcuexcar 168
Aldeanueva del Arzobispo 180
Algaba 179
Almazán 174
Almedina 184
Almendral 183-185
Spain (cont.)
Almendralejo 167 168 175 182
Almería 181
Andújar 181
Antequera 185 186
Aracena 177 189
Arahal 173
Arançana 168
Arçiniega 172
Arcos 179 188
Arenillas 169
Aroche 174 181
Arroyuela 183
Astorga 170 172
Avila 165 174
Axpuru 175
Azanchal 174 175
Azuaga 179
Badajoz 166 167 169 171-173 177-181 184
Baeza 165 188
Basaurti 176
Beçeda 178
Becerril del Campo 171 184
Béjar 169 170
Benavente 174 187
Bollullos 185
Bovadilla 185
Briviesca 186
Burgos 174
Burguillos 170 171 176 179
Cabril 172
Cáceres 166 178 184
Cadiz 119 180
Çalduendo 178
Campos 169
Canizal 180
Castilleja de la Cuesta 174
Castrocalbón 186
Castrojeriz 170
Castro Nuño 176
Castroverde 186
Cazorla 188
Celleros 172
Cheles 167
Cidaler 180
Ciudad Real 180 182
Ciudad Rodrigo 183

INDEX OF PERSONAL NAMES

Alvarez (cont.),
Teresa 171 182
Alvarez de Balboa,
Inés 170
Alvarez del Canto,
Mari 170
Alvarez de Losala,
Marì 185
Alvarez de San Bicente, Francisca 177
Alvaro, Beatriz 167
Alward, John 10
Amand, Francois 210
Amanville 190
de Amarilla, Juan 174
Ambila, Juan 187
María 187
Miguel 187
Ambrose, Abraham 10
Amburger, Conrade 91
de Amor, Juan 173
Amstutz, David 161
Analin, Abram 32
Ancona, Augustine 223
Anderson, Andrew 227
George 91
Hannah 91
James 17
John 17 91
Moentz 10
Peter 13
Andibert, Pierre 190
del Andrada, Alonso 180
Andrei, John William 96
Andrew, Anthony 34
Andrews, George 107
Jocomb 24 41
Thomas 134
William 31 133
Andriot 198
Androi, Manuel 224
Andros, William 64
Angas, Catalina 183
Angeliere,
Elizabet 88
de Anguis, Diego 172
de Anguis (cont.),
Juan 172
de Angulo, Alonso 172
Juan 167 172
Leonardo 167
Pedro 172
Anleton, Peter 10
Annet, Vincent François 204
Annot, Marie Claire 211
Anríquez, María 173
Anoy, P. 225
Ansau, Thomas 218
Anselme, Claude 213
Ansiot, Nicolas 216
Anthonie, John 62
Anthony, John 134
Antoine, Claude 205
François 205
Antonia, Juan 225
Appeal, Barbary 162
Magdalen 162
Appleby/Apleby,
Robert 91
William 33 35
Appler, David 117
Apples/Applen/Appler,
David 104
Appleton/Apleton,
Richard 30 57
Arbuthnot, John 19
Archer, William 109 111
Arens, Charles 196
Arenson, Cornelis 10
de Arévalo,
Alonso 170
Pedro 172 187
Argière,
Marguerite 191
de Argote, Alonso 187
Isabel 187
Arias, Diego 172
Pedro 172
Arias de Saavedra,
Hernán 184
Armaud, Francis 224
Armaud (cont.),
L. 225
Armistead, William 79
Armstead, William 74
Armestronge, Jocky 34
Army, John 29 57 68
Arnandé, Jeanne 211
Arnaud, Isaac 89
Arney, Joseph 96
Arndell, John 63
Arno, Lewis 228
Arnott, John 96
Arras, Nicholas 27
Arreau, Pierre 206
Arrie, Elisabeth 222
de Arroyal, M. 177
de Arroyo, Juan 176
Rodrigo 176
Arrundell,
Elizabeth 29 50
John 29
Margret 29 47
Peter 29
Richard 24 41 49
Arteser, John 109
de Artezón,
Beatriz 185
Arthur, Joseph 33
Ascomb/Ascombe,
Abigail 25 42
John 31
Mary (--) 42
Ash, Christo. 34
Ashbury, Robert 74 80
Ashley, Ann 25 42
Ashmore, William 9
Ashton, Joseph 158
Leonard 115
Askew,
William 23 45
Askume, John 64
Asree, Cathrine (--) 224
Assay, Louis 218
de Astorga 184
Astombe, Mary (--) 25
Aston, Robert 56
Atkins/Attkins 33 36

Bardon, Claud 88
de Barette,
Barbara 10
Bargan, Pierre 200
de Bargas, Pedro 176
Rodrigo 176
Barke, Frances 33
Barker, Henry 25 42
Jacob 109
John 36
Stephen 55
William 126
Barkley/Barkly,
Ed. 30 54
Jane 54
Barlow, Henry 27
Barn, Mark 223
Barnaby/Barnabie,
John 31 58
Barnard, Robert 96
117
William 29 56 67
Barnehouse 77
Barnes, Edward 29
Phillip 35
Robert 40
Barnett, John 32 51
Thomas 23 50 126
William 47
Barnier, Vincent 214
Barniellos,
Hernando 182
Baron, Chas. 225
Barr, Thomas 109
de Barra, Inés 186
Barrait, Antoine 192
Barreto, Juan 172
Barrett, Francis 30
54
Walter 61
William 23
de Barrette,
Isaac 10
de Barrionuevo,
Marcos 165
Barrow, Thomas 33
William 126
de Barrutia, Juan 170
de Barrutia (cont.),
Pedro 170
Barry, David 39
Francis 109
James 109
James D. 104
Richard 109
Robert T. 110
William 29 62
Barteaud, Paul 10
Bartlett, Edward 125
Richard 28
Thomas 125
William 125
Bartley, James 17
Bary, Jean 196
de Basaras,
Miguel 189
Pedro 189
de Basarte, Juan 176
de Basconcelos,
Andrés 167
Bascough, Richard 35
Basingthwayte,
John 38
Baskins, W. M. 91
Baskem, Silvain 221
Basnett,
Theophilus 85
Basneve,
Catalina 223
Basse, Nathaniel 29
56 66 67
Samwell 29
Bassett, Asa L. 122
William 36
Bastillon,
François 202
Bastin, François 202
Baston 156
de Bastrop 220 221
Bataillard, Jean 204
Batalle, Nicolas
Francois 209
Batchelor, Edward 125
Bate, John 56
Bates, John 47
Thomas 110
Bath, John 69
Batisier, Claude
Emanuel 215
Bats, Thomas 38
Batson, Abraham 126
Elizabeth 126
Rose 126
Batt, Ellin (--) 49
John 28 67
Michael 25 49
Battalter, J. 227
Batten 75
Andrew 72 76
Batteon 194
Batteton, Chris. 195
Batty, Eliza. 135
Baudeson, Nicolas 202
Baudet, Francois 218
Baudouin 208
Baudot, Philbert 214
Baugh, Thomas 23 43
Baugton, Isacke 24
Baujou 190
de Baulne 190
Baumgart, Anna 162
Bautista, Juan 168
Miguel 177
Bawde, Randall 45
Baxter, John 9
Richard 73 79
Roger 110
Bayard, Peter 10
Pierre Dominique
208
Bayliffe,
Temperance 23
Baynam, Elizabeth 30
John 30
Bázquez, Alonso 175
Andrés 175
Barbola 174
Bartolomé 181
Catalina 177 187
Francisca 187
Gonzalo 177 187
Juan 174 177
Leonor 181
Bázquez Caballero,

Berte, Paul 10
Bertel, Claude 194
Berthelot, Francois 219
Bertin, Elie 195
Francois 210
Marie 195
Bertrand,
Jacques 212
Natalis 212
de Berwick 215
Besnard,
John 131 134
Besoin, Gabriel 215
Bessac, Michel 193
Besse 23
Bertrand 190
William 23
Best,
Christopher 25 42
Thomas 30
Bettner, Godfrey 110
Betton, Samuel 33
Betts, Margaret 17
Betuchet, Pierre 217
Beuret,
Jean Guillaume 205
Beverley, William 19
Bew, Robert 25 27 42 50
Bewbricke, John 34
Biat, Jean 218
Marie (Vasseur) 219
Bibbeau, Jaques 89
Bibbie, William 64
Biberon,
Jacques Michel 199
von Bibra, Friedrich Heinrich 128
Bickers, Robert 91
Bickley, Richard 54
Bidas, Pierre 192
Bideau, Pierre 205
Bidet, Jean 195
Biggs, Richard 23 44
Sarah (--) 44
Thomas 23 33
William 23
Bignell, Jan 135
Bignoll, Marmaduke 18
Bigord, Jean 209
Bigsby, Nathl. 98
Bikar, William 37
Bileux, Nicolas 209
Bill, A. T. F. 97 102
Charles 121
Billecault,
Francois 217
Billiard, John 30
Billingsley,
Francis 91
Billot, Catharine 89
Francois 88
Bincks 27
Binks, Ann (--) 49
William 49
Binsley, William 63
Biondi, Antonio 110
Biot, Jacques 213
Birch, Richard 15
Bird/Byrd 86 87
Samuel 91
Birth, James 98
Bishop, Henry 9 110
Bisseret, Remis 202
Black, Ann 153
Christian 153
Donald 152
Duncan 153
Ewen 153
James 100
Jannet (--) 152
John 152
Mary 152
Sam 223
Thomas 91
Blackborne, James 63
Blackburn, Benjamin 131
Robert 110
Blackett, Joshua 17
Tobiah 133
Blacklocke, Thomas 32
Blackman, Nicholas 22 45
Blackwood, Susan 25
Blackwood (cont.),
Susan (cont.) 50
Bladen, William 13
Blagden/Blagsen,
George 105
Blair 87
Alexander 91
Blake, John 18
Walter 23 55 74 80
Blakswik, James 132
Blampin, Leonard 202
Blanc, Silvester 227
Blanca, Catalina 179
Blancard 211
Blanchard, Louis 218
William 96
Blancks, Thomas 48
Blanco, Juan 175
Bland 75
Edward 104
Blane, R. 227
Blaney, Edward 25 42 50
Lewis 10
Blankenbacker,
Zachariah 94
Blankenstein,
William 10
Blasco, Pedro 170 187
Blasco Milano,
Alonso 187
Blasdell,
Nicholas 100
Blas García, Mari 175
Blav, Louis 206
Bleutlingers,
Conrad 20
Blewer, John 161
Blewet, John 37
Margery 37
Blochet, Louis 218
Blore, Francis 64
John 64
Blondell, John 12
Blood, J. R. 228
Blount, Thomas 125
Blowe, Joseph 72
Blower, Gody 32

Boyse (cont.),
Christopher 82
Chyna 45
Humphrey 33
Luke 44
Braby, Elizabeth 24
Stephen 24
de Bracamonte,
Diego 180
Brackenridge,
Alex. 91
Brackley, Jane 30
Bradford, Henry 50
Bradley, Thomas 51
Bradshaw/Bradshawe,
Giles 35
Richard 23
Bradston, John 30
Bradstreet,
Francis 91
Bradway/Bradwaye,
Alexander 22 44
Giles 36
Sisley (--) 44
Brady, Peter 97 115
Thos. 111
William 91
Braford, John 37
Bragado, Francisco
167
Brakley, William 34
Brame, John 228
Bramham, Francis 91
Bramford, John 23
Branch,
Christopher 22 43
Mary (--) 43
Thomas 43
La Branche 189
Branchet, Michel 219
Brandon, Martin 38
Brandy, John 19
Branlin, Ann (--) 46
William 46
Brannan, John 97
Bransby, Thomas 28 52
Brashear/Brasheare/
Brasheere/Brasheers/
Brasseur 73 75
Robert 77 78
Brasington, Thomas 35
Brassard,
Estienne 193
de Brassee 216
Brau, Nicolas 217
Braun, Francisco 226
Brava, Marina 180
Bravo, Baltasar 166
Hernan 180
Luis 166
Brawdrye, Mary 33
Brawford, Samuel 91
Bray 38
Breau, Jean Bte. 199
Breckinridge, William
Dunlop 111
Brerton, Samuel 97
le Breteche,
Antoine 204
Breton, Jean Pierre
159
Nicolas Le 200
Brevier, Jean 216
Brewood, Th: 39
Brewster, Edward 39
Richard 66
Brial, Ana 185
Brian, Alain 208
Bribby, William 31
Brice, Ann 127
William 127
Bricke, Edward 24 41
Bricks, William 27
Bride, Chirst. 140
Flora 141
Bridges, Henry 35
Thomas 53
Bridgewater/Bridgwat-
ter, Isbell (--) 48
Richard 26 48
Bringvan,
Nicholas 204
Brindonneau,
Rene 205
Brion, Vidalle 214
de Briones,
de Briones,
Esteban 185
Hernando 185
Brisard, Louis 193
Briscoe, John 74
Brisebois, Louis
Theodore 194
Brishitt, Peter 33
Brispoe, Anthony 10
Brisson, Madeleine
211
Bristow, Richard 40
Brit, James 111
Britel, Guillaume 202
Briton, James 227
Brittaine, Robert 30
Brittin, Robart 58
de Briviesca, Pedro
188
Borron 223
Broadbeck/Broadback/
Brodbeck, Jacob 97
111
Broadhurst, Thomas 13
Broadshaw, Richard 48
Broat, Jeanne 194
Brock, Robert Alonzo
90
William 44
Brocke, John 62
William 24
Brockwell, James 17
Brodbanke, Thomas 35
Broderick, Thomas 111
Brogden, John 34
Bromage, Henry 38
Brook, Sam 103
Brooke, W. J. 116
Brooks/Brookes 31
Cutberd 35
Francis 97
James 29 62
Thomas 23 47
William 31
Broord, James 10
Broret, Jaques 88
Brösing, Andrew 165
Brossard, Mathieu 193

Burt/Burtt,
Anthony 62
Jane 41
Lane 24
William 26 54
Burton, Charles 97
George 41
John 39
Richard 61
Busbee, Edward 26
Bush, Elloner 126
John 31 33
Martha 126
Martha (--) 126
Sarah 126
Susan 59
William 126
Bushel/Bushell,
Alice (Crocker) 68
Henry 36 68
Nicholas 33
de Bustamante,
Gonzalo 179
Pedro 179
Bushrod, Thomas 79
Buss, Hans 160
de Bustillo,
Gutierre 184
Butcher, Frances 26
Butler, John 38
Ann (--) 134
Edward 24
Francis 48
John 91 134
Buttal 159
Butter, Thomas 13
Butterey, Richard 33
Butterfield/Butter-
feild, John 32
Button, Thomas 27
Buwen, Thomas 35
Bygrane/Bygrave,
Elizabeth 28 55
Bykar, William 37
Byrne, Charles 102
Henry 91
James 112
Patrick 123
Byrnes, Walter 227

Caballero,
Hernando 178
Cabanis, Henry 88
de Cabrera, Pedro 189
Cabulot, Andre 209
de Cacavelos,
Lorenzo 185
Cacho, Alonso 180
de Caçorla,
Catalina 174
de Caçuera,
Leonor 184
Caden, James 112
de la Cadena,
Alvaro 171
Lope 171
Cadet, Blondelet 190
Cadge, Edward 50
Cadiou, Francois 212
Caesar, Jules 226
Cage 75
Edward 81
Cagnerel 190
Calame, Jacob 159
de Calçada, Antón 180
Calcker 25 42
Calder, James 104
Thomas 63
Calderón, Alonso 186
Ana 172
Bartolomé 186
Favián 174
Juan 171
Pedro 166 182
Rodrigo 166
Çalduendo, Pedro 178
Caldwell, Geo. 91
J. F. 121
James 91
Calewell, Daniel 140
Calet, Charles 217
Calfiel, Mich'l 162
Callan, John F. 119
Nicholas 98 102 111
112 123 124
Patrick 98 112
Callay, Jacques 200
de la Calle, Juan 184
Callon, Nicholas 98
Calmers, Thomas 90
Calston, James 13
Calthrop, Charles 29
de Calvarrasa,
Toribio 185
de Calvente,
Francisco 173
Calvert, Charles 112
George 9
Leonard 9
de Calzada, Juan 180
Çamarrón, Tomás 166
Cambran, Elvira 173
Çambrano, Esteban 175
Cameron, Allan 141
Angus 141
Duncan 19
Finley 13
John 14 19
Katrine (--) 141
Caminge, John 23
Caminos, Catalina 182
Campbell/Camble,
Alexander 12 141
145 155
Ann 141
Archibald 154
Cathn. 141
Colin 132
Dan 98
Daniel 141
Donald 149
Dugald 91
Duncan 150 153
Girzie 154
Hector 145
Jean 138 139
John 91
Katherine (--) 150
Lachlan 154
Mary 154
Neil 153
Patrick 91
Peter 11
Robert 150

Causey (cont.),
Nathaniel 23 40 46
Thomas 28 46 81
Thomasine (--) 46
Caussepain, Charlotte (Vendue) 195
François 195
Marie 195
Pierre 195
Cautepie, Jean 88
Michell 88
Catalano, Salvadore 113
Catanoch, John 144 147
Catenat 194
Catesby, John 34
Catherine, Joseph 202
Cathey, James 91
Catinois, François 196
Caton, Isaac 157
John 98
de Catroverde, Hernando 185
Catton 201
de Cavallos, María 184
Cavenaugh, Philemon 91
de la Cavex, Domingo 178
Cawt, Bryan 25 42
Çaydino, Rodrigo 172
Rodrigo Alonso 172
Caynhoo 81
Parson 74 75
de Caytán, Catalina 177
Caze 201
François Nicolas 197
Jacques 197
Cazin, Expietienne 156
de Cazorla, Catalina 168
de Çeçeyl, Andrés 177
de Çeçeyl (cont.),
Juan 177
Ceeley, Thomas 66
Ceinturier, Marie 211
Cesar, Jean B'te 207
Chabanas, Isaac 88
Chabert 211
Chagneau,
Catherine 193
Estienne 193
François 193
Jean 193
Marie 193
Chaigneau, Jacques 207
Chailloux, Therese 193
Chalmers, James 139
Chaloner, Morris 33
Chamberlin/Chamberline 39
Frances 35
Francis 31 60
Rebecca 31 60
Chambers, Alice 50
Elizabeth 91
James 32 54
John 14 47
Thomas 47
Chambery, Marie (Giraude) 219
Chamboux, Jedron 88
Champ, John 33
Champagne, Pierre Camusat 196
Champer, Robert 22
Champin, Pasta 30
Champion, Pascoe 57
Chanat, Jean 214
Chandler/Chandeler/Chaundler, Arthur 26 48
John 30 58
Richard 39
Chaney, Joseph 91
Chantreau,
Antoine 207
Catherine (Aubry)
Chantreau (cont.),
Catherine (Aubry) 207
Francois 207
Madeleine 207
Marie Michel 207
Chantry/Channtree/Chauntree, Robert 25 27 42 53
Chanuallon, Genevieve 211
Chapelle 228
Claude 209
Guillaume 217
Chaplaine,
Isacke 24 46
John 24 46
Mary (--) 46
Chapman/Chappman,
Ann (--) 46
Frances 25 42
Francis 53
Henry 17 131
James 19
Luke 56 67
Nicholas 22 53
Phillip 30 59
Samuel 85
Thomas 23 46
Chapon, Rene 212
Charbonnier 215
Chard, Ann (--) 44
Joshua 22 44
Charinton, Thomas 9
Charles, Jean 206
Charlton, Henrie 63
Charpentier,
François 199
Marie 213
Charreau 216
Charte, William 36
Chartier, Joseph 202
Charvau, Mathurin 207
Chastain 90
Estienne 88
Pierre 87
Chastatain, Quintin 88

Corcoran, Thomas 96
99
Cordea, Hester 10
Cordell, Thomas 73
Corder, Thomas 27
Corderoy, John 39
de Cordoba, Anton 173
Antonio 173
Corme, William 102
de Corne, Pierre 89
Cornejo, Alonso 169
186
Antón 186
Francisco 169
Pedro 168
Cornelly, Jean 195
Cornie, William 30
Corning, Ziporah 106
Cornish, Thomas 31 63
Cornu, Pierre 88
Cornwallis/Cornwal-
lys 74
Thomas 9 79
Corona, Rodrigo 178
de la Corredera,
Juan 188
Corresux,
Alexandre 213
Cosins, John 10
de Costa, Matthias 10
Costard, John 39
Coste, Jacques A. 223
Costigan, Joseph 99
Cotet, Marie
Ferdinande 200
de Coto, Alvaro 167
Cottive, Dauphin 191
Cottler/Kotiger,
Antony 161
Cotton, Joseph 91
Robert 40
Coubber, Rebecca 31
Couch, Josiah 122
Coucham, John 14
Coulter, E. Merton
163
Coumba, William 99
Countivane, John 33
Countway, John 33
Couper, Walter 62
Coupet, Francoise 88
de Cour, Mathieu 214
Courbec, Nicolas 212
Courbette 211
Courbier, Simon 195
Courcel, Louis 195
Courcy, Jean 195
Couronnay, Francois
191
la Courru, Pierre 88
Courson, Pierre 214
Court, Francois 210
Courtableau,
Jacques 195
Courten 216
Courtenay, John 99
Courtez, Louis 198
Courtine, Antoine 214
Courtineau,
Mathieu 208
Courts, John 15
Coussins, John 110
de Coustillan 203
de Coutelier, Marie
Francoise 211
Couttant, Francois
218
Coutte 200
Couturier 195
Jeanne (Gaudin) 203
Covell, Gresham 77
Cover, George 100
Cowan, Hugh 114
William 19
Cowman, Thomas 135
Coxe, Richard 109
William 61
Coyle, Andrew 114
Cradocke, Alice
(Cooke) 68
Christopher 68
Craft/Croft,
Michael 161
Craigin, Robert 19
Cramer, Frederick 19
Crampe, Thomas 31
Crampson, James 14
Crampton, John 69
Cranch, William 107
Cranfield, Edward 9
Cranich, John 56
Cranmer, Andreas 162
Crapplace 33
Crashaw, Rawleigh 29
Crauch, William 107
Crawford, John 91
Patrick 91
William 91
Creager, George 20
Creaser/Creasor,
Thomas 114
Cred, Manuel 225
Credy, Julius 161
Creniella, George 123
Cretien, Francoise
(Gaguet) 214
Jullien 214
de la Creuse, Jean
205
Creutzfeldt,
William 114
de Crèvecoeur,
Elzear Felix 217
Crew, Joseph 48
Joshua 26
Randall 45
Robert 52
Crewer, Philip 108
Cripps, Zachary 54 66
Crisman, George 20
Crismand, Joseph 10
Crispe, Thomas 31
Zacharia 27
Cristóbal Méndez,
Bachiller 181
Criswell, Robert 225
Crochet, Nicolas 207
Crocker, Alice 68
Henry 49 55
Jone (--) 55
Richard 28
Crocket, Robert 91
Crody, Henry 162
Croft/Kraft,

Croft (cont.),
Catherine 161
Croggan/Croggon,
Henry B. 114
Isaac N. J. 114
Croliés, Charles 204
Crompe, Thomas 51
Crompton, Thomas 69
Cronenberger, Anna
Catharina 160
Elizabeht 160
Gertrues 160
Henrich 160
Nicolas 160
Cropen, Humfrey 39
Cropley, Edward S.
114
George 99
Richard 99
Croppe, William 74 80
Croshaw, Raleigh 41
Crosnier 190
Jean François Le
190
Cross/Crosse,
Ellioner 91
Richard 91
Thomas 25 49
Croston, Edmund 85
Crotty, Patrick 114
Crouch, Richard 25 70
71
Thomas 42 53
Crouth, Thomas 25 27
Crowder, Hugh 53
James 45
Crowley, Timothy 99
Crozar 155
Crozimier, Nicolas
195
Cruder, Hugh 27
Cruit, Robert 114
Crust, Thomas 50
de la Cruz, María 174
Cuadrado, Gonzalo 175
Cuderington, John 41
de Cuebas, Juan 174
de la Cueva, Beatriz
de la Cueva, Beatriz
172
de Cuevas, Juan 174
Cuffe, Martin 34
Cugley, Danniell 64
Cull, John 114
Culley, Samuel 56
Cultey, Samuel 28
Cummings/Cummins/
Cumins, Alex. 91
Christopher 99
James 114
Patrick 114
William 12
Cumplido, Antón 171
Francisco 171
Cunningham,
Robert 120 139
Samuel 114
Cunnington,
Michael 115
Cunstable,
Robert 26 71
Cupper, Pierre 89
Curley, James 115
Curling 135
Curner, Joh. 162
Currie, Catharine 154
Curry, Kate Singer 20
Curswell, Jeanne 220
Mathiew 220
Robert 220
Samuel 220
Curtis/Curtise,
John 30 60
Michael 10
Thomas 30 60
Cushing, Charles 227
Cussin, Claude
Nicolas 219
Jeanne (Fremy) 219
Pierre 219
Cussins, Richard 91
Custis, Eliza 95
Martha (--) 95
Cutler, Robert 40
Cuttin, Vandre 200
Cuvillier, Joseph 115
Dabzall, Willson 135
Daça, Juan 185
Daffour, Benjamin 11
Daivlen, Henry 26
Dalavier, Denis 213
Dalby/Dalbie,
William 22 53
Dale, Niccolas 61
Thomas 82
Daley/Daily, James 91
John 115
Dalrymple, Ann 137
Archibald 137
James 137
Janet 137
Jean 137
Jno. 137
Mary 137
William 138
Damel 219
Dameron, Bridget 35
Damford, Jeremy 73
Damiel, Ollivier 189
Damiens, Guillaume
192
von Damnitz, Hans
Hermann 128
Damont, Louis 199
Damport/Dansport,
Lawley 53
Lanslott 25 27 42
Dancy, John 54
Danel, Louis 213
Dange, Louis 205
Dangerman, Xtopher 11
Daniau, Philippe 193
Danison, Daniel 11
Danney, E. 228
Danning, Elizabeth 92
Darbonne 203
Darby, John 133
Jonathan 195
Daries, James 27
Darling, Jean 195
Darmuseau,
Nicolas 202
Darnaud, Antoine 190
Jacques 190

Dunham, John 19
Dunkersly,
Benjamin 17
Dunlop, John 139
Dunn/Dun, Arthur 92
John 116 141
Peter 34
Thomas 49 100
Dunthorne, Elzabeth
61
Thomas 61
Dupain, Charles 195
Louis 199
Du Plessix 189
Dupper, Edward 35
Dupré, Jean 217 218
Thomas 218
Dupuy 90
Durand, Jean 213
Louise 211
Marie Charpentier
213
Durendy 201
Durham, John 92
Durisse, Marie 218
Durmmond, John 136
Dürninger, Abraham
127
DuRouvroy 193
Duru, Jeanne (Letril-
lard) 210
Roland 210
Dusaussoir,
Antoine 209
Dutartre/Dutitree,
Claude 219
Claudius 11
Dutrieul, Jos. 224
Duval, Charles 217
Charlotte 197
Claude 204
Jean 204
Duverger 193
DuVernay 193
Duvivier, Philippe 87
Dyer/Dier, Edward 112
James 92
John 70
Dyer (cont.),
Joseph 135
Mary 33
William 33
Dzierozynski,
Francis 117

Eakins, James 17
Earl, Enoch 227
Robert 117
Earle, Nathaniel 37
Early, Thomas 126
East, Richard 31
Easton, William C.
123
Eastwood, Sarah 135
Ebeleng, Frederick
117
Henry 117
Eberback, Henry 117
Ebsworth, Agnes 30
Anthony 30 57
Ellallowe, Peter 59
Eckardt, Henry 117
Eckin, John 9
Eckles, John 138
William 138
Eckloff/Ecloff,
Christian 100 117
Godfrey 117 122
Ederife, Ester 50
Edgar, John 11
Edger, William 32
Edgear, William 92
Edlow/Edlowe, John 64
Mathew 22 43 64
Tabitha (--) 64
Edmiston, David 92
Edmonds, John 32
Richard 33
Robert 32
Edmunds, Jacob 17
Robert 54
Edward, Jane (--) 132
John 132
Edwards, Arthur 33
Hayden 223 227
John 27 54
Edwards (cont.),
Richard 61
Robert 9
Thomas 126
William 33 87
Edwyn, William 9
Eester, Thomasin 61
Egan, William 117
Eglin, Richard 14
Stephen 135
Eichler,
Abraham 161
Eigler, Jacob 117
Einbroet, John 117
Elbert, William 13
Elbet 218
Elbridg, William 34
Elexon, John 10
Elie, Nathaniel 37
Ellatt, John 52
Ellen, John 36
Ellerlee, Thomas 126
Elliott/Elliot/Eliot,
Alfred 113
John 36
Johnathan 100
Mary 18
Samuel 108
Ellis, David 24 25 41
49
Henry 117
I. 223
Margaret 18 49
William 126
Ellison/Elison,
Ellin (--) 52
John 27 52
William 59
Elloustardo,
Miguel 225
Elsword, Hener 28
Elvans, Richard 117
Elwood, Henry 55
Ely, Elizabeth 62
Walter 29
Eman, John 69
Ember, Edward 36
Emerson, Ann (--) 55

Fenn (cont.),
Samuel 73 77
Fennell, Robert 31 64
Fenox, Ann 125
James 125
Robert 125
Fenton, James 34
Fenwick, Benedict 103
Enoch 110
Fermont 75
Feratier, Pierre 214
Fereby, Richard 36
Ferguson/Fergusson/
Farguson,
Duncan 14 19
Dunham 19
J. W. 86
John 140
Patrick 19
William 15 118
Fermignac, Marie 207
Fermont, Samuel 74
Fernall, Robert 53
Ferne, Phillis 84
Fernley, Thomas 32
Fernández,
Alonza 186
Catalina 167
Diego 186
Elvira 175 176
Francisca 180
Francisco 170
Isabel 179
Juana 169
Juan 167 176 186
Leonor 180
Luis 188
María 167 169 170
P. 226
Fernando, Peter 11
Ferrand, Jean Bte.
206
Laurent 219
Ferrar, John 34
William 45
Ferrarois 189
Ferrell, Honner 92
Ferrera, Beatriz 180
Ferret, Francoise 211
Ferrier, Pierre 89
Ferris, Thomas 39
Ferrity, Nicholas 118
Ferry, Thomas 227
Field/Feild,
James 58
Thomas 40
William 53
Fields/Feelds,
Henry 58
Mary 92
Fierfax, William 38
Fiesler, Henry 161
Fightig, Christian 20
Figowido, John 227
de Figueroa,
Hernando 175
Filatreau/Fillatreau,
Pierre 194
Thoynoud 198
Filenst, Thomas 23
Fill, John 118
Fillery, Andrew 19
Filmer, John 26
Finch 75
Frances 46
Ludovick 162
Fine, Hubert 202
Richard 56
Fink, Mark 92
Finkman, Conrad 118
Finlason, John 92
Finley, Patrick 92
Fischer, George
Andrew 118
Fishbourne,
Philip 20
Fisher, Edward 26 48
Henry 23
Jane 34
John 25 31
Katherine 46
Robert 46
Samuel 33
Sarah 48
Thomas 33
Fister, John 118
Fitch, Joseph 36
Fitchut, William 158
Fithiol 221 222
Fitt, Ann (--) 51
Robert 51
Fitts, Alice 27
Robert 26 43
Thomas 27
Fitz Redmond, W. 13
Fitzgeffrey 70 71
George 69
William 69
Fitzgerald, David 118
James 118
John 118
Fitzhugh, William 121
Fitziefferys 33
Fitzpatrick,
James 118
Flack, Francis 18
Flaherty, William 118
Flaming 198
de Flande, Louis 192
Olne (la Force) 192
de Flandre, Fermin
Fermin 192
Flanders, William 92
Flannigan,
Michael 118
Flar 159
Flatt, James 136
de la Flèche, Jean
Chesney 206
Fleet, Beverley 79
Fleming, John 118
Fleshman, Peter 94
Fletcher, Angus 139
Edward 33
Euphame 139
Katrine (McIntyre)
139
Nancy 139
William 106
Fleury, Antoine 219
Elizabet 88
Jean 215
Flinn, Lawrence 101
Flint, Thomas 29 66

Fridig (cont.),
J. J. 161
John 162
Martin 161
Fries,
Adelaide L. 127
Frisbie, Richard 62
Frisle, Margery 34
Frizon, Antoine 211
Froger, Vincent 218
Frogmorton, John 25
Frogneux, Lievains 202
Fromm, Clemens 162
Fry/Frey, Casper 161
Henry 33
Johann Gustav 128
John 31 32
Philip H. 91
Fryer/Frier/Freyer,
George 26 48
Joh. 162
Ursula (--) 48
Fuchs/Fouks/Fookes/Foockes, William 30 57 78
de Fuente/de la Fuente, García 171
Juan 180
de Fuentes,
Florestán 188
Luis 171
Fuerte, Mari 185
Fuertes/de Fuertes,
Inés 176
Luciana 188
Teresa 182
Yvan 176
Fulham, Thomas 35
Fullalove, James 119
Fulshaw, Samuel 34
Fulton, Samuel 126
Fulwood, John 28
Furlow 33
Fuus, Christian 160

Gable, John 162
Gabriel, Antoine 205
Gaddis, Adam 119
Gaffer, Francoise 219
Gage 153
Gaget, Antoine 192
Gaguet, Francoise 214
Gahagan, Thomas 92
Gahan, William 119
Gaile/Gaill,
Elias 25 42
Gaillard, Jean 88
Gaines, James 92
Gaither,
Greenberry 98
Galabrun/Gallibrun,
Louis Jean 119
Galbán, Juan 177
Galbreath, Angus 139
Katrine (Brown) 139
Gale, John 23
Gales, Joseph 107
Galisteo, Blas 175
Gallant, William 120
Gallas, Francois 192
Gallasper, John 161
Galle, Catherine (Nicole) 200
Louis 200
Gallego, Alonso 175
Juan 183
de Gallegos,
Beatriz 186
Rodrigo 186
Galochero/Calochero,
Antonio 172
Francisco 172
Galván, Francisco 177
de Gamarra,
Cristóbal 186
Gambier, Michel 216
Gambs, Georg G. 127
de Gámez, Diego 174
Hernando 165
Juan 165 174
Luis 166
Pedro 165 166
Gammon, Nath. 29
William J. 125
Gannon, James 101
Ganey/Gany,
Anna 31 61
Henry 31 59
William 31 61
de Gaona, Agueda 171
Gaondet, Michel 212
Gape, Henry 37
Garand, Pedro 226
Garant, Jacques 195
García 225-227
Alonso 167 170 179 183
Alvar 181
Andrés 169 170
Antón 187
Asencio 168
Bartolomé 179
Beatriz 168
Bernal 166
Catalina 171 173 183 187
Cristóbal 170
D. 181 188 225
Elvira 174 175 188
Francisco 178
Inés 169 170 172 180
Isabel 176 187
Juan 168 178 181
Juana 168 180
Luis 181
Mari 169 170 185
María 174 180
Marina 178
Martín 181
Mayor 170
Pascual 178
Pedro 170 180
García Calderón,
Alvaro 171
García Caro, Juan 171
García de Arroyal,
Gutiérrez 177
García del Campo,
Pedro 175
García de León,
Diego 170
García del Espino,

Goodall (cont.),
Thomas 101 113
Goodby, Jone 31
Goodchild,
Chrisenus 35
Richard 35
Goodison, Raymond 40
Goodman, Robert 29 62
Goodrich, Francis 14
Goodwyn/Goodwine,
Reinold 29
Samuel 37
Gookins/Gookin/
Gookines 73 75
Daniel 68 78
Frederick William 68
John 78
Gorda, María 180
Gordon/Gorden 189 190
Alexander 12 143
Charles 143
George 148
J. 226
James 120
John 143
Marg. 137
William 143
Gorganus, Francis 126
Gorham, Allen 226
Solomon 226
Gorman, John B. 101
Gormans, John B. 112
de Gormaz, Isabel 166
Gormlay, Philip 120
Goss, Francis 119
Gotee, John 11
Gottard, Jean 219
Gottefrin, Jean 218
Gottlieb, Geo. 162
Gouard, Philbert 213
de la Goublaye,
Antoine 193
Gouet, Denis 217
Jacques 217
Gough, Stephen H. 110
Gouin, Claude 204
Gould, John 120
Gould (cont.),
Peter 33
Goulding/Gouldinge,
Sara 59
Thomas 55
Gouldocke, Sara 30
Gouldwell, Henry 30
Goulson, John B. 226
Gouturier, Jeanne 203
Gowsh, Francis 35
Gowton, John 69
Grace, Ann 92
William 101
Gradon, Richard 40
Grady, Mary 92
Grafton, John 133
Graham, David 14
Peter 12
Grajero, Alonso 169
Pedro 169
Grammer, Gottlieb Christopher 101
de Granada,
Andrés 186
le Grand,
Augustine 190
Grande,
Francisco 183
Miguel 183
La Grandeur 189
Jean Bary 196
Grandin 193
Michel 205
Grandjean, Jean 189
Grandrin,
Barthelemy 205
Granes, Thomas 31
de la Grange,
Arnoldus 11
Granger/Graunger,
Jean 213
Nicolas 31 63
de Grañón,
Bernardino 181
Grant, Alex. 92
Allen 19
Augus 19
Daniel 15
Grant (cont.),
George 147
John 19 92
William 12
Granville, Pierre 215
Grar, Solomon 157
Grassi, John 102
Grave, Elnor (--) 50
George 50
Graves, George 25 42
Robert 47
Thomas 41 63
William 17
Gray/Graye/Grey,
Cyril Vernon 120
Joan 25 42
John 19 37
John B. 115
Margrett (--) 52
Robert 39
Thomas 25 42 52
William 25 42 92
Grays, Lawrence 94
Greason, William 120
Green, Edward 92
Elizabeth 17
Farnifould 126
Henry 11
James 120 227
Joseph 227
Owen 120
Patrick 120
Robert 92
Thomas 9 74
William 17
Greene, Aderton 33
Anne 37 68
Griffine 26
Henry 9 72 75 76
John 25 28 34 42
Richard 27
Robert 22
Sisely 24 42
Solomon 32 64
William 61
Greening, Albert 11 12
Greenleafe,

Greenleafe,
Robert 44
Susan (--) 44
Greenless, John 140
Mary (Howie) 140
Greer, George
Cabell 71
James 102
Greeves, Thomas 101
Gregory, Richard 23
49
Grelet, Pierre 89
Gresham, John 12
Grevett/Greevett,
Ėllin (--) 51
John 26 43 51
de Grieu 189
Griffin/Griffine/
Griphin, John 39 51
Mathew 33
Raph 26
Rice 30 57
Richard 32 35
Thomas 34
Griffith, Ambrose 29
Grigges, John 73
Grigsta, Thomas 9
Grillon, Marie 211
Grimes, Ann 24 41
George 32
Guy 120
John 126
Robert 80
Grindall/Grindal,
Edward 27
Thomas 27
Grindry, Jone 31
John 31
Mary 31
Grintor, William 97
Grivell, Pooley 23
William 40
Grize, Marie Anne 211
Groda, Jose 226
Groom, Ann 17
Charles 18
Grove, Richard 52
Groves, Edward 18
Grubb, Thomas 51
Grube, Bernhard
Adam 128
Gruffin, John 33
Grundman,
Claudia R. 21
Grundy, Robert 13
Grupe, William 120
Grusitive, Jacob 227
Guegan, Louis Henry
102
Guemel, Louis 219
Guenée, Claudine 218
Guerard, Jacob 156
P. 156
Guerard de Grand
Camp, Pierre 206
Guerin 198
Guerdon 193
Guerie, Antoine 194
Guerin, Jacques 199
Marie (Fermignac)
207
Guerra, Isabel 186
de Guerrera,
Bartolomé 180
la Guerrera,
Juana 172
Guerrero, Alonso 173
Juan 173
Guery, Joseph 190
Guevin, Etienne 88
Guezo, Pierre 190
Guibert, Joshua 11
Lenneur 194
Guichard, Samuel 11
Guignard, Jacques 208
Guilder, Gilbert 162
Guillam,
Christopher 38
Guillaume, Claude 205
Jean 205
Guillén, Leonor 186
Guillett, Annette 190
Guilloy, Jean 206
Guine, Thomas 33
Guiñi, Francisco 188
Guirand, Jean 190
Guirao, Mari 169
Guisada, Juana 179
Guisado, Andrés 179
Bartolomé 172
Hernán 184
Lorenzo 172
María 184
Pedro 184
de Guisse, Paquet 205
Gullever, Joan (Pie)
68
Robert 68
Gully, Thomas 92
Gulstons, Chad. 35
Gun, Donald 148
Gundrie, John 59
Marie 59
Gunston, Chad 32
Gunton, Thomas 120
William 120
Guntor, William 97
Gurgana, Edward 40
Gurr, George 27
Gussis, Jean 214
Gutiérrez, Alonso 166
Alvaro 179
Cristóbal 179
Gómez 183
Isabel 166 169 184
Juan 169
Leonor 173
Mari 172 176
María 183 188
Mencía 169
Gutiérrez Castel-
lanos, Juan 188
Guttensohn, John 120
Guttschride,
Ernest 101
Guttslick/Gutt-
schlick, Ernest 102
Guy, James 44
Robert 23 55
Whitney 35
de Guzmán,
Francisco 167 182
Gwyn 19

Hernández (cont.),
Juana 168 170
Juan 166 170 172 175 179 188
Leonor 182
Manuel 171
Mari 175 179
María 171 173 174 181 183
Martín 166 168 183
Mayor 173
P. 177
Pablos 183
Pedro 171 174 177 179 186
Toribia 179
Toribio 170
Hernández Bejarano, Diego 169
Hernández Barreto, Gonzalo 172
Hernández Biedma, Luis 170
Hernández de Diosdado, Alonso 186
Hernández de Grado, Mencía 172
Hernández de Hernan Núñez, Francisco 175
Hernández de Hinistrosa, Luis 181
Hernández de la Bera, Pedro 179
Hernández de Montiel, Martín 170
Hernández de Osorio, Juana 182
Hernández de Sevilla, Alonso 168
Hernandez Faudiño, Pedro 180
Hernández Soto, García 183
Hernández Terrón, Francisco 166
Hero, Oble 63
Herode, Marie Ficlou 211
Heroulx, Pierre 204
Herr, Peter 162
de Herrada,
Bartolomé 188
María 188
Herrendon, John 92
Herrera/de Herrera,
Francisco 183
Hernard 173
Inés 171
Isabel 171
Jerónimo 167
Juan 183 186
Leonor 184
María 167 171
Hervia 226
Hess, Jacob 121
William 121
Hesse, H. 226
Hesselius, Gustavus 11
Hethersall, Thomas 31
Hetten, John 227
Heyworth, Robert 107
Hewes, Thomas 60
Heydon, Edward 36
Heytas, M. 225
Mamie 226
Hibbs, Charles 121
Hickmore 25 42
Hickroat, Henry 20
Hicmott, James 50
Hiden, Martha Woodroof 43 64 72
Higgenson,
Elizabeth (--) 77
Humphrey 77
Higgins,
Elizabeth 30
John 44
Patrick 121
Higglet, John 37
Hilbus, Jacob 124
Hill, Edward 30
Elizabeth 30
George 40
Frances 31
Hill (cont.),
Francis 63
Hanna 30
James 13
Jane 45
John 9 30 59
Joseph 12
Marmaduke 45
Nicholas 77
Thomas 31 137
William 31
Hilliard/Hilliord 41
Gregory 34
John 9 34
Hillier, Mary 158
Hillman, Jno. Hendrich 162
Hills, Ismale 32
Hilton, Hugh 22 44
Hind, Geo. 162
Hindry, James 13
Hine, William 122
de Hinistrosa, Luis 181
Hinton, Elias 27
Elizabeth 31
Joane 31
John 25 42
Hipp, Geo. 162
Hitchcock/Hitchcocke/ Hitckock/Hichcocke 34
Kilibett 24 41
Thomas 26 32 55
William 28
Hitz, Florian 122
John 122
Hobbes, Judith 73
Hobreman, Passerasse 199
Hobson 37
Edward 22 43
Thomas 22 36
de Hoces, Beatriz 166
Gonzalo 166
Hodges, Elizabeth 26 49
John 34
Thomas 9

Kearnan, Patrick 123
Kedglie, John 123
Keffer, Peter 40
Kehl, John V. 123
Keie, Sarah (--) 47
Thomas 47
Keily, Jeremiah 123
Keinnston, Thomas 34
Keiser, Henry 123
Keith/Keitch,
John 123
Keleher, James 123
Keller, John F. 105
Jonas 123
Jonas P. 109 119 124
Michael 124
Kelloway, William 69
Kelly, Bernard 124
Michael 92
William 92
Kelso, Elizabeth 155
Keltridge,
Elizabeth 74
Kemp, Anthony 70
Margrett (--) 48 70
Richard 78
William 26 30 48 58 69 70
Kempff, Gregorius 20
Kendall, Henry 92
Kengla, Jacob 118
Keniston, Allen 48
Kenna, A. R. 228
Kennburgh, James 138
John 138
Kennedy/Kenneday,
Arch. 13
Daniel 15
Hugh 12
John 11
William 135
Kennell, Samuel 62
Kennery, John 14
Kent, Humfrey 47
Joane (--) 47
Keobel, Jacob 124
Keogh/Keogle,
Keogh (cont.),
Matthias 103
Keppler, Henry 124
Kerchler, Mathias 92
Kerfitt, Thomas 51
Kerill, John 34
Kerr, Alexander 102
Kersey, Philip 14
Kersly, Henry 30
Kerton, William 33
Keth 31
George 58
John 59
Keyman, Benomy 37
Keyworth, Robert 99
de Kgoet 203
Kid/Kidd, Roger 25 49
Kiddall, Sara 26
Kiernan, Charles 120 124
Hugh 103
Kildrige, William 30
Killingbeck,
Richard 40
Killson, Thomas 59
Kincaid, James 103
Kinchley, Paul 103
Kindle, Thomas 92
Kines, John 92
King, Benjamin 108
Charles 105
George 101 115
Henry 55
James 19
James C. 98
Robert 92
W. W. 95
William 92
Kingman, Sarah 16 17
Kingsley, William 53
Kingsmell/Kingsmeale 26 65
Jane (--) 52
Richard 52 78
Kingston, Thomas 66
Kinkee, Herman 11
Kinney, Jeremiah 124
Kinsley, Benjamin 124
Kinton, John 32
Kipps, William 18
Kirkwood,
Jonathan 124
Kitchin, Justus
Englehead 11
Kithly, Phillip 54
Klein, Madtz Jensen 127
Kleindienst,
John P. 124
Sebastian 124
Klotz, George 124
Kneller/Kueller,
George 103
Knight, Ben. 32 63
John 35
Mordecay 54
Richard 33
Robert 131
Kniston, Thomas 49
Knoblock, John 97
Knoll, Evea 162
Knott/Knatt,
James 31 64 74 80
Knowles, Israel 35
Kohl, Anna Barbara 159
Anna Marill 160
Jaquer 159
Luis 159
Margaritha 160
Maria Margaritha 160
Nicolas 159
Kohling/Kahling,
John Michael 123
Kolman, Anthony 103
Königsdorfer,
Gottlob 129
Korff, John 124
Kotiler/Kohla,
Christian 161 162
Kraft/Krafft/Kroft,
Christopher 124
George 124
John 124
Krebs, Charles I. 124

Kroes, Peter Paul 124
Küffer,
Anna Margarita 159
Elizabeht Catarina 159
Elizabeht Margaritt 159
Jaque 159
Margaritt 159
Maria Ottillia 159
Theobald 159
Kugel, Elisie 221
Jean 221
Marthe 221
Kuhl, Henry 124
Kullaway, John 24 42
Kuller, Joh. 162
Kurter, Abraham 222
Catherine 222
Hamilton 221
Henry 222
Jean 221
Jeannette 221
Joseph 222
Mathieu 221
William 221
Kyne, Mathias 98 103

Laboureau, Jean 193
La Bonté, Nicolas 204
Labrille, Louis 109
Lacon, Mary 33
LaCoste, John 224
Joseph 223
La Cour, Charles 206
Lacroix, Antoine Derville 213
Lacton, Henry 50
La Farge 189
La Feuillade 215
La Fleur, Babet 211
Lafon 208
Francois 214
La Fontaine 190
Jean 192
Marie 211
La Franchise, Jacques 212
La Geurd 29
La Girardière 189
de Lagrange, Jean Janson 200
Marie Ferdinande (Cotet) 200
L'aîné, Cezille 193
Roussel 193
Laine, Simon 205
de Lair/de Laire 190 194 197 200
Laird, John 103
Lake 28
George 104
Lakemeyer, Frederick 124
Lallemand 201
Laloix, Louis 210
La Marche, Louis 199
Lamb, Richard 92
Lambert, Chevalier 216
Jacques 218
William 32
Lambotte, Edward 32
Lambright, George 104 109
Lamby, William 124
Lamee, John 11
Lamontagne, Jean 202
Simon Lucas 213
La Motte, Pierre 198
Lamouveaux, François 193
Lampart, Edward 92
La Navette 196
La Lancette 193
Lançon, Frances 181
Lancour, Harold 9-12 14 15 18-22 40 43 64 67-69 71 72 84 86 90 91 125 127 129 155 158 163-165 189 223
Land, Richard 17
Lander, David 14
Landman, John 23
Landriker, Jno. 161
Landro, Juan 167
Landrot, Marie 201
Lane, Alice 60
Henry 46
Thomas 29 60
Langevin, Pierre 193
Langden, Peter 29
de Langle 193
Langley 35
Hezekiah 123
Sarah 24 42
Langman, Mary (--) 51
Peter 51
Langlois, Andre 209
Antoine 216
Bonnere Francois 208
Jean 205
Lankfeild, John 29
Lanphier, Robert G. 119
Lantheaume 191
La Pensèe 189
Lapham, Oliver 112
La Plume 189
Laport, Anne 216
Laporte, Etienne 212
Lapp, Jno. Geo. 162
Lapworth, Michael 53
Robert 43
de Lara, Juana 181
de Larbre, Marguerite 199
Larcebault 189 190
Larence, James 223
Larick 227
La Rieux, Jean 207
Marie 207
Larkin/Larkum,
John 37
Thomas 12
William 38
Larmeron, Jacques 207
Larmount, James 29
Larnagan 225
Larner, Martin 118
La Roche, Durand 193
Jacques 216

Miguel, Alonso 169
Andrés 184
Mari 166
de Míguez, Pedro 165
Milain, Gabriel 193
Jean 192
Milborn, Andrew 136
Christopher 136
Miles, Betty 126
Henry 14
Sarah 126
Mill, James 19
de la Milla, García 182
Millar, Daniel 11
Millard, Joshua 117 118
Miller, Christopher 20
George 116 228
Grover 100
Guill. 222
Jacob 19 95
James 73 75 77
John 20 225
Jno. F. 226
Mary (--) 77
Michael 19
Robert 99 100
William 33
Millet[t], Frances 33
Jacques 207
Millner, Mary Magdalen 162
Mills, David 12
Elizabeth 136
James 93
John 137
Peter 11
Milman 41
Milmer, Richard 40
Milner, Robert 45
Milnhouse, John 48
Milton, Richard 46
Milver, Robert 22
Milward, Henry 36
Mimes, Thomas 23
Minard, Louis 213
Ming, Joseph 125 126
Thomas 126
Mingot, Elizabet 88
Minors/Miner/Minor, Philip H. 114
Minozet, Jean B'te 209
Minstrid, Andrew 73
Mintren/Mintrene, Edward 59
Richard 31 59
Miquel, Jean 214
le Mire, Louis 216
de Miruena, Hernando 168
Juan 168
Misère, Antoine 194
Mitchell, Ann (Campbell) 141
David 93
Francis 57
James 13
John 17 93
M. 224
Maudlin 57
Robert 141 224
William 93 137
Mobbery, William 13
Moffet/Moffit, John 105
Mary 105
Robert 105
Mocaye, John 74
Mogenor, Peter 227
Moguet 203
Moise, Timothy 38
Moises/Moyses, Theodore 22 44 46
Moize de Moizne, Peter 11
de Molina, Juan 173
Teresa 181
Molley 134
Momieur, Francois 209
Monant, Lewis 225
Moncel, Nicolas 209
Monet, Jean Bte. 213
Mongon, Pierre 195
Monier, Laurent 208
Monro[e]/Munro[e], Hugh 146 149
Philip 106 110
Thomas 114
William 93 147
de Monrroy, Diego 184
Isabel (--) 184
Montagne, Tranche 196
de la Montague, Nicholas 11
Montais, Jacob 216
Jeanne 216
Joseph 216
Marie 216
Simon 216
Montal, Jean 218
Marie (Durisse) 218
Montaner, Juan 226
Montanet, Maria 224
Montaño, Juan 178
Montecue, Peter 53
de Monterde, Gaspar 182
Monterde, Pedro 182
Monternant 224
Montgomery, Peter 11
Montoro, Francis 228
de Montplaisir 190
Montreuil, Pierre 205
Montulet, Martin 214
Monville, Louis 197
Moone/de Moone, John 48
Martine 27
Moor/Moore/More, Dorothy 73
Elizabeth 62
G. 226
Henry 39
James 105
Jarrat 36
John 29 62 79 157
Joseph 74
Leonard 22 43
Mordecai 13
Robert 29 62

Moore (cont.),
Sara 24
William 32 98
Mooreton, Thomas 73
Moper, Nathaniel 29
Mora, Beatriz 166
Morage, Joseph 202
de Morales,
Bartolomé 184
Isabel 180
Moran, A. 225
Morân, Pedro 180
Morân de Valderas,
Francisco 180
Morano, Florencia 187
Morant 225
I. 226
Moras, Jean 207
Morcillo, Alonso 174
Morcock, Revoll 48
Moreau, Ambroise 200
Francois 217
Jacques 190
Jacques Francois 191
Jean 88
Jeanne (Paul) 200
Sebastian 215
Morecocke,
Reignold 26
Morel 190
Moreland, Thomas 63
Moreno, Alonso 169
Francisco 187
Isabel 182
Juan 169
Luis 170
Pedro 168
Moretti, Juan 226
Morgan/Morgaine,
Edmond 57
Edward 30
George 147
John 17 93
Mary 93
Patrick 19
Robert 35
Roger 9
Morgan (cont.),
Thomas 33 93
William 58
Moriarty, Ambrose 102
Moriatta, Ambrose 105
Morice, Marguerite 213
de Morillo, Isabel 165
Morin, Jean 192
Martial 215
Pierre 209
Morisset/Morriset,
Charles Antoine 207
Pierre 88
Morley 41
Morphet, John 93
Mornon, Claude 214
Morris, James 137
Jane 93
John 30 57
Mary 57
Richard 33
Samuel 25 56
William 93
Morrison/Morison,
Alexander 147
Edward 139
Hannah 126
Richard 126
Susanna 126
Mortimore, Alex. 13
Morton/Morten,
Ralph 40
Thomas 72
William 30 59
Morzillo,
Hernando 174
de Moscoso, Luis 186
Mosewood, Richard 24
Mosley, Joseph 30 57 68
de Mosquera/Mosquera,
Cristóbal 186
Diego 176
Galador 176
Mosse, Richard 37
Moul, Timothy 89
Moulin, Abraham 88
Pierre 214
Moulston, Thomas 24 41
Mounday, Mary 30
Robert 30
Mount, Thomas 112
Mountfort,
William 38
Mountney,
Alexander 30 61
Leonard 61
Mounts,
Christopher 11
Movant 224
Moy, Francois 214
de la Muce 86
Olivier 89
Much, Roger 32
Mudd, Jerh. 98
Mudge, William 25 42
Mudo, Pedro 177
Mugenbourg,
Martin 11
Mulero, Rodrigo 184
Mulholland/Mulhalan,
John 93
Owen 93
Mulledy/Mullidy,
Thomas 105
Müller, Ludwig 165
Mullinax, Richard 40
Mullock, Andrew 11
Mulsin 225
Munday, Robert 57
Munier, Jacques 192
Munnes, William 63
Muñoz, Alonso 176 179
Bartolomé 180
Diego 169
Francisco 169 178
Hernando 172
Juan 172 176 180
Munsell, Joel 64
Murchie, Finlay 154
Murdoch, John 103
Murdock, William 19
de Murga, Martín 169

Murphy 224
  Edward 105
Murray/Murry,
  Henry 14
  Michael 105
  Patrick 19
  Thomas 97 102 104-106 121
Mutch, Margery (--) 51
  William 51
Myers, John 17
  Samuel 17
Mynkie, John Samuel 11

Naccoon 19
Nace, Pierre 87
Naffager, Peter 20
Naile, William 27
Namblard, Pierre 207
Namond, Anne 211
Nant 76
  Thomas 83
de Nantes, Pierre 207
de Narbáez, Juan 186
Nasebitt, William 126
Nasfeild, Henry 60
Nash, Prudence 125
Naudin, Jean 213
  Rennes (Raquin) 213
de Nava, Francisca 172
Nave, Alexandre 13
Nayle, William 52
Naylor, John 85
  Thomas 32 85
Neals, Henry C. 100
Neares, Thomas 29
Nedelec, Simon 212
Nedin, William 110
Needome, John 27
Neil/Neill/Neale 10 35
  Edward Duffield 11 64
  Francis 101 106
  James 11 117 118
Neil (cont.),
  John 73 77
Neisser, Augustin 164
  George 164
Neitzell, John 20
Nelly, John 14
Nelson/Nellson,
  Ambrose 11
  Elizabeth 127
  George 24 41 48
  Joan 127
  John 127
  Mary 127
Nelstrop, Rawland 40
Nengfinger, William 11
Nerisson, Pierre 189
Nesmith, John 19
Nevill, James 126
  Richard 9 126
Newcome, William 31
Newman/Neuman,
  Elizabeth 126
  Jane 126
  Robert 31 60
  Thomas 126
  William 29 57 67
Newola, Seriaco 224
Newport, John 93
Newsome, A. R. 129 130
Newton, Clemt. 98
  Isaac 228
  John 19
  Samuel 123
Nicholas/Nicolas/Nichollas, Claude 196
  William 22
Nichols/Nicholls,
  James 134
  John 18 40
  Robert 74
  Thomas 34
  William 46 93
Nicholson/Nicolson,
  Alexander 144 147
  Francis 86 87 89
  William 12
Nickcott, Hugh 35
Nicod, Abraham 88
Nicolay, Jacques 87
Nicole, Catherine 200
Nieto, Alvaro
  Juan 166
  Pedro 166
Nimond, Jean 213
Ninger, Alphonse 207
Nithery, James 12
Nitschmann, David 164
Noer, Andrew 122
Noiron, Jacques 218
Nolland 204
Nomers, John 11
Nonn 34
Norman, Priscilla 74
Normandin, Jacques 208
Normansell,
  Edward 33
Norres, Joan 84
North, Thomas 29
Norton, Thomas 41
Norvil, Adam 19
Nourse, Joseph 104
Nowell, John 56
Noyes, Jacob 97
Nuce, George 29
Nuelson, George 14
Nugent, Nell Marion 21 76
Null, Conrad 20
Nun, Charles 223
Núñez, Constanza 176
  Fernán 180
  Luis 176
  Juan 176 180 184
  Mari 178
Núñez de Herrera,
  Juan 184
Núñez de la Parada,
  Elvira 171
Núñez de Prado,
  Juan 173
  Pedro 173
Núñez de Vargas,
  Vasco 170

Pran, George 27
Praromand 204
Pratt/Prat,
Isabell 26 52
John 41
Prater, Thomas 58
de Pravia, Juan 172
Preciado, Alvaro 167
Juan 167
Presson, François 192
Prester, Nich. 162
Preston, Richard 74 79
Roger 23 45
William 106
Pretty, George 40
de Prevon, Noël 193
Prevost, A. 156
Adam 88
Adrien 214
Annette 202
Antoine 202
Elizabeth 202
Jeanne 202
Marie 88
Price/Prise,
Ann (Johanna) 17
Ann (--) 44
Edward 25 33 42 51 93
Elizabeth 17
Henry 39
Hugh 22 44
John 22 44
Judith (--) 44
Thomas 32
Walter 46 65
William 22 43 90
Prichard/Pritchard/
ap-Richard, Henry 30
Thomas 25 33 37 49
Prichett/Prickett,
Margery 31
Miles 31 57
Thomas 34
Priest, John 70
Walter 24
Prime, William 105
Prime (cont.),
William (cont.) 106
Primptems 196
Prinfse, Henry 28
Proctor, Allis (--) 52
John 27 52
Prodger, Richard 40
Prophett, Jacob 33
Protest 193
Provinçal,
Hyacinthe 204
Prowse/Prouse,
George 28 52
Master 39
de la Puebla,
Elvira 181
de la Puente,
Alonso 182
Francisco 182
Puffet, William 37
Pugeol 201
Pugh/ap Hugh,
David 41
Pugett/Puggett,
Cesar 55
Christopher 23
Pulizzi/Pulitizi,
Felice 98
Venenando 98 115
de Puncarreda,
Catalina 184
Purfrey 27
Purfry, Thomas 58
Purnell, William 157
Purry 158 159
Purser, Thomas 73 78
Pussin, Antoine 212
du Pyn, Loys 88

Qacharie, Yve 222
Quarie, Ann 33
Quary, Robert 126
Queen, John 107
de Quemada,
Marina 173
Querke, William 31 59
Quertems, Jacques 216
Quictet, Jean 88
Quills, William 32
de Quintana, María 188
de Quirós, Bernaldo 185

Radcliffe/Ratcliffe/
Ratclife/Ratlife,
Ann (--) 45
Elkinton 24 42 54
Richard 85
Roger 22 45
Thomas 37
Raddin, George W. 110
Radeau, Nicolas 214
Raffin, Joseph 219
Railey, Andrew 52
Rainbird/Raynberd,
Nicholas 63
Rakestraw 93
Ralye, Andrew 25 42
Ralson, Robert 93
Ramage, Alexr. 150
Ramée, Pierre 189
Ramenstein, Chris. 162
Ramírez, Isabel 177
Juana 173
Ramo, Vincent 224
Ramos 225
Alonso 167 172
Domingo 172
V. 226
Ramsey/Rhamsey 226
John 13
Robert 93
Ramshaw/Ranshaw/
Ransham 75
Thomas 81
William 28 55 81
Rancon, Jean 195
Raney, John 93
Ranke, Richard 32
Rapier, Richard 28
Raquin, Rennes 213
Rashoon, Stephen 11
Raspasser, Martin 205

Ruiz de Çaras,
Juan 170
Ruiz de Contreras,
Antón 185
Ruiz de Ibarra,
María
Ruiz/Ruyz de Ocampo,
Francisco 175
Ruiz de Porras,
Pedro 188
Ruiz Quiebrabrazos,
Jorge 181
Rumell, Adam 28
Rumy/Rury, Samuel 116
Rush, Clinton 48
Rushmore, George 28
Russell/Russel,
David 19
Dennis 75 82
Doctor 40
John 27 41 50
Maximilian 38
William 41
Rutherford, James 15
Ruthven, Dugald 154
Rutten, Elizabeth 27
Ryale, Joseph 48
Ryan, John 93
Solomon 93

Saavedra, Juana 184
de Saavedra, Lope 188
Sabin/Sabyn,
Robert 31 59
Sablet, Abraham 88
Sabureau 190
Sacie 227
Sack, Johann
Christoph 127 128
Sacker, John 63
de Sagredo, Alonso
176
Bartolomé 176
de Sailly/de la
Sailly 86 87
Charles 89
St. Amant, Benoist
Monder 199
Michel 205
St. Blaise 211
St. Clair, George 98
Ste. Brissy, Jean 209
Ste. Forsine,
Jean 213
Ste. Nottard,
Jean 218
Marie (Durisse) 218
de St. Esteban 216
Ste. Tringuar,
Jean 218
de St. Frouly,
Albert 200
de St. Georges,
Joseph 190
St. Germain,
Romain 215
St. Jacques,
Pierre 205
St. Jago 223
Saint Jean 189 190
Jean 204
St. Joseph, Joseph
Jouvens 196
Saint Julien 189
St. Just 208
St. Laurent, Joseph
Pomart 196
Saint Louis 189
Barthelemy 205
Saint Martin 189 190
St. Michel,
Pierre 205
St. Olive,
Philippe 218
St. Olivier 207
Sainton, François
Augustin 204
Pierre Charles 204
St. Paul, Jean Louis
Achard 196
St. Prix 193
St. Quentin,
Samuel 198
de Saintray 198
Saint Sauveur 189
Saire, William 9
de Salamanca, Cosme
168
de Salamanca (cont.),
María 186
Salande, Felicity
(--) 223
de Salas, Cristóbal
187
Gabriel 187
Lope 180
Pedro 180
Salazar/de Salazar,
Cristóbal 178
Diego 184
Francisco 174 177
Gregorio 184
Juan 184
María 178
Salcedo/de Salcedo,
Luis 185
Nicolasa 180
de Saldáñez,
Elena 188
Juan 188
Salford/Safford,
Christopher 23 46
John 30 59
Mary 31 59
Robert 30 59
Sara 32
de Salinas,
Aldonça 174
Salisbury,
William 33
de Salle,
François 205
Salmon, Jacques 200
Salomon, Louis 204
Salouin, Mathieu 205
Salter, Elizabeth 24
42 50
John 30
de Salto, María 166
Saltzer, Chris. 162
Salvadge, Robert 29
Salván, Alonso 180
Salvador, Felix 224
Juan 175
Salvadore, M. 225
Sambage, William 41
Samon, John 39

Stamp, Thomas 78
Stanard, William
Glover 72
Stanbridg,
Nathaniel 34
Standish, James 49
Staneling, Mathew 34
Stanley, Morris 63
Roger 49
Sarah 17
Stanton,
Elizabeth 94
John 32
Matthew 94
Staples, Richard 38
Starborough,
Sampson 125
Starkey,
Elizabeth 25 42
Starusquy,
Vincelle 205
Stead/Steed 72
Thomas 76 135
Steele, Michael 19
Steelman, John Hans
11
Steinhauser,
Johann 127
Stelly, Simon 200
Stemple, Christian 21
Stephens/Steephens/
Stevans, Edward 107
John 28 55
Richard 25 34 42 51
Thomas 37
Stephenson/Stevenson/
Steavenson,
Clotworthy 100 101
105
David 93
John 93
Thomas 93
Stepney, Thomas 61
Sterling,
Philippe 199
Stettinius,
Samuel 102 103
Steven, Chrn. 137
James 137
Steven (cont.),
Sarah 137
Thomas 137
Steward, Daniel 14 15
David 13
Stewart/Stuart,
Alexander 151 152
Allan 151 153
Archibald 151
Banco 152
Charles 151
Christian 152
David 221
Dougald 151
Elizabeth 150
Elizabeth (--) 150
George 94 221
Guillaume 221
Isobel 152
James 17 151
Janet 150
John 14 150-152
Kenneth 152
Lilly 151
Margaret 150
Mary 221
Michel 221
Patrick 150
Rachel 221
Robert Armistead 21
Salli 221
Thomas 151
William 17 19 124
152
William H. 105
Stichy, Gaspard 204
Stiles, James 17
Stille, Axel 11
Stin, Gregoire 202
Stinebrenner,
Christian 21
Stobbs, Robert 13
Stockdell, Edward 30
Elizabeth (--) 77
Timothy 73 77
Stocker, William 26
54
Stocks 26
Stockton, Jonas 31 61
Stockton (cont.),
Timothy 31 61
Stoiks 43
Stokes/Stoaks,
Ann (--) 51
Christopher 66
Elizabeth 94
John 51
Samuel 126
Stolea, Hanna Maria
161
Stone/Ston,
Elizabeth (--) 55
James 75 82
John 27 28 54 55
Maximilian 55
Moyses 25 42 57 70
71
Richard 34
Sisly (--) 55
Stoneby, Henry 97
Storks, Richard 37
Stowell, Caleb 158
Strachey, William 23
55
Strange/Straimge,
William 23 49
Street, Thomas 18
Stringer, Ann 17
Frederick 117
Samuel 36
Strouse, Henry 21
Struck, John 162
Stuiger, George 97
Sturter, Gabriel 89
Stutton 19
Suárez, Juan 166
Juana 166
Suersby, John 37
Suiveyor, Joseph 224
Sullivan, Daniel 17
Jeremiah 107 115
117 121
Sully/Sulley,
Maudlyn 58
Thomas 26 58 73 78
Sumerville, James 15
Summerfield/Sumfill/
Sum̄erfild, John 31

Summerfield (cont.),
Nicholas 63
Summonton,
John W. 223
Summers, Sarah 17
Sunnfill, John 31
Surge, Bernard 90
Surgis, Symon 22
Sussames, Alex^{r} 34
Suter, John 19
Sutherland, Adam 150
John 150
Thomas J. 107
William 94 143 150
Worthington 107
Sutton,
Nicholas 24 47
William 27
Swagert,
Hans Michael 162
Swancoat, John 73
Swandal, William 35
Swarbeck, John 48
Swart, Margaret 162
Sweeney/Sweeny,
George 97 108 118
James 121
Sweet/Sweete,
Robert 30 59
Swift/Swifte 27
Thomas 54
Swineyard, John 11
Swinger, Alex. 13
Swinhow, George 37
Thomas 37 49
Swinton, Charles 12
Swope, Christopher 21
Sword, Humphrey 15
Swormstead,
Christian 11
Syberrye/Siberry,
George 69
Henry 70
Thomas 71
Syserson, Marius 11

Tabarre, Jean 207
Tachon, Jean 193
Tachon (cont.),
Louis 193
Marie 193
Tacy, Jeanne 211
Talas, Martin 228
Talu, Pierre 190
de Tamayo, Isabel 172
Tanneberger,
David 164
John 164
Tanner, Daniel 30 58
Josias 52
Tanns 190
Tanson, Jacques 190
de Tapia,
Francisco 177
Inés 177
Pedro 184
Tapic 197
Tapye 201
Tarascon,
Francisco 166
Jacques 205
Tarborer, Richard 27
Tardieu, Jean 88
Tarleton, Edward 84
Tarmigan, Isaiah 125
du Tartre,
Francois 88
Tasker, Benjamin 13 15
Tastet/Tastel,
Nicholas 107
Tatam/Tattam,
Nathaniel 22 45
Tathill, William 24
Taure, Daniel 89
Taverner, George 133
John 40
Tavert, John 11
Taylor/Tayler/Taluar/Tailour 28
Dorothy (--) 44
Elias/Ellis 74 80
Fortune 24 42
George 212
Jasper 34
John 19 38 60 74
Marion 141
Taylor (cont.),
Mary 140
Rebecca 60
Richard 22 44
Robert 33 37
Samuel H. 121
Saunders 19
Thomas 36 109 124
William 41
Teage, Katherin 74 79
Teasdale 227
de Tejada, Catalina 165
María 170
Tejedor, Gómez 184
Teller, Jno. 161
Téllez de Vega,
Gonzalo 173
Juana 173
Tellier, Michel 209
Tellown, Peter 126
Temin, Benoise 198
de Temiño, Leonos 182
Temple, Edward 24 32 44
Templeman,
William 134
Tepper, Michael 10 71
Terasse, Louis Vincent 205
de Termanda, Hernando 176
de Terreros,
Teresa 178
Terret, Nathaniel 94
Terriell, Abel 225
Terrill, Honner 94
Tessendier 216
Tesson, George 218
Teusse, Robert 206
Texier, Pierre 194
Tezé, François 197
Theiler, Jac. 160
Theyler, Jno. 160
Thibou 155
Louis 156
Thimbleby,
Nicholas 33
Thomas 75 163

Welchman (cont.),
John 29
Lewis 29
Welder, William 22
Weldon, William 43
Weller, Adam 21
Wells, Cornelius 119
John 16
Joseph 18
Welton 75
Wendmile,
Christopher 28
Went, James 16 17
Werkslagen, Paul 19
Werner, John Jacob 21
Werryfield, Jacob 19
Wescott, Philip 134
Wesell, Nicholas 29
Wessingher, Jno. 161
West, Anthony 25 42 54
Francis 24 27 41 61 62
Henry 34
John 26 27 37 43 51 65 69 71 135
Nathaniel 32 37
Thomas/Rhomas 26 43 70
Westalot, Andre 225
Weston 36
Ann 135
Thomas 45
William 24 45
Wetherell,
Sackford 62
Wethersby/Wethersbie,
Albiano 30
Bartholmew 30 59
Dorythie 59
Wetzel, Lawrence 161
Wharfield,
Benjamin 12
Wharton, Henry 14
James 96 98 99
Wheeler, Henry 29 62
John 94
Whitby, Richard 28
White, Abigail 135
White (cont.),
Andrew 9
Edward 54
Francis 125
Frank F. 15
George 125
Hugh 15
James 13
Jeremy 53
John 94 125 134
Juan 226
Lee 224 225
Luck 125
Mary 125
Media 125
Robert 137
Sarah 125 134
Whitehand, George 55
Whitehest,
William 228
Whitfield/Whitfild,
Gilbert 30 57
Whitinge, James 59
Whitman, William 94
Whitmore,
Christian 49
Robert 25 42 53
Whitt, Edmond 27
Jereme 27
Robert 34
William 24
Whittaker 39
Whittakers,
Elizabeth 29
Isaac 29
Mary 29
Wicks, John 18
Widgen, William 126
von Wiedebach,
Friedrich 128
Wigge, Edward 56 67
Wiggins, William 126
de Wildenberg, Jean Henri de Planta 127
Wilcox/Willcockes,
Charles G. 112 123
Elizabeth 58
John 31 63
Wilcox (cont.),
Mandlin 31
Michael 31 58
Wilder, John 14
Wiles, Bishop 40
Wiley, John 106
Wilne, André 221
Wilhite, John 94 95
Michael 94
Tobias 95
Wilkins/Wilkines,
Briggett 64
Giles 36
John 32 39 64
Wilkinson, Isabel 85
Willer, Thomas 34
Williams/Williames,
Ann 18
David 22
Edward 51
Elizabeth 27
Henry 23 46
Hugh 41
James 117
John 123 131
Lewis 35
Pierce 47
Rice Axr. 27
Robert 27 33 35
Roger 53
Rowland 29 63
Susan (--) 46
Thomas 23 45 94 108
Thomas Hollaway 108
William 32
Williamson, Andrew 137
Arch'd 11
Willis, Ann 50
T. 223
Walter 73 77
Willowbey/Willoby,
Thomas 30 58
Wills, Thomas 9
Wilmose, John 26
Wilmott/Willmott,
Samuel Devonshire 108
Wilson/Willson 75

Yeamans, Benjamin 126
Yeardley/Yardley/
Yearlley,
Argall 24 41
Elizabeth 24 41
Frances 24 41
George 24 37 41 49
80
Temperance 24 41 49
Yeats, Leonard 23
William 19
Yeaw, Richard 37
de Yelbes,
Francisco 178
Gonzalo 178
Yemanson, James 24 42
Yeoman, Robert 36
Yerkardt, George 20
Young/Younge/Yonge/
Jung/de Young 24 41
Benjamin 228
Jacob 161
Jacob Clause 10
Joan 25 42 58
Richard 25 42 57
Robert 94
Samuel 12
Thomas 139
William 40 98
de Yrue, Clara 177
Ysquain, George 204

Zains, Esedro 223
de Zamora/Çamora,
Leonar 179
Maria 187
Zapata/Çapata,
Alonso 172
Zeisberger, David 164
165
Rosina (--) 164
Zellich, Michael 128
Zembrano/Zambrano,
Esteban 188
Isabel 178
Zenger, John Peter 11
Zerrato, Francis 176
de Zevedo, Diego 187
Isabel 187
von Zezschwiz,
Hans Ernst 127
Zimmerman, John 94
Zino 227
von Zinzendorf,
Christian Renatus
128

No Surname Given
Alexander 19
Alexander ----agie
19
Allen, servant 26
Alonso 183
Ambrose 57
Ana 171
Angelo, Negro 24 41
Angelo, Negro woman
50
Ann, maid 24
Anthony, Negro 23
28 30
Antonio, Negro 56
67
Beatriz 170
Bernardo 182
Betty, Indian 126
Catalina 177
Charles, servant 45
Charles I, King 64
Charles II, King 64
Charles Edward,
Prince 18
Chouponke, Indian
30
Cisely, maid 34
Collins, Thomas
Wood's man 35 36
Daniel 32
Daniel, Mr. Dombe-
lowe's man 37
Datis, Negresse 222
Diego 183
Donald 19
Edward 31 32 39
Edward, Negro 26
Elinor 25 42
Elizabeth, maid 34
36 44
No Surname Given
(cont.),
Eve Elizabeth 159
Frances, Negro 28
Francis, Irishman
37
Francoise 191
Frederick St--ger
99
Frederick St--ges
99
George 31
Gilbert 34
Henry 29 31
Henry, Welshman 38
Hosier 33
Hugh 39
Isabella, Negro 30
James, Frenchman 28
James, Irishman 34
James ---ity 122
John, Mr. Pearis'
servant 33
John, Irishman 34
John, Negro 23 27
John ---nald 19
Juana 168
Lorenzo 182
Margaret, blind old
maid 37
Margarett, Negro 28
Margarita 169
Marie, Negresse 191
Mary 30
Mary, maid 28 36
Mary, Negro woman
56 67 225
Mathew 36
Mathew, maid 39
Methusalew 36
Nathaniel, servant
68
Nice, Negresse 222
Nicholas 35
Olaria 188
Ozenda 175
Parnel, maid 39
Peter 29 57
Peter, servant 68

No Surname Given (cont.),
Phillip 31
Pius V, Pope 10
Rebecca 39
Richard 36 39 59
Robert 38 39
Robert, Mr. Ewins' man 33
Robert ------ 19
No Surname Given (cont.),
Salvador 188
Stephen 33
Steven 35
Susan 58
Syman, Italian 34
Thomas 31 34 58
Thomas, boy 28
Thomas, Indian 31
No Surname Given (cont.),
Thomas, servant 68
Thomas, Henricke Peterson's man 36
William 31 37
William, Negro 23 126
William ------ 19
Zorobabell 32

INDEX OF VARIANT SURNAME SPELLINGS

The following index is intended to assist the reader in locating variant spellings or forms of surnames in the foregoing index of personal names. It is not a complete index of the variant spellings in that those variations which would not be out of order, such as Browne with Brown, are not listed.

Adie, Addy
Alnutt, Allnut
Anríquez, also Enríquez
Apleby, Appleby
Apleton, Appleton
Applen, Apples
Attkins, Atkins
Bailey, Baly
Baillie, Baly
Baley, Baly
Balley, Baly
Bayley, Baly
Bayly, Baly
Benet, Bennett
Brien, Bryan
Brodbeck, Broadbeck
Byrd, Bird
de Calçada, also de Calzada
de Calzada, also de Calçada
Çamora, de Zamora
Çapata, Zapata
Celive, D'Celive
Chaundler, Chandler
Chauntree, Chantry
Cheney, Cheyney
Chisman, Cheeseman
Clerk, Clark
Comes, Combs
Coombe, Combs
Coomes, Combs
Conly, Connelly
Covell, Coffield
Croft, Craft
Descobar, also Escobar
Desteban, also Esteban
D'hospital, Hospital
Díaz, also Díez
Dier, Dyer
Díez, also Díaz
Dowtie, Doughty
Dreher, Trayor
Duboisson, Dubuisson
Duglas, Douglas
Dun, Dunn
Dutitree, Dutartre
Enríquez, also Anríquez
Esbey, Espey
Escobar, also Descobar
Esteban, also Desteban
Falkoner, Faulkoner
Farguson, Ferguson
Feelds, Fields
Feild, Field
Floid, Floyd
Fludd, Flood
Foockes, Fuchs

Pacquet, Packet
Paquet, also Packet
Parish, Parrish
Passmore, Pasmore
Peirse, Pierce
Perce, Pierce
Perse, Pierce
Prise, Price
Pritchard, Prichard
Rae, Ray
Ratcliffe, Radcliffe
Ratlife, Radcliffe
Raynberd, Rainbird
Reed, Read
Reid, Read
Reignolds, Reynolds
Reinolds, Reynolds
Rhamsey, Ramsey
de Ribera, de Rivera
ap-Richard, Prichard
Riemensperger, Remensperger
Rinfton, Rinston
Rodelsperger, Rottlesperger
Rodgers, Rogers
Ruyz de Ocampo, Ruiz de Ocampo
Ryly, Reily
Safford, Salford
Sançoucy, Sans Soucy
San Soucy, Sans Soucy
Scottismore, Scotchmore
Semmes, also Simms
Sheaperd, Sheppard
Siberry, Syberrye
Simmes, Semmes
Slayter, Slater
Smyth, Smith
Soothey, Sothey
Sower, Sauer
Steavenson, Stephenson
Steephens, Stephens
Stuart, Stewart
de Sygura, de Segura
Symon[d]s, Simons
Tailour, Taylor
Taluar, Taylor
Tattam, Tatam
Tiler, Tyler
Througood, Thoroughgood
Tomson, Thompson
Vaghan, Vaughan
le Warre, Delaware
Wasborne, Washborne
Wats, Watts
Watters, Waters
Wattkins, Watkins
Wattson, Watson
Worldige, Worlidge
Yardley, Yeardley
Zembrano, also Çambrano